I0605521

King George's War

Also by Michael G. Laramie

King William's War:
The First Contest for North America, 1689–1697

Queen Anne's War:
The Second Contest for North America, 1702–1713

The Road to Ticonderoga:
The Campaign of 1758 in the Champlain Valley

Gunboats, Muskets, and Torpedoes:
Coastal North Carolina, 1861–1865

Gunboats, Muskets, and Torpedoes:
Coastal South Carolina, 1861–1865

By Wind and Iron:
Naval Campaigns in the Champlain Valley, 1665–1815

Colonial Forts of the Champlain and Hudson Valleys:
Sentinels of Wood and Stone

The European Invasion of North America:
Colonial Conflict Along the Hudson-Champlain Corridor, 1609–1760

The Third Contest For North America, 1714–1748

King George's War

and the

Thirty-Year Peace

MICHAEL G. LARAMIE

WESTHOLME
Yardley

Westholme Publishing, LLC
904 Edgewood Road
Yardley, Pennsylvania 19067
Visit our Web site at www.westholmepublishing.com

ISBN: 978-1-59416-430-9
Also available as an eBook.

Printed in the United States of America.

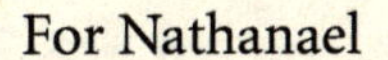

For Nathanael

Contents

PART FOUR
Delenda est Canada

PART FIVE
War, Privateers, and the Treaty of Aix-la-Chapelle

MAPS AND PLANS

Preface

First, I should point out that the title of this book should technically be the thirty-year peace and King George's War, but it did not have quite the same ring. Regardless of the title, this work continues the contest for North America from the end of Queen Anne's War (1702–1713), which marks the start of the thirty-year peace, through the end of King George's War in 1748. With the French examining the lessons from Queen Anne's War, this period would produce a number of key fortifications along regions of contention, such as Fort St. Frederic on Lake Champlain, the naval fortress of Louisbourg on Cape Breton Island, as well as Fort Niagara and the British response, Fort Oswego on Lake Ontario. The first two would prove to be central points of contention in King George's War (1744–1748), while matters with the last two would be settled in the Old French War (1754–1763), as the last French and Indian War is sometimes called.

Although there would be limited direct conflict between the three primary colonial contenders in North America during the thirty-year peace, with the Franco-Spanish conflict of 1719 and the Anglo-Spanish conflict of 1727-1729 being the few exceptions, proxy wars, economic competition, and internal conflicts with former Native allies would strike at the French and English colonies, with the Three Years' War, the Yamassee War, and the Natchez and Chickasaw Wars being primary examples. In fact, the thirty years of peace did not prove to be exceptionally peaceful.

They would, however, prove to be the setting for the War of Jenkins' Ear (1739–1748), those parts of which pertain to North America are spoken to in detail in this text. Here the conflict would begin as the settling of old scores, with attacks on Spanish St. Augustine and a counter campaign targeting the new British colony of Georgia. While this Anglo-Spanish conflict would shift farther south into the Caribbean, to the north, news of war between France and Britain would arrive in 1744. King George's War, the North American component of Europe's War of Austrian Succession, would start in Nova Scotia with French attacks on the weakly held British colony. Here it was not just the missed opportunities that would haunt the attackers but the response to their efforts that would spawn one of the boldest expeditions of the colonial period—Governor William Shirley's campaign against the French fortress of Louisbourg on Cape Breton Island.

To the west the recently constructed Fort St. Frederic at Crown Point, New York, not only extended French power over the Champlain Valley but proved a launching pad for the French pursuit of the old policy of *petite guerre*, the war of raids, raiders, and terror aimed at forcing the American colonies to switch to the defensive and divert their resources to defend an undefendable frontier. With an advanced position in the Champlain Valley the French would dispatch raids deep into New England and New York, and on a much larger scale than those seen during King William's War (1689–1697) and Queen Anne's War. Towns, hamlets, and even colonial forts became targets of this activity, which proved so intense that the American colonies would revive the old invasion plan calling for simultaneous attacks on Quebec and Montreal.

While the rallying cry of *delenda est Canada* (Canada must be destroyed) rang out in the American colonial assemblies and a fleet of warships assembled in Britain to capture Quebec, France, still buoyed by Count Maurice de Saxe's victory at Fontenoy in 1745, responded to news of Louisbourg's capture by launching a large naval expedition to retake Cape Breton and Nova Scotia. Thus, for both the British colonies and New France, the destiny of the conflict would hinge on a pair of fleets from Europe. Neither expedition nor the Treaty of Aix-la-Chapelle, which ended the fighting, would settle matters between the two, but the heightened level of military involvement of both mother nations had set the stage such that the next war, The Old French War, would.

HUDSON BAY
RUPERT'S LAND
Lake Winnipeg
James Bay
Big R.
Albany R.
Rupart R.
Rupart's Fort
Moose R.
Nottaway R.
Hamilton R.
LABRADOR
NEWFOUNDLAND
St. Johns
Placentia
CANADA
Lake of the Woods
UPPER COUNTRY
St. Lawrence R.
GULF OF ST. LAWRENCE
Saguenay R.
CHIPPEWA
Lake Superior
ALGONQUIN
Cape Breton Is.
Louisbourg
NEW BRUNSWICK
St. Johns R.
Quebec
Beaubassin
Canso
OTTAWA
Three Rivers
WABANAKI
MENOMINEE
Ottawa R.
Fundy Bay
Lake Nipissing
Fort Richelieu
Montreal
Fort Chambly
Penobscot R.
Kennebec R.
Port Royal
Fort Michilimackinac
FOX
Mississippi R.
Wisconsin R.
Lake Huron
St. Lawrence R.
Lake Champlain
Falmouth
Fort Frontenac
Fort St. Frederic
Connecticut R.
Merrimack R.
Lake Michigan
Lake Ontario
Oswego
Portsmouth
POTAWATOMI
Fort Niagra
IROQUOIS
Albany
Boston
Lake St. Clair
Fort Detroit
Lake Erie
MOUNTAINS
Allegheny R.
Delaware R.
Hudson R.
NEW ENGLAND
Newport
Des Moines R.
ILLINOIS
KICKAPOO
Fort Pimiteoui
ERIGAS
New York
LONG IS.
N
E
W

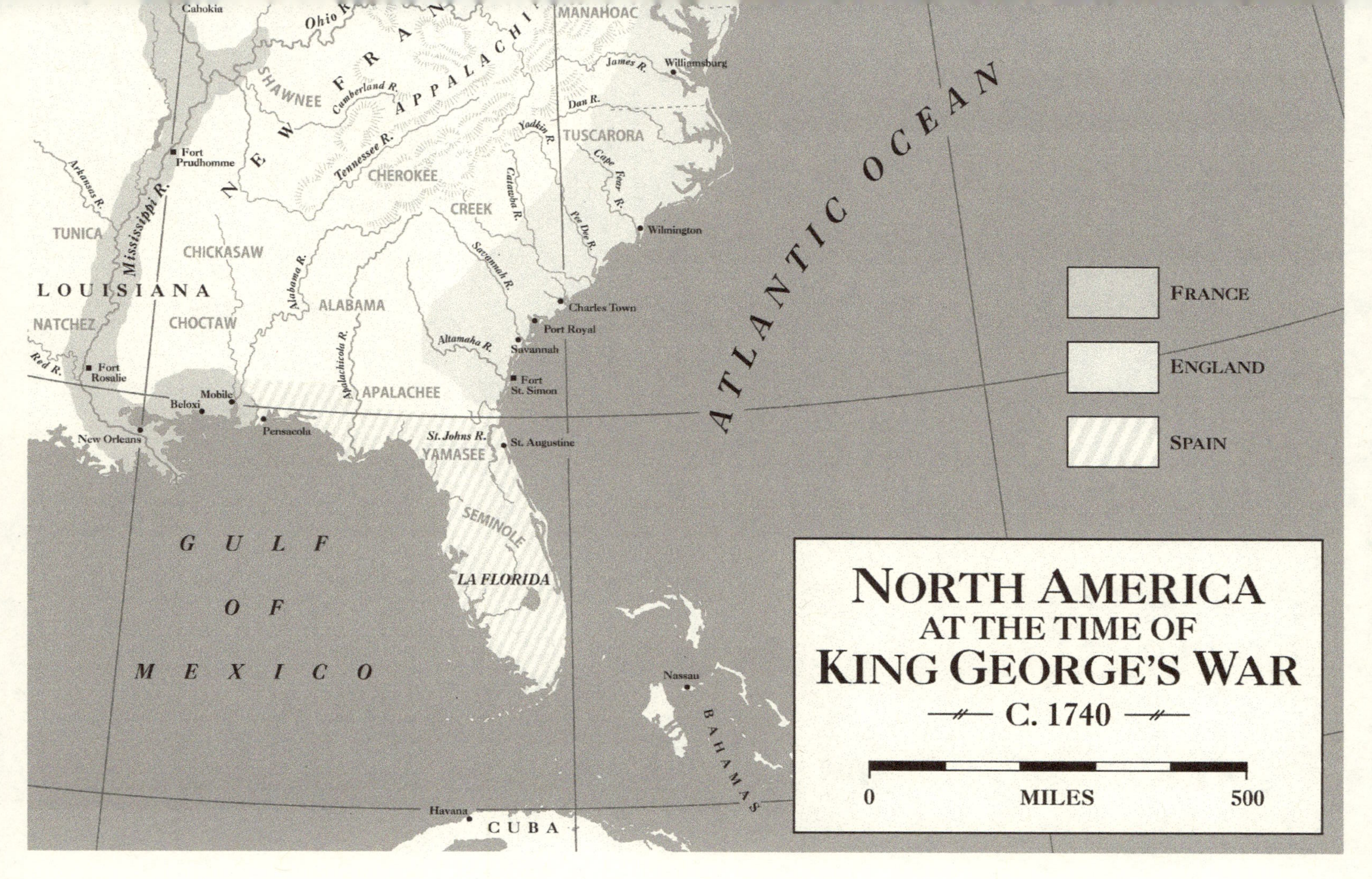
NORTH AMERICA
AT THE TIME OF
KING GEORGE'S WAR
C. 1740
0
MILES
500
FRANCE
ENGLAND
SPAIN
ATLANTIC OCEAN
GULF OF MEXICO
LOUISIANA
LA FLORIDA
BAHAMAS
CUBA
Havana
Nassau
Cahokia
Fort Prudhomme
Fort Rosalie
New Orleans
Beloxi
Mobile
Pensacola
St. Augustine
Fort St. Simon
Savannah
Port Royal
Charles Town
Wilmington
Williamsburg
Ohio R.
Cumberland R.
Tennessee R.
Mississippi R.
Arkansas R.
Red R.
Alabama R.
Apalachicola R.
Altamaha R.
Savannah R.
Catawba R.
Yadkin R.
Pee Dee R.
Cape Fear R.
Dan R.
James R.
St. Johns R.
MANAHOAC
SHAWNEE
TUSCARORA
CHEROKEE
CREEK
TUNICA
CHICKASAW
NATCHEZ
CHOCTAW
ALABAMA
APALACHEE
YAMASEE
SEMINOLE

Part One

The Thirty-Year Peace in the North

CHAPTER ONE

From Cape Breton to Îsle Royale

In 1713, the Treaty of Utrecht brought an end to the War of Spanish Succession and its American counterpart, Queen Anne's War. Although New France had weathered the conflict, it lost at the peace table. Under the terms of the treaty the colony ceded its holdings in Newfoundland, on Hudson Bay, and in part of Acadia, which became known as Nova Scotia. The latter agreement dealing with the boundaries of Nova Scotia was couched in such vague language that it was destined to create future problems, but for the moment at least, the verbiage was acceptable to both parties. The treaty opened parts of the west and the Mississippi Valley to English traders and called for the formation of a joint commission to demarcate the boundaries of the French and British colonies in North America. It was also agreed under article fifteen of the treaty that the Iroquois were British subjects, a simple statement that would lead to innumerable arguments and eventually help fuel a final confrontation between the two colonies. In the meantime, a long peace settled over North America, although one not completely free of conflict.[1]

The ink on the official peace treaty had barely dried when the sound of hammer and saw could be heard coming from Cape Breton Island in the Gulf of St. Lawrence. The idea of fortifying Cape Breton was first seriously proposed in 1706 by Jacques Raudot, the Intendent (Chief Financial Officer) of New France. The location made sense not only as an anchorage for the French Navy to protect the Gulf of St. Lawrence but as a staging point for privateers and naval elements looking to raid the American coast in time of war. Just as importantly, it would also prove an ideal place to move the French fisheries. There were numerous good harbors and abundant shorelines to dry fish, and the weather was more tolerable than Newfoundland. Nor was it lost on Raudot that an expansion of this trade would damage New England commerce without firing a shot. In addition, the heavily wooded island would be able to supply masts, planks, and a host of products to the navy, with shipbuilding on the island logically following.

The observations were symbolic of the logistical damage the English were causing New France, but with war raging in North America and Europe it was simply noted and filed away. The proposal would resurface, but it was not until the end of Queen Anne's War that Cape Breton once again took on importance. French ambassadors at the peace negotiations ceded Newfoundland and a large portion of Acadia, but they were instructed to do what was necessary to preserve French control over Cape Breton, signaling the acceptance of the idea to occupy and fortify the island.

There was really little choice in the matter. Unlike the British colonies to the south, Canada was not self-sufficient. Occasionally the colony would have a bumper crop and sell some of the surplus to colonies in the Caribbean, but in general, it relied on France not only for food but gunpowder, arms, tools, and almost every other element of life. If Canada was to maintain this lifeline as well as a market for its primary export, furs, it had to control the Gulf of St. Lawrence. In theory, this could be accomplished by naval elements operating out of Placentia, Port Royal, or several other harbors along the coast of Nova Scotia. In practice, however, this approach proved unsatisfactory. The loss of Port Royal during Queen Anne's War, coupled with the limited naval facilities at Placentia and along the shoreline of Acadia, had created a situation where the weakened French Navy had been unable to prevent British privateers from infesting the gulf. Now with Placentia, the home port of the French fishing fleet, and part of Acadia scheduled to be turned over to British control, implementing Raudot's proposal had become a necessity.[2]

To deal with this problem, Paris had agreed to build a fortified naval port on the island, but the question was where? There was little time to decide, as the garrison and citizens of Placentia were scheduled to leave in late 1713. The temporary choice, ironically enough, was English Harbor. This would soon be renamed Louisbourg when Cape Breton became officially known

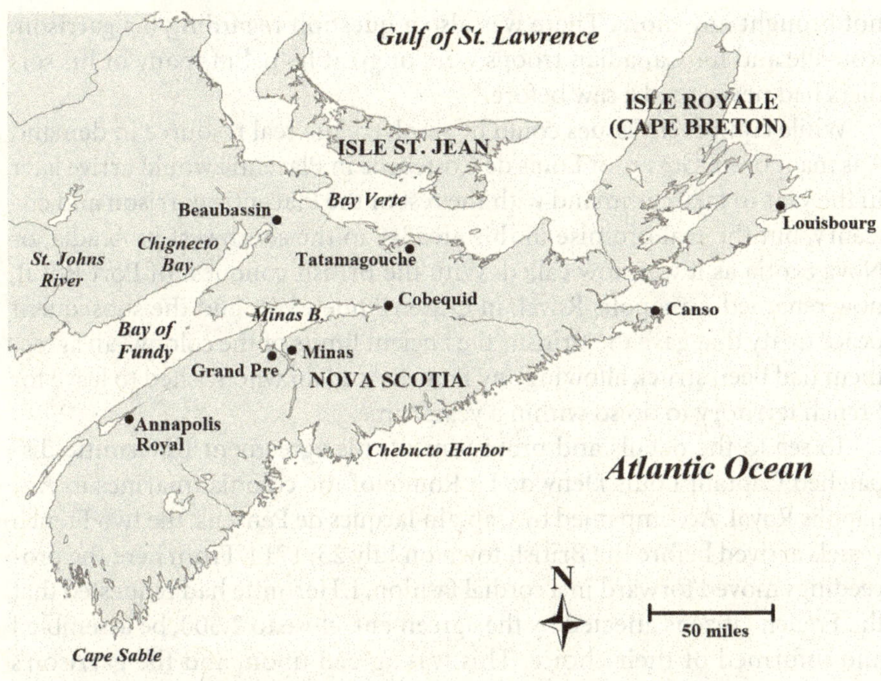

Nova Scotia and Îsle Royale.

as Îsle Royale. As the British were not ready to assume control of Placentia until 1714, only a small number of citizens and soldiers under the command of Placentia's engineer, Major Jacques L'Hermitte, traveled to Louisbourg aboard a supply ship sent from France. Governor Philippe Vaudreuil in Quebec supplemented this force with fifty Canadians, many skilled foresters under the leadership of the well-known partisan Jean Hertel de Rouville.

Crude shelters were erected from the dense forests that lined the shores, and in these the 150 men, women, and children of the new colony weathered a difficult winter. The supplies sent did not prove sufficient, and by spring the garrison had consumed three of its horses and nineteen of the twenty-one cattle they had brought with them. In fact, the weather was so bad that there was still snow on the ground and ice drifts off the coast when the first supply ships from France arrived in late May 1714. Governor Vaudreuil had arrived as well, along with Intendent Michel Begon. The trio discussed the projected fortifications for the harbor, which were to be built of stone, before L'Hermitte pointed out that there was no stone quarry nearby or lime for such construction. Not that it mattered, as currently he was equipped with only a few dozen axes and picks, and the supply vessel had not brought any more. There was also a question regarding his garrison. Rouville and his Canadian troops were of great help, but many of his soldiers had never used a saw before.[3]

While equipment issues could be resolved, the real resource in demand was manpower. Governor Louis de Costebelle in Placentia would arrive later in the year to take command with the rest of the Placentia garrison and citizenry, but the real promise in this area lay to the southwest in Acadia, or Nova Scotia as it was now called. With the British conquest of Port Royal, now renamed Annapolis Royal, in Queen Anne's War and the subsequent peace treaty that gave the British "the ancient limits of the colony," an agreement had been struck allowing any French Acadian who wished to leave for French territory to do so within a years' time.

To see to the details and provisions of this agreement L'Hermitte dispatched Captain Louis Deny de La Ronde of the colonial marines to Annapolis Royal. Accompanied by Captain Jacques de Pensens, the two French vessels arrived before the British town on July 23, 1714. From here the proceedings moved forward in a cordial fashion. L'Hermitte had requested that the French citizens affected by the agreement, close to 2,500, be assembled and informed of their choice. This was agreed upon, and the garrison's major, Paul Mascarene, soon to be a prominent name in Nova Scotia history, was appointed to accompany the French ambassadors to the surrounding townships.

If the French government had high hopes of moving a significant portion of the citizenry to Louisbourg, they would be disappointed. The first meeting concerned the inhabitants in the area of Annapolis Royal. A total of 916 men, women, and children circled La Ronde and Mascarene as both representatives gave their side of the agreement. The French citizens were free to stay, Mascarene pointed out to the crowd. They could keep their land and possessions and remain unmolested so long as they took an oath of allegiance to the British Crown. Otherwise, they must leave. La Ronde spoke next. The animated oration started with an appeal of loyalty to the French king and progressed in a free-flowing string of promises that the captain was not authorized to make. The king would furnish vessels for transport and provide provisions for a year for those who would relocate to Louisbourg. In addition, there would be no duties on their trade for a year, and there would be no seignorial land system. While L'Hermitte pointed out that La Ronde's "flatteries and lies would trouble the universe," it did not convince the bulk of the attendees.

One hundred forty-six inhabitants agreed to relocate, but the rest chose to stay on their land. The reasons were twofold. First, Nova Scotia was a far

A portion of a 1768 map showing Cape Breton Island and Canso, Nova Scotia. (*Norman B. Leventhal Map Collection, Boston Public Library*)

more prosperous location than the forest-ensconced lands of Cape Breton. Second, there was real skepticism regarding the French Crown's ability to deliver on its promises. Too many had seen how Port Royal had been neglected during the last conflict, and they applied this lesson to their decision.

The towns of Cobequid and Minas were visited next. At these locations another 156 individuals agreed to go to Louisbourg. Satisfied with the proceedings, La Ronde returned to Louisbourg with a handful of Acadians.[4]

Another attempt to move inhabitants to Îsle Royale came from the Baron Bernard-Anselme D'Abbie de St. Castin. Upon his father's death in 1707, Bernard assumed the title of Baron Castin. With his mother being the daughter of a prominent Wabanaki sagamore (chieftain), near the end of the Queen Anne's War he had been appointed lieutenant by Governor Vaudreuil, and along with several missionaries, he was sent to Acadia to keep the Wabanaki and citizens there loyal to France. This Castin was able to accomplish through his reputation among the colonists and kinship to the Wabanaki. However, he was unable to convince any of the Wabanaki, mostly Micmac, to move to Îsle Royale, although a Micmac village was established close to the island at the northeast end of Nova Scotia. Father Felix Paim, a Recollet Missionary at Minas, explained the reasons behind the hesitancy. "The Indians say," he wrote Costebelle,

> that to shut them up in the island of cape Breton would be to damage their liberty, and that it would be a thing inconsistent with their natural freedom and the means of providing for their subsistence. That with regard to their attachment to the king and to the French, that it is inviolable; and if the queen of England had the meadows of Acadie, by the cession made by his majesty of them, they, the Indians, had the woods, out of which no one could ever dislodge them; and that so they wished each to remain at their posts, promising, nevertheless, to be always faithful to the French.[5]

When La Ronde dropped anchor at Louisbourg, he found that Governor Costebelle and the Placentia garrison had arrived with the guns and supplies from the fort there. The inhabitants of Placentia would follow a few months later in their fishing vessels after a storm-tossed voyage, but only a few Acadians undertook the trek to Louisbourg on their own. Together with the garrison and those already on station it raised the population of the colony to around eight hundred by early 1715.

The year brought merchants to the location, and the fishing was found to be better than expected. In addition, the weather was far milder than Newfoundland. While this point helped the transplanted citizenry, there was much to worry about. The fortifications were going slowly, in part because the materials had not been delivered and in part because of a lack of funds to pay the troops for the additional work. The officials tended to blame each other for many of the issues but all agreed on one thing; there was too much liquor in the colony. The ill effects of this soon showed in the mutinous conduct of the garrison, which, according to one French officer, were the best paid, fed, and clothed troops he had ever seen.[6]

An Englishman, Jethro Furber, who was forced to take shelter at Louisbourg in 1715, noted that there were forty vessels and six warships in the large harbor. He had also been told that the fishing was so good that the boats returned to port twice every day to unload their hauls and that the new inhabitants preferred the location over Placentia so much that the feeling was the "English gave them a Wedge of Gold for a piece of silver." Others, such as Samuel Vetch, the first governor of Nova Scotia after Port Royal's capture in 1710, listened to such reports with worry. The French colony was growing quickly, and should it attract a sizable portion of the French Acadian population it could prove problematic. "Their skill in the Fishery, as well as the cultivating of the soil," Vetch wrote, "must inevitably make that Island [Îsle Royale], by such an accession of people, at once the most powerful colony the French have in America, and of the greatest danger and damage to all the British Colony's as well as the universal trade of Great Britain."[7]

As reports on the French colony's progress and complaints from the British reached him, the French minister of the marine, Jerome Phelypeaux, the Count de Pontchartrain, began to arrive at a similar conclusion. "The English are well aware of the importance of this post, and are already taking umbrage in the matter," he informed the French court.

> They see that it will be prejudicial to their trade, and that in time of war it will be a menace to their shipping, and on the first outbreak of trouble they will be sure to use every means to get possession of it. It is therefore necessary to fortify it thoroughly. If France were to lose this Island the loss would be an irreparable one, and it would involve the loss of all her holdings in North America.[8]

While such thoughts were true, they were also premature, as there had still not been a decision on whether Louisbourg, Port Dauphin, or Port Toulouse was to be the principal anchorage on the island. Each had its merits and advocates. The last of these, Port Toulouse, was favored by the Acadians and Governor Costebelle. At first the water was considered too shallow to make the port serviceable to heavy vessels, but three deep-water channels were eventually mapped out that altered this view. While the channels possessed a number of unexpected twists and turns, it was nothing that could not be marked out with buoys, and in time of conflict these buoys could be removed to make the passage extremely hazardous to an enemy vessel. The nearby land was suitable for an agricultural community and the proximity to Nova Scotia was desirable, but it was farther from the French fishing grounds than Louisbourg. The real problem, however, was the broad entrance to the bay, which would prove extremely difficult and costly to fortify. The next choice, Louisbourg, had a number of desirable features. It was the closest of the three to the fishing grounds, it possessed a large deep harbor that was accessed through a narrow passage that could be easily defended, and although the extent of its beaches, which would be used to dry and prepare fish, were not as great as Port Dauphin, it was adjacent to a number of smaller harbors along the coast that could be used to supplement this activity. Port Dauphin was the last choice. The port's narrow confines made it the easiest and cheapest of the three locations to fortify. The nearby land was quite fertile, and the extent of the beaches here was greater than Louisbourg, although not quite as useful given their restricted nature. The real problem lay with the fact that it was the farthest of the three from the fishing grounds, meaning that larger vessels would have to be employed to take advantage of this trade.

Port Toulouse was quickly dismissed, and the choice between Louisbourg and Port Dauphin distilled down to the fishing trade versus the costs of fortification. The French court chose the latter and selected Port Dauphin. Louisbourg would still be garrisoned and protected by smaller forts and a battery or two of cannons, but Port Dauphin would be the primary fortified anchorage on Îsle Royale.[9]

While this process was underway Costebelle encountered another problem. Nova Scotia Governor Francis Nicholson had given the French Acadians until the fall of 1715 to depart; otherwise they would be forced to take the oath of loyalty or have their lands confiscated. This matter had been resolved by La Ronde, and at least three hundred or so had expressed a desire to remove to Îsle Royale. While a few had returned with La Ronde, and a handful of others had sailed in their small vessels to the island, the bulk of this group was still in Nova Scotia awaiting the promised transport. The problem was that France had not sent out a vessel to see to this matter. Nor had any of the promised provisions to support these immigrants arrived.

It would not be until August 1716 that Costebelle dispatched a ship to Nova Scotia. The commander of the vessel returned empty handed in September. He informed the governor that the Acadians were no longer interested in coming, in part due to the failure to carry through with the promises made by the French envoys. One French official saw the real reason; they would not leave a good land for a poor one. Costebelle did not push the issue, which he feared might lead to a confrontation with the

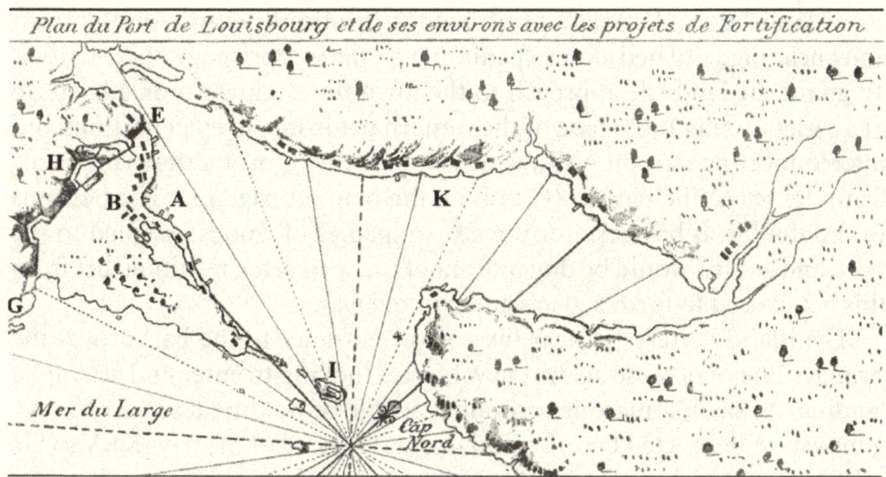

A 1719 plan of Louisbourg Harbor and the proposed fortifications. Key: A. Dockyard, B. the Town, G to E. Landside wall, H. King's Bastion, I. Island Battery, K. Royal Battery. (*J. S. McLennan,* Louisbourg, from its Foundation to its Fall, 1713-1758)

British. The Acadians would stay where they were. In fact, leaving them in Nova Scotia presented a number of useful opportunities in the way of trade and striking at the British when the time called for it.[10]

With a number of conflicting reports before them, and questionable estimates from the engineers on station regarding the costs involved in fortifying Louisbourg, Port Toulouse, and Port Dauphin, the French court dispatched a senior military engineer to take charge of the project. The task fell to Jean-Francois de Verville. Commissioned in the prestigious royal engineers in 1704, Verville had fought in a number of engagements in Spain and Germany during the War of Spanish Succession, earning a coveted Cross of St. Louis and knighthood in the process. He was wounded at the siege of Landau during the Rhine campaign of 1713 and later would be stationed in Flanders before being nominated for the position of director of fortification for Îsle Royale in June 1716.

Verville's first order of business was to survey the three primary ports on Îsle Royale before returning to France with an estimate of the cost to secure each. By late 1716 the engineer had accomplished this task. He first recommended that Louisbourg be the center of the fishing trade and the colonial capital. Fortification work should start there, with Port Dauphin and Port Toulouse being given secondary considerations.

At Louisbourg, Verville's projected fortifications began with the town and anchorage situated along a peninsula on the western edge of the harbor. To guard the landside approach to the town the engineer took advantage of a series of hills at the base of the western peninsula to erect bastions and interconnecting curtain walls, which would stretch over a thousand yards from the sea to the harbor (G to E on the map on page 11). The bastions would double as barracks for the six companies of troops assigned to the port, and a ditch would be dug in front of the works, the resulting dirt from this being used to form a glacis and covered way.

The island battery (I) near the narrow entrance to the harbor was the primary line of defense against naval forces looking to enter and attempt a landing. As such, a masonry redoubt capable of holding a score of heavy guns was to be erected here. Behind this, at the head of the bay (K), Verville called for a redoubt and a battery of heavy guns that could not only target the narrow entrance and support the Island Battery, but bombard any intruders that made their way into the upper harbor. Known as the Grand or Royal Battery, the position would become a fixture in the defenses of Louisbourg even though isolated, and with suspect landside defenses, it was of questionable use. There were other issues Verville addressed. He called for state officials not to be involved with the fishing trade, and he complained of the slow progress made by the garrison on the current defenses, recommending that a contractor be employed to construct the proposed works.

It is clear that the Verville opinion carried a great deal of weight, in part given the status French engineers had amassed under the leadership of the founder of this organization, Marshal Sebastien Vauban, and in part as a result of his own reputation. The use of masonry construction would be costly, as there was no nearby quarry or brickyard, meaning a source would either need to be found or everything would have to be imported. Fortunately, limestone was discovered at nearby Canso, which would simplify logistics and reduce the costs for this important component. Satisfied with the engineer's report, the French court approved his plan in July 1717, and the fortress of Louisburg took a major step toward becoming a reality.[11]

CHAPTER TWO

Nova Scotia

QUESTIONS REGARDING the bounds of ancient Acadia and the fate of its citizens were addressed in March 1715 by the Board of Trade in London, which was responsible for colonial matters. The boundary issue focused on two points. First, was Cape Breton part of the ancient limits of Acadia, and second, did these limits extend along the coast of modern-day New Brunswick and Maine to the Kennebec River? As to the first point, the French argued that given the physical separation of Nova Scotia and Cape Breton by the Gut of Canso, it had never been considered part of Nova Scotia. More importantly, it did not matter. French officials pointed to the Treaty of Utrecht, which explicitly spoke to Cape Breton being French territory.

A more worrisome push came from those who wished to enforce the ancient claims along the New Brunswick and Maine shoreline. The reasons for wanting to do this were clear; it was a fertile land teeming with a host of ports and much better adapted to settlement than Nova Scotia or Cape Breton. While objections and counter protests continued along these lines from both sides, any actual attempt at settlement by the British came at a substantial risk. The region had long since been claimed by the Wabanaki Confederacy, and while they had submitted to British authority under the Treaty of Portsmouth the year before, any attempt to push these claims would likely bring the northern colonies into another conflict with their old adversaries. With the memories of King William's and Queen Anne's Wars along the Maine, New Hampshire, and Massachusetts frontiers still fresh in their minds, few in New England were interested in letting this happen.[1]

The next matter discussed, pertaining to the French citizens of Acadia, was the most pressing one before the Board of Trade. When Nicholson captured Port Royal in 1710, all the citizens were given a choice; they could take an oath of allegiance to Queen Anne and remain on their lands, or they had one year to remove themselves from Nova Scotia. These conditions were reflected in the Treaty of Utrecht signed by the British and French on April 11, 1713, essentially resetting the one-year clock established by Nicholson.

It would take several months for news of the treaty and its terms to reach the concerned parties in North America, but by the fall of 1713 most colonial officials had been informed. Even so, it would not be until the following summer that the French sent representatives to Annapolis Royal to ascertain those who wished to leave and those who wished to stay. The lieutenant governor of Nova Scotia, Thomas Caulfield, acted in a courteous and professional manner as the citizens were questioned as to their decisions. With who would stay and who wished to go resolved, it now became a question of transportation. The French representatives were able to take a few citizens back to Louisbourg, and a few families who possessed vessels sailed on their own, but the majority had livestock and households to transport. It was agreed that transportation would be provided by France and that materials to allow the inhabitants to build vessels for their own transport would be sent. The net effect of this arrangement had been to reset the clock once again.[2]

The initial inclination, pushed by Nicholson and Vetch, had been in favor of the Acadians' departure. They had previously taken oaths to the Crown only to break them. Allowing them to stay, especially under the influence of their Catholic priests, would just lead to trouble when a rupture appeared between France and Britain. However, the delay in the Acadians' departure had raised a number of questions, which Vetch, who had been replaced by Nicholson in the fall of 1712, addressed in a November 24 letter to the Board of Trade.

Vetch placed the number of Acadians affected at 2,500, and information reaching him was that almost all, under threat of repercussions and the lure of promises by the French envoys, had elected to leave. If so, it would be a disaster on multiple levels. The flight would leave the colony "entirely destitute of inhabitants." Basic food production, fisheries, and over five thousand head of cattle would leave with them. In turn, the net effect on Îsle Royale would be to double its population and create an agricultural base on the island, which would normally take a decade or more to establish. Not only would the prosperous trade associated with these people be lost, but the Wabanaki in the area, primarily Micmac and Maliseet, would likely leave with them, which also meant the loss of the Indian trade, a considerable amount according to Vetch. Beyond strengthening Îsle Royale, which was hardly in the interest of Great Britain, it would have a crushing effect on Nova Scotia. It would take years to replace the cattle and livestock production on the island, all of which would have to be purchased and transported from New England at a sizable cost. It would also be difficult to attract future settlers, who clearly understood that they would be exposed to the wrath of the French and their Micmac allies should any rupture in the peace occur.[3]

Caulfield was coming to a similar conclusion. With news arriving of the death of Queen Anne and the coronation of King George I on October 20, 1714, the lieutenant governor, his garrison, and the nearby English inhabitants had taken an oath of allegiance to the new British sovereign. Caulfield then used the event to dispatch a number of envoys among the Acadians to see if they would also take the oath. What he found was puzzling. Most refused but not always for the reasons he suspected. Many responded that they would not sign the oath because they had elected to leave and were just awaiting transportation. However, they were happy to sign that they would "do nothing contrary to the service of King George" while they remained in Nova Scotia. Others expounded on this point, officially stating that, "I promise and swear faithful allegiance to King George so long as I shall be in Nova Scotia, and permitted to retire where I judge fitting with all my moveable goods and effects when I judge fitting without hindrance." Some claimed that, without guidance from the governor of New France, they were unable to agree. A large element of this last group was the Wabanaki. When the envoys spoke with the Passamaquoddy sagamores, the latter shrugged and said, until they heard word from Governor Vaudreuil, they could not take the oath. The spokesman for the Penobscot was more direct, saying, "I do not proclaim any foreign King in my country," before vehemently objecting to the idea of the English settling on their lands.[4]

While it appeared that many of the French inhabitants were planning to leave, well over a hundred had taken the oath, and a number of communities had not been asked. Among many the matter appeared up in the air, and in the meantime, most agreed to conduct themselves by the laws of the land. Perhaps more telling was the testimony of a group of six representatives chosen from several towns and hamlets. They commended Caulfield's administration, which had maintained the peace and in their opinion was the best government, French or British, to date. Even so, they would not take the oath. "If it were not that we naturally cannot refuse the grace and favours which our good Most Christian King offers us," they reluctantly informed the lieutenant governor, "we should choose to live and die under his government."[5]

On May 3, 1715, the promised French transport having failed to materialize, Caulfield wrote the Board of Trade about his dilemma. "Ye Inhabitants of this country, being most of them french refuse the oaths, having as I am informed refused to quit this colony intirely and to settle under ye French Govrmt." With a large part of the population in limbo, and no guidance having arrived from London concerning their status, Caulfield desired "to be informed how I shall behave to them." Furthermore, the new government at Annapolis Royal had no money to purchase supplies from New England, and as such, were dependent on the local inhabitants for food. Caulfield pointed out that, if the Acadians were to actually leave, without immediate relief, "it will be impossible for this place to subsist the ensuing winter."[6]

As the Board of Trade considered the matter, Vetch, who had pointed out the perils of an Acadian exodus from Nova Scotia, proposed a simple solution; do not let them leave. According to the language in the Treaty of Utrecht, the French had one year to remove the Acadians who elected to exercise this option. This time had expired. True, a de facto extension was agreed upon the previous summer, but even this agreement was over a year old. Nothing in the treaty said that the British had to honor such an extension or abide by French timetables. At Vetch's urging the board interviewed a recent denizen of Nova Scotia, William Shirreff. Shirreff, one of Caulfield's clerks, had lived in Annapolis Royal for four years, during which time he had met and dealt with large numbers of Acadians as part of his duties. "Itt was with abundance of reluctancy that a great many of them, especially some of the principall amongst them whom I have seen cry, resolved upon going," Shirreff testified. "If itt is possible to prevaile upon them to stay, itt will certainly be of considerable advantage to that Collny." He then went on to confirm the concerns expressed by Vetch and Caulfield regarding the detrimental effects on the colony should the Acadians depart, especially on the garrison of Annapolis Royal. He expounded on the potential of the colony, which beyond the flourishing fishing trade along its coast was a bountiful source of pitch, tar, masts, and other naval products, and then ended by noting that "if industriously sought after, and itt probably may be brought sooner to perfection by the French remaining in the country."[7]

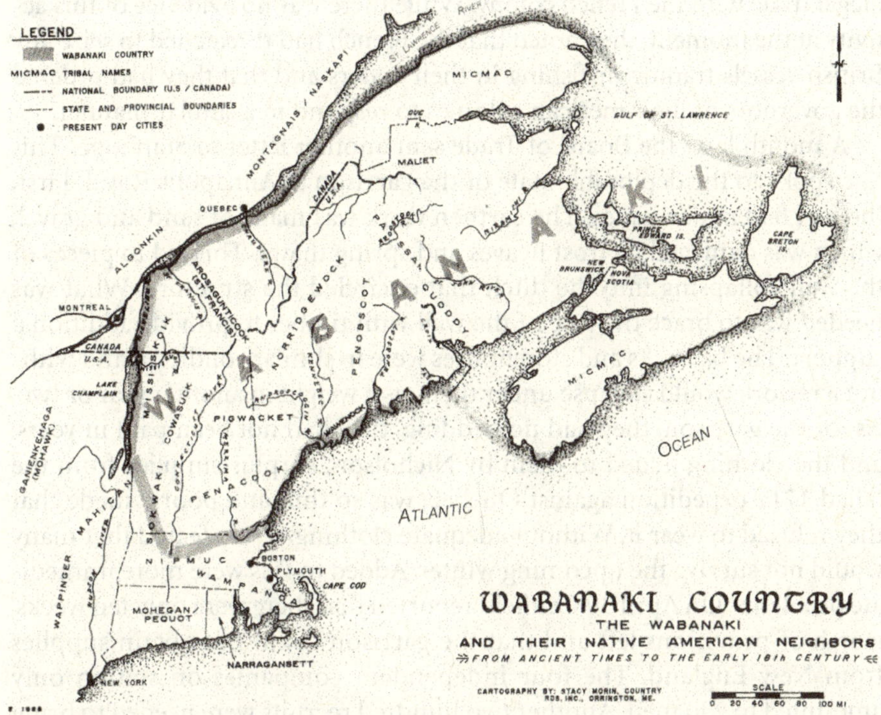

The Wabanaki Confederacy and nearby tribes. In this map the Eastern Abenaki have been represented by the Penobscot and the Norridgewock (Kennebec) who are but two of eleven tribes that make up the Eastern Abenaki. Likewise, several of the fourteen Western Abenaki tribes, the Penacook being the most prominent of these, are shown covering western Maine, New Hampshire, Vermont, and parts of modern-day Quebec. This pro-French confederacy would fight alongside their allies until the conquest of Canada in 1760. (*Morin County, Maine*)

It would not be until the end of May that the Board of Trade would write Secretary of State James Stanhope with their recommendations. They forwarded complaints that the ancient limits of Acadia encompassed Cape Breton, but even Vetch considered Cape Breton a separate territory. With this territory specifically stated as French in the treaty, the matter was a nonstarter. The matter of the departing Acadians was the main concern, and here they recommended a modification of Vetch's position. Any Acadian who wished to leave was free to do so, but as the allotted time under the treaty had passed, they would no longer be allowed to take their possessions, particularly their livestock, with them. There were also matters concerning illegal trade with the French colony. While there was no evidence of this activity at the moment, they noted that the French had threatened to seize any British vessels trading or fishing in their waters and that they had ordered the governors of the American colonies to respond in a similar manner.

A month later the Board of Trade sent another letter to Stanhope. This one spoke to the deplorable state of the garrison at Annapolis Royal. First, the fort had major issues. The earthen work was made of sand and gravel, which was damaged by frost heaves and spring thaws. This led to pieces of the wall collapsing into the ditch that encircled the structure. What was needed was to brace the face of the wall with timber to provide additional support. The barracks and storehouses were in similar condition and without a rework would collapse under their own weight in another year or two. As for the garrison, they had no bedding, they had not been paid in years, and the clothing issued to them by Nicholson, surplus supplies from the failed 1711 expedition against Quebec, was so thin and poorly made that they refused to wear it. Without adequate clothing, it was feared that many would not survive the upcoming winter. Added to this were more immediate problems. On April 30 Caufield reported that there were only ten weeks' worth of provisions left and that the garrison could not obtain supplies from New England. The four independent companies on station only amounted to 230 men. Another two hundred recruits were needed to bring these companies up to establishment, but even this might not prove enough, as conditions had deteriorated to the point that desertion seemed a better option for many.[8]

By November, when no signs of an Acadian exodus appeared, Caulfield once again made the case for their staying. He noted that, while the current generation might prove troublesome, their children, "in process of time may be brought to our constitution." They were an industrious people who the governor had not found issue with since his arrival. When asked, they had always been willing to help, and he noted that he had found "several well meaning people among them." It seemed clear that the best policy to follow was to either let them stay or, if need be, entice them to stay.

While Caulfield's approach was reminiscent of Colonel Richard Nicholls, the first English governor of New York after the conquest of the Dutch colony, there was a problem. Governor Nicholson, who had captured Port Royal in 1710 and become a prominent colonial figure after doing so, had a much different view of the matter. When he arrived at Annapolis Royal in August 1715 for a brief visit, he forced some of the French inhabitants to depart and "shut ye gates of the Garrison against those that remained and declared them traytors." He then informed the garrison that he would see to their supply issues and that they must be able to weather the winter without any help from the populace or perish in the attempt.[9]

Although this boosted the desertion numbers, fortunately the garrison was relieved, and Nicholson no longer became a problem when Vetch once again became governor of Nova Scotia. Nor did the Acadians leave, even when a French ship sent by Governor Costebelle appeared in the summer of 1716. The matter of an oath of allegiance to the British Crown, however, still remained one of the primary obstacles to a more permanent solution. Vetch was not surprised, expressing his opinion a few months earlier that, "As to the French inhabitants, there is not many removed, notwithstanding the discouragements they mett withal some time ago, and will no doubt gladly remain upon their plantations (some of which are considerable) provided they may be protected and encouraged by the Crown." What remained to be seen, in the governor's eyes, was whether they would remain loyal to Britain in the event of a conflict. In the fall of 1716 Caulfield summoned together the Acadians and secured an oath of allegiance from close to a thousand men, several of whom had returned from Cape Breton. The lengthy process, coupled with matters still under debate and trifling arguments, led the lieutenant governor to write London with a change of heart. "There is but little dependence on their friendship, tho' at the same time I am persuaded it will be with reluctancy that they leave the country."[10]

When Lt. Governor John Douchett arrived at Annapolis Royal in late October 1717 to replace the deceased Caulfield, he was surprised to discover that a large number of citizens had still not taken the oath of loyalty. The new lieutenant governor called together the Acadians in the vicinity of Annapolis Royal and informed them that, if they did not sign the oath of allegiance, they would not be given the rights of British citizens to fish along the shores of Nova Scotia. The Acadians still refused to sign, this time claiming that if they did the French authorities would use the Wabanaki against them, and at present, there was no way for the British to protect them from this threat. Thus, they proposed a neutral state, where they would take up arms for neither the French nor British. The idea was immediately dismissed, and Douchett viewed the Wabanaki claim as dubious, informing London that he believed "they fear'd their preists much more than the Indians," the former of which were "contually doeing all in their power to prevent an English settlement in this Country." Even with the power of these individuals over the populace, Douchett was optimistic. While his initial attempts had only netted a handful of signatures, after the meeting he found "severall inclin'd to signe rather then loose the profitt they reap in the fishing season, which begins here in spring and lasts till the winter, so that I expect as the spring aproaches, if advantage can biass them more then their preists, some (if not all) will declare themselves subjects to H.M."[11]

Another concern for the new lieutenant governor were reports that French citizens from Cape Breton were fishing around Canso and using the nearby shores to dry their catch. Douchett wrote the new commander of Louisbourg, Joseph de St. Ovide, on May 15, 1718, to complain about the infringement of the treaty and inquire into the intents of the French toward the Acadians who wished to leave. Douchett then wrote a letter to Governor Vaudreuil in Quebec, informing him of his new appointment to Nova Scotia and his commitment to upholding the peace treaty between the two nations. He asked that Vaudreuil make the terms of the treaty clear to his Native allies and requested that the Bishop of Canada direct his missionaries in Acadia not to engage in anything "contrary to King George's interest," otherwise, he warned, "I must be oblidged to use such methods, as would not be pleasing to me or to them."[12]

St. Ovide responded that he would "neglect nothing to maintain the peace" but claimed no knowledge of illegal fishing activities. He then pointed out that the ancient border of Acadia only went as far east as the St. Mary River, and as such Canso and the area about it was French as per the treaty. As for the Acadians, the threat of not letting them take their possessions should they depart and the British interference in allowing the French to send naval supplies for the small boats many had built to leave was at fault for the current situation. "You must know how impossible M. Nicholson and other Governors of Nova Scotia made it for them to fulfill the agreement," St. Ovide pointed out to Douchett. The response from Vaudreuil also contained a surprise. First, the French governor agreed that the priests should confine themselves to their ministries. "I can hardly believe them so ill advised, as to stir up the people who have submitted," he wrote Douchett. Vaudreuil then protested the British policy of not letting the Acadians take their possessions as part of their departure. Another option, Vaudreuil noted, was to allow the Acadians to withdraw with their cattle and other possessions to the St. Johns River (New Brunswick), which, being outside the ancient limits of Acadia, was still French territory.[13]

Governor Samuel Shute of Massachusetts had also heard of French fishing violations near Canso. When confronted with complaints by Yankee fishermen, Shute, a decorated British cavalry officer who had served with the Duke of Marlborough during the War of Spanish Succession, took a more direct approach to resolving the matter. Like Douchett, he wrote a letter to St. Ovide calling for the immediate withdrawal of any French vessels and settlers from the area. "I therefore ask the proper redress from you," Shute wrote, "before I proceed to other methods of asserting and vindicating the rights of the King of Great Britain." To accentuate his last point, the governor dispatched Captain Thomas Smart and the 24-gun frigate H.M.S. *Squirrel* to deliver the letter. Shute informed Smart that, if he did not receive a satisfactory answer to the summons, he was to begin enforcing British fishing rights.

Shute had also sent Captain Cyprian Southack, a well-known New England mariner who had served in both King William's War and Queen Anne's War, and had charted much of the area, to act as his envoy. On September 11, Southack and Smart met with St. Ovide and his senior officers at Louisbourg and presented Governor Shute's letter. St. Ovide's argument centered not of the activities of French fishermen but on an interpretation of the "ancient limits" of Acadia. Southack countered this with his charts and knowledge of the area, making it clear that the old limits of Acadia embraced the entire peninsula to the east of the Gut of Canso. In fact, this was spelled out when Cape Breton was to remain French. The two men began to disagree concerning the twelfth and thirteenth articles of the Treaty of Utrecht when St. Ovide pointed out that this is what the Treaty Boundary Commission in Paris was to settle. The kings of France and Britain had not appointed St. Ovide or Governor Shute to decide such matters. The French commander then suggested that perhaps it would be best if the area in question, Canso, not be used by either side until their respective governments had reached an agreement. The conference convened for the day, but the next morning Smart was more direct. He demanded that St. Ovide give orders for the French who were fishing and drying their catches at Canso to withdraw. He would accept any reasonable time period for this withdrawal, but the order must be made now. St. Ovide simply reiterated his previous point that the matter belonged in the hands of their respective Crowns. Smart openly registered the complaint once again before assuring St. Ovide that his decision would be "resented by the English Government and that measures would be taken accordingly."[14]

With nothing resolved, the meeting ended, and the next morning the *Squirrel* raised sail and departed Louisbourg Harbor. Captain Smart followed the governor's directives and anchored the frigate near Canso for several days in hopes that the French would withdraw. When they did not, he sent marines ashore to rip down their fishing huts and drying stations. He then pounced on French fishing vessels near Canso. Several were chased away, and a pair loaded with a sizable amount of fish were seized. Content with his work, Smart triumphantly entered Boston Harbor in late September with his prizes in tow. While Shute and the town's merchants applauded the results, few stopped to realize the potential repercussions.[15]

St. Ovide was taken by surprise when news of what had transpired reached him. He impressed a 30-gun ship in the harbor and, after assembling a crew of 250 soldiers and sailors, ordered Jean-Joseph D'Allard de Ste. Marie to proceed immediately to Canso. The crew and ship's captain, however, were so disorganized that they were not ready to leave until the next morning, and when storms appeared at daylight St. Ovide called off the venture. While some were critical of St. Ovide's response, it was clear at this point that he chose to take a diplomatic approach to the matter. He sent St. Marie to Canso to make an accurate assessment of what had occurred and to begin removing any French inhabitants he found there. When this was complete, he seized a pair of British vessels in retaliation and then filed a long complaint with the French treaty commissioners in Paris. St. Ovide's correspondence arrived about the same time as Governor Shute's letter reached London. Both sides complained of ill conduct from the other and argued their interpretation of the borders of ancient Acadia. Both also found unreceptive audiences. The French court, with numerous other issues before it, sought a diplomatic solution as part of the upcoming discussions on demarcating the colonial boundaries in North America. London, while it approved of Shute's stern approach toward illegal trade in Nova Scotia, held a similar view and was not interested in escalating the matter. At the moment, with current negotiations concerning the borders of Hudson Bay proceeding in a harmonious manner, there was little to be gained by straining the relations between the two nations.[16]

News of the War of the Quadruple Alliance pitting France, England, Austria, and the Dutch Republic against Spain arrived at Louisbourg and Annapolis Royal in the spring of 1719. While such events would have great bearing on the colonial powers in southeastern North America, in the northeast the issues between the British and the French in Nova Scotia would take on a different character. The new governor of Nova Scotia, Richard Philipps, would not arrive at Annapolis Royal until the middle of April 1720. As with his recent predecessors, his first order of business was to once again offer the Acadians an opportunity to take the oath of allegiance to the British Crown. The Acadians were torn by their decision. It was of no fault of their own that the French had not sent transport, and should they comply with Philipps and take the oath, the French at Îsle Royale would view them as traitors and launch the Micmac against them. At the moment, they could do nothing until the matter of French assistance was resolved. Philipps suspected that the latter case was not true, but he had neither orders to forcibly remove the Acadians nor the military strength to do so. The governor extended the evacuation deadline and then wrote the Board of Trade in London for directions. He believed that most inhabitants would choose to stay but that the French priests were behind the lack of commitment. Given his current strength he asked for reinforcements, an armed sloop to patrol the shores, and a few hundred Mohawk from New York to keep the local Micmac in check should the Acadians leave or stay.[17]

"As to the French inhabitants of Nova Scotia, who appear so wavering in their inclinations," the Board of Trade replied to the governor, "we are apprehensive they will never become good subjects to H.M. whilst ye French Governors and their priests retain so great an influence over them." The agreement among the board was that they should be removed as soon as sufficient reinforcements had reached Philipps, but under no circumstances was he to "attempt their removal without H.M. possitive orders for that purpose." In the meantime, Philipps continued his cautious approach toward the inhabitants and assured them that they would be allowed to practice their religion should they choose to stay.[18]

Larger issues would soon cloud the matter. Governor Shute's attack on French fishing activities was not to go unpunished. Just before dawn on August 8, 1720, a detachment of fifty French and Micmac crept into the fishing village of Canso. A portion of the war party broke into small groups and dispersed among the sleeping homesteads while the remainder proceeded toward the docks. A few moments later, a shot rang out setting off a chorus of war whoops and shouts as doors quickly gave way before the attackers. A few resisted and paid the price, but most were dragged out of their beds and led to a large building where they were held while their homes were ransacked. At the docks the French and Indian war party dashed upon the waterfront, and while they quickly captured over half a dozen vessels at the wharf, a number of fishermen were able to reach their ships anchored in the harbor.

As suddenly as it had started it was over. At sunrise most of the town and its inhabitants were in the attackers' hands. Leaving the prisoners behind, the war party sailed away to a nearby island with their booty. The location—owned by Captain Thomas Richards, who was currently aboard a ship in Canso Harbor—had been seized before the attack, netting the raiders sixteen prisoners and one of Richards' sloops. Part of the English fishing fleet rallied and approached the island only to be chased away by musket fire. That afternoon, after the French had set sail for Îsle Royal, Richards outfitted two small vessels and set off in pursuit. It proved a well-timed response, as six vessels, holding much of the plunder, were recaptured along with fifteen of the attackers.[19]

The prisoners made it clear to Philipps that the attack was in retaliation for Captain Smart's attack on Canso and that the governor of Louisbourg was behind the effort. He had sent an emissary to the Micmac villages to elicit their aid with presents of powder and shot. Philipps sent the prisoners depositions along with a letter of complaint to St. Ovide, as a company of soldiers was dispatched to Canso with orders to erect a fort. St. Ovide blamed the action on brigands, and as far as the Micmac were concerned, he responded by saying that he had no say or control over their actions. Fearing a larger problem, Philipps met with Wabanaki envoys. Thus far, his relations with the Wabanaki had been cordial and peaceful, and this was no different. He personally met with several sagamores who had pledged their commitment to the peace treaty. He then presented them with the customary gifts. "But I am convinc'd that a hundred thousand will not buy them, from the French interest while the priests are among them," he later wrote London.[20]

One of the governor's first letters to the Acadians concerning the attack on Canso was to the French deputies of Minas, ordering them to incarcerate a number of nearby Micmac who had participated in the plundering of an English vessel. The response from the citizens was somewhat expected; they had nothing to do with it, did not wish to be involved, and claimed to be far more afraid of the Micmac than the English. Unexpectedly, the Micmac sent a letter to Philipps clearly stating their position. They informed him that his threats would not succeed. "We have assembled to tell you that this land which God has given us and to which we belong cannot be claimed by anyone else." Philipps responded by sending an envoy to the Passamaquoddy on the St. Johns River. The latter pointed out that they had nothing to do with the Micmac or their attack on Canso and had no intention of disturbing the peace. Their reason for doing so, however, did nothing to comfort Philipps. "We desire to do so," they explained, "for so long as our great King Louis of France shall be at peace, we shall be so too, being assured of his favour and protection. We can only obey his commands, he being our ally and having always protected us."[21]

While frustrated and lacking options, at least Philipps took some consolation in that it appeared that the Canso incident would not develop into a wider conflict that would threaten the weak colony. Little did he realize that this would come from a larger issue brewing to the west.

CHAPTER THREE

The Road to War

THE ATTACK ON CANSO by the French and Micmac was just an extension of a long-running dispute between traditional opponents: New England and the Wabanaki Confederacy. Under the Treaty of Portsmouth in 1713, the Wabanaki were proclaimed British subjects and were to abide by British law, trade regulations, and "never entertaine any treasonable conspiracy with any other nation." Just as importantly, the English settlers would return to their homes along the coast of Maine without molestation, and the lands east of the Kennebec River, as stated in the earlier treaties, were to remain Wabanaki.

There was really little choice but for the sagamores to agree to the terms of the treaty. After two wars and almost twenty-five years of continuous fighting, the Wabanaki Confederacy was exhausted. Their numbers had gone from an estimated fighting force of a thousand at the opening of King William's War to three hundred at the time of the treaty. During Queen Anne's War their traditional ally, New France, had once again failed to supply the confederacy with the goods they required and the military aid they had promised. Thus, when Governor Joseph Dudley of Massachusetts proposed that all lands to the east of the Kennebec would remain Wabanaki, the sagamores agreed to the terms, which fulfilled their biggest demand.[1]

Many settlers were anxious to return to their old homes, and within a few months the Massachusetts assembly had authorized funds to promote the resettlement of Saco, Scarborough, Falmouth, North Yarmouth, and Arrowsic Island. Falmouth, which had maintained a garrison at Fort Loyal during Queen Anne's War, was quickly repopulated. The damaged old homes were repaired, but soon this was not enough and new homesteads began to appear at nearby Purpooduck, Spurwick, and later New Casco. Saco followed a similar path, rapidly filling the old town and spilling out into hamlets nearby. Scarborough took longer but resulted in several settlements in the area. North Yarmouth and nearby Cape Porpoise, which had been devastated during Queen Anne's War, took even longer, but the latter officially became known as Arundel (Kennebunkport in 1820).

Smaller towns and villages to the west of the Kennebec River followed. Thus far, the Wabanaki remained friendly, trading and bartering with the settlers when they encountered them. A push to establish Brunswick, Topsham, and Harpswell on the west bank of the Kennebec, near the mouth of the river, drew more attention from the Wabanaki, as did the settlements on Arrowsic Island and Georgetown on Parker's Island. From these locations fish, particularly sturgeon, and vast quantities of timber were transported downriver and forwarded to markets in Boston and elsewhere. Fields were cleared and fishing vessels clustered at new wharfs in a host of harbors along the southwest coast of Maine. None of this activity bothered the Wabanaki, and even some of the settlements near the mouth of the Kennebec, such as Georgetown on Arrowsic Island, which were technically to the east of the river, were shrugged at.

The construction of Fort George at Brunswick and Fort Menaskoux on Arrowsic Island, however, was a different matter. At the moment, the balance of power worked. The Wabanaki villages were vulnerable to an attack, but so too were the colonists. However, should the New Englanders erect a line of fortifications along their border, this balance of power would shift in their favor, particularly if these fortifications were built in stone like Fort George. The Wabanaki had been consistent in their opposition to fortifying the frontier, and given that this point had been a primary component in several major conflicts with New England, it is not surprising that a return to this practice would elicit a similar response. Nor did matters improve when rumors arrived that the English were looking to construct another fort on the west bank of the Kennebec and, worse yet, were planning to rebuild the stone fort at Pemaquid.[2]

The sudden resurgence of settlements along the Maine frontier had also created a number of petty incidents. New Hampshire Lt. Governor George Vaughan and several representatives met with a pair of Wabanaki spokesmen at Portsmouth in June 1716. The emissaries were quickly questioned

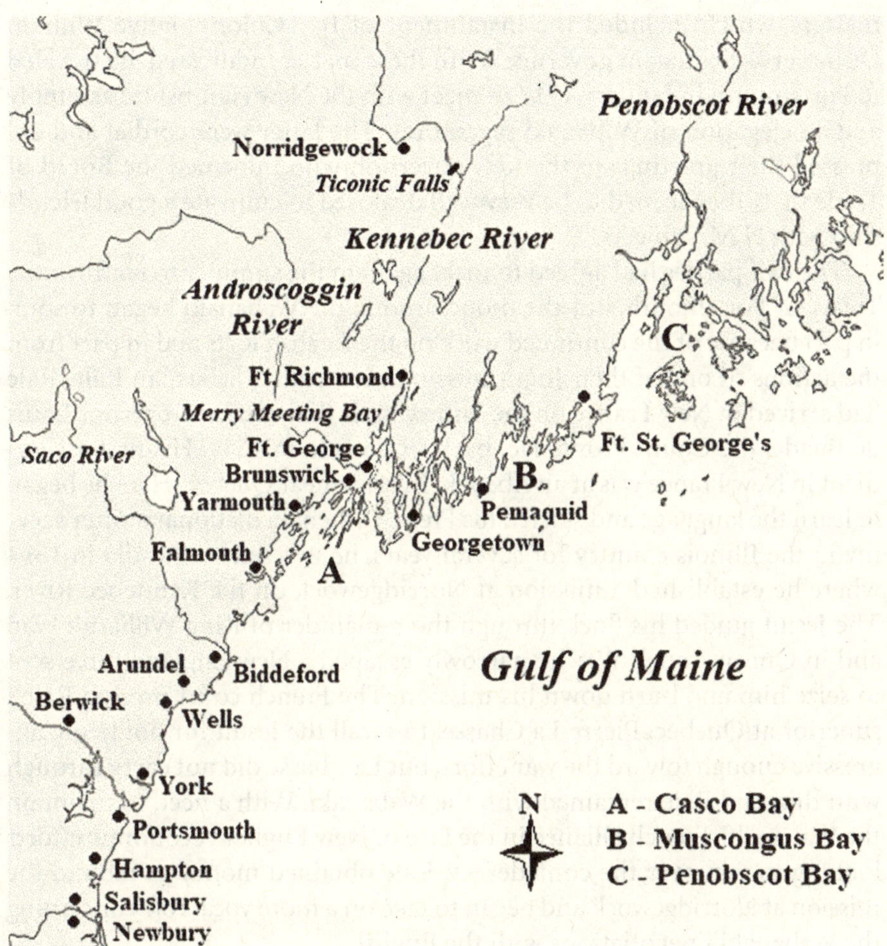

The New England Coast from Newbury, Massachusetts, to Penobscot Bay.

by Vaughan as to a rumor that had reached him. "We are informed from Albany ye Indians had a design against the English this spring as soon as the grass was grown." The Wabanaki spokesman, Abombasein, nodded and said, "We heard some such thing but had it from ye English." Vaughan advanced to questions on a number of minor incidents, but in the end Abombasein shrugged. "There are a great many storys you tell us, we are sorry for them but are ignorant about them."[3]

When the new governor of Massachusetts, Colonel Samuel Shute, arrived at Boston on October 4, 1716, he first focused his attention on local matters, which included the installment of Bay Colony native William Dummer as lieutenant governor. With these matters addressed, he traveled to Portsmouth in January 1717 to meet with the New Hampshire assembly and a delegation of Wabanaki sagamores. The latter were cordial and expressed their greetings to the new governor, who informed the Board of Trade that "they seem'd to be very well disposed to cultivate a good friendship with H.M. subjects."[4]

The two parties had agreed to meet again in the summer to reaffirm the Treaty of Portsmouth, but the mood among the Wabanaki began to sour, in part because of the continued work on the English forts and in part from the actions of one of their Jesuit missionaries, Father Sabastian Rale. Rale had arrived in New France on the same vessels that carried Governor Louis de Buade, the Count Frontenac, back to Canada in 1689. His first assignment in New France was at an Abenaki mission near Quebec. Here he began to learn the language and started his French-Abenaki dictionary. After serving in the Illinois country for several years, he was sent to Acadia in 1694 where he established a mission at Norridgewock on the Kennebec River. The Jesuit guided his flock through the remainder of King William's War, and in Queen Anne's War he narrowly escaped a New England force sent to seize him and burn down his mission. The French court pressed Rale's superior at Quebec, Pierre La Chasse, to recall the Jesuit for not being aggressive enough toward the war effort, but La Chasse did not carry through with this, and Rale remained with the Wabanaki. With a need to maintain the Wabanaki-French alliance in the face of New England economic efforts looking to win over the confederacy, Rale obtained money to rebuild the mission at Norridgewock and began to take on a more vocal role concerning the Wabanaki's negotiations with the English.[5]

On August 9, 1717, the H.M.S. *Squirrel*, carrying Shute and a number of representatives from Massachusetts and New Hampshire, dropped anchor at Georgetown-on-Arrowsic. Onshore was a cluster of settlers and sagamores. Shute sent an officer to notify the party that the governor would set up his tent and raise the Union flag around three o'clock. That afternoon, Shute, flanked by colonial officials and a small guard, met with sagamores from the Norridgewock, Pigwacket, and Penobscot nations led by Moxus and his father Bomazeen.

After a long oration by Shute, which expounded the "great, good and wise" virtues of their mutual king, George I, the governor pointed to the recent resettlement of the region and how peace and trade was of mutual benefit to both parties. He then emphasized that the Wabanaki could depend on him, the king's representative, to justly deal with any of their complaints. The Wabanaki spokesman, Winuirna, thanked the governor for his address and asked that the sagamores be permitted to respond the next morning, to which Shute agreed.

At 9:00 a.m. the conference reconvened. Shute had the terms of the Treaty of Portsmouth read aloud and asked the sagamores if they agreed with these articles. They signaled that they understood the governor but wished to speak to a pair of issues. The first dealt with the provisions in the treaty that all English claims to lands along the coast of Maine would be returned to their ancient state. That is, pre-King William's War. It was true that the lands east of the Kennebec were Wabanaki, Shute responded, but the previous coastal settlements up to the St. George River would be restored. The Wabanaki asked that no further settlements be made, but Shute was clear on the point that the old settlements, to which deeds and purchases could be shown, would be restored.

After consulting among themselves, the sagamores returned with a proposal. "We are Willing to cut off our Lands as far as the Mills, and the Coasts to Pemaquid," Winuirna informed the governor. Shute shook his head after the interpreter finished. "We desire only what is our own, and that we will have," he returned. The question then became one of the new forts being erected. When Winuirna pointed out that no new forts were to be built in the area, the governor shrugged and said such practices were for both the English and the Wabanaki's protection. This line of questioning went on for several minutes until Winuirna stood. "We are a little uneasy concerning these Lands, but are willing the English shall possess all they have done, excepting Forts."[6]

The Wabanaki could see the expression on the governor's face. "Tell them we will not take an Inch of their Land," Shute informed the interpreter, "nor will we part with an inch of our own." The answer did not seem to satisfy any of the chieftains, who suddenly rose and walked off. Shute threw up his hands and returned to the *Squirrel*. A few hours later a letter arrived from Rale. The Jesuit pointed out that, when Governor Vaudreuil was recently in Paris, he had conferred with the king on whether he had given away any Indian lands under the recent treaty. The king informed him that he had not and was prepared to defend these Natives from any aggression. Shute tossed the letter aside and was prepared to leave the next morning when a pair of canoes halted his departure. The Wabanaki apologized for their behavior and wished to meet again to ratify the treaty. Shute agreed, and with a new Wabanaki spokesman, the terms of the Treaty of Portsmouth were reaffirmed.[7]

While the Arrowsic Treaty was good news, it was clear to Shute and several others that Rale and a number of French envoys were seeking to undermine the agreement. Shute even wrote to Rale in February, reminding him of his "Management & Conduct" toward the Eastern Indians, who were British subjects by treaty, meaning he would be held accountable to King George for any infractions against his rule. He assured the Jesuit that old land claims, which owners had disposed of during the various conflicts, would be restored, but "As to the Lands lying to the Eastward of Pemaquid, I know of no Settlement Designed at present from hence in those parts." After expressing a number of other complaints, the governor concluded by warning Rale that if a fracture with the Wabanaki should occur he would lay responsibility for it at the Jesuit's feet.

Matters were about to become worse in this regard. The following year a "Memoir respecting the Abenaquis of Acadia" appeared before Governor Vaudreuil. The author admitted that the Treaty of Ryswick, which had ended King William's War, had fixed the border at the St. George River but that "the Abenaquis pretend that the whole of that coast, and all the rivers to be found therein, belong to them. And it is our interest to sustain them in their pretensions." If this was not done and the Wabanaki fell under English control, the entire French Maritimes would be in jeopardy. Thus, in order to maintain this alliance, it had to be made clear to the government of Massachusetts that the French would support their allies if they attempted to encroach upon their lands. There was really little choice in the matter.

> 1st That this Nation is the only support of the Colony against the English or the Iroquois. 2nd If we do not admit or pretend to admit their right to the country they occupy, they will never be induced to take a part in any war for the defence of this same country, which is the rampart of Canada. 3rd If some interest be not exhibited in their defence, they will divide themselves between the French and the English, and in as much as they experience better terms in regard to trade from the latter than from the former, it will not be long before they are wholly attached to them. More than half the tribe is already English by inclination, and retained only by Religion; their Missionaries alone have the power, it is admitted, to persuade them to submit to the will of the Governor-general. 4th If matters be allowed to proceed ever so little in the course they have been for some time pursuing, New France will be bounded on the South by the River St Lawrence; it will be necessary to abandon all our posts and settlements on that side, and nothing will prevent the English and the Iroquois making irruptions into the very heart of the Colony.[8]

The author was careful to point out that, although some wished to see a conflict between the Wabanaki and the English, even if the former were armed by the French, it was not the answer. First, the current Wabanaki were not the Wabanaki of old. Their fighting strength was now only a few hundred men. If they were "not to be aided by some men, can we, with honor and in conscience, precipitate it into a war against an enemy greatly its superior?" the author questioned. Then, pointing to the logical outcome of such an action, he asked, "What will become of ourselves if these Indians be worsted, and the English become masters of their villages, some of which are in our midst?"[9]

The mood of the confederacy was certainly changing. A number of Norridgewock, unhappy with the recent agreement at Georgetown, sent deputies to Quebec to speak with Governor Vaudreuil. After detailing their plight, they asked the governor if he would help them if they went to war with the English. Vaudreuil nodded and said that he would always come to the assistance of his allies. The Wabanaki spokesman thanked him and pointed out that, "as they had assisted him at the expense of their blood on every occasion that he had required," what manner of aid would he send? He would send hatchets, powder, and guns, Vaudreuil informed the Native representatives. The comment brought forth a murmur and a number of frowns. "Is this the way, then," the spokesman returned, "that a Father aids his children, and was it thus we assisted you?" Vaudreuil then promised that he would send the other Native allies of New France to help them. Seeing that this brought forth yet more grumbling among the delegation, the governor ended the matter by standing and saying, if necessary, he would personally lead this force. The conference broke up with the Wabanaki unconvinced as to French promises of assistance.[10]

The situation would only worsen over the next few years as more settlers arrived on the Maine frontier. The Wabanaki watched as Fort William Henry at Pemaquid was repaired, and work was started on Fort St. George's on the St. George's River in what is today Thomaston, Maine. In the summer of 1719 Wabanaki behavior toward the colonists seemed to turn suspicious, causing Shute to send fifty soldiers to reinforce the garrisons across the frontier. Little materialized, although Shute blamed the mood on Rale and the other missionaries among the Native nations and even petitioned the French court to have these offenders recalled. On July 4, 1720, Massachusetts representatives met with several Norridgewock sagamores at Falmouth to discuss current grievances between the Wabanaki and the settlers. The commissioners ascribed the problems to complaints that English settlements were springing up east of the Kennebec River and to the influence of Rale, as well as the promise from the governor of New France that he would march to their assistance in the event of hostilities.

The incidents of theft, property damage, and threats against settlers had only intensified with news of the French and Micmac attack on Canso in August, but another conference was arranged on November 25, 1720, at Georgetown. Colonel Shadrach Walton and Samuel Moody spoke for the Massachusetts government, while Warraweuset, alias Mogg, spoke for the Norridgewock and other sagamores that were present. Walton addressed his credentials and power to speak for the government of Massachusetts. When he asked Mogg to demonstrate his credentials, the sagamore stood holding a belt of wampum over his head for all to see as his commission to speak on the behalf of those present. Satisfied, Walton announced that the talks could proceed, at which point Mogg also expressed his satisfaction, saying, "We desire we may go on with Our talk, first that the people that are upon Our land at Merry Meeting [Bay] may be removed." [11]

Walton ignored the comment and proceeded with English grievances against the Wabanaki, which, regardless of past promises, seemed to have grown worse. The mischief and insults would not be allowed to continue. Mogg shrugged and conceded that some of the young men had gone too far. They had been spoken to about such matters. The real issue, however, was not these acts but the settlement at Merry Meeting Bay. "If all those people were removed from Merry Meeting Bay, all other Differences between us would be easyly composed."[12]

Walton chastised the spokesman for diverting the conference away from the damages incurred by settlers and the Wabanaki's former promise to compensate the injured parties. Mogg pointed out that none of the sagamores had heard of such an agreement. They asked what price was to be paid and for time to collect the required payment. Walton, not believing the delegates, finally proposed a solution. "You are the Heads of your tribes and must answer for what they do," he informed the sagamores, "But to make short of the matter we demand 200 skins of you which is but a small matter in comparison of the Injuries you have done us." Walton, however, was not finished. He berated the chieftains on the conduct of their young men, which, if not controlled, would bring the English in search of justice. He then blamed many of their ills on Father Rale—that his lies and deceit were leading the Wabanaki down a path of "Utter ruin & Distruction."[13]

Negotiations then ensued, in which to the surprise of Walton, the sagamores agreed to return in twenty-five days' time with the skins, and as a pledge to carry through with this promise they would leave four sagamores as hostages. Walton, who had taken a heavy-handed approach to the matter, then pressed the hostage conditions further, saying even after the agreed upon payment, the hostages would continue to be held as assurance of the Wabanaki's good behavior. In addition, any other number of hostages demanded by the government would be delivered in fulfillment of this continuing pledge. Walton had a small document drawn up to which several of his officers signed and Mogg as well as five other sagamores affixed their seal. Since the matter seemed settled, Walton expressed a final warning to the sagamores. The deeds to the lands up to the St. George River, some seventy years old, would be restored, by force if need be.

For Father Rale, whose new church at Norridgewock had just been finished, news of the agreement arrived with warnings that the English had put a bounty of £100 on him. The latter was disconcerting but not surprising given that the Jesuit was instantly blamed for every action undertaken by the Wabanaki. The charge leveled by the Massachusetts assembly was that the Jesuit had "been the Incendiary that has instigated & stirr'd up those Indians to treat his Majesty's Subjects setling there, in the abusive, insolent & hostile manner that they have done." This time, there was some truth to the charges. There were two factions forming within the Norridgewock and nearby Wabanaki nations. One was in support of Rale, who opposed the English encroachments and was vocal about it, and one which favored a more peaceful, negotiated settlement with the English.[14]

In pursuing his path Rale had two motives. First was his view that English deed claims were meaningless, particularly the seventy-year-old ones. It was nothing more than a land grab, aided by the twisting of arms if need be. Having lived among the Wabanaki for years he knew that no one, including sagamores, had the right to sell the land, which was viewed as common property. All knew such a gesture was meaningless, and as such, they would sell the land from east to west for a simple iron pot or a musket. In just the last year he had seen several plots of land sold to English traders, without any question as to the validity of the purchase under the Treaty of Portsmouth. As a respected voice among the native nations, he objected and soon found support from many who saw a familiar theme emerging from the English.

The Jesuit's second motive was tied to his means to continue to tend to his flock. Rale admitted that his converts' Catholic faith naturally aligned them to the French cause, but the lack of French goods and the proximity to cheaper products among the growing villages of Maine and New Hampshire had naturally shifted Wabanaki trade toward the British. In doing so, it had also allowed the English to build towns along the Kennebec River to meet this need. In the Jesuit's mind this economic connection was not only a threat to a Franco-Wabanaki alliance but a test of his and his flock's Catholic faith in the face of Protestant New England. Here Rale was convinced not only that they would triumph but that he would do everything in his power to help them succeed. "This is the tie which binds them to the French. It has been tried in vain to break it, either by traps which have been held out to their simplicity, or by acts of trespass, which could not help irritating a Nation infinitely zealous of its rights & of its liberty," he wrote his nephew on the troubled relationship between the British colonists and the Wabanaki. "These beginnings of misunderstandings fail not to alarm me, & make me fear the dispersion of the flock, which Providence has confided to my care so many years & for which I would willingly sacrifice that which remains of my life."[15]

Rale coordinated his actions with his superior La Chasse and Governor Vaudreuil at Quebec. The latter found his hands tied by a directive from the king to refrain from open hostilities with the English. The question of the land rights surrounding the ill-defined meaning of ancient Acadia had spilled into the question of the Wabanaki from Kennebec to St. Johns. At the moment, diplomatic talks were underway to address the matter, and the king did not wish to interrupt their deliberations. On the other hand, King Louis XV was pragmatic about the situation. Should the English attempt to press their claims before this commission had ruled, the governor was to use "his prudence to prevent it, either by means of the Indians or in any other way that would not, however, bring about any cause of rupture with England." With the proxy approach being the only option before him, Vaudreuil used Rale to forward this agenda. Just as the English encroachments along the coast of Maine appeared cyclic, so too was Vaudreuil's decision to push the Wabanaki toward another confrontation with New England.[16]

The second faction, the peace party in this case, looked to avoid conflict and pointed to the benefits of trade with the English. So what if they took their old settlements back? Three conflicts with the New Englanders had left the confederacy a shell of its former self while the English showed up in greater numbers every year. Talk of the French intervening was nonsense. True they would send arms and supplies, but one only needed to look at French support in the last two conflicts to understand what this promise really meant.

For the moment, the peace party had triumphed at Georgetown, agreeing to hostages and paying the required retribution of two hundred skins. The thought of accepting such conditions infuriated Rale and many within his party. The Jesuit wrote Vaudreuil with news of the treaty and what had transpired. The governor was dismayed by "the faint hearts of your Indians in giving hostages for damages done to those, who would drive them from their native country, have convinced me, that the present is a crisis in which a moment is not to be lost." Vaudreuil informed Rale that he was sending Father La Chasse with a few dozen Abenaki from the St. Francois and Becancour Missions along with a handful of Huron from Lorette to stiffen the resolve of the sagamores.[17]

On July 28, 1721, both Rale and La Chasse, who had formerly served among the Wabanaki, gave fiery speeches in front of several hundred Wabanaki. They pointed to the fact that the payment of two hundred skins had been made but the prisoners had not been returned, and how the English had once again violated their own treaty. These words were followed by those Abenaki war chiefs who had made the journey from Canada and soon found a home among the growing crowd of angry voices and defiant shouts. A few days later La Chasse, Rale, and Baron Castin led a procession of ninety canoes to Georgetown. Flying the French flag, the flotilla of 250 men, almost the entire fighting strength of the Wabanaki Confederacy, appeared before Fort Menaskoux and demanded to speak with the garrison's commander, Captain Samuel Penhallow. Penhallow, certainly uneasy about the sudden appearance of such a large French and Wabanaki delegation, agreed to meet with La Chasse, Rale, Castin, and Lt. M. de Croisel of the French Marines. The party gave Penhallow a letter addressed to Governor Shute, stating they wanted the prisoners returned, and if the questionable English settlements were not withdrawn in three weeks, they would return to burn them to the ground.[18]

In the Bay Colony the response to the threat was to raise three hundred troops to reinforce the garrisons along the frontier and to issue an edict calling for the Wabanaki to immediately turn over Rale and any other rebels who supported him. Otherwise, any Indian found would be taken prisoner and sent to Boston. As with the Wabanaki, there were many in Massachusetts who were in no rush to beat the war drums, remembering the visions of the frontier in flames. They questioned the government's failure to live up to its obligations under the Treaty of Portsmouth as being partly at fault. The promised trading posts had never been built to exchange furs and skins for provisions, ammunition, clothing, and other desired articles. Nor had the smiths or armorers been provided, as agreed upon in the treaty. These failures had only strengthened French influence over the Wabanaki, thus, before pushing measures further, perhaps these matters should be addressed.

One thing most of the citizens of Boston agreed with was that Father Rale was the lynchpin behind the Wabanaki's new attitude. A dead-or-alive reward was to be offered on the Jesuit, but Shute brought such talk to an end, rightly pointing out that it would only further aggravate the situation. However, this did not stop Baron Castin, a lieutenant in the French Marines and a Penobscot sagamore, from being apprehended on no specific charge after a friendly encounter near Georgetown. After several months of incarceration in Boston, Shute ordered the influential Castin to be released, in hopes of calming the situation.

As fall progressed into early winter there was talk that war would arrive in the spring. The Massachusetts assembly had convinced the governor that, to prevent this, a preemptive strike should be put into place to seize Rale. Shute had been skeptical of such an approach in the past and had frowned on Castin's arrest, but he finally agreed to the operation. In December, Colonel Thomas Westbrook led two hundred men up the Kennebec River to its junction with Sandy Creek. Ahead, the village of Norridgewock lay in the stark winter moonlight, its lower walls traced in fresh snow. Westbrook's timing was excellent. Most of the men were away hunting, leaving Rale in the village with the young, old, and sick. Fortunately for the Jesuit, a pair of young boys had seen the English boats struggling against the creek's current and outran them back to the village. Ordering the young to help the old and sick, Rale directed everyone into the woods. With time short, the Jesuit only had a few moments to gather together the sacred vessels in a small box before fleeing into the tree line. Westbrook's men arrived to find the village deserted. The next morning, they conducted a search and came within a handful of steps of discovering Rale hiding behind a tree. Having missed their quarry the New Englanders pillaged the mission, finding a chest containing Rale's correspondence with Vaudreuil, which pointed to the two men's efforts to stir up the Wabanaki against the English. Westbrook then ordered his men to carry away anything of value, including Rale's chapel bell, before putting the village to the torch and returning to the detachment's boats.[19]

While the letters would confirm what all suspected, their price was not worth the proof. Combined with the English having refused to return the four sagamores taken hostage and the illegal abduction of Castin, the attempt to capture Rale and the subsequent destruction of his mission had not only failed to defuse the situation and prevent a war, but in fact, had started one.

CHAPTER FOUR

The Three Years' War

ARMED WITH PROOF of Rale's and Governor Vaudreuil's attempt to rupture the peace along the New England frontier, Shute reinforced the garrisons and forwarded the evidence on to London. Many believed that the Wabanaki would strike once the snow receded and the rivers and streams opened to navigation. This, however, was not the case, as spring passed with a hopeful calm along the New Hampshire and Maine frontier. While some began to draw wishful signs from the lull, Governor Shute was not convinced, informing the Board of Trade that war would break out this summer unless the government of Canada could be forced to abide by the Treaty of Utrecht.[1]

Shute was remarkably close in his estimation. After returning home from their hunting trips, the Norridgewock and their allies discovered what had transpired with Castin and the attack on Rale's mission. Messengers were sent with the news for all able-bodied men to assemble at Norridgewock after the crops had been planted. The war song rang out as the Wabanaki tribes, joined by some of their brethren from the St. Francois and Becancour Missions as well as a number of Huron from the Lorette Mission, struck at the war pole and vowed to push back the English intruders.

On June 13, 1722, a string of twenty canoes filled with sixty brightly painted Wabanaki and a few French partisans descended the Kennebec River. At Merry Meeting Bay the war party encountered several small vessels, which they took without firing a shot. On board were nine families, the entire settlement of a nearby hamlet. Five of the prisoners were kept, in response to the four Sagamores being held in Boston they were informed, while the rest were set free. Small groups of Wabanaki surprised craft along the coast, but the next major effort was directed against Fort St. George's on the St. George's River. Here they surprised and burned a sloop, taking half a dozen captives in the process. A detachment then advanced on the newly built fort but were soon halted by musket and swivel gun fire from the walls. The two sides exchanged fire for several hours while the remaining attackers killed livestock and burned several homes. When this was accomplished the war party retreated with its captives.[2]

A few weeks later a more concerted attack was launched along the frontier. A war party of Penobscot quickly overran the settlement of St. George's and laid siege to Fort St. George's for twelve days, "being very much encouraged by the influence of the Friar that was with them." In fact, it was a Jesuit, Father Etienne Lauverjat of the Penobscot mission at Pentagoet. Under drizzling skies, the garrison watched from the fort's walls as the black-robed figure directed the war party to implement his limited, but by no means insufficient, knowledge of siege craft. A main trench was carved out of the ground and slowly advanced against one of the fort's walls. The plan was not without its merits. While Lauverjat did not have cannons to erect a firing parallel, if the trenchwork could place his forces close enough to the wall, he could attempt to either burn the structure or storm it at night from this advanced position.

The garrison did not panic and fired on the advancing sap with muskets and small cannons, but even here the Jesuit had an answer. Logs had been cut, lashed together, and then covered with branches and tied into a large bundle to yield a makeshift sap roller. The trench was dug behind this rolling barricade, which covered the working parties from the enemy fire. While Lauverjat had employed his knowledge of siege craft to create a tangible threat to the fort, he had failed to brace the trenchwork, and when heavy rains arrived it turned the hard work into mud and disappointment. The war party broke up shortly thereafter and disappeared into the forest.[3]

To the west, isolated farmsteads, if not already abandoned by their owners, were attacked, as was the town of Brunswick. A large war party descended on the town in early July, burning most of the buildings and killing or capturing a number of citizens. Fort George was alarmed by a fleeing soldier and the nearby settlements warned by other citizens that had taken flight. Satisfied with their work, the war party withdrew with their prisoners to a home on nearby Fish Hill. Unfortunately for them, it was within cannon range of Fort George, which now began to pepper the dwelling with grape and chain shot. Having seen enough, the Wabanaki took to their canoes and paddled to Pleasant Point at the confluence of the Kennebec and Androscoggin Rivers.

A messenger was sent to Captain Johnson Harmon, posted on Arrowsic Island with a company of men, informing him of the attack and that the raiders had departed toward Pleasant Point. Harmon would not receive the warning. Having already seen the smoke coming from the direction of Brunswick, he concluded that it had been attacked. Hoping to cut off the attackers' retreat, he had a pair of whaleboats outfitted and set off for Merry Meeting Bay.

It was after dark when Harmon's boats entered the bay. In the distance to his left, he could make out campfires near Pleasant Point. His men, thirty-four in number, landed quietly near the enemy's canoes and, finding the war party asleep, arranged themselves to the left and right. The Wabanaki soon awoke with surprised shouts only to be drowned out by a volley of muskets, and as they scrambled to get away, a second volley ripped through their ranks. A few escaped and a smaller party encamped not far away fired a few scattered shots at Harmon's men as they pushed off in their canoes. The entire engagement lasted only a few minutes, but as Harmon surveyed the camp he counted fifteen fallen opponents, as well as an English prisoner they had slowly dispatched a few hours before. Harmon and his men returned to Arrowsic unscathed, having made it clear to the Wabanaki that the frontier was not as poorly guarded as they might have thought.[4]

When news of the first attacks on Merry Meeting Bay reached Governor Shute on the evening of June 18, he penned a quick letter to the secretary for the Board of Trade, Alured Popple, detailing the assault and the seizure of five Englishmen. "I'm afraid there will be no avoiding a war with them," he concluded. It would actually take a little longer than the governor anticipated. Shute was for declaring war, but he was new to the colony, and unlike the assembly and the citizens of New England, he did not recall the horrors of King William's War's most mournful decade and its repeat during Queen Anne's War. One of the first measures considered was to convince the Iroquois to intervene on the side of the English, but this was soon dismissed for fear of sparking a larger conflict between the Five Nations and New France's native allies.

Instead, an olive branch was extended to the Wabanaki. The assembly demanded an explanation, an exchange of prisoners, and satisfaction for the damages. The action did lead to a prisoner exchange but little else, and as the reports came into Boston over the course of July it appeared that only one path remained. This was made clearer when Shute received a letter from Governor Vaudreuil. In response to the Massachusetts governor's complaints, Vaudreuil informed him that, "he has and will assist the Indians, and that he has orders from the Court of France to do so." With the assembly now signaling to the governor that they supported military action, on July 25, 1722, Shute formally declared war on the Eastern Indians.[5]

The conflict known as Rale's War, Lovewell's War, Greylock's War, Dummer's War, the Three Years' War, or the Fourth Anglo-Wabanaki War, depending on your preference, was by a statistical point of view as futile as they come. Two years before, in response to a series of questions posed by the Board of Trade, Governor Shute had computed the population of Massachusetts at ninety-four thousand, of which, "the Regular Militia as they have been returned to me by the Officers of the Several Regiments &c: Amount to Fifteen thousand Six hundred and Eleven Men." Added to this would be several thousand more militia from New Hampshire, colonial naval elements, as well as transports and maritime resources from both colonies. Although this force could potentially amount to well over twenty-thousand men, it was, of course, impossible to bring this many men to bear. Even so, it was feasible to raise several thousand men and with control of the sea lanes launch expeditions against the Wabanaki in numbers that they could not challenge.

In the same letter that Shute unveiled his computations, he described the state of the colony's old Wabanaki adversaries.

> In the Neighbourhood of this Province to the North East or towards Nova Scotia there are two Tribes of Indians one of them known by the name of the Kennibeck (Kennebec) Indians One hundred fighting men who live chiefly at a place called Neridgiawack (Norridgewock) within a Sort of Fort made of Wood and where, is a small Chappel and a Jesuit. There are two or three other small Settlements of Indians that may make out in all fifty fighting men at Pennicook (Pennacook), Amarascogin (Androscoggin), and Pegwoket (Pequawket). One other Tribe called the Penobscot Indians lying up the River of that name One hundred and fifty fighting Men, both Tribes too much inclined to the French Interest thro the Influence of the Jesuits who have allways one among them, and during the late Warrs between England and France they have been bloody Enemys to the English.[6]

On the other side of this equation was Rale and the Wabanaki. While Shute's estimation of three hundred men was fairly accurate, it did not in-

Governor Philippe Vaudreuil, the Marquis de Vaudreuil. Vaudreuil would guide the French colony through Queen Anne's War and would remain Governor until his death in 1725. His son Pierre would later go on to become the last Governor of New France. (*National Archives of Canada*)

clude the Maliseet and Micmac who, less effected by Queen Anne's War, could bring several hundred men to the field. However, the governor was correct in assuming that both the Maliseet and Micmac would be more concerned with Nova Scotia and therefore would not be his problem. While the last two nations would not be of much help dealing with Massachusetts and New Hampshire, there would be help in the form of war parties from the Abenaki and Huron Missions near Quebec and material support from Governor Vaudreuil in the way of arms and provisions. Supplemented by a few adventurous French partisans, the entire Wabanaki force facing northern New England might have approached 350 to 450 men at its peak. While this number could impose chaos and fear on the coastal settlements, it was considered too small to effectively raid the Massachusetts frontier, thus, the conflict became centered on Maine and New Hampshire. Given the size of the Wabanaki force any large-scale efforts on towns or fortified positions where significant losses might be incurred were eyed with caution. Instead, to mitigate these risks and magnify their numbers, it was agreed to focus on small war parties that would strike at softer targets.

While these detachments patrolled the wood-lined roads of Maine and New Hampshire, ambushing men returning from their fields, Governor Philipps in Nova Scotia had a much larger problem on his hands. In June the Wabanaki targeted the English fishing fleets in the Bay of Fundy. Lying in wait in a number of small harbors, they pounced on these vessels in the early-morning hours, taking their crews captive. One of the first was Captain George Lynham of the sloop *Prosperity*. Surprised and taken by a Wabanaki war party in Chignecto Bay, Lynham and his crew were forced to sail the ship closer to shore where forty-five Wabanaki were loaded aboard the vessel. With this task accomplished, Lynham was then ordered to set sail for Annapolis Royal where the war party expected to rendezvous with others for an attack on the British post. The *Prosperity* was delayed, however, when his captors spied another British sloop and, after a short chase, captured it, adding it to their growing flotilla. Captain Joseph Bissell of the sloop *Dove* was another victim. Seized in Penobscot Bay, when he asked why he was being held he was told it was in retaliation for the Sagamores held against their will in Boston. Bissell escaped and watched from a safe haven as the captured vessel was loaded with supplies and part of the French and Indian war party before putting out to sea.[7]

With a handful of vessels at their command it did not take long for the Wabanaki to accumulate a fleet. Many fishing vessels were simply hailed, and when they approached close enough, they were either boarded or quickly surrendered when a score of muskets was leveled at them. Others made a dash for it, creating brisk chases over the waves, punctuated by shouts and war whoops as the woodland warriors fired on the fleeing vessels from the prow of their ships. Within a month over a dozen vessels were in Wabanaki hands, giving them for the first time a naval component to their martial endeavors and, surprisingly, temporary control over the Bay of Fundy. The plan had been to organize an assault on Annapolis Royal, but Lt. Governor John Douchett, who was in command with Philipps having traveled to Canso, wisely took twenty-two Wabanaki that he found in town prisoner. The move damped any enthusiasm toward an attack on Annapolis Royal, leaving the Wabanaki content to raid the coast and attempt to blockade the port.

Matters were just as bad on the southern coast of Nova Scotia. As in the Bay of Fundy, primarily Micmac and Maliseet detachments seized fishing vessel after fishing vessel until they too had a force of eighteen craft. Beyond the devastation to the English fishing fleet there was real fear of an attack on Canso, perhaps aided by French forces from Louisbourg. After the attack on Canso in August 1720, Philipps had dispatched Lt. Colonel John Armstrong and two companies of troops from Placentia to build and garrison a fort at the fishing village. Matters started poorly when one of the detachments' supply vessels, the sloop *William*, carrying food, clothing, and part of Armstrong's personal effects, was seized by a Spanish privateer. Even with these handicaps, Armstrong was able to raise an earth and wooden palisade fort and arm it with cannons taken from English vessels in the harbor. Now, as Armstrong and Philipps surveyed the situation before them, they both agreed that an offensive action was preferable to relying on their crude defensives.[8]

With a number of ships in the harbor refusing to sail on account of the Wabanaki fleet off shore, Philipps chose two craft to outfit as warships, and reinforcing each of them with a detachment of twenty soldiers from the garrison, sent them out to sea in search of the enemy. The first vessel, under the command of Captain John Elliot of Topsham, cruised the coast until July 29, when he discovered seven sloops and schooners anchored in a small harbor. Realizing he had found what he was looking for Elliot passed the word for the crew to man their stations and enter the harbor.

Given their numbers, the Wabanaki chieftains thought they had snared another victim and called on Elliot to surrender. Instead, Elliot responded by running up his flag, pulling astride the largest vessel, and discharging his small cannons into its side while his troops launched a volley on the surprised Wabanaki on deck. Numbers, however, were not on Elliot's side, and after the initial shock the Wabanaki began fighting back. For half an hour the two ships lay side by side exchanging musket fire as the small cannons onboard the English warship splintered the side of the enemy vessel. Elliot had been wounded several times by birdshot, and the weight of the enemy's fire from the vessel in front of them, as well as from onshore, was shifting the odds. At this point, the officer in charge of the British troops onboard dragged a box of grenades up onto deck and quickly changed the direction of the engagement. The explosives burst on the deck of the enemy schooner, sending the Wabanki over the side. The water provided little protection as Elliot's crew fired upon them, killing several as they swam to shore.

When the last of the Wabanaki disappeared into the tree line, Elliot seized the remainder of the captured vessels and freed eighteen English prisoners. He would return to Canso and along with the commander of the second English sloop, Captain John Robinson, would go back out to sea, recapturing a sloop and schooner a week later. Philipps was impressed with the two captains, informing the Board of Trade that their efforts "had the good effect that in three weekes time I retook all the vessels and prisoners."[9]

In New Hampshire and Massachusetts, the declaration of war was followed by raising troops to patrol the frontier and the authorization of new defenses. One of these measures was to cut a road to Lake Winnipesaukee and erect a blockhouse there to prevent the Wabanaki from using this area as a staging point for attacks on coastal New Hampshire. The work went forward, but it was soon clear that the task had been badly underestimated, and as such, it was abandoned. Massachusetts agreed to outfit a pair of armed vessels to patrol the coast and equip a thousand men with whaleboats and arms. Two hundred men would be sent to reinforce the garrisons at York, Falmouth, North Yarmouth, Maquoit, Arrowsic, and Fort Richmond, while two detachments would be formed to strike back at the enemy. The first, consisting of three hundred men would ascend the Penobscot River, while the four hundred men in the second expedition would advance up the Kennebec River. To entice volunteers, the assembly returned to a practice that had raised the objection of many—scalp bounties. These started at £8 for a women or child, and £15 for an adult male, but "The general assembly not finding the former bounty sufficiently encouraging to volunteers," the bounty was raised to £60 and even escalated to £100 under the conditions that the soldiers took no pay and provided their own rations during the expedition.[10]

While these forces were being recruited news arrived that, on September 10, a Canadian Abenaki and Micmac contingent, reputed to be some five hundred strong, had landed at Arrowsic Island. As the war party advanced on Georgetown and Fort Menaskoux, they were discovered by a detachment Captain Penhallow had sent out to protect citizens harvesting their corn. The sentries fired warning shots that alerted the local populace and provided enough time for the citizens and forward parties to retire inside the fort.

The Wabanaki exchanged fire with the fort for a time but soon tired of the task and turned to slaying livestock and burning over two-dozen homes. Late that afternoon, Colonel Walton and thirty reinforcements appeared in a pair of whaleboats. After consulting with Penhallow it was agreed to counterattack with Walton's men and forty men from the garrison. The gates soon opened and the English force pressed forward, spreading to the left and right as it advanced.

The attack surprised the Wabanaki, in part because of its foolishness. The response was swift as dozens of muskets halted the English advance, while the scattered elements of the war party moved toward the sound of the guns. It did not take long for Walton and Penhallow to realize how badly outnumbered they were, and when parties of Wabanaki began to press along their flanks, Walton gave the order to retire to the fort. The last of the English troops reentered the fort as the sun began to dip below the horizon. Thus far, the casualties had been few with a number of wounded and one man killed while peering out of a firing port. It was impossible to tell what the enemy's casualties might be, but there was fear they would attempt to storm the structure under the cover of darkness. Instead, the war party used the opportunity to withdraw.[11]

In Massachusetts, a different war was beginning to interfere with the prosecution of the real one. With the declaration of war, Governor Shute assumed the mantle of captain general and began appointing officers to lead the planned expeditions. He had also reengaged with Governor William Burnet of New York about employing the Mohawk against the Wabanaki and appeared to have made great headway. The Massachusetts assembly, however, was more interested in weakening the governor's powers and securing these for themselves. As part of the resolution on supply for the war effort the assembly had inserted a clause that the monies could only be used for the specifically stated clause and nothing else. When combined with the assembly's oversight duties, it gave them *de facto* control over the governor and the war effort.

Shute objected when the legislature interfered with troop deployments and scouts that were under his control but in general agreed with the basic plan of the campaign. Matters took a turn for the worse when the assembly rejected the appointment of Major Samuel Moody, based on past complaints. Shute asked how the assembly could do this without speaking with the officer first, but in November the assembly focused their attention on Colonel Shadrach Walton. As part of the planned attack on the Wabanaki, Walton and his forces had been ordered to ascend the Penobscot River. When enemy forces attacked Arrowsic Island in September, Walton had rushed his forces to their aid, and although he arrived after the battle was over, he posted his troops in the area of Georgetown to protect the inhabitants. The assembly called out the change in plans, and although Shute explained why the decision had been made, the assembly demanded that Walton report to them to account for his conduct. Walton reported to Shute, but he refused to meet with the assembly. While this was a minor setback, the assembly's control over the money for the expedition and pay of the troops involved was sufficient to weaken the governor, giving them the measure of control they sought.

In fact, Shute had seen enough and departed for England in December, never to return. The colony's system was unworkable and left the governor powerless. The only question in Shute's mind was whether Parliament would bring this practice to an end or if the colony would travel further down the path of self-government. Shute wrote the king and testified to the Board of Trade regarding the colonial assembly attempts over the last few years "to undermine the few Prerogatives that have been reserved to ye Crown." The governor's detailed letter spelled out a number of instances and problems that supported this point. Enough so that the Board of Trade urged the intervention of Parliament. "Hence your Excellencys will be appriz'd of what importance, it is to H.M. service, that so powerfull a Colony should be restrain'd within the due bounds of obedience to the Crown and be more firmly attach'd to the interest of Great Britain than they at present seem to be," the board concluded, "which we conceive cannot effectually be done without the interposition of the British Legislature, herein in our humble opinion no time should be lost."[12]

While this issue was being addressed in London, the Massachusetts assembly was using their power to coerce Lt. Governor Dummer, who was now acting governor. Dummer was forced to dismiss both Moody and Walton, which further delayed the colonial campaign. It was not until early February 1723 that Colonel Westbrook, who had replaced Walton, and Captain Harmon appeared off the coast of Maine. Westbrook took a sizable force up the Penobscot River but, beyond burning a small chapel and a few buildings, found nothing. Harmon, who ascended the Androscoggin River, found even less before the two parties withdrew and returned to Boston. A third expedition consisting of a company of scouts under Captain John Sayward went as far as New Hampshire's White Mountains before turning back with nothing to show for the effort but a few cases of frostbite. In fact, there was little to find, as most of the Wabanaki had moved to the missions of Canada for the winter to ensure their safety.

The return of spring also signaled the return of raids on the Maine and New Hampshire frontiers. War parties struck Scarborough, Cochee, and the Lamprey River in New Hampshire. At this latter location they attacked the homestead of Aaron Rawlins. Rawlins's wife was outside with their young son and daughter, and the trio were captured before anything could be done. Rawlins and his twelve-year-old daughter, however, were in the home and put up a furious defense. With his daughter loading, and plenty of powder and firearms, there was a good chance that he could dissuade the attackers and they would move off. The thoughts were correct, but a shot through one of the windows slew Rawlins early in the engagement. With a shout the Wabanaki dashed upon the home, and when they found the twelve-year-old with powder stains on her hands, they unleashed their fury, decapitating the youth and scalping her dead father.

There was no lack of similar displays across the frontier as the season progressed. Although Massachusetts possessed sixteen regiments of foot and fifteen troops of horse in its militia, to the dismay of many it acted defensively throughout the year. Efforts to bring the Iroquois to the aid of the colonists appeared certain after a conference was held in Boston, which, as part of the entertainment phase, contained a demonstration of an early breechloading rifle. The delegates from the Six Nations expressed interest in the £100 bounty being offered and promised to fall upon the Wabanaki should they seriously insult the New Englanders, but nothing came of the negotiations and no major intervention by the Iroquois would occur.[13]

Close to thirty people were either killed or carried away, and probably as many wounded along the Maine frontier over the summer and fall of 1723. The year ended with a Christmas Day attack on Fort St. George's. The sixty Wabanaki were acting on information from a soldier they had captured who spoke to the poor state of the garrison. For thirty days, much of it consumed by freezing rain, they pressed on the garrison, but it was clear that the information was in error, and when Colonel Westbrook arrived with reinforcements the Wabanaki departed.

"I know not what you now think of the war with the Abenaki," Vaudreuil wrote Lt. Governor Dummer in late October. "You may see that it is not so easie a Thing as you Thought at first to reduce those Indians." There was a good deal of truth to the statement. The snows of January 1724 arrived to find that, thus far, the Wabanaki had fared well in their conflict with the English. True, they had suffered losses, but most of these came early on and were more than made up for by the participation of the Huron and Abenaki Missions in Canada. In addition, by wintering at these missions they had also undermined the enemy's favorite tactic, which was to strike at the Wabanaki villages in the dead of winter. The English appeared on the defensive, and overtures of peace both from the Iroquois and the English were rejected "until the English had left their lands and repaired the wrongs and injustices they had done them."[14]

Vaudreuil admitted that the thought of the Iroquois declaring against them "had seriously intimidated" the Wabanaki, particularly those of the missions who were easily within reach of Iroquois war parties. To deal with this the governor turned to the Iroquois missions at the Lake of Two Mountains and Sault St. Louis for an answer. He had the Huron and Abenaki chieftains approach these missions and ask for their help in the conflict. Both missions agreed and asked Vaudreuil for permission to go to war. The governor was happy to oblige and provided all the necessities required for their war parties. The move not only added several hundred more men to the Wabanaki cause but effectively nullified any Iroquois threat. The Five Nations might be willing to help their English allies against the Wabanaki, but once news arrived that they might find themselves fighting against their Christianized family members, they were no longer interested. The English could solve their own problems.

For Vaudreuil, the success with the Iroquois missions turned his attention to more promising prospects. While New France could not take a direct part in the conflict, the Ottawa, Algonquin, Neppissing, and a host of other nations to the west were not under such restrictions. His argument to them was simple; if the English were free to take the Wabanaki's land, who was next?[15]

CHAPTER FIVE

Lovewell's Pond and the Treaty of Casco

Spring brought a return to the raids. In mid-April 1724, a small war party took several settlers working in their fields before falling upon and capturing a sloop at Kennebunk. Two weeks later, the Wabanaki would score an even greater success when Captain Josiah Winslow led sixteen volunteers in a pair of whaleboats out of Fort St. George's on a reconnaissance patrol. While nothing was found, the two vessels were ambushed from a riverbank on their return voyage. The second whaleboat under a sergeant named Harvey, being closer to shore and behind Winslow's vessel, was brought to a standstill by a volley from the shoreline. Another volley followed before, with a shout, the Wabanaki dashed out of the woods with their canoes. Harvey and his men fought back as best they could, but Winslow could see the badly outnumbered vessel being surrounded. The captain ordered his crew to reverse course, but before he had gone far two-dozen Wabanaki canoes swarmed about his craft. A long fight of defiant yells and flashing muskets ensued as the Wabanaki circled, looking for an opportunity to close on their enemy. By sundown it was clear to Winslow that they could go no farther. Harvey's boat had been taken hours before, several of his men were wounded, and his leg had been broken by a musket shot. He ordered his men to pull for shore. Three escaped into the woods, but the rest were soon surrounded and fell in a desperate last stand.[1]

The next several months brought more small-scale attacks. War parties skirmished with Penhallow's garrison at Arrowsic and raided Purpooduck and Spurwink, although in the latter case they were pursued and scattered after being surprised. These actions accomplished little to push the English out of their settlements. The Wabanaki and their allies also found their traditional targets much better prepared this summer, enough so that the raiders shifted their attention along another path. Taking a cue from the Micmac success in Nova Scotia the year before, the Wabanaki along the Maine coast began targeting fishing vessels, and just as in Nova Scotia, they found immediate success. Waiting along the shores of several harbors they watched the English ships drop anchor for the evening or send boats ashore to dry their catch. That night the war party quietly took to their canoes, often helped by wind and rain, and crept alongside the fishing vessels. Once aboard, a handful of shots and war whoops followed, and within a few minutes it was over. The tactic proved so successful that by mid-summer the Wabanaki were in possession of close to thirty vessels along the coast of Maine, one of which was a large Marblehead schooner armed with a pair of swivel guns. About half the crews were retained to sail the vessels while the rest, a little over a score, had been dispatched during the attacks. When these vessels began to merge with those taken by the Micmac along the coast of Nova Scotia, there was a sudden realization that the British colonies had once again lost naval control of the Bay of Fundy and perhaps even the Gulf of Maine.[2]

Using this newly acquired naval power the Wabanaki descended on Fort St. George's. Late on the afternoon of July 21, the sentries notified the fort's commander, Lt. William Canady, that five vessels were approaching and that an Indian delegation was coming ashore under a white flag. Canady met with the Wabanaki spokesman a little before sunset. The envoy, using a captured fisherman as an interpreter, demanded the surrender of the fort, offering to send the garrison back to Boston in one of their captured vessels. Canady refused and informed the spokesman that he would fire on the vessels if they approached any closer. The Wabanaki signaled for the ships to stop, but, already closer than Canady was comfortable with, a warning shot from one of the fort's cannons brought them to a halt. The meeting soon broke up, and after dark the Wabanaki invested the fort, making their presence known with shouts and the occasional shot.

The next morning negotiations resumed, which led to a brief conversation on land rights. When Canady proved defiant, the spokesman threatened the garrison with no quarter if the Wabanaki were forced to attack. Canady informed him that, if they wanted the fort, "you must take it by

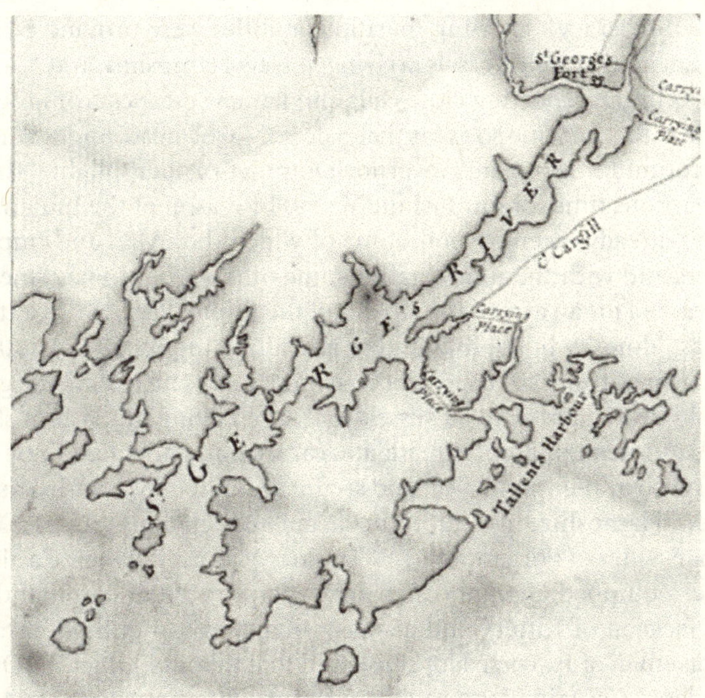

Detail from a 1759 map of the St. George's River showing the location of Fort St. George's. (*Norman B. Leventhal Map Collection, Boston Public Library*)

force of Arms which you nor all ye Indians in the Eastern Country can do." A few more words passed between them before the Native ambassador threw up his hands and departed. The garrison watched as the enemy sailed a pair of small vessels into a cove and began loading them with wood and other combustibles. Late that afternoon the two fireships, bellowing smoke and flames, approached the fort under full sail.

The intent was to burn the fort's blockhouse near the shoreline, and according to the fort's commander, the unexpected attack almost succeeded. The fort's cannons scored a hit on the first vessel, which likely damaged its steering as the abandoned craft sheared away and, with the help of the tide, went harmlessly ashore. The second vessel was more problematic. Striking the ship several times with the fort's guns did nothing to halt its progress, and it passed near enough that Canady noted, "we had ye good fortune to escape." There was another attempt at negotiations, and several unsuccessful efforts to seize the handful of British vessels in the harbor, after which the Wabanaki, short on powder, abandoned the siege and sailed away.[3]

The confederacy's growing maritime abilities were proving a problem in New England as well. Vessels arriving at New Hampshire and Massachusetts ports began reporting close calls and narrow escapes from the Native fleet. The threat became so great that Salem, Marblehead, and a number of nearby communities wrote Governor Dummer of their plight. "Its now a very hazardous time for our Fishing Vessels by reason of the Indian Enemy who have already taken Several, some of which they Man and Improve as Privateers and with them have taken some others of our Fishermen." The petition asked for an armed ship to escort the fishing fleet, which at the moment was "almost wholly discouraged and afraid to proceed." Another victim of the privateers was more direct in his assessment, calling the growing Wabanaki fleet "a terror to all vessels that sailed along the eastern shores."[4]

For Dummer, the reports made it clear that an effort had to be undertaken to destroy the enemy fleet and secure the Gulf of Maine. It was agreed that New Hampshire would equip a pair of shallops under Captains Johnathan Salter of Portsmouth and Thomas Mannery of New Castle, while Dummer equipped a twenty-man schooner under the command of Dr. George Jackson of Kittery and a sixteen-man shallop under Captain Sylvanus Lakeman of Ipswich. Not convinced that this was sufficient, Dummer then ordered Captain Thomas Durrell of the 20-gun frigate H.M.S. *Seahorse*, currently anchored in Boston Harbor, to outfit three fishing vessels and man them with sixty of his crew.[5]

While Durrell's sailors prepared their vessels, the fleet of two New Hampshire and two Massachusetts vessels put out to sea. By July 17 they were off Montinicus Island, a little over a dozen miles from the western entrance to Penobscot Bay. After a few days of having seen no sign of the enemy, the flotilla turned back east on July 21. Around three o'clock that afternoon, both Mannery and Salter spied a large schooner laying near Green Island. Mannery came alongside Salter's vessel and asked him if he planned to attack. Although Lakeman's shallop and Jackson's schooner were only half-a-dozen miles behind them, it was agreed to proceed without them. Salter, however, thought better of the matter when he saw movement on the enemy schooner and broke off the attack. Without Salter's support, Mannery's men would not go forward, and the two vessels sailed off, having accomplished nothing.

Lakeman and Jackson would arrive on the scene a little under an hour later to discover the schooner moving toward the western entrance of Penobscot Bay. The vessel seemed to be missing some of its rigging and was proceeding slowly, which perhaps gave a false sense of security to the two Massachusetts captains. With their Union colors flying, Lakeman and Jackson maneuvered to within pistol range before launching a volley of musketry at the ship. Small arms flared to life aboard the schooner, but it was the bark of swivel guns that splattered the British ships with grapeshot which proved worrisome. In a slow-running fight, the three vessels exchanged fire until just before sunset, when the schooner came close enough to the mainland that Wabanaki detachments ashore could bring their firepower to bear. As it was, both British captains had seen enough and agreed to return to Boston. Jackson and several of his crew were wounded, and both ships had their rigging badly cut up.[6]

A few days later, on July 27, a pair of Massachusetts schooners under the command of William Cox, whom Dummer had also commissioned, lay at anchor at Mt. Desert Island. A little after 7:00 a.m. an unidentified schooner began to enter the harbor. The English warships raised sail and moved closer to investigate. After hailing the vessel, it abruptly made for shore. Cox tacked to close the distance only to be greeted by a score of Wabanaki muskets. The three ships exchanged gunfire until the schooner went aground and its crew abandoned the vessel for the safety of the tree line. Cox and his men launched a few volleys at the retreating Wabanaki, wounding three of their number, and appeared to have put them to flight. However, once the war party reached cover it halted and began a concentrated fire on the English vessels, pelting them with musket balls and buckshot. For several hours the two sides, no more than sixty yards apart, exchanged shots while a landing party was assembled to board the now-abandoned schooner. Although it cost Cox four wounded, including himself, the New Englanders were able to get the stranded schooner off the beach at high tide, and the three vessels returned to Boston on August 6. Captain Durrell's three converted warships would appear in the area a week later, but after an extensive search they found nothing. The reason was simple. Finished with the vessels, the Wabanaki had either hidden or destroyed them and returned to their villages.[7]

Although the maritime threat had been dealt with, the repercussions and damage to the fishing trade coupled with the constant incursions along the frontier had pressured Dummer to act offensively. As Father Rale had been identified as one of the primary agents behind the conflict, plans were once again prepared to seize him. Four companies under Captains Johnson Harmon and Jeremiah Moulton would rendezvous at Fort Richmond in early August, and from there, ascend the Kennebec River to Rale's chapel at Norridgewock. Departing in seventeen whaleboats the force of 208 men came ashore at Ticonic Falls, some two-dozen miles below the village, where they left their boats under guard. The march was resumed on foot the next day, and that evening the advanced guard encountered a party of Wabanaki and, believing them to be scouts, fired in response. One of the party, a young woman, fell dead while an older male dashed for the river and was shot while trying to swim to safety. The remaining old woman was taken prisoner and informed Moulton and Harmon that they had killed her husband, Bomazeen, and their daughter. She also confirmed that the town was only a day's march and was ill prepared for an attack.

Part of this lack of diligence may have come from Rale himself. A few weeks before, several war parties had returned with rumors that over two hundred English were being sent to drive them out of their village. The Jesuit shook his head at the news. "How could that be," he asked the concerned sagamores, "seeing that we are daily surrounding and making inroads against them everywhere in the midst of their land, and they not coming out of their fort?" Seeing a few unconvinced faces, Rale shifted to another point. "Besides," he remarked, "in all the wars you have had with them, did you ever see them come to attack you in the spring, summer, or in the fall, when they knew you were in your habitations?" There were nods and murmurs of agreement that would have tragic consequences.[8]

Around noon on August 23, Harmon and Moulton found themselves within two miles of Norridgewock, and thus far, there were no indications that the enemy knew of their presence. At this point Harmon, who was senior commander, led a detachment of eighty men to approach the village via its cornfields. It was nearing harvest, and there was a good chance that many in the village would be tending to these fields. Securing them would cut off their escape. In the meantime, Moulton would take the rest of the detachment and march on the village.

Moulton pushed forward and around three o'clock appeared out of the woods before the town, which, without a palisade, consisted of a few dozen wigwams and small cabins clustered around the newly built chapel. Dividing his men into three detachments he advanced through the tall grass and thickets to surround the village. When Moulton's central group came within a pistol shot of the town, a Wabanaki exited his wigwam to start a fire. When he saw the line of troops approaching, he shouted out a warning and raced for his musket. There were some fifty to sixty fighting men in the village and perhaps twice as many women, young and old. For the former, who quickly appeared with their arms, it was not a question of winning the upcoming fight. The English were already on them; it was too late for this. It had become a question of buying time for their families to escape.

The rattled Wabanaki fired a few scattered shots at the advancing enemy but with no effect. Moulton, who had ordered his men not to fire until fired upon, ordered the line to halt and gave the command to fire. The volley rippled through the disorganized Native ranks as the order to advance rang out again. There were a few more shots from the defenders, but the situation soon turned into a rout. Shots could now be heard to the left and right of the village as fleeing groups of Wabanaki ran into Moulton's two other detachments. The only path open was the river, and the English troops were slowly funneling the villagers to this point. The river was not deep at this location, but the current was strong. Some were swept away, others were shot as they attempted the sixty-foot crossing, and a few, thinking they had found safety in a canoe, realized they had no paddles and drifted downriver as dozens of muskets focused their fire on them.

While most of the town quickly emptied, there were two huts that continued to fight back. The first held the sagamore Mogg and his family. Firing out of a window Mogg had killed one of the three Mohawk scouts that had accompanied the expedition. Enraged, the brother of the Mohawk and a handful of Moulton's men stormed the home, slaying Mogg, his wife, and their two children before their fury subsided. The second structure that still held out was Rale's cabin. Moulton had informed his men that he wanted the Jesuit alive, but when a well-aimed shot from Rale wounded one of Lt. Richard Jacques's men, he had seen enough. Dashing forward he kicked in the cabin door and fired on the sixty-eight-year-old Rale, striking him in the head while he was reloading his musket.[9]

It was all over in fifteen minutes. The bulk of the villagers had escaped across the river, but close to thirty, a number of sagamores and Rale counted among them, lay dead along the banks of the river and in a line that led down to the shore. Harmon would arrive half an hour later, and after pillaging the town the expedition made camp for the evening. The next day, with their plunder secure, the town was fired and the detachment marched back to its whaleboats. On the western bank of the Kennebec the 150 survivors of the attack watched as a black column engulfed their village the next morning. The remaining warriors wanted to pursue the retreating English, but, short on powder and provisions, they turned their backs to the flames and began to lead the long column of Norridgewock refugees to Canada.

The destruction of Norridgewock and the death of Rale was a long-sought-after victory for the war-weary New England colonists. For the first time in the conflict, they had found the enemy in number and inflicted a crushing defeat upon them—all at the cost of a few wounded. It appeared the tide might be turning. While the news made its way through the taverns and meetinghouses, Dummer harvested one of the fruits of the victory.

Among the items found in Rale's cabin was his correspondence with Vaudreuil. The papers left little doubt as to French involvement in the conflict. Dummer complained directly to the governor of New France and then forwarded the papers on to London.

As for Rale, his role in the conflict as well as the nature of his demise depends on one's perspective. A product of the Counter-Reformation or a devoted spiritual caretaker? A defender of his flock or an agitator that brought about his own and his followers' destruction? Or all of these? There is little doubt that both Vaudreuil and Rale's superior, La Chasse, pressured the Jesuit along his fateful path, and with this it seems clear that Rale understood that, if he did not accept the approach, he would simply be replaced and another would be appointed to carry it out. This was perhaps his greatest fear. Tales of the Jesuit's death also varied. French accounts have him standing before his converts in defiance of the attackers and riddled with a cloud of bullets for this noble effort. The official colonial account was questioned as well, particularly when the missionary's scalp was brought to Boston, but given that Jacques had witnesses and admitted to killing Rale against orders, it is far more likely than the French account. Even so, cries of murder were leveled against the New Englanders. One author clarified both points. "In conclusion, Rale cannot be properly denominated a martyr, nor the English murderers. There can be no doubt that he was killed in the excitement of battle, while in a building from which a defense was being made, and against the intentions of the English commander."[10]

The expedition did not slow the raids on the Maine and New Hampshire frontiers. These continued throughout the summer and fall of 1724, aided by Wabanaki allies among the Catholic missions in Canada. Dummer sent several expeditions into the interior waterways of Maine, looking to repeat the success of Norridgewock, but these failed to halt the attacks, as the Wabanaki had moved their villages farther inland or had departed for the Canadian missions. As the snows began to fall over the Northeast it appeared to the weary citizens of New England that, despite the successes of summer, the war was no closer to ending.

Not all would agree. Captain John Lovewell of New Hampshire, looking to stem the raiders and take advantage of the £100 bounty on scalps in the process, had organized several successful expeditions near Lake Winnipesauke in late 1724 and early 1725. In one case, he had ambushed and killed a war party of ten that appeared to have originated in Canada. As the woodsman's acclaim grew so too did his numbers. In April 1725 he raised a company of seventy men, with the aim of targeting the headwaters of the Saco River where he suspected there were several Pequawket villages. The

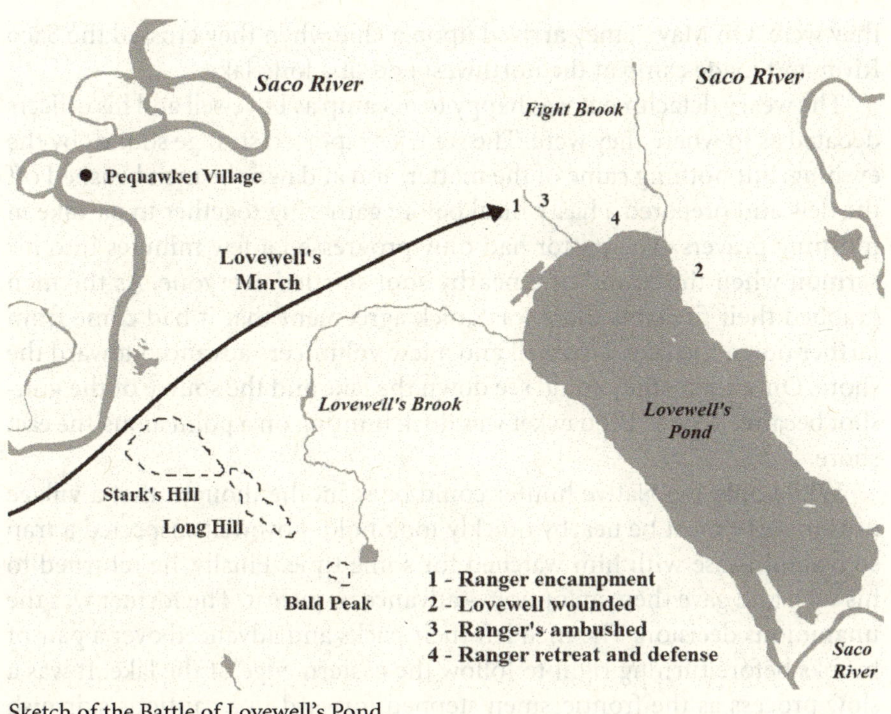

Sketch of the Battle of Lovewell's Pond.

preliminaries seen to, on April 16 Lovewell left Dunstable, New Hampshire, with forty-six volunteers, his limited supplies forcing him to dismiss the rest of the troops. Long raining days and fast-flowing creeks gorged with runoff hindered the war party as they made their way north along the bank of the Merrimac River. A few weeks later, after having sent two men back who could not continue the march, the detachment passed Lake Winnipesaukee and soon found itself on the western shore of Lake Ossipee when one of their number, Benjamin Kidder, fell ill. It was agreed to build a small palisade fort at the location where the surgeon could tend to Kidder. A sergeant and seven men would be left to guard the location, and just as importantly, it was agreed that the stronghold would be a point of retreat if things went wrong.[11]

From here the remaining thirty-four volunteers began their trek toward the headwaters of the Saco River. Following deer trails and breaks in the wilderness the war party marched northeast through endless clusters of pines, budding trees, and patches of snow spending their last days in the shadows and hollows. No one, including Lovewell, knew precisely where they were. On May 7, they arrived upon a clue when they crossed the Saco River and made camp at the northwest end of a long lake.

The weary detachment was happy to encamp as Lovewell and his officers debated as to where they were. The sentries reported strange sounds by the evening, but nothing came of the matter, and at dawn the men brushed off the dew and prepared a hasty meal before gathering together to partake in morning prayers. The pastor had only progressed a few minutes into his sermon when the sound of a nearby shot startled everyone. As the men grabbed their firearms there was quick agreement that it had come from farther down the lake. Lovewell and a few volunteers advanced toward the shore. Once there, they could see down the lake and the source of the gunshot became clear. A Pequawket was duck hunting on a point along the east shore.

While only the Native hunter could be seen, the thought that a village or war party must be nearby quickly took hold. Lovewell suspected a trap so he and those with him watched for some time. Finally, he returned to his men and gave them an option—advance or retreat. The former was the unanimous decision. The men left their packs and advanced over a pair of brooks before turning right to follow the eastern edge of the lake. It was a slow process as the frontiersmen stepped forward in a cautious skirmish line, the dense thickets and pines disrupting their ranks. Suddenly the Native hunter appeared out of the brush before a section being led by Lovewell and Sgt. Samuel Whiting. There was instant surprise on both sides until the Pequawket lifted his musket and fired a load of shot into Lovewell and Whiting. Another shot quickly followed from behind Lovewell, dispatching the attacker and bringing the encounter to an end. Seeing no signs of anyone else, a wounded Lovewell ordered his men back to where they had left their packs.[12]

Although Lovewell did not realize it, his path to the northwest end of what would become known as Lovewell's Pond had taken him within a mile of the lower Pequawket village on the Saco River. While the occupants of the village were unaware of Lovewell's presence, two returning war parties led by sagamores Paugus and Whawa had discovered Lovewell's tracks and followed them to the detachment's encampment. Neither Paugus or Whawa, who together fielded forty-one men, were interested in attacking without knowing the enemy's strength. Instead, they waited until nightfall and then moved forward hoping to catch a glimpse of their opponent, but it proved a dark evening and nothing could be confirmed.

The war chiefs pulled back before daylight and began to formulate their next steps. To their surprise, a shot rang out over the lake that morning.

Not long after, a scout returned with news that the English had marched off, leaving their packs behind. Paugus ordered the war party to move forward and then gave an approving nod to Whawa when a quick count showed thirty-four packs. With the numbers in their favor, the packs were removed and an ambush arranged for the retuning detachment. Two distant shots followed an hour later, but with no idea what this meant, the war party shifted about a bit and waited in silence.

Around mid-morning the first of Lovewell's men returned to the site where they had left their packs only to stop and question one another if they were lost. More began to appear in the clearing asking the same questions when a shot from Paugus set off a volley that ripped through the disorganized New Hampshire ranks. Lovewell received what would be a mortal blow, and his two lieutenants, Josiah Farwell and Jonathan Robbins, were both wounded along with eight others. The gunfire was followed by war whoops as the Pequawket launched themselves at the dazed colonials. Lovewell's men, however, had no intention of giving up so easily, and the charge was met by a volley of muskets that blunted its advance.

Still, Lovewell's men could not stay where they were. They had no idea of the enemy's strength and might soon be outflanked and surrounded. Ensign Seth Wyman, the only officer not injured in the opening shots, organized a retreat to the shores of the pond. Here, with their backs to the water, a spot was chosen with Fight Brook on the right, a bog in their front, and a cluster of rocks anchoring their left. Wyman deployed the detachment in a crescent, ordering the men to take cover behind fallen trees, rocks, or whatever else they could find. The Pequawket followed, pushing on the defenses in an attempt to overrun Wyman's position before it was formed, but they were met with such a concentrated fire that they soon fell back.

The battle would now become one of sniping exchanges, shouts of defiance, and bursts of gunfire that settled back down into sporadic shots. For ten hours the two sides sparred in this fashion, with a number of Pequawket, including their shaman, falling victim to English muskets, while on Lovewell's side Chaplin Jonathan Frye and Lt. Robbins were badly wounded. Around 3:00 p.m. Lovewell was struck again. Already in a dangerous state, he died from his wounds not long after. Paugus called on the English to surrender throughout the afternoon, but in each instance he was responded to with insults and musket fire. When the well-known sagamore was killed near sunset the war party disengaged and slipped away under the cover of darkness, carrying away their dead and wounded with them.

For Wyman it was clear that they needed to leave, but when he called out the roll, he discovered there were only twenty men left, eleven of whom were seriously wounded. Of this latter group three would not be able to travel. One of these, Lt. Robbins, asked Wyman to load his musket so he might have one last shot at the attackers when they returned. Of the other two, Farwell and Frye, both attempted the march back to the fort at Lake Ossipee, but neither had traveled far before Wyman was forced to leave them to perish in the forest.

When the party arrived at Lake Ossipee they were dismayed to find the fort deserted. Early in the battle one of Lovewell's men had bolted, and when he reached the fort, he informed the handful of men there that Captain Lovewell was dead and his company defeated. With the devastating news it was agreed to abandon the post and return to Dunstable. A few provisions were left behind in case a survivor or two made it back to the fort. Wyman shook his head and divided up the provisions, and after a short rest, the detachment marched to Dunstable.

When the news of Lovewell's defeat reached the governor of New Hampshire, John Wentworth, he ordered a rescue party to assemble and march to the scene of the battle in an attempt to recover any survivors. This force discovered Lovewell, Robbins, and those who had fallen near the pond and buried them on the battlefield. A quick search also revealed a shallow grave that held three Pequawket, one of whom was Paugus. The nearby Pequawket village was deserted, and there were no signs of the enemy during the rescue mission.[13]

The Battle of Lovewell's Pond has become steeped in New England lore, much like Robert Rogers at the Battle of Rogers' Rock in 1758. In reality, it was a crushing defeat that cost Lovewell and many of his company their lives. The Pequawket had arranged a near-perfect ambush, and had their numbers been slightly greater, they would have overrun and annihilated the New Hampshire detachment. As it was, they had inflicted greater losses on their enemy for a few of their own. Even so, it was a bitter victory. The loss of Paugus combined with the understanding that they would now have to relocate their villages did little to motivate celebration. More importantly, a greater realization was coming to the forefront. The New Englanders could easily make up their losses, but for the Pequawket and the rest of the Wabanaki, such losses, even small ones, were beginning to take their toll, especially among the leading sagamores. Just as in Queen Anne's War, the conflict had devolved into a war of attrition, and no matter how successful the Wabanaki were, it was losing trajectory.

Governor Vaudreuil would not hear news of the fight at Lovewell's Pond for several weeks, but he already feared for his allies. In late 1724 he wrote Paris describing the loss of Father Rale and the state of the Wabanaki in their ongoing conflict. Yet more had arrived at the Becancour and St. Francois missions near Three Rivers. They were clearly being forced to do so as New England expeditions had called into question the safety of many of their villages. While the governor understood the king's orders to avoid direct intervention, it was also clear that what assistance New France could lend in terms of supplies and raids by sympathetic nations was not enough. "Should the Court not think proper to assist the Indians publicly in this war, which is waged by the English against them," he wrote the court,

> it seems at least expedient that it complain loudly of the contravention by the English of the treaty of Utrecht; adopt measures to put an end to them, and have it settled at the Congress at Cambray, that the English shall not be permitted to molest the Abenaquis by encroaching on their territory and establishing themselves, contrary to the law of Nations, in a country of which the said Indians have been from all time in possession.[14]

Vaudreuil also made clear the consequences of not intervening either politically or militarily on the side of their allies. The Wabanaki would tire of the war and make peace with the English. This, in turn, would send some to seek refuge in the missions of New France while those who remained would soon be won over by the English who would freely point out "that France has cared nothing for them except when she had need of them, whilst now, when it is her interest not to embroil herself with England, she refuses to take any part in their quarrel with the English." This, he concluded, would resonate among the Wabanaki and detach them from New France for good.[15]

In March 1725, Vaudreuil arrived at Montreal only to be informed that four English delegates were at Fort Chambly, wishing an audience with the governor. The next day Vaudreuil met briefly with Colonel William Dudley and Colonel Samuel Thaxter, representing Massachusetts, Thomas Atkinson representing New Hampshire, and their traveling companion, Colonel John Schuyler of New York. The governor noted Schuyler's presence and his family's close connections to the Iroquois. The English ambassadors, who had taken four months to reach Montreal, gave Vaudreuil a letter from Dummer and requested a conference, being empowered to speak for Massachusetts and New Hampshire.

Vaudreuil met with the representatives for several weeks. The envoys demanded the return of English prisoners taken by the Wabanaki, that French aid to the Wabanaki cease, and that English claims along the coast of Maine be validated by treaty and purchase. The governor shrugged at the accusations and requests. First, he claimed that the aid given to the Wabanaki was yearly presents, much like the English made to the Five Nations. If the Wabanaki wanted to use these for war, that was their decision. Second, the Wabanaki had informed him that they had never sold any of their lands and that the documents the English held were forgeries. Lastly, as to the prisoners, the governor could do little. Some prisoners had been sold to the French, but the rest belonged to the Wabanaki, and he had no say over these individuals. However, he could be of some assistance by organizing a conference between the New England representatives and the sagamores at St. Francis and Becancour.

It was not until late April that this meeting took place. It quickly fell apart when the St. Francis and Becancour chieftains demanded all the land from the Saco River through Nova Scotia, minus Port Royal, be returned to them, the church at Norridgewock be rebuilt, and a new priest assigned to it. Dudley responded that they might as well ask for Port Royal as well, to which the Wabanaki spokesmen responded that they were justified in laying claim to Massachusetts and New Hampshire, but as these were established, "they were still inclined to tolerate them." Little else came from the meeting other than an understanding of how far apart the two sides remained.[16]

While the raids on the Maine frontier did not stop after Lovewell's expedition, they did subside as peace overtures reached the English. As Vaudreuil had predicted, the Wabanaki had begun looking for a way to end the conflict. As a result of these efforts, a Massachusetts delegation met with thirteen sagamores at Fort St. George's in July 1725. While the outstanding issues between the two parties were not resolved, enough progress was made that it was agreed to meet again, this time in Boston. There was no official truce at this point, but both sides agreed to refrain from any military action, though it would take time to notify everyone of this.

There were indeed several raids during the next few months, some by war parties out of Canada and some by the Wabanaki, but this did not disrupt the planned talks at Boston, which started in early November. It was clear that both sides wanted peace, and by December a treaty had been signed bringing the conflict to an end. It was agreed that all Wabanaki nations and their allies would cease hostilities, including those in Canada and Nova Scotia, and a general prisoner exchange would take place. The English would keep their claims to all purchased lands, and everything else would be retained by the Wabanaki. The English also agreed to set up trading houses to supply the tribes' needs, something that had been promised by Governor Shute but never carried into fruition, and that all future points of contention be directed to the Massachusetts governor for resolution. It was also agreed that the final treaty should be ratified in a public place and should include representatives from all the nations involved. In keeping with this, both sides met at Falmouth in late July 1726, and after a few days of deliberations, the Treaty of Casco was signed on August 5, 1726, ending the Three Years' War.

"It is surprizing to think that so small a number of Indians should be able to distress a Country so large and populous," Captain Penhallow wrote of the conflict. It was perhaps something of an understatement. A few hundred Wabanaki, supplemented by the occasional aid from the Canadian missions, had held off twenty times their numbers for three years. They had damaged the fishing trade, challenged for the Gulf of Maine, and defied New England efforts to bring them to bay. The cost to the government of Massachusetts was estimated at £250,000, and the lost productivity in New Hampshire and Massachusetts was likely far larger.[17]

For the Wabanaki, who lost perhaps a third of their fighting strength and had their villages decimated or forced to relocate, there had been little choice but to yield. Without the direct intervention of New France, the conflict was simply not sustainable. Yet the terms of the treaty were no different than when the war started, which certainly points to New England's desire to end the conflict by whatever means necessary. The results were as Vaudreuil had predicted. A number of Wabanaki moved to the missions at St. Francois and Becancour, which certainly helped in securing Canada, but the majority stayed. Had the English failed to live up to the terms of the treaty, there might have been a chance to bring these allies back into the French orbit, but to his credit Dummer was more diligent than Shute in such matters. One of the key elements, English trading houses, was fulfilled with a post at Fort St. George's, one on the Saco River, and another on the Kennebec River. The trade was regulated by the Massachusetts government, which meant that prices undercut not only French merchants but English merchants as well, leading to a well-regulated system that fulfilled Vaudreuil's worst worries and led to a generation of peace along the Maine, New Hampshire, and Nova Scotia frontiers.

While correctly foreseeing the consequences of the conflict, Vaudreuil would not see its outcome. He died in Quebec on October 10, 1725, at the age of eighty-two. Vaudreuil, who had served as governor for twenty-two years, had guided New France through the perilous days of Queen Anne's War and had successfully maintained the fragile French trade alliance on the western frontier against English intrigues. He also saw the future of the colony and leveraged French alliances in an attempt to keep English expansion in check, which, much to the detriment of the Wabanaki Confederacy, meant involving them in two conflicts with their more powerful neighbors. For Vaudreuil, there seemed no other option. Like Count Frontenac two generations before, he rightly deduced the threat the British colonies posed to New France. "The projects set on foot by the English, since the Treaty of Utrecht," he wrote the minister of the marine shortly before his death, "indicate that Canada is the object of their constant jealousy, and the Colony has not a more dangerous enemy."[18]

CHAPTER SIX

A Stone Sentinel

THE ANGLO-WABANAKI CONFLICT in Nova Scotia was more subdued than in Maine and New Hampshire. In one of the major incidents, a Maliseet and Micmac war party, numbering around sixty, attacked the fort at Annapolis Royal in June 1724. The garrison, underestimating the enemy's size, sallied out into an ambush. The attackers killed and scalped two of the detachment while the rest, realizing their mistake, retreated back to the fort carrying their wounded with them. The war party was not interested in exposing itself to the fort's cannons, so the attackers occupied their time slaying livestock before putting a few homes to the torch and moving off under the cover of darkness. Canso was threatened, and the fishing fleet had been raided, but the feared full-scale conflict that would have brought the French citizenry over to the Wabanaki side never materialized.[1]

Lawrence Armstrong, the new lieutenant governor of Nova Scotia, arrived in May 1725 and posted himself at Canso. As Governor Philipps had returned to England in 1722, Armstrong became acting governor while Douchett remained governor of Annapolis Royal and head of the town's council. After touring the island's defenses and consulting with Major Paul Mascarene, who had been appointed chief engineer of the colony in 1717, he wrote London in September 1725 concerning his "allmost forgotten Province." Armstrong was impressed and informed the court that there was no reason why Nova Scotia would not be every bit as profitable as the New England colonies, at least in terms of fishing and the maritime trades. The problem was enticing settlers, as the current ones "are as yet discouraged, having no shelter from the daily insults and cruel massacrys of the Indians, who are supported and clandestinely encouraged by the French." The real problem, Armstrong pointed out, was Louisbourg and its governor, "who had distributed arms and supplies to the Micmac and Maliseet by which we British subjects do greatly suffer."[2]

Fortunately, news had arrived from Massachusetts that the Wabanaki were willing to meet and negotiate a peace. Armstrong appointed Mascarene to represent Nova Scotia in these proceedings, which would lead to the Treaty of Casco, which Mascarene signed. As far as Armstrong was concerned the war could not end soon enough. The disruption of the fishing trade and the sorry state of the colony's defense, combined with the growing threat posed by French Louisburg, was enough to worry about. The peace treaty also simplified his ongoing negotiations with St. Ovide at Louisbourg. Much as Dummer had sent ambassadors to speak with Vaudreuil about French involvement in the war, so too had Armstrong sent ambassadors to Louisbourg armed with the same questions. These received similar answers, which were no longer pressed after news of the peace treaty arrived. In mid-September Armstrong traveled to Annapolis Royal for a meeting with the Micmac and Maliseet to confirm the Treaty of Casco. At the same time, with news arriving of the death of George I and the coronation of George II, the governor sought to settle an old problem: oaths of allegiance from the French Acadians.

He accomplished the first of these tasks on September 17 in a conference with the sagamores of the tribes, who quickly pledged that they would uphold the treaty. The second task proved as elusive as ever. A number of Acadians had traveled to Îsle Royal with their livestock, but most had stayed. The governor summoned the French representatives from the area around Annapolis Royal and demanded their oaths. Once again, there was hesitation but not because the bulk of the citizens held an allegiance to France. The resistance had now focused on bearing arms for the English if they took the oath. They asked to be excluded from militia service and wished nothing more than to remain neutral in any conflict. At first Armstrong attempted to assure the representatives that, as Roman Catholics, they would not be called upon for military service. This, however, did not satisfy the representatives, and Armstrong had language inserted into the oath that excluded them from this obligation "in order to get them over by degrees." The effort enticed 133 inhabitants to take the pledge to King George and encouraged the governor to send representatives to Minas in the spring in order to propose the same arrangement with the villages in this region.[3]

As for the defenses of Nova Scotia, they were a disaster, as could be attested to by Philipps's and Mascarene's reports. Fort Anne at Annapolis Royal, poorly constructed from the beginning, was slowly falling apart under the ravages of the seasons, leaving "breeches in the ramparts sufficiently wide for 50 men to enter abreast." The magazine was not secure, the barracks were near collapse, and many questioned the wisdom of even firing a cannon for fear of bringing down more of the walls. Even the most basic elements to defend the fort from shovels to ramrods for the cannons were in short supply, and the garrison needed almost everything from arms to clothing. After inspecting the structure, Philipps noted that "A thorough repair thereof is by no means adviseable, in regard that a new fort of smaller dimension may be built at less expense, which the circumstances of that post will admit." Plans previously drawn up by Mascarene, as well as financial and resource requirements were sent to the Ordinance Office the next year, but nothing came of the effort. By 1727 matters had become so bad that Armstrong and his officers paid for the construction of wooden palisades to close the gaps in the fort's walls. Sixteen of them then signed and sent a petition to the Board of Trade regarding "the increasingly ruinous condition of the magazine and fortifications."[4]

Although there was a battery of twelve cannons at Canso, the earth fortifications on which they were mounted were crumbling, and the makeshift barracks were incapable of serving the large garrison required to defend the location. Beyond money and material for new fortifications, money for repairs and manpower was just as important. Philipps noted that the nine companies of his 40th Regiment numbered only 360, which was well below establishment and barely enough to secure Canso and Annapolis Royal much less enforce British rule throughout the predominantly French-populated colony. Mascarene, when submitting his plans for a new fort at Annapolis Royal spoke to the necessity of seven hundred to eight hundred men to first build the stronghold and then reinforce the troops on station. It was clear that the colony desperately needed men and money to put it on a secure footing.

Neither would appear. Furthermore, the following spring the French villages near Minas Basin and along Chignecto Bay refused to take the oath. Philipps and Armstrong recommended that small forts be built in these areas and garrisoned with five companies of troops to encourage the inhabitants to moderate their behavior toward the government, and they requested a new fort be built at Canso, but this led to little. With the reconfirmation of Philipps as governor of Nova Scotia and Placentia in the summer of 1728, there was hope that some of the proposed measures would be adopted to encourage the growth and security of the colony. Instead, problems with the lieutenant governor of Placentia and his interference with the fishing trade had caused the Board of Trade to split Placentia away from the government of Nova Scotia, placing it under the captain of the seasonal naval contingent that visited the island.[5]

Philipps arrived in Canso aboard the H.M.S. *Rose* with his renewed commission in late June 1729. Here he found 250 vessels and 1,500 to 2,000 souls involved in the fishing trade. He insisted in a letter to the Duke of Newcastle, the secretary of state, that many more would settle if a proper fort and garrison were established at the location. After a storm-tossed voyage Philipps arrived at Annapolis Royal on November 20. Here he was met with a grand reception. After his commission was read, he turned to the old task of collecting oaths of allegiance from the populace and enticing new settlers. Around Annapolis Royal the governor met with some success in this first effort, in part because he allowed the local Acadian priest, Father Rene-Charles de Breslay, to return from his fourteen-month exile with the Micmac. By January 1730, Philipps had collected 227 signatures at Annapolis Royal and expected that more would be forthcoming.

Philipps also found a problem between Lt. Governor Armstrong and Major Alexander Cosby, in command of the garrison at Annapolis Royal. After rectifying this issue in late April, Philipps traveled to the settlements near Minas Basin and along Chignecto Bay. Here he obtained the oath of allegiance from all but seventeen families in the region. In September he wrote London on the status of this task. "I have the satisfaction to have seen fully completed and have now the honour to congratulate your Lordships on the entire submission of all those so long obstinate people and H.M. on the acquisition of so many subjects."[6]

Philipps was summoned back to England in July 1731 to settle the accounts of his regiment, but it would not be until August 27 that he departed. The governor had accomplished a great deal during his return to Nova Scotia. While some of the proposed settlement plans did not proceed as hoped, he did restore some sense of order, and after collecting the long-sought oaths of allegiance, he brought some calm to the region. With Philipps's departure Lt. Governor Armstrong, who had recently returned from England with Philipps's recall orders, once again became acting governor. Land issues, both concerning the claims made by the French inhabitants that had never been surveyed and the inability on his part to make land grants for new settlers, was a continual problem. So too were the political differences

Fort Anne at Annapolis Royal and the nearby vicinity c.1753. A number of settlements can be seen near the fort, with the rest of the town extending to the southeast in the direction of (A) on the map. While a fort would be maintained at this location for over half of a century it spent the majority of its existence in disrepair. (*Norman B. Leventhal Map Collection, Boston Public Library*)

between Mascarene and Major Cosby, which greeted Armstrong's return to "this much neglected (and as I may venture to say) distracted colony."[7]

At least peace reigned for the next decade. The fishery at Canso slowly became the domain of the New England colonies, with fewer ships from

Britain arriving every year. The location also became a regional center for New England whaling efforts, which comprised seventy vessels by 1733. This in turn would heighten British concerns for Canso, which was at best ill defended and likely a French target in the event of a conflict. Mascarene, who was now lieutenant governor, informed London the next year of the "naked and defenseless" condition of the colony's primary fishing port, noting that there were not even barracks for the four understrength companies of Col. Philipps's regiment stationed there. Should the French move against this location, there was little that could be done given that he had, "no vessels of force to curb the insolence of their privateers nor proper instructions and power to proceed against your Majestie's French subjects in case any of them shall be suspected or convicted of treacherously aiding, assisting or counternancing any insults made against us or concealing any such design." This latter issue would be addressed again the next year by Royal Navy Captain Thomas Coram, who pointed to the need for loyal subjects to settle in the area, concluding that "in case of a rupture with France, that whole province will without doubt be utterly lost for want of good and faithfull inhabitants." These pleas would fall upon deaf ears. Armstrong was right; it was a much-neglected colony.[8]

For the growing colony of Louisbourg, the years following the Three Years' War were filled with trade, a good portion of which was illegal, pirates, internal command disagreements, and the threat of war with the British. By 1726 Louisbourg, counting the garrison, numbered some 1,300 inhabitants, which would swell to several times that number when the seasonal fishing fleets appeared. Just as importantly, thirteen other settlements had been established along the coast that harbored another 2,200 denizens. Commerce was steadily increasing as ninety-six vessels arrived at the port in 1726 from France, Canada, and the West Indies, with another twenty-two calling upon the smaller ports along the coast. With the confines of the French and British navigation acts restricting commerce and profits, a robust illegal trade appeared. A good deal of this was between New England and Louisbourg. While official records showed only a few visits to the French port by English vessels, the collector of customs at Canso spoke more honestly on the levels of this activity:

> They will without any Restraint Load and carry from thence to several Ports in his Majtys Plantations, Brandy, Wine, Iron, Sail Cloth, Rum, Molasses & several other French Commoditys with

> which there is from 80 to 90 Sail generally Load with in a Year, these Vessels generally carry Lumber, Bricks & live stock there, they commonly clear out for Newfoundland, tho never design to go farther than Lewisburg, often they sell their vessels as well as Cargoes.[9]

Trade between Îsle Royal and the French in Nova Scotia also flourished, bearing out Verville's earlier comment that the French who stayed in Nova Scotia were of far more use to Louisbourg than had they relocated. This trade was seldom interfered with, and a surprising number of government officials on both sides were involved in this profitable business. In fact, it was so prevalent that the merchants at the French port claimed it placed them at a severe disadvantage.

Unfortunately, this increased commerce also brought pirates. Many were British from the Caribbean, but a number of Spanish vessels seem to have been involved in this trade as well. The threat was serious enough to find French and British warships patrolling the fishing banks together, and in Louisburg the idea of a pirate raid had led to the mounting of heavy cannons at the Island Battery and accelerating the work on the town's fortifications. There were also disagreements between Governor St. Ovide and Intendent Jacques Ange Le Normant De Mezy. From De Mezy's appointment in 1716 he and St. Ovide seldom saw eye to eye in matters. De Mezy's questionable accounting practices and his failure to enforce regulations led to his replacement by his eldest son Sabastian in 1732, but if St. Ovide thought that relations might proceed more smoothly with the change, he was mistaken.

The next few years proved exceedingly difficult for the colony. A vessel carrying smallpox infected the town, striking down a significant number of the inhabitants and a number of the garrison. Famine followed the next year. Matters became so desperate that St. Ovide pleaded for De Mezy to release funds to send a pair of vessels to New York to acquire supplies. When the latter refused, the governor ordered a pair of ships to be sent to France to explain the peril the colony faced. The ploy worked, and De Mezy released the funds. As it was, the two vessels sent to New York did not return until spring, and had it not been for a vessel from Quebec and another from New England arriving, the suffering over the winter months would have been much worse.[10]

Throughout this period work on the fortifications pressed forward, although not always at the desired rate. Verville's initial plans for a defensive work at the head of the harbor called for a small battery, with the guns firing *en barbette*, that is, over a parapet, but he was to change his mind. In 1723, the engineer addressed this matter in a paper outlining the construction of a much larger structure, which would become the Grand or Royal Battery. The proposed fortification had two functions. First, working with the guns of the Island Battery, it was to prevent an enemy vessel from forcing its way into the harbor. Second, should an enemy vessel gain entrance to the harbor, the cannons of the Royal Battery were to deny it a safe anchorage, especially to the northeastern portion of the harbor. In Verville's opinion, this task called for a large battery of thirty heavy guns and would dictate the layout of the stone fortification to accommodate the desired firing patterns. There was yet another element that dictated a large structure—the likelihood of an attack from the landside. There were plans for a glacis and a covered way fronted by a *cheval-de-frise* on this side of the structure, as well as provisions for several cannons and a pair of flanking towers on either end of the stronghold. Even with these defensive provisions, it was clear that the proposed work would require a sizable garrison to prevent an enemy from simply storming the landside of the structure while the battery's cannons were engaged.

Building the earthwork and clearing the site started in 1723, and for the next few years stone was hauled to the site and lime kilns were erected before work began in earnest. By the summer of 1728, the fortification was pronounced complete. Of course, there were still many items to perfect, and the violent nor'easters that traveled the region guaranteed that there was always work to be done. As such, it would not be until 1732 that the fortification took on its regular garrison.[11]

The key to the harbor's defense was the Island Battery, and it was not until August 1, 1722, that Verville could report that the excavation of the site was underway. The work was "pushed with vigor," and by December seven cannons had been mounted at the makeshift works. The following year brought more clarity to the project. Verville laid out a battery for thirty-eight heavy cannons, ten of which were focused on vessels approaching the harbor's entrance, four on vessels in the harbor, and the rest on the narrow straits between the island and the lighthouse peninsula. An elevated twenty-three-foot-thick wall was raised along the north shore with a turnback at either end to capture a tall rocky bluff to the south, which formed a natural fourth wall facing the sea. Ramparts and firing platforms would be fashioned for the predominantly northern and eastern facing cannons, which fired *en barbette* over a two-foot parapet, while the barracks, storehouses, and powder magazine were laid out in the interior.

Work began on this project not long after, but by mid-November 1724 the wall was not complete. While all involved realized the importance of

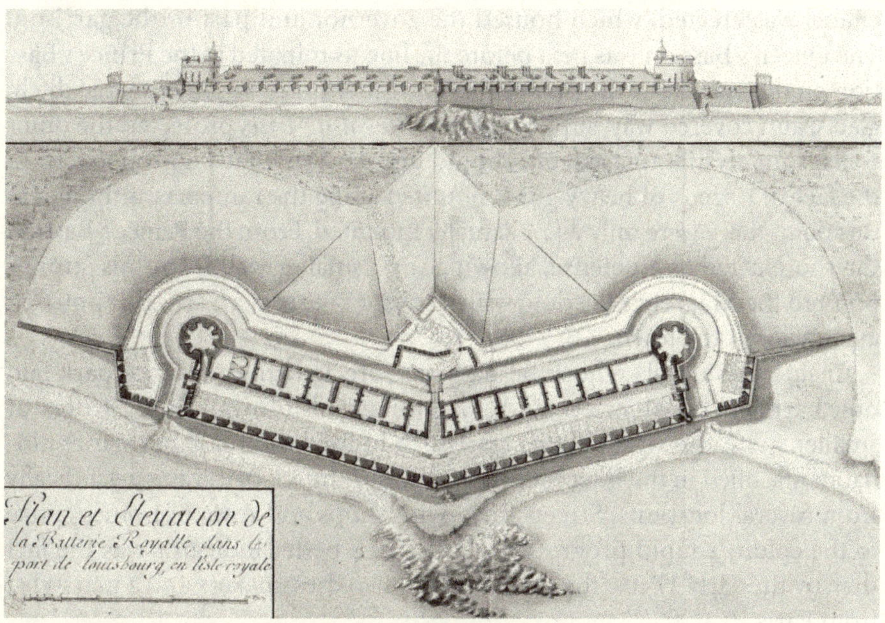

A plan of the Royal Battery. The landside defenses of this self-contained fortress were not complete when Louisbourg was besieged in 1745. Even so, the seaside battery of over thirty 42-pound naval cannons presented a formidable challenge to enemy vessels looking to enter the harbor. (*Norman B. Leventhal Map Collection, Boston Public Library*)

this battery, manpower shortages, bad weather, and high seas had stunted the effort, bringing all work to a halt until spring. Little was accomplished the next year, as efforts were focused on the Royal Battery. In fact, it would not be until December 1730 that the Island Battery's powder magazine was finished, the platforms constructed, and the cannons mounted along the ramparts. There was still a cistern to construct and a number of items to finish within the interior, leading to the official declaration of completion in June 1732. Even so, like most North American fortifications, it would always be a work in progress.[12]

By 1738 work on the fortified town on the southern shore of the harbor had been declared complete. The landside defenses consisted of a series of stone bastions built on a string of small hills and connected by thirty-six-foot curtain walls that stretched from the harbor's edge to the seashore. At the western end of this chain was the Dauphin's Bastion, which guarded the most commonly used gate into the town. Next was the King's Bastion. This was the centerpiece of the line, behind which the four-story-tall stone citadel was erected, which housed the governor and part of the garrison. The Queen's Bastion was next before the line terminated at the Prince's Bastion on the sea side of the peninsula. To further brace this line, a large ditch, glacis, and covered way, supported by a *cheval-de-frise*, protected the outer walls from an infantry assault, should one dare risk such a proposition in the face of dozens of heavy guns mounted along the ramparts, although at this point there were only a few actually mounted. From the Prince's Bastion the shore acted as a defense, allowing for a smaller wall from this strongpoint to the Maurepas Bastion, which covered the eastern seaside approach and enclosed the town.

Inside these walls a hospital had been erected, an ordinance park laid out, barracks constructed, and government buildings raised. Scores of smaller stone and wood buildings, which housed the 1,500 permanent inhabitants, filled in the intervening spaces, and church bells rang periodically from several locations. Streets lined with shops and rows of homes spoke to the colony's rapid progress, but perhaps a better indicator was the fact that, by the early 1740s, the town boasted two dressmakers and a hairstylist from Paris.[13]

The garrison now consisted of a company of artillery, eight companies of the Free Companies of the Marine, and three companies of the Swiss Regiment Karrer, which had been raised in response to a shortage of marines. Together these troops and their officers would amount to over 650 men, but none of these units were ever at full strength, and with detachments at several outposts on the island, it placed the effective force guarding Louisbourg at less than five hundred men. In a time of crisis, the garrison would be augmented by some three hundred to four hundred militia and whatever naval personnel or fishermen happened to be in port, likely doubling or tripling their overall numbers.

While over a thousand men guarding a fortified city supported by heavily armed stone fortifications might appear sufficient, the quality of the troops would have more bearing on the outcome than numbers. Of particular importance at Louisbourg was the lack of skilled gunners. With the works in a constant state of construction, and shortages a way of life, there had been little time to drill the gun crews, many of which were only vaguely familiar with the loading, aiming, and firing of a cannon. The governor had attempted to rectify this problem in the spring of 1736 when he drafted two men from each company to train and serve as artillerymen. Although they were not officially a *Compagnie des Bombardiers*, as was commonly seen in fortifications along the French coast, St. Ovide was looking not only for the same function, but just as importantly, the same appearance so as to change the perception of "foreigners, who say openly that though we have many cannon, we have no one to serve them."[14]

While the defenses of the French naval port neared completion, or some semblance of that, news arrived of France's involvement in the War of Polish Succession. While this conflict did not include Britain, there was genuine concern that it soon might and that Louisbourg could suddenly become a target. The possibility led to a series of proposals by St. Ovide. He noted that the French port was considered a major threat to New England and as such was likely to be attacked by a force from these colonies. Preferably, news of war would reach Louisbourg first, giving an opportunity to take the offensive. If this were the case and the king wished to act, two men-of-war, a frigate, four companies for the garrison, and six hundred well-armed and well-supplied regular troops should be sent with the news. This force, when combined with elements of the Louisbourg garrison and a detachment of Micmac, could easily seize both Annapolis Royal and Canso. The former location was in ruins while the latter post was so poorly defended that reports had reached St. Ovide speaking to its abandonment upon the outbreak of hostilities.

One of the most likely scenarios was an attack on Louisbourg by New England militia and elements of the Royal Navy. This would probably come in the spring, before the supply ships and the fishing fleet arrived. Here St. Ovide had taken a number of measures to secure the port. The fortifications were in an advanced state, although the wall between the King's and Dauphin's Batteries still needed to be finished, and with the exception of the Island Battery, only a handful of cannons had been mounted. In addition, there was still work to do to protect sections of the harbor's shoreline with a *cheval-de-frise* to discourage any enemy landings. As he found it unlikely that an enemy fleet would attempt to run the narrow channel past the heavy guns of the Island Battery and those mounted in the Royal Battery, a landing and advance on the fortress from nearby Gabarus Bay or Mire Bay was the best approach before them. This would certainly lead to a formal siege, and given the questionable abilities of New England militia, especially in a siege operation, St. Ovide was confident that the garrison would triumph under such circumstances.[15]

St. Ovide would travel to France in the fall of 1738 to answer accusations concerning his involvement in illegal trading activities, never to return to

Overleaf: A plan of the town and fortifications of Louisbourg, 1745, by Capt. John Henry Bastide, Royal Engineers. (*Norman B. Leventhal Map Collection, Boston Public Library*)

PLAN OF THE
TOWN AND FORTIFICATIONS
OF LOUISBOURG.
E
F
G
D

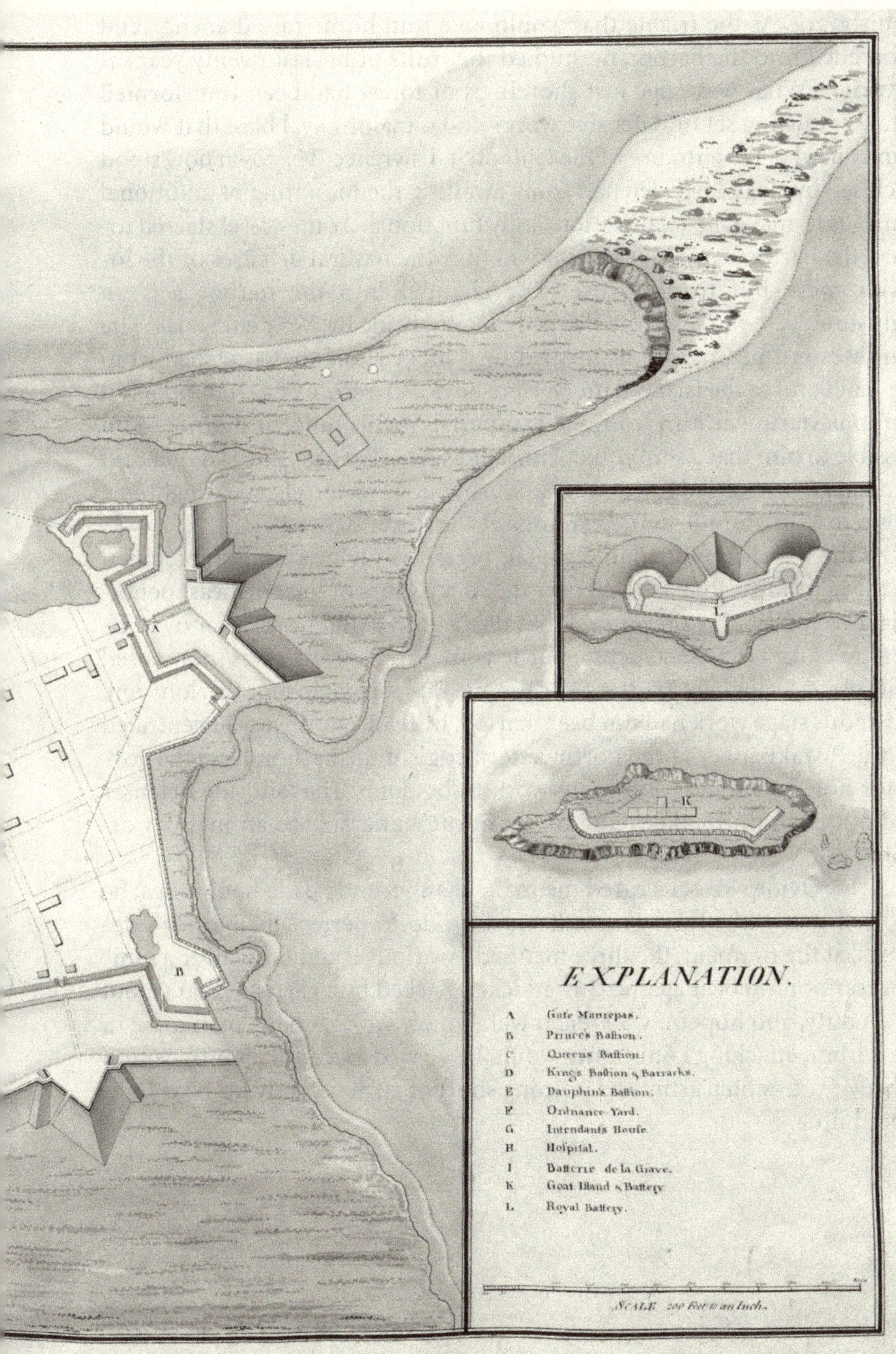
A
B
L
K
EXPLANATION.
A Gate Maurepas.
B Princes Baſtion.
C Queens Baſtion.
D Kings Baſtion & Barracks.
E Dauphin's Baſtion.
F Ordnance Yard.
G Intendants Houſe.
H Hoſpital.
I Batterie de la Grave.
K Goat Iſland & Battery
L Royal Battery.
SCALE 200 Feet to an Inch.

Louisbourg. As the frigate that would take him home raised anchor and proceeded into the harbor, he studied the fruits of his last twenty years as governor. What was once just shorelines of forest had been transformed into a sprawling set of defensive works and a major naval base that would stand guard at the entrance of the Gulf of St. Lawrence. The town now stood enclosed by siege-level defenses, only awaiting the mounting of additional cannons to make the fortifications fully functional. As the vessel steered toward the harbor's exit St. Ovide noted how the natural defenses of the location were put to good use. The channel into the harbor was an eight-hundred-yard expanse flanked on either side by two peninsulas. The southwestern peninsula was formed by a rocky shoal that stretched from the mainland to the Island Battery. Here he noted a score of 42-pound naval cannons staring at him from the ramparts. At this range it did not seem possible to him that a ship could withstand such a barrage, but as he glanced to the rear, he realized it was worse. The intruder would also be caught in a crossfire from the 42-pound cannons at the Royal Battery.

As the vessel continued under a fair breeze St. Ovide's attention focused on the lighthouse that towered over the rocky shore of the northeast peninsula. Erected in 1734, it was said that the beacon could be seen for over fifteen miles. In 1736 the structure burned down, but another was soon raised in its place. Originally a battery of cannons was considered for this location, but at this stage work had not been started. Instead, effort was concentrated on the Royal Battery at the northwestern edge of the harbor. Here the governor noted there was still more work to be done. The landside defenses had not been finished, leaving the position vulnerable to an infantry attack.[16]

As St. Ovide's vessel cleared the main channel and headed out to sea, he realized that while there was still much to do to perfect the harbor's defenses, at the moment, the three fortified positions could bring over a hundred cannons to bear against any attacker. Backed by a garrison that would do its duty, and hopefully a French warship or two that happened to be in the harbor, attacking Louisbourg would be viewed as a difficult proposition for any professional army and nothing short of an act of folly for New England militia.

CHAPTER SEVEN

The Hudson and Champlain Valleys

WHILE CONFLICT and intrigue engulfed Acadia, Maine, New Hampshire, and eastern Massachusetts, along the natural invasion route formed by the Hudson and Champlain Valleys the thirty years' peace took a different path. The region, dominated by the Hudson River, Lake Champlain, and the Richelieu River, cut a path out of the primeval forests stretching from the St. Lawrence in the north to New York City in the south. This chain of waterways posed a grave risk as well as an opportunity for both sides, given that most of this waterway was navigable to small craft, meaning that an army with cannons could move quickly from one end to the other.

Here French Canada and New York examined the lessons of Queen Anne's War and made efforts to strengthen their defenses. For the governors of New York, Albany was the key to the New York frontier and its defenses. The town marked the northernmost point of navigation on the river and was a key trading and diplomatic post with the Iroquois Confederacy, who were now British subjects. Fortunately, the old wooden Fort Albany, so dilapidated by northern winters and neglect that there was fear the walls would collapse, had been replaced with a stone one. Fort Frederick, as the new structure was named, measured two hundred feet to a side and boasted fourteen-foot walls between its four bastions. A twenty-foot ditch circled the structure, and a pair of two-story buildings slightly higher than the fort's walls ran down the length of two sides. These twin structures served as barracks, storehouses, workshops, and the commandant's quarters. Armed with two dozen cannons and garrisoned by nearly one hundred men, Fort Frederick was a powerful addition to the defenses of Albany.

By the mid-1720s there was talk of replacing Fort Frederick, but instead the existing structure was refurbished. In the mid-1730s minor repairs were made to the fort while work commenced on replacing the stockade around the town. Portions of the wooden structure were replaced with stone, a ditch was added about its length, and a number of blockhouses, armed with small cannons, were erected at key points along the perimeter. By 1738 the work was complete, making Albany the most secure post on the New York frontier.[1]

A proposed stone redoubt at Half Moon never materialized, and instead the old palisade fort at this location was revived at various points during the intervening peace. At Saratoga, the most northerly defensive point along the Hudson, a small stockade fort was erected in 1721 to provide refuge for the handful of Dutch farmers in the area, but the scarcity of funds and general disinterest in the project resulted in such a poor fortification that the twelve-man garrison often complained that it was impossible to keep their arms and supplies dry. More concerted efforts were made at Schenectady. Portions of the town were rebuilt after the devastating attack in 1690, but it would be another five years before the wooden palisades that originally encircled the village were reconstructed, this time with blockhouses at various points along their length. Although much to the citizens' and the governor's dismay, a proposed stone fort was never undertaken, in 1705 a one-hundred-foot square palisade fort with bastions at each corner was built at the eastern edge of the town. With the exception of frequent repairs, the "Queen's Fort," as it was known, would remain unchanged for the next thirty years. In 1734 the weather-battered structure was torn down and a new one of the same dimensions erected in its place. Christened Fort Cosby, this new stronghold was far sturdier, being built by laying horizontal timbers one upon the other on a stone foundation as opposed to the palisade method of the old fort. Capable of holding several hundred men, the new structure housed small 4-pound cannons in each of the bastions and a 6- and 9-pound gun on carriages in the parade ground. A garrison of seventeen men, maintenance issues, a perpetual lack of supplies, and the positioning of the fort at the eastern edge of the town undermined the overall strength of the works.[2]

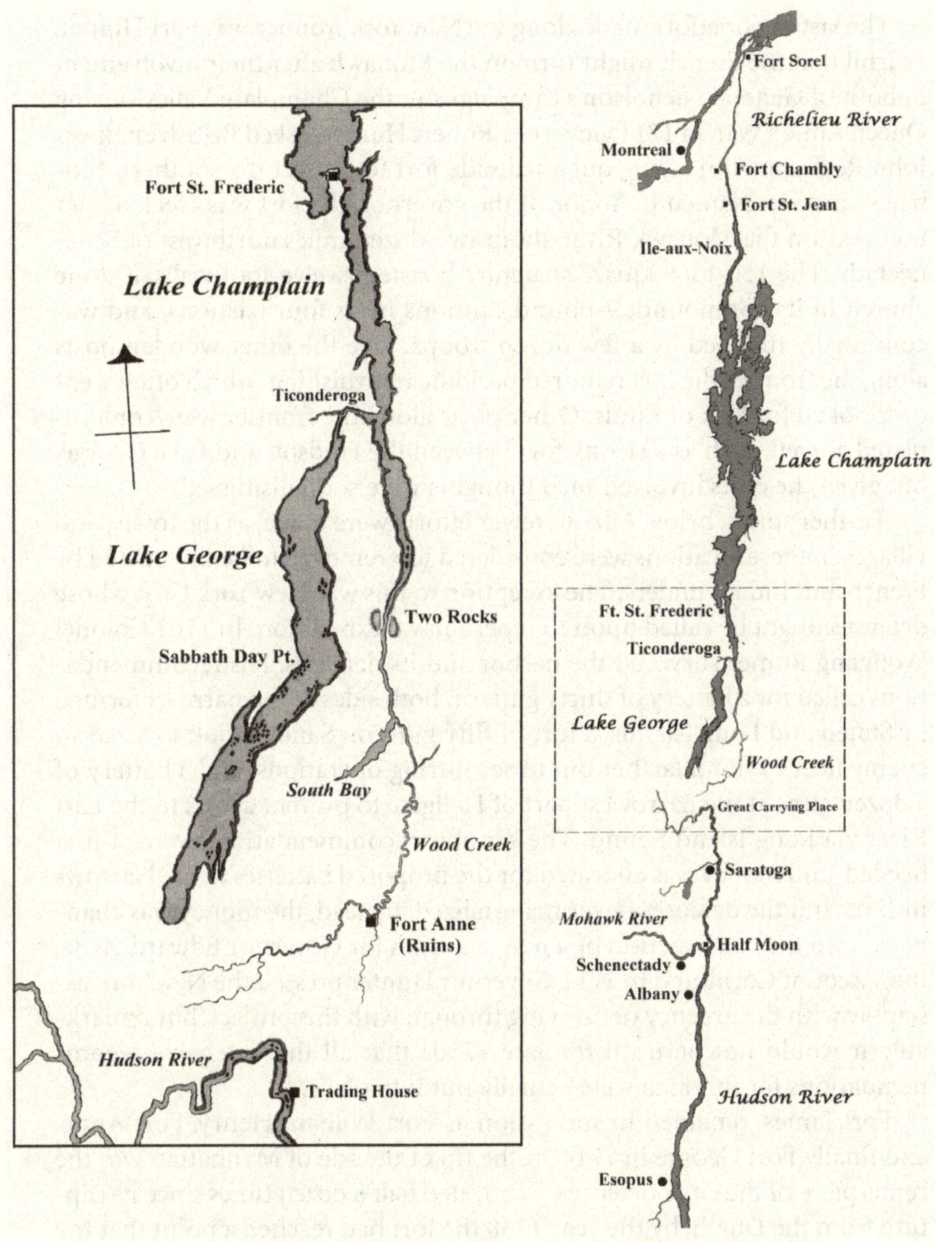

French and British positions in the Champlain and Upper Hudson Valleys, 1748.

The last major effort made along the New York frontier was Fort Hunter. Fearful that the French might turn on the Mohawk after their involvement in both of General Nicholson's campaigns in the Champlain Valley during Queen Anne's War, in 1711 Governor Robert Hunter tasked British engineer John Redknap with laying out a palisade fort to protect the southern Mohawk cantons. Named in honor of the governor, the fort was erected later that year on the Mohawk River about two dozen miles northwest of Schenectady. The 150-foot square structure boasted twelve-foot walls, a stone church in its compound, 9-pound cannons in its four bastions, and was continually manned by a few dozen troops. Like the other wooden posts along the frontier the fort required periodic refurbishing, which often went overlooked for lack of funds. Other posts along the frontier were contemplated as well, such as a strong fort between the Hudson and Lake George, but given the costs involved such thoughts were soon dismissed.[3]

Farther south, below Albany, fewer efforts were made, as the towns and villages in these locations were considered too removed to be threatened by French and Indian raiders. The exception to this was New York City, whose defenses might be called upon to repel a naval expedition. In 1701 Colonel Wolfgang Romer surveyed the harbor and its defenses. His recommendations called for a battery of thirty guns on both sides of the narrows formed by Staten and Long Islands, a fort of fifty guns on Sandy Hook to force an enemy fleet to stand farther out to sea during operations, and a battery of a dozen guns at the narrowest part of Hellgate to prevent access to the East River via Long Island Sound. The sensible recommendations were at first heeded, and money was allocated for the proposed batteries at the Narrows in 1703, but the defenses never materialized. Instead, the money was channeled into the construction of a new mansion for Governor Edward Hyde, the Viscount Cornbury. In 1711 Governor Hunter pressed the New York assembly with the urgency of carrying through with this project, but remarkably it would not be until the late 1750s that all the defensive recommendations for this area were actually put into place.

Fort James, renamed in succession as Fort William Henry, Fort Anne, and finally Fort George in 1714, at the tip of the Isle of Manhattan was the centerpiece of the city's defenses. Renovated half a dozen times since its capture from the Dutch, by the year 1738 the fort had reached a point that the governor of New York complained of its ruinous condition and the lack of military supplies within its walls, most of which had been sent over for the Canadian expedition of 1711. Fortunately, the fort was backed by a nearby battery of fifty guns erected in 1735 to control access into the upper harbor. As for Fort George itself, the interior buildings were renovated after a fire

The defenses of Albany, c.1738. While Fort Frederick to the northwest of the town was dominated by the nearby heights, the belief was that the French could not transport the cannons needed to besiege the fort to this location. The ruined fort to the south of the town is the old Dutch fortification and trading post, Fort Orange. (*Hulbert,* The Crown Collection of Photographs of American Maps, Series I/2 *[1907]*)

in March 1741 destroyed most of them, but from this point on, the fort, mounting only 9- and 12-pound cannons, took on a secondary importance to the nearby battery.[4]

TO THE NORTH, New France had also been busy making improvements to its defenses along the Montreal-Albany corridor. After Queen Anne's War the foremost post along this route was Fort Chambly, and initially, it received the bulk of the attention. In the winter of 1702, the thirty-seven-year-old fort was severely damaged by a fire. With relations between the two colonies deteriorating, there was little choice but to rebuild the fort. The second fort was a wooden structure like the first. The walls were fashioned from vertical logs supported by a filled ditch and a network of horizontal support logs. The old redans were replaced with bastions at the corners of the fort. Along the south wall a building called the "King's Store" was constructed, which functioned as a barracks and storehouse. A second building of a similar nature appears to have also been placed along the inside of the north wall, and a powder magazine was placed below the southeastern bastion. After Nicholson's threatened invasion in 1709, it became clear that the current wooden fortification was insufficient. The next year Governor Vaudreuil ordered engineer Josue Boisberthelot de Beaucours to construct a stone fortification over the site of the current wooden one. The fort was only to be capable of withstanding light artillery fire, primarily because it was considered unlikely that the English could haul heavy cannons over Lake Champlain.

Beaucours laid out the new Fort Chambly in a square with three-story-tall bastions at each of its corners. Thirty-foot-high curtains constructed of limestone and masonry linked the bastions, making the entire structure approximately 168 feet to a side. A fortified entrance was placed on the west wall facing the Chambly Basin. The bastions and the wall along the side facing the Richelieu were pierced for cannon, and firing ports were set into the four-foot-thick walls. Long buildings were built against the eastern, southern, and western walls. These buildings served as the storehouses, workshops, and barracks for the garrison. Powder magazines and covered wells within the lower parts of the bastions completed the works. When it was finished in the summer of 1712, it was an impressive structure, so much so that Governor Vaudreuil informed the minister of the marine that Fort Chambly was "now beyond insult."

The fort underwent major modifications between the years 1718 and 1720. Colonial engineer Chaussegros de Lery rebuilt the north wall, which was already showing damage from the periodic ravages of the Richelieu River. De Lery also added watchtowers to the bastion corners, reworked some of the embrasures and loopholes, and oversaw the construction of a ditch, drawbridge, and machicolation to better protect the fort's gate. In the 1730s the fort again had its north wall reworked after years of flooding threatened to undermine its integrity. It was a persistent problem, and it would not be the last time that such repairs had to be undertaken. The fort was typically garrisoned by thirty to fifty troops of the Free Companies of the Marine. In addition, there were approximately forty families that lived

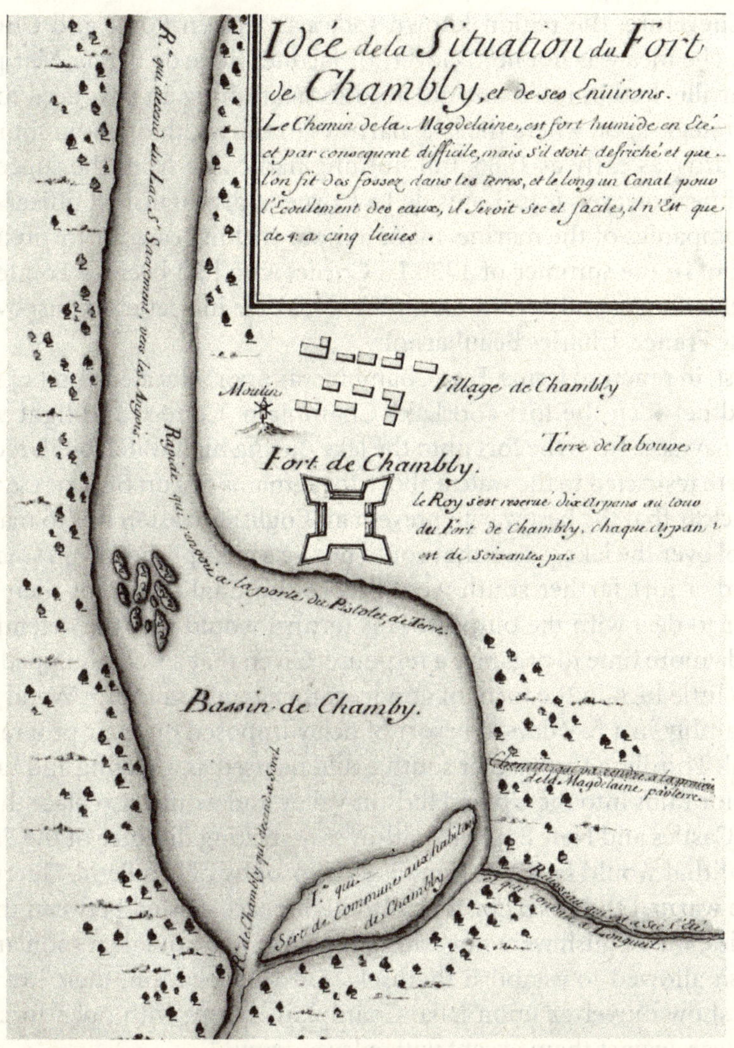

Fort Chambly and the nearby village of Chambly. The fort guarded a set of rapids on the Richelieu River and the anchorage in the Chambly Basin. Note that north, toward the St. Lawrence River, is at the bottom of this image from 1717. (*Norman B. Leventhal Map Collection, Boston Public Library*)

in or about the hamlet that had taken shape around the fort. In a crisis, these individuals would take refuge within the fort, effectively doubling its garrison.[5]

For New France a secure Fort Chambly was a necessity, but in the late 1720s talk began to circulate about locating a fort farther south at Pointe-à-la-Chevelure, the region known today as Crown Point and Chimney Point. The idea was not new. Governor Jacques Rene de Brisay, Marquis de Denonville, had pointed out the need for stationing an advanced force at this strategic spot, where the lake narrows to the width of about four hundred yards, as early as 1686, but nothing had come from the suggestion. This time, however, Jean-Louis de La Corne, a distinguished officer in the free companies of the marine, made a more striking case for fortifying the location. In the summer of 1730 La Corne, who had been to Pointe-à-la-Chevelure on several occasions, outlined his case in a letter to the governor of New France, Charles Beauharnois.

First, in practical terms, Fort Chambly was poorly located. A set of rapids existed between the fort and Lake Champlain. Canoes and light vessels could navigate from the fort onto the lake during high water, but larger vessels were restricted to the waters above the remains of Fort St. Therese. Thus, it was clear that the best way to prevent an English invasion was to maintain control over the lake, a task that could not be accomplished from Chambly. Second, a fort farther south would force the English out of their boats sooner to deal with the outpost. This in turn would give the defenders of Canada more time to organize a response. Given that a well-equipped army, with a little luck in the form of good weather, could sail from Wood Creek to Chambly in a few days, any sort of delay imposed on their progress was crucial. Thirdly, a fort farther south could be used as a staging and rallying point for raids into the Upper Hudson Valley and would also place the Mohawk Castles and New England within easy striking distance of the French, a point that would facilitate Canada's philosophy of "La Petite Guerre." La Corne warned the governor that, although peace existed between the two colonies, the English were not asleep. If action was not taken soon and the English allowed to establish themselves at this location, then "we could never show ourselves upon Lake Champlain except with open force, nor make war against them except with a large army."[6]

Beauharnois was in complete agreement. The recent English establishment of a British fort at Oswego on Lake Ontario made it clear that some form of action was necessary. He sent La Corne's memorandum to the king and requested permission to fortify Pointe-à-la-Chevelure. In the meantime, as it would take some time for a response from France, he dispatched a small party to Pointe-à-la-Chevelure to trace out and prepare the ground for a stockade fort.[7]

Beauharnois's request was met with a receptive court in Versailles. The governor was directed to take the steps necessary to erect a palisade fort at the location until a more permanent structure could be undertaken. With the English erecting a post at Oswego on Lake Ontario the French court did not need many reasons for agreeing to the idea, but as it turned out they had another purely political reason for wanting a fort at Pointe-à-la-Chevelure. As the commissioners met to determine the limits of the English and French possessions in North America, the king's councilors at Versailles began formulating a "water-shed" theory to define their boundaries. In its basic form it claimed that all the waters drained by the St. Lawrence River and the lands that were contained therein belonged to New France. In the case of Lake Champlain, it was true that the French held the right of discovery, but occupation was just as important when it came to making a boundary claim. The establishment of a post on Lake Champlain then would not only bar the English but would solidify their territorial claims over the entire Champlain Valley. There was also another point that entertained the court's imagination. The fort at Point-a-la-Chevelure could be used as a bargaining chip in the current boundary negotiations, perhaps in an exchange for the English fort at Oswego.[8]

Work on the wooden fort began in August of 1731 under the watchful eye of Rocbert de la Morandière, an officer in the Free Companies of the Marine. The task was nothing new for Morandière, who had built a dozen palisade forts across New France. The fort was laid out as a four-bastioned hundred-foot-by-hundred-foot structure located on a bluff near the water's edge on what is today called Chimney Point. Inside were a series of buildings for lodging the twenty-man garrison, their munitions, and their supplies. A chapel had even been constructed to meet the occupants' spiritual needs. By mid-October the task was complete. So too was the letter of complaint from the English ambassador at Versailles, the Earl of Waldegrave, who had received numerous reports over the course of the summer regarding the French endeavor. The ambassador claimed that the fort was built on Iroquois lands, and as such, it was in violation of article fifteen of the Treaty of Utrecht, which made the Iroquois British subjects. He called for its immediate destruction and the withdrawal of any French troops encroaching upon these lands. Contrary to issuing such an order, the king responded by commending Beauharnois on his vigilance and ordering work to proceed on erecting a more permanent fortification at the site.[9]

In keeping with the king's wishes, Beauharnois asked de Lery to draw up a set of plans for a stone fort at Point-a-la-Chevelure. De Lery, who was responsible for the design and construction of most of the major fortifications in Canada, took to the task and by the end of the month had completed a preliminary set of plans for a stone fort on the west bank of the lake at modern-day Crown Point. The governor winced when he examined the engineer's design. Instead of a regular bastioned fort, de Lery had centered his design about a four-story-tall *redoute à machicoulis*, a structure that resembled a rook or corner battlement on a medieval castle. He circled this structure with a more conventional stone wall in which the redoubt roughly occupied the position of the easternmost or waterside bastion. A ditch and a wooden palisade protected the outer wall, and the main gate, a small blockhouse in and of itself, was located along the northern wall. Taken as a whole, the design looked more like a product of the Middle Ages than the military dictums of Vauban.

De Lery must have noticed with some amusement the quick glances that passed between the governor and the intendent, Gilles Hocquart, as they pored over his drawings. "Unusual," one imagines the governor to have commented. "And expensive," the intendent would have returned. The engineer gave them their moment and then explained his work. Contrary to discarding Vauban, he had abided by one of his first principles, that being that fortifications should be adapted to peculiarities of the surrounding terrain. He had dismissed the idea of a regular bastioned fortress for several reasons. First, the long and harsh winters would make servicing and manning the cannons along the outer walls next to impossible. This was not the case with the current design. The fort's cannons were mounted in firing ports along the upper levels of the redoubt, all of which could be closed to the elements by means of wooden shutters. Secondly, the redoubt would be difficult if not impossible for attackers to scale. The firing ports could be closed and the other windows covered with iron bars to prevent access. This was not true of a regular fort, and as such, a regular fort required a larger garrison to maintain its security. With his design, a few sentries posted at advantageous points could survey the entire landscape, which, when coupled with the natural security of the redoubt, meant a far smaller garrison would be required, perhaps fifty in peacetime and twice that if hostilities broke out.

The reduced garrison costs pleased Hocquart as much as the reduction in manpower pleased the governor. The outer walls, de Lery continued, like the redoubt, were loopholed and provided with a covered way that traversed their parameter. When called upon, small cannons and swivel guns could be mounted along these walls to provide for a first line of defense. But like the keep of a castle, even if these walls were breached, the defenders could still fall back upon the redoubt, which overlooked the entire compound.

Beauharnois and Hocquart were convinced and transmitted the plans along with their recommendations to Versailles. De Lery followed with a letter to the minister of the marine outlining his thoughts on the matter. The

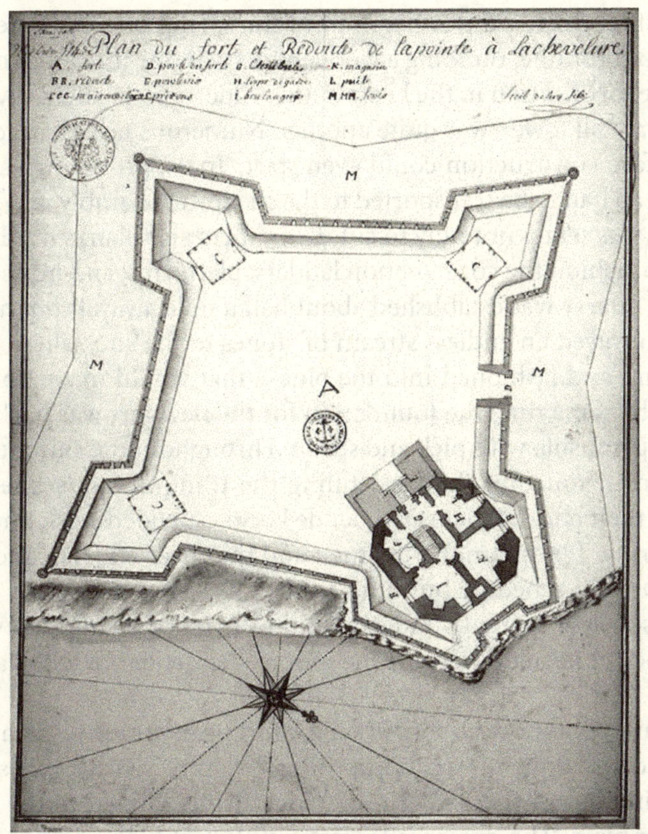

A 1737 plan of Fort St. Frederic. (*Archives Nationales d'Outre-Mer, Aix-en-Probence, France [FR CAOM 03DFC511B]*)

court was at first receptive, but in April of 1733 the minister of the marine expressed concerns over the costs involved and questioned whether the current wooden fort or a small regular stone fort would not meet their requirements. No, the governor answered. No, the intendent seconded. The fort at Point-a-la-Chevelure was the first line of defense against the English. A palisade fort was fine for protection against raiders but would not last a day before English cannons. A more significant structure was required, and it was required soon, as there were already reports arriving of English designs on the area. A statement in the form of a major fortification was required not only for the security of New France but to prevent further English expansion into the region. The court relented on the projected costs and gave the order to start work on the fort, to be named St. Frederic, early the next year.[10]

The actual work did not begin until the spring of 1735. The task was anything but routine. Building a wooden fort was one thing, but constructing a stone fortification in the heart of the wilderness, particularly one with a four-story-tall tower, was quite another. Numerous tasks had to be completed before construction could even start. Tools, provisions, and beasts of burden all had to be transported to the site from Chambly and Montreal. A sawmill was set up not only to cut the timbers and planks needed for the fort but to fashion the construction ladders, platforms, and hosts as well. A limestone quarry was established about half a mile away. From here teams of oxen conveyed an endless stream of stones to the site, where they were cut by hand and fashioned into the blocks that would make up the fort's walls. At the same time the foundation for the new fort was hacked out of the rocky peninsula with pick and spade. Throughout the summer months crews of men toiled at the task, filling the tranquil landscape with the sounds of their effort. In late October de Lery suspended work until the following spring. Illness among the men and the sheer effort of the task had put him behind schedule but not as much as might have been expected. The garrison was currently lodged within the redoubt, and the works, although "not perfected," were for the moment sufficient to withstand an attack.[11]

The finishing touches were put on the fort nearly three years later. When all was said and done it was an imposing structure, a black limestone barricade rising out of the wilderness, a lock firmly affixed to the waters of Lake Champlain. The outer walls were twenty feet high and two feet thick with bastions protruding like the points of a compass. A twenty-foot-wide ditch crowned with a row of sharpened stakes circled the walls, creating a deadly trap for those who elected to storm its ramparts. Within the flagstoned compound there sat a small stone church and numerous other buildings to house the garrison and their supplies, but it was the four-story-tall tower that held the eye. A dark sentinel standing over the edge of the lake, from a distance it might be mistaken for a lighthouse, but as one approached closer they would discern the bristling cannon and arched bombproof roof that indicated the structure's true purpose.[12]

The fort was not without its critics. A stone windmill was placed just east of the fort and doubled as a lookout post, having a better view up the lake than the fort, causing Peter Kalm, the Swedish naturalist who traveled the length of the lake a decade later, to question whether the fort should not have been placed at this location. There were also concerns as to the rising ground some four hundred yards to the west, which flanked and dominated the fort's interior. But such items were undue criticism. All forts have their inherent weaknesses. Fort St. Frederic was not a Gibraltar. What mattered was that it would take a battery of 12-pound cannons and a formal siege to secure its works, an act that would afford enough time for an army to be assembled and marched to its relief.[13]

Fort St. Frederic had been in place only a few years when it became clear that the fort's supply chain was incapable of meeting its demands. Forwarding supplies from Fort Chambly was a tedious and expensive proposition given the sets of intervening rapids and the limited capabilities of the small bateaux and canoes that traversed the route. What was needed was a heavier vessel, plying an established supply route. Such a vessel would serve another purpose as well. Armed with small cannons and superior to anything the English could slip past Fort St. Frederic, it would assure French control of the waters. Soundings had pointed out that the lake was more than capable of taking such vessels, and although not all the navigation hazards had been charted, enough had been found that by the early 1740s it was agreed to build a thirty-five-ton vessel on the lake. The problem was where to build it and where to anchor the vessel when it was not at Fort St. Frederic. Beauharnois, Hocquart, and de Lery discussed the issue at length and arrived at a solution. A wooden fort should be constructed on the west bank of the Richelieu River just south of the St. Jean rapids where there was still sufficient water for a small schooner. The fort would act as a supply depot and magazine for Fort St. Frederic and a staging point for reinforcements going to its relief. The idea was attractive but suffered from one problem. Since the water route to the proposed fort was impractical, a road would have to be cut to the fort from La Prairie, which, although an expensive proposition, was agreed upon as the only practical alternative.[14]

It would be several years before Fort St. Jean would be erected to complete the northern end of Fort St. Frederic's supply line, but in the meantime the presence of the new French stronghold at Crown Point was not lost on the citizens of New York and New England, nor the Iroquois. Lt. Governor George Clarke of New York, in a series of letters to the Board of Trade on the matter in late 1737 and early 1738, explained the French watershed theory, which would make most the Iroquois homelands French and would restrict the English colonies along the eastern coast of the continent, "but I presume to think those pretensions vain," he concluded. Of more importance was the military advantage Fort St. Frederic gave the French and how little there was he could do about it. "I know of no regulations for determining the boundaries between New York and Canada," he informed the board. "It is probable each will endeavour to extend themselves as far as they can. The French have lately made a wide step by building a fort at

Crown Point which alarms the English colonies by it being a pass of great importance. By this pass only, there is access to Canada from the English colonies and from this the French will be able in wartime to send out parties to harass and plunder the colonies of Massachusetts Bay, New York, and Connecticut."[15]

His assessment was correct. The French had won the battle of position in the Champlain Valley, and New York had done nothing in response. They would soon pay the price for this indecision.

CHAPTER EIGHT

Niagara and Oswego

Arguments and political maneuvering between New York and Canada were not just confined to the Hudson and Champlain Valleys. Along Lake Ontario a similar scenario would take hold, one which would primarily center about two events: the establishment of a French trading post at Niagara and a corresponding British trading post erected to the east at Oswego.

Niagara had long been identified as an important post by the French. In early December 1678 a small ten-ton brig carrying sixteen men under the command of Pierre de la Motte-Lussiere dropped anchor near the mouth of the Niagara River. It had proven a perilous voyage, and at several points it appeared the vessel would be lost, but it had arrived intact with its cargo. This advanced guard of Rene La Salle's exploration of the Great Lakes and the Mississippi Valley had departed Fort Frontenac with supplies to build a vessel on Lake Erie and establish a portage on the Lake Ontario side of Niagara Falls. The site selected for the latter task was on a peninsula along the east bank of the Niagara River near its confluence with the lake. Here La Salle planned to build a fort, but after speaking with the Seneca, on whose land it would be constructed, the adventurer found a suspicious audience, enough so that one of La Salle's companions wrote, "we were obliged to give over our Building for some time, contenting ourselves with a Habitation encompass'd with Pallisado's."[1]

With the construction of the sloop *Griffon* on Lake Erie and the departure of La Salle and his expedition to the west, the cluster of warehouses and barracks that comprised Niagara turned into just another remote French post on the edge of the wilderness, occasionally occupied by traders but more often than not abandoned. Matters changed in 1687 when French Governor-General Jacques-Rene Brisay, the Marquis de Denonville, looking to halt Iroquois attacks on New France's Great Lakes allies, organized an expedition against the Seneca. As part of this effort Denonville dispatched two veteran bush fighters, Daniel Greyson D'Lhut and Louis-Joseph Durantaye, to the upper lakes to recruit a force of Native allies and French woodsmen, while La Salle's former lieutenant, Henri Tonty, was to do the same with the Illinois nation. The war parties were to rendezvous at Niagara and from there join the governor at Irondequoit Bay.

For Niagara the sudden burst of activity as some 180 Frenchmen and 400 of their allies descended on the peninsula was short lived. After receiving word from Fort Frontenac a few weeks later, they took to their canoes and traveled east to rendezvous with Denonville. The governor's expedition skirmished with the Seneca and destroyed several of their villages before setting sail for Niagara on July 30. Here Denonville put his men to work improving the fortifications. It did not prove an easy task. The ditch had to be hacked out of the rocky soil and the nearest stands of trees were located farther upriver, but with the surplus of manpower the main work went quickly. With the stockade progressing the governor assigned a garrison of a hundred men and gave command to Captain Pierre de Troyes, who the year before had seized the English trading posts on James Bay. A few days later on August 3, Denonville and the bulk of the army departed for Fort Frontenac.[2]

Work continued on the fort, and the supply vessel that Denonville had promised arrived a few weeks later. Matters would turn bleak after this ship departed for the winter. The food supplies sent by the governor were suspect and soon spoiled, forcing the garrison to hunt for its food. The nearby Seneca, who had not been seriously damaged by Denonville's efforts, stalked de Troyes and his men. It soon reached the point that hunting, wood cutting, or any other activity outside the fort's walls only became possible in large groups. Sickness then struck, claiming the lives of over half the fort's garrison including de Troyes. The starving survivors clung to hope that spring would bring the supply ship, and in early April the brig *La General* appeared on the horizon. When the relief force came ashore, they were stunned to find most of the garrison including the commandant dead and the rest too weak to continue. Men and supplies were funneled to the

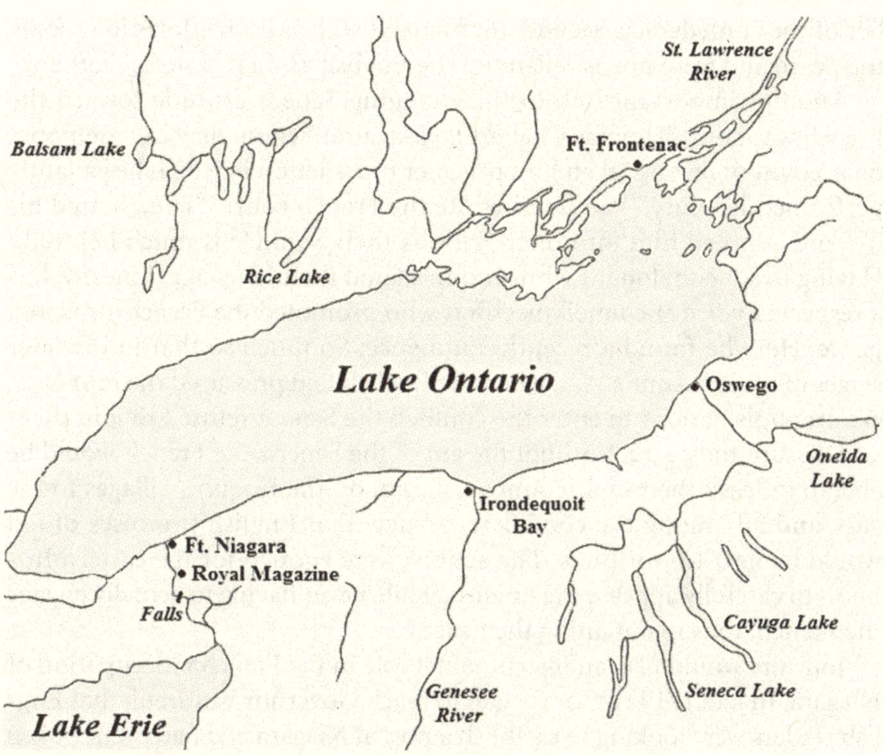

French and British posts on Lake Ontario during the Thirty-Year Peace.

stronghold over the summer, but with the deteriorating conditions between New France and the Iroquois, Denonville decided to abandon the stronghold in September 1688.[3]

The broken remains of Fort Denonville sat on the Niagara peninsula for over thirty years, a reminder of two brief expeditions and the importance both placed in this strategic location. There was talk of reestablishing the post, but little came from the proposals. During this period King William's War and Queen Anne's War had altered the position of the Iroquois Confederacy to a path of neutrality. It had also fractured the Five Nations. The eastern members of the confederacy, the Mohawk, Oneida, Onondaga, and Cayuga, respected the peace treaty but remained reluctant allies of the English primarily due to trade relationships. The Seneca on the other hand had swung from anti-French to pro-French in their thinking. First, most of the attacks by French-allied nations during King William's War and the days leading up to the Peace of Montreal in 1702 had fallen on this western member of the confederacy. Second, they agreed with French efforts to enforce the peace and were not as reliant on the English as their eastern brothers.

Another important link to the changing Seneca attitude toward the French was Louis-Thomas Chabert de Joncaire, "whom they call their Son, on account of having taken him prisoner in an action in which he gallantly performed his duty," Vaudreuil wrote the French court. "They spared his life and adopted him into their Tribe as their Son. He is much beloved." Having lived with, fought with, and mastered their language, Joncaire was a respected voice at council meetings who promoted the French-brokered peace. Here he found a receptive audience. So much so that in the later stages of Queen Anne's War, when the English had pressured the four eastern Iroquois nations to enter the conflict, the Seneca refused to join them and disrupt the peace. Without the aid of the Seneca, the French would be able to unleash their high-country allies upon the Iroquois villages to the east, and all among the confederacy knew that English promises of aid would be next to worthless. The actions were enough for the eastern Iroquois to carefully appease the English, while never having to actually engage the French, thus maintaining the peace.[4]

Joncaire would play an instrumental role in the French reoccupation of Niagara. In late 1719 rumors began to reach Governor Vaudreuil that English traders were looking to establish a post at Niagara and had even spoken with a Seneca sachem about the idea. It was alarming news. An English post at Niagara was a dire threat to New France. From this position it could intercept all trade from the western lakes that passed through the Niagara portage. It would also place the English in a position to trade directly with New France's Great Lakes allies. The cheaper and more plentiful English trade goods, coupled with the strategic location, would soon undermine all French efforts in the west.

The problem was how to approach the idea of rebuilding a fort at Niagara. The Seneca had maintained their neutrality and were not likely to suddenly agree to a French stronghold or a stone fort on their lands. It was at this point that the governor turned to Joncaire, who offered a unique solution. Traveling to the Seneca country in early 1720, Joncaire met with the Seneca council. They expressed their delight in seeing their son return home, to which Joncaire pointed out that was the purpose of his visit. He would like to be able to visit more often and would like to build a homestead and facilities for his fur trading business. The chieftains shrugged and pointed out that they had asked him many years ago to settle among them, "granting him liberty to select on their territory the place most acceptable to himself for the purpose of living and in peace, even to remove their vil-

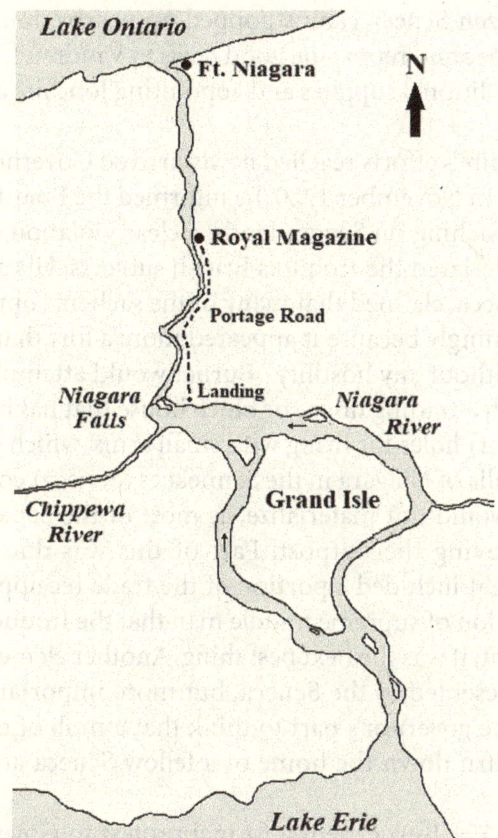

French posts along the Niagara portage from Lake Ontario to Lake Erie.

lages to the neighbourhood of his residence in order to protect him." Joncaire nodded and said he would now like to do this and asked for a piece of land. Again, the chieftains shrugged and told him that he was their son, and as such he could pick whatever land he wished. Joncaire thanked the council and selected a piece of land along the east bank of the Niagara River in modern-day Lewiston, New York. The location was at the north end of the portage road around the falls and long rapids and marked the beginning of water navigation down the river into Lake Ontario.[5]

Joncaire acted quickly, and soon several canoes loaded with supplies and men appeared. The initial efforts consisted of a fortified garrison house, which, much like its New England counterparts, was surrounded by a palisade. Known as the Royal Magazine, this wooden structure had barely finished when a dozen Seneca cabins popped up nearby. Joncaire was quick to return to Quebec and report the good news to Vaudreuil, who responded by forwarding additional supplies and appointing Joncaire as the commandant of Niagara.

Word of Joncaire's efforts reached newly arrived Governor William Burnet of New York. In November 1720, he informed the Board of Trade about the French encroaching on Seneca lands, a clear violation of the Treaty of Utrecht, which declared the Iroquois British subjects. His agents, who had met with the Seneca, claimed that many of the sachems opposed Joncaire's blockhouse, seemingly because it appeared more a fort than a trade house. In the spring "without any hostility," Burnet would attempt to get "our Indians to demolish a trading house or block house that has been made musket proof with port holes for firing with small arms, which the French have set up near the falls of Niagara in the Sennekees [Seneca] country." Such efforts, however, would not materialize, as most of the Seneca were not interested in removing the outpost. Part of this was due to an offer on Joncaire's part that included a portion of the trade receipts. Although this was not the position of supreme middle man that the Iroquois Confederacy had always sought, it was the next best thing. Another element was the trading choices it presented to the Seneca, but more importantly it showed a disconnect on the governor's part to think that a mob of outraged Seneca were going to burn down the home of a fellow Seneca at the behest of a British official.[6]

In mid-July 1721 Burnet sent a formal protest to Governor Vaudreuil. Burnet complained that reports were reaching him that Joncaire was inciting the Seneca, British subjects, to revolt against the Crown. This, along with the construction of a fort at the north portage in Iroquois lands, was a clear violation of the Treaty of Utrecht and should be immediately rectified. Vaudreuil replied a month later that Burnet was the first governor of New York to complain about the French establishment at Niagara, a location occupied by the French off and on for over forty years. Given that the post predated the treaty and was not mentioned in the treaty, Vaudreuil did not recognize Burnet's claims regarding the location.[7]

Burnet's response to French influence on the Five Nations called for banning trade in Indian goods with the French, building forts at both ends of the Niagara portage and several others on Lake Ontario, and opening avenues of trade with Canada's western allies. This was a sensible plan and precisely what the French feared, but executing such a project was another matter. First, the fortifications of New York, from Fort George at New York City to Fort Hunter on the Mohawk River, were in disrepair and decay. So too was trade with the Iroquois. The governor would need trade goods and presents, but more importantly, he needed money and men to see his plan through. Men he hoped he could obtain from London, asking for two more independent companies to be sent to man the new posts. This did not occur. Nor were funds immediately dispatched, as the British Ordinance Department pointed to the colony's delinquent accounts from previous fortification work. The New York Assembly, which would not meet again until spring, was not anxious to supply the funds either, although a 2 percent duty on imported European goods was agreed upon, but only if it was approved by London.

The following year the Board of Trade delivered a long report on the state of the British plantations. In this they supported Burnet's plans and looked for financial assistance to see this venture through. Fortifications, trade bans, new posts, and diplomatic endeavors aside, the board pointed to a simple change that was likely to yield far more lasting effects.

> There is however one other method left for gaining the good will of these Indians, which providence has put into our hands, and wherein the french could not possibly rival us, if we made a right use of our advantage, & that is, the furnishing of them, at honest & reasonable prices, with the several European commodities, they may have occasion for, but even this particular, from the unreasonable avarice of our Indian traders, & the want of proper regulations, has turned to our detriment, and instead of gaining us friends, has very probably created as many enemies.[8]

Lack of funds handicapped Burnet's efforts in 1721, leading one colonist to write a friend that "The French at Canada are still busy with our Five Nations, and take much more pains to gain them than we do to keep them." However, after meeting with the Five Nations representatives at Albany in early September, the governor was able to report some progress. The Iroquois had agreed to avoid trading and corresponding with the French. In addition, they would open trade connections to the French high-country nations and would speak with the French about pulling down their trading house at Niagara. With the reaffirming of the Covenant Chain, between the confederacy and the British, Burnet was able to fund a small trading post among the Five Nations at Irondequoit Bay, where ten British traders would spend the winter. From here he hoped to entice a portion of the fur trade away from the French.

While Burnet would claim that his ban on selling Indian goods to the French and the efforts of the trading post at Irondequoit Bay had diverted a sizable portion of the fur trade away from the French, little was done to challenge the French position at Niagara. The Seneca did not demand that the post be torn down, in part because they saw no real action on the part of Governor Burnet to challenge the post, and thus, at the moment there was no reason to do anything that might provoke a problem.[9]

Gatherings of British traders at Oswego over the next few years, and rumors that a permanent trading post was to be established at this location, forced Vaudreuil into action. If the British established themselves at Oswego, Vaudreuil wrote the French court on May 25, 1725, there was little choice but to fortify Niagara to protect the western trade lines. To facilitate this action the governor ordered two barks to be built at Fort Frontenac. These would be used to carry the materials needed for the construction of the stronghold at Niagara. Once the work was completed, these craft would act as supply vessels and would cruise the eastern end of the lake to intercept French trading parties headed for Oswego. The next step was to obtain permission from the Iroquois to build a stone trading house, which the Vaudreuil informed Paris, "will not have the appearance of a fort, so no offense will be given to the Iroquois, who have been unwilling to allow any there, but it will answer the purpose of a fort just as well."[10]

The matter of expanding the French position around Niagara had been a theme of Joncaire's conversations with the Seneca for the last several years. The tribe had agreed to a small palisade fort at Niagara capable of holding three hundred men in the past, and when Joncaire spoke with the sachems in June 1725 regarding Vaudreuil's plans, the primary condition was once again that the fort not be built of stone. By the time this news arrived, Vaudreuil had already dispatched the governor of Montreal, Charles Le Moyne de Longueuil, to the Onondaga to meet with a council of representatives from the Five Nations. In this delicate matter Longueuil was inadvertently aided by a large number of British traders at Oswego, who halted his delegation and demanded a pass from the governor of New York. Longueuil objected to the Iroquois envoys who were traveling with him, accusing them of no longer being masters of their own land. The words had the intended effect. "You have been permitted to come here to trade," the Iroquois informed the British, "but we will not suffer anything more."[11]

As Vaudreuil and Intendant Michel Begon reported, "He repaired next to Onontagué, an Iroquois village, and found the Deputies from the other four villages there waiting for him; he got them to consent to the construction of two barks, and to the erection of a stone house at Niagara, the plan of which he designed." There is a good deal to suspect in this statement. The council did give him permission to replace the old wood building at the portage with a new one that might "be safe from rain" and act as a depot for the two vessels being built. There are, however, no direct mentions of it being built of stone, although a letter to the minister of the marine in October speaks to the agreement being "a house of solid masonry, where all things needed for trade with the Indians could be safely kept."[12]

With the two barks still under construction and fall approaching, it was agreed to dispatch colonial engineer Gaspard-Joseph Chaussegros de Lery to survey the location in anticipation of construction beginning next spring. Born in Toulon in 1682, Lery had studied under his father who was a military engineer. He had fought throughout the War of Spanish Succession, being wounded at the siege of Turin in 1706, and participated in an abortive mission to land a Jacobite force in Scotland a few years later. Now an infantry captain, Lery transferred to the Department of the Marine after the conflict. With the lessons of Queen Anne's War now digested, concerns about Quebec, which was only spared due to the wreck of Admiral Hovenden Walker's fleet in 1711, came before the ministry. To better understand the problem in 1716 Lery was dispatched to Quebec to make plans of the current fortifications and recommend improvements. What was to be a simple survey would lead to an appointment as chief engineer and a say in most of the important posts in Canada for the next forty years including the defenses of Quebec and Fort St. Frederic at Crown Point.

On June 6, 1726, Lery, a detachment of workmen, and one hundred troops arrived at Niagara in the two barks. The original plan had called for the stone house to be placed on an elevation at the north end of the portage, near the old Royal Magazine. Lery, however, selected Denonville's old location at the mouth of the Niagara River. The engineer had several good reasons for the change. First, control of the river was paramount. A post at the portage was only viable if it was secured by a post at the mouth of the Niagara River. If the English were to seize this latter position, they would cut the supply lines to the portage fort and, from there, could simply starve the garrison into submission. Second, a post at the mouth of the river would cut English efforts to trade along the north bank of the lake. Given that almost all of this trade was conducted by canoes that wisely did not brave the lake crossing but skirted the shores, a post at this location would be in a position to disrupt this traffic. There was also the matter of the supply vessels, which would have to struggle against the strong currents of the river to reach the portage, versus the easy anchorage at the mouth of the river. The engineer would not ignore the portage. He would build a small wooden structure here which would suffice in times of peace but, as he noted, would prove untenable if war broke out with the Iroquois.

By early September the new commandant of the fort, Charles Le Moyne, wrote that the stone house was nearing completion and the site was securely enclosed within a wooden stockade. Lery designed the "French Castle," as the stone trading house would later become known, to be as fireproof as possible, as he considered this the greatest danger for the forts of Canada. Instead of wood framing, the engineer built stone loadbearing walls inside the two-story structure and paved the floors with stone. The windows in the 125-by-60-foot structure had shutters on the top floor that housed a string of cannons, and those on the ground floor were protected by iron bars. Lery had also taken the time to trace out a series of bastions and curtain walls that in the future could be used to fortify the entire site. While he had hoped to finish work on the trading house by years' end, illness had struck his work force, preventing the castle's completion. Even so, three-quarters of the work was done, and the stronghold was capable of lodging the garrison and any traders for the winter.[13]

While Lery lamented over not being able to finish the new post, Governor Burnet met with the Iroquois in Albany. The governor asked about the French fort at Niagara and if the Iroquois had allowed this. The Onondaga admitted that they had given the French permission to build the structure, even though it was on Seneca land. When Burnet asked how that could be, the Onondaga representative shrugged and responded, "One Nation often makes a Proposition and gives their consent to a thing in the name of all the rest, which, if they afterwards consent and approve of, it is well, but if they disallowed it, it was void."

After quickly querying the representatives present it appeared that the idea was now void. While Burnet had won this small victory, it did not translate into anything. Although the Iroquois had agreed that the French post was not desired, other than a few diplomatic protests, they were not interested in doing anything about it. This attitude was adopted in part because it was clear that many Seneca did not object to the structure and because the Iroquois, which were now the Six Nations with the inclusion of the Tuscarora in the confederacy, were not interested in starting a conflict that would bring New France's allies upon them. Regardless of Burnet's words, they understood that the British would not be in a position to intervene in this conflict. In this Burnet could not argue. While he had the delegations' agreement concerning the French encroachment on their lands, any intervention on his part would likely start a war, which London had made clear it was not interested in pursuing. Thus, the best Burnet could do was assemble the pertinent documents and send a formal protest to London.[14]

The "French Castle" at Niagara. The stone building on the left did not exist at the time, and the trading house would have been enclosed within a wooden stockade. Note the open shutters on the third floor. These are actually gunports for the fort's cannons. (*Library of Congress*)

The governor had more success when it came to his plan to erect a trading post on Lake Ontario. He found the Iroquois ambassadors in favor of the idea and negotiated an arrangement with them to build a trading post at Oswego. Located across the lake from Fort Frontenac, the governor was sure that it would divert yet more of the French fur trade. The following spring a work party was sent to the location to erect a stone house. Several hundred traders who typically spent the summer at the location followed, as did a company of soldiers. The governor had heard reports that a large French party was headed to Niagara, and fearing that they might interfere, he had raised a company of militia to protect the expedition.

In July 1727 a letter was delivered to the commandant of Oswego from Governor Beauharnois demanding that the post be demolished and abandoned in fifteen days. As might be expected it was ignored. This was followed a few days later by a letter addressed to Governor Burnet where Beauharnois called the new post a violation of the Treaty of Utrecht, as the commission assembled to demarcate the boundaries of New France and the English colonies had yet to issue a ruling. Burnet shook his head when he read the letter and replied that he had only established Oswego because of the French violation of the treaty with their construction of a fort at Niagara, which was clearly on Iroquois land.

Beauharnois's initial response to the establishment of Oswego was to call out the militia and march on the post. The merchants of New France favored this approach, but the governor soon reconsidered and halted any thought of military action. Such an act would certainly rupture the peace with the English and the Iroquois, contrary to his standing orders. With his hands tied the best Beauharnois could do was issue diplomatic protests to Burnet's actions, while the latter continued to pen his own regarding the French post at Niagara.[15]

While the complaints crossed the Atlantic, work on Niagara and Oswego continued. The long letters filled with objections and references to the Treaty of Utrecht accomplished nothing, as both forts were completed without interference. For Niagara, the late 1720s and 1730s proved a trying time. Although the fort served its purpose in guarding the portage from the western Great Lakes, the anticipated trade at the new post never materialized. Part of the problem was the ordinances passed preventing the sale of brandy, which only encouraged native and French traders to visit Oswego, where rum was sold in plentiful quantities. Supply problems led to several mutinies by the garrison and further complicated trade by forcing those who wished to sell their furs to press to Oswego or Fort Frontenac. While there was little that could be done to prevent native traders from visiting Oswego, French traders were another matter. Small boats were dispatched from Niagara and Fort Frontenac to patrol the lake and seize any Frenchmen looking to trade at the British post. A few traders were caught, but it was not enough to dissuade many from seeking the quick profits to be found at the British post.

The only real answer to this problem was to stock Niagara with the goods required to draw the native and French traders away from Oswego. This approach was first proposed only a few years after the establishment of the French post and, although agreed upon, was never truly addressed. For instance, on several occasions the trade goods from France arrived too late in the year to forward them to the western posts. This in turn created artificial shortages and lured more traders to Oswego, which was always well supplied. In 1736 Beauharnois informed the minister of the marine that "as for the commerce now carried on at Fort Frontenac and Niagara, it becomes every year more inconsiderable in comparison to the expenses the King incurs there. These two posts which produced some years ago, as much as £52,000 of peltries have these four years past returned only £25 to £35,000." While the lack of trade goods explained a portion of this, the governor and many others ascribed it to another reason. "This falling off has occurred merely since the discontinuance of the distribution of Brandy to the Indians, whereof it is the King's pleasure that Messrs. Beauharnais and Hocquart be very sparing." In fact, sparingly had turned into none at all as storekeepers at the French posts

Charles Beauharnois de La Boische, Marquis de Beauharnois, Governor of New France. An experienced naval officer and able administrator Beauharnois served as Governor for over twenty years, spending much of his time countering English threats to the colony's system of native alliances, guiding the colony through a period of westward expansion, and negotiating the crisis posed by King George's War. (*National Archives of Canada*)

had been told by local priests that they would be refused communion if they were caught selling liquor to the natives. It proved a particularly frustrating issue for Beauharnois. While he agreed with the policy, it was clearly damaging trade and undermining the French position in the west, and to make things worse, the English at Oswego placed no such restrictions on their rum. Matters would not improve for the French post over the next few years, although all agreed that Oswego had now become a major threat.

On August 24, 1727, Governor Burnet reported that he had finished "a stone house of strength at a place called Oswego." At the moment the garrison and the structure appeared secure, the latter having four-foot-thick walls made of "large good stones." The governor was convinced that it would require siege cannon to take the stronghold, so long as the garrison remained diligent. This was perhaps for the best, as rumors had reached Oswego in July that four hundred French and eight hundred Indians were preparing to descend upon the British post. Burnet dismissed the intelligence, but just in case, he forwarded supplies for six months and doubled the garrison. Nothing materialized, and by fall, he was writing the secretary of state, the Duke of Newcastle, that "The Assembly seem very hearty to support it, as the best thing that ever was done to secure the Indians in our interest, and to check the encroachments of the French."[16]

The next several years were spent looking for ways to fund the crucial outpost. At the start of the New York Assembly's 1730 session Governor John Montgomerie scolded the legislature for not providing an effectual means to support the trading post and garrison at Oswego. "Every man who knows the Interest & circumstances of this province must be very sensible of the importances of that place on which chiefly depends the prosperity & success of your Indian Trade, the fidelity and obedience of the Six Nations to the Crown of Great Britain and a protection and Defence of your frontier settlements." The assembly wished to finance this task through a tax on the Indian trade but finally relented when Montgomerie informed them that taxing Indian goods would only raise prices and drive the Natives back into the hands of the French. The governor suggested a land tax to distribute the costs throughout the colony, but the assembly rejected this advice and instead implemented a tax of three shillings on anyone who wore a wig. Thus, the most important post on the New York frontier was to be financed by the whims of fashion. The matter of supporting Oswego would prove problematic for years, and although it was less than ideal, it was finally agreed to accomplish this via a tax on the Indian trade. Of more concern to the inhabitants of the growing post were rumors in 1737 that the French were planning to establish a trading house along the southern shore of Lake Ontario at Irondequoit Bay, a mere fifty miles from Oswego. While these fears would not come to fruition, there was a sense that a clash between the two rivals on Lake Ontario was not far away.[17]

Part Two

The Thirty-Year Peace in the South

CHAPTER NINE

The Yamassee War

THE SOUTHERN COLONIES, primarily South Carolina and its principal city of Charleston, had been one of the few victors in Queen Anne's War, although the means of this accomplishment were questionable on multiple levels. Alliances with the Creek and Yamassee had not only fueled a robust Indian slave trade but also expanded the British realm through a series of ventures. The Spanish Missions in Georgia and Florida, ill prepared to defend themselves and with little in the way of Spanish resources available to respond to such onslaughts, collapsed under the weight of muskets and tomahawks. By knitting together a series of alliances with the Chickasaw, Alabama, and Creek, among others, the South Carolina government had even managed to press on French Louisiana and the network of Native alliances the fledgling colony had erected to protect itself.

While successful in expanding the influence of the colony, and commercially successful in its main aim of expanding the Indian slave trade, the war had left many unsettled problems. One of these issues concerned South Carolina's allies. The Yamassee and a number of Creek tribes had secured power and status by siding with the English. Yet with their success and the expansion of the colony's influence, the South Carolina traders had now become more interested in the Chickasaw and Cherokee, powerful nations that could better further their trade and territorial ambitions. Such a practice of discarding old allies for more powerful ones was a well-established pattern in the colony. The Westro, early allies of South Carolina, had been replaced by the more powerful Savannah, who in turn had been supplanted by the Creek.

The approach had worked in countering Spanish and French expansion, but it came with a significant risk as Thomas Nairne, one of the first Indian commissioners for the colony, pointed out when efforts were made to win over the French-allied Choctaw in 1708. "Wee believe Tho a friendship should be Contracted with the said Indians it will not be Lasting unless it Can be done with the consent of the Creek." The possibility of losing its economic and political status would certainly raise the ire of the Creek, but when coupled with abuses in the Indian trade, it created a volatile situation. Exorbitant prices for trade goods, the continuation of the Indian slave trade, forced labor practices, and questionable land sales by the traders had concerned the South Carolina Board of Indian Commissioners. Efforts were made to halt these practices, and those complaints that reached the commissioners were addressed, but the majority of the infractions were never reported.[1]

One of the most insidious practices was the accumulation of Indian debt. The traders sold rum, gunpowder, and metal goods on credit, charging ridiculous interest. Huge debts were amassed that surpassed an entire year of the Carolina fur and skin trade. When the individual defaulted, the traders turned to collecting from the tribe. The Board of Indian Commissioners responded with several steps to address this issue. First, rum debt was outlawed, and the board finally arrived on a ruling that banned selling on credit unless it was formally acknowledged by the debtor's kin or the chieftain of the tribe. Even so, with the offending traders at such a distance it did little to halt the practice, and a number of traders lived like kings throughout the Creek and other Native nations.

The combination of these issues led to a plan of rebellion that involved the Creek, Yamassee, Choctaw, Catawba, Cherokee, and a number of smaller nations. Only the Chickasaw rebuffed the offer, perhaps sensing the outcome and the position it would award them for staying neutral. English accounts point to French and Spanish intrigue behind this plan, but while it seems likely that both English rivals would benefit from such an action, and if asked would express their approval, there is no evidence of either's direct involvement.[2]

The conflict would start among the Yamassee, which consisted of ten principal villages, five among the islands of Port Royal Sound in South Carolina (Pocotaligo, Pocosabo, Huspah, Tomatley, and Tulafina) and five southern ones on the Altamaha River in Georgia. On April 12, 1715, a pair

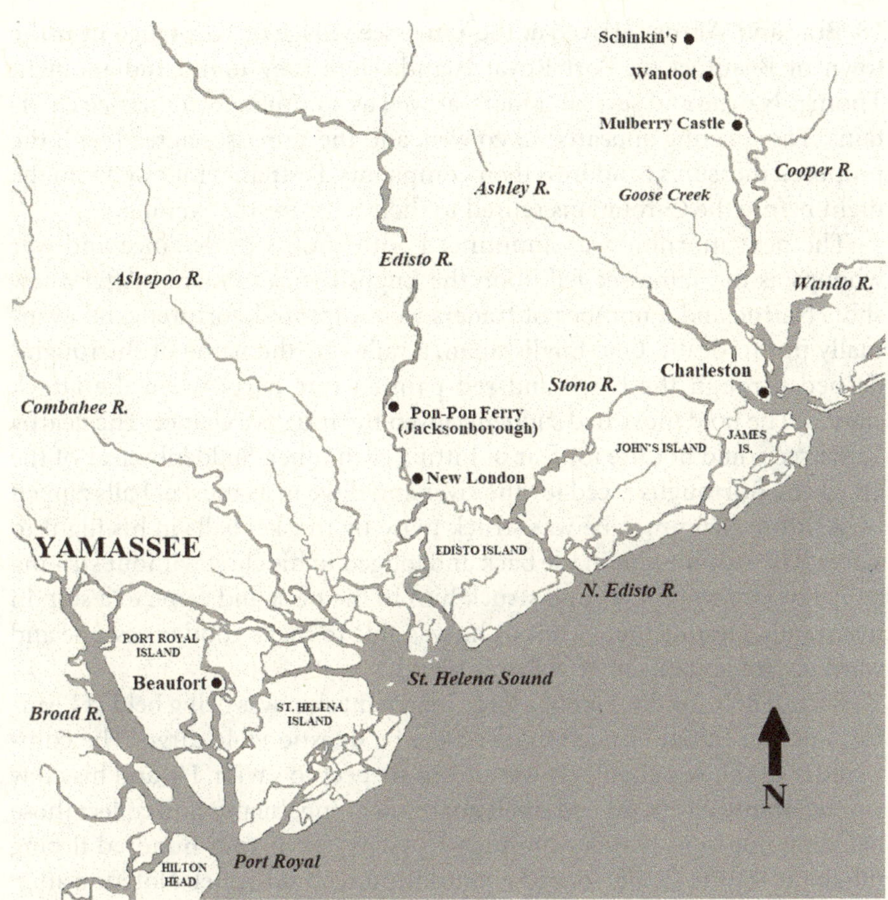

The colony of South Carolina, c.1715. Beyond Charleston and the immediate area, the primary colonial settlements and plantations (not shown) ran up along both banks of the Ashley and Cooper Rivers for much of their lengths, and to a lesser extent along the Stono and Edisto Rivers.

of traders named William Bray and Samuel Warner arrived in Charleston requesting an immediate audience with Governor Charles Craven. Bray reported that he and his wife had spoken to a sympathetic Yamassee who warned them that "the Creek Indians had a design to Cut off the Traders first and then fall on the settlements and that it was very near." Warner confirmed the news through another source, which informed him that the Yamassee would strike "at the first affront from any of the Traders."[3]

Craven sent Bray and Warner back to the Yamassee with news that he would immediately dispatch an agent to address their grievances. On April

18, Bray and Warner arrived at the Yamassee village of Pocotaligo near the town of Beaufort on Port Royal Island. Here they found Indian agent Thomas Nairne and several traders, as well as a number of Yamassee chieftains. The meeting appeared to go well, and the Yamassee agreed with the proposed measures to address their complaints. Festivities followed into the night before the Carolinians retired to their tents for the evening.

The next morning was announced with shouts of defiance and war whoops as the Yamassee fell upon the English encampments. After a few shots Nairne and a number of traders were captured, tortured, and eventually put to death. One Englishman, a sailor by the name of Burroughs, dashed through the black-and-red-painted war party when the attack started. The bold move had suddenly given Burroughs a chance. The nearby Yamassee could not fire for fear of hitting each other. Suddenly clear of the attackers, Burroughs raced for the river and dove in as musket balls zipped by. A strong swimmer, he was struck twice by musket balls in his flight to safety. The first hit him in the back and lodged in his chest without striking a vital organ, and the second struck him in the neck and came to a stop in his mouth. Despite these wounds he was able to make good his escape and warn the inhabitants of Port Royal Island.[4]

Fortunately for the colony, a large merchant ship was being held at Beaufort after an initial inspection discovered a questionable cargo. The commander of the vessel quickly went from suspect to savior. He and his crew worked frantically to unload small boats full of inhabitants and collect those deciding not to wait and swimming to safety. Some four hundred fleeing inhabitants were finally loaded aboard the anchored vessel. Not long after, a large Yamassee war party, finding the plantations and town apparently deserted, appeared along the shore. From here they fired on the crowded merchantman, but after a few volleys of grapeshot from the ship's cannons and swivel guns, they gave up any idea of attempting to board and instead sniped at the vessel throughout the night. The next morning the war party took to slaughtering the livestock and burning any buildings they came upon. The handful of inhabitants that had chosen to hide rather than seek refuge on the ship soon paid for their mistake. Many perished in the flames, others were dispatched in a chorus of war whoops and falling hatchets, and the truly unlucky met their demise in a more gruesome fashion. As columns of smoke rose over the settlements on Port Royal and St. Helena Island a second Yamassee war party struck St. Bartholomew's Parish to the northeast. Here they achieved far more surprise, burning a dozen plantations, capturing or killing close to one hundred settlers, and sending the rest streaming down the country roads toward the safety of Charleston.[5]

When word of the attack reached Craven, he reacted quickly. Looking to strike at the Yamassee before any other Native nation could join the conflict, he gathered together several mounted militia companies, some 240 men in all. He also dispatched a messenger to Colonel Alexander Mackay and Colonel John Barnwell, ordering them to raise as many men as possible and sail to the relief of Port Royal. From there they would advance up the Broad River to attack the Yamassee village where Nairne and his companions were slain. Craven would support this effort by advancing on the village by land.

A few days later Craven's detachment was near the Combahee River, sixteen miles from their objective. Here they encamped in a long field flanked by bands of forest a gunshot away. That evening scouts warned Craven that the Yamassee were in the woods on either side. The governor shifted his troops to meet the dual threat and at dawn was greeted by a barrage of several hundred muskets. A number of the Carolinians broke under the onslaught but were quickly rallied by Craven and his officers. The two sides fired on each other for forty-five minutes until Craven and his men charged the tree line with a huzzah. Having seen enough, the Yamassee broke off the engagement and disappeared into the countryside.

Craven had lost eleven killed and a score wounded in the bitter engagement, but the Yamassee were hit hard as well. Several of the dead included leading chieftains. One known as "Smith" was found with a letter in his pocket addressed to the governor "in which he advised him to quit the country, because they had determined to seize it, adding that all the Indians of the Continent had joined or would join them." Given the nature of the terrain before them and the real threat of a larger Yamassee-Creek force assembling to strike at Charleston, Craven called off the expedition and returned to the colonial capital.

Mackay and Barnwell had more success. With the Yamassee having left Beaufort and the surrounding plantations, Mackay continued on and landed his forces a few miles from the Yamassee village of Pocotaligo. After a short march he surprised the village. There were a handful of shots, but the rout was complete as the Yamassee fled, leaving Mackay and Barnwell in control of the town, and among other things, the English plunder taken from the nearby plantations and homesteads. News soon reached Mackay of a nearby Yamassee fort. Leading 140 men, he attacked the wooden palisade. The Yamassee put up a stiff resistance until a colonial scouting detachment of sixteen men appeared. Mackay used the sudden influx of manpower to rush the fort. Soon the Carolinians were over the wall, and the struggle became hand-to-hand along the parapets and in the parade ground. The moment would not last long, as a counterattack by the Yamassee pushed Mackay and his men off the wall and back to their original lines. Walking down the firing line, the colonel called on his men, reminding them of why they were here. With his men rallied, Mackay ordered a charge. Once again, the Carolinians surged over the wall, fighting hand-to-hand with hatchets, knives, and musket butts to force the Yamassee off the ramparts. Their numbers dwindling, the defenders decided on retreat and went over the opposite wall under a hail of musketry.[6]

Attacks came to the north as well. A Catawba and Cheraw war party pushed on Goose Creek, burning plantations and settlements as they moved toward Charleston. Captain Thomas Barker threw together ninety militia and rode forward to engage the war party. The sight of the mounted corps riding past brought some measure of hope to the refugees now traveling the various roads to Charleston, but it would not end well for Barker. The Native guide he had selected led the party into an ambush. Scores of muskets flared from the woods, killing Barker and a number of the advanced guard. Another volley followed, forcing the main column to dismount, but with their commander dead and their casualties quickly mounting to well over two dozen, the retreat was sounded.

This defeat was followed by an even greater one. Near the headwaters of the Cooper River lay three plantations: Schinkin's, Wantoot, and Mulberry Castle. This latter location was a large brick and wood two-story garrison house built with four flankers and armed with a few small cannons. Located at the very edge of the colony, Schinkin's and Wantoot were no more than palisade works. Even so, with a resolute garrison they would not be easily taken. The approaching four-hundred-man Catawba and Cheraw war party, which also included some seventy Cherokee, was more than capable of taking these last two forts by storm, but as it would prove a costly venture, the war party turned to deception to accomplish the task. At Schinkin's on the Santee River, the uniformed garrison allowed a number of local Cheraw and Catawba into the fort during a celebration, much as had been done in the past. This time, however, the visitors produced hatchets and knives and opened the gates. Almost every member of the garrison, some twenty-two in all, were quickly overwhelmed and dispatched with only four being taken prisoner. One young Black slave, however, had escaped over the wall and sounded the alarm at Wantoot.

The war party set about plundering the fort and celebrating their success deep into the night. When morning came, they were completely unaware that a relief column of 120 men from Goose Creek under Captain George Chicken was only a few miles away. Chicken divided his party into three sections so as to cut the war party's escape routes, but a pair of Catawba laying in ambush forced him to start the attack early. Caught completely off guard, the war party crumbled before the sudden onslaught. A few dozen were killed or wounded as they abandoned the fort and took flight. Chicken was able to recover four of the garrison and took a pair of prisoners. The freed prisoners informed him that the Cherokee had left the night before when news arrived that a peace delegation was being sent to their nation by Governor Craven.[7]

To the south Mackay would burn the captured Yamassee fort and village before returning. Together with Craven's expedition and Chicken's well-timed counterattack to the north, the quick actions had blunted the assaults on the colony. More importantly, the colonial response made some of the larger supporters of the Creek and Yamassee reconsider their position. The offending traders in the Choctaw, Cherokee, and Creek villages had been quickly dispatched. A few managed to escape, some seeking refuge among the Chickasaw, but the bulk had been dealt with, which solved the Indian debt problem, temporarily at least. While it was true that the estimated combined native force of eight thousand greatly outnumbered the South Carolina colonists, this would not remain the case, as the other English colonies would send troops and supplies to aid them. As such, the Choctaw, Cherokee, and many of the Creek adopted a wait-and-see attitude.

For Craven and the citizens of the colony, many of whom now found themselves in Charleston, the opening attacks had been devastating. Beyond the loss of the Indian traders and some forty men in a number of engagements, the loss of life among the populace was at least several hundred, and vast parts of the colony were now abandoned. "The Town (Charleston)," one citizen informed the Board of Trade, "may perhaps hold out some months, but in what a miserable condition must the poor people be, drove from their plantations, imprison'd between mud walls, stifled with excessive heats, oppress'd with famine, sickness, the desolation of their country, death of their friends, apprehension of their own fate, despairing of relief, and destitute of any hopes to escape." Another was more succinct in appraising the effect on the colony, claiming that "The Southern parts, which include a fifth of the Province are entirely depopulated." Appeals for aid not only went out to the Board of Trade but also to Virginia, North Carolina, and the lord proprietors of the colony. For the latter, the magnitude of the attack and the numbers of Native nations involved left them incapable of bearing the cost to send the requisite number of men and arms to defend the colony. Instead, they appealed to the king for aid in order to prevent the "utter destruction of his faithful subjects in those parts."[8]

The first to respond was Virginia. Upon being informed of the events Governor Alexander Spotswood dispatched a ship with powder and arms. This was followed on July 18 by the landing of the last elements of a 120-man Virginia detachment under Captain Arthur Middleton. Five hundred muskets were also coming from Rhode Island, and North Carolina had raised a detachment of 120 militia and allied Indians under the command of Colonel Maurice Moore. They were marching south toward Cape Fear where they would rendezvous with another detachment before pushing farther south.

The influx of guns and manpower were enough for Craven to form an expedition against the Catawba and Cheraw who had raided the northern plantations. The governor assembled a hundred militia, forty Black slaves, and a detachment of allied Indian scouts, about two hundred men in all. On July 18 the mounted detachment departed the Ponds (Summerville) bound for the Santee River. The ultimate aim was to link up with Moore's North Carolina troops and then, as a combined force, strike a blow against the "Northern Indians." Craven had just finished crossing the Santee River when a rider informed him that an Apalachee and Yamassee war party, reputed to be from five hundred to seven hundred strong, had crossed the Edisto River and attacked the settlement of New London or what is now Willstown Bluff, South Carolina. The nearby citizens were able to reach the palisade fort held by a garrison of fifty men. The war party tested the will of the defenders, and when they saw their response, they shifted to easier and more lucrative targets. After burning a few homes about New London, they moved down the Stono River, burning twenty plantations and numerous smaller homesteads to within a dozen miles of Charleston. Here they attempted to cross over the Stono River but found the crossing guarded. Craven retraced his steps upon hearing the news, but the war party easily outdistanced him, burning the barge they had used to cross the Edisto after them.

Believing themselves safe on the other side of the Edisto River would be a mistake. A detachment under Colonel Robert Fenwick arrived at the Pon-Pon Ferry a day later and, after repairing the damaged vessel, advanced toward the Combahee River. As he approached the river scouts returned with news that the Yamassee were at Jackson's plantation near the ferry. Fenwick used the information to creep into position around the plantation that evening. At daybreak the detachment completely surprised the sixteen Yamassee at the homestead, and after a few minutes of defiant shouts and bursts of gunfire, it was over. Nine of the Yamassee had fallen, and two more were in Fenwick's hands. The rest had fled. Fenwick had also seized four periaugers—flat-bottomed vessels that could be sailed or rowed. Suspecting more Yamassee vessels on the river he dispatched a captain by the name of Palmer in one of the captured craft with orders to lay in wait at the mouth of the river.

The next day Palmer discovered three vessels. After advancing on them and firing a few long-range shots, the Yamassee onboard thought better of the matter and abandoned their craft, swimming ashore and disappearing into the tree line. With his newly captured vessels Palmer proceeded to Port Royal, where he joined two other English captains. It was agreed among the trio to set up an ambush at Daufuskie Island, near the outlet of the Savannah River. A party was landed on shore while the vessels sat nearby. The hope was to force the enemy craft ashore where the colonial detachment lay in wait. A few days later the trap proceeded exactly to plan as eight Yamassee periaugers came into sight. The crews of two of these vessels abandoned their craft and escaped, but the other six were forced ashore and decimated by the waiting colonial muskets. The prisoners taken had useful information. They spoke of the Yamassee villages on the Sapelo River, which spurred an expedition under the command of Lt. Governor Robert Daniell. The Yamassee, however, heard news of this effort, and when Daniell arrived at the settlements, he found them deserted, their inhabitants having departed for Spanish Florida.[9]

By fall the fighting had slowed to sporadic small-scale raids, but the war was hardly over. Craven spoke with Governor Robert Hunter of New York about enlisting the aid of the Iroquois. Hunter pushed the idea forward, holding several conferences with the sachems of the Five Nations and even offering to provide them with firearms and supplies should they undertake such an expedition. While this effort would not materialize into any tangible aid, it did serve two purposes: first, to raise the morale of the colony's beleaguered citizens, and second, to send a warning to the Native nations involved in the conflict.

In October 1715, overtures of peace to the Cherokee appeared to have succeeded when a large Cherokee delegation, over a hundred strong and led by eight senior chieftains, arrived at Charleston. Peace was made between the Cherokee and South Carolina, and the two parties agreed to punish the Creek with a pair of expeditions. It was the best news the inhabitants of the colony had heard in half a year. With the Chickasaw remaining neutral, the Yamassee retreating south, and the Cherokee now on the side of the colony, which was finally receiving the firearms and supplies it needed to raise 1,200 additional soldiers, it appeared the war would soon come to an end. Elated by news of the Cherokee treaty, some of the colonists began returning to their plantations and homes.[10]

For the Upper and Lower Creek, many of whom were never interested in the conflict, the news posed a major problem. They, like the Cherokee and Choctaw, had dispatched the Carolinian traders among them but had done little in the way of participating in the fighting beyond a few individuals who had volunteered their services to the Yamassee, Catawba, and Cheraw. News of the current arrangement between the Cherokee and the English threatened not only their villages but their position with the English. It had been the Creek who had swelled South Carolina's numbers during Queen Anne's War and laid waste to the colony's Spanish enemies. It had been the Yamassee and Creek who taken over the position of the Westro and Savannah as principle English allies and suppliers of product for the lucrative Indian slave trade. Fear that the colony wished to replace them with the more powerful Cherokee and Chickasaw was part of the reason behind the conflict. Now, as events had unfolded, the rebellion appeared to be accelerating this process.

Creek diplomats traveled to the Lower Cherokee villages upon hearing the news and sought peace. The Cherokee accepted the Creek declaration and did not appear at the planned rendezvous in November with the South Carolina troops. Looking to understand what had occurred Colonel Moore marched to the Cherokee village of Tugaloo with three hundred men to meet with a council of chieftains from the Lower villages. Here Moore found that the Cherokee were of two camps. The Lower villages were against war with the Creek and in general for peace amongst all parties involved. Their spokesman informed Moore that they had already accepted the Creek envoys' request for a truce and a parley with the English. As this seemed the best path to resolving the conflict, Moore agreed to wait two weeks for the Creek and Yamassee chieftains to be summoned for a conference.

The colonel then traveled to the Upper or Over Hill Cherokee villages on the Little Tennessee River, led by the Chieftain Caesar of Echota, who had negotiated the agreement with Governor Craven. Moore found Caesar in favor of carrying through with his promise and attacking their old enemies the Creek. Moore explained the verdict of the Lower villages and the sudden opportunity for peace via a conference between the Creek, Yamassee, Cherokee, and English. In doing so, he was able to convince a wary Caesar to wait on any attack.

It was several weeks before a sizable Creek and Yamassee delegation arrived at Tugaloo and met with their Cherokee and English counterparts. Finally, late on the afternoon of January 26, 1716, news came that the participants were all in place. The next morning Moore and those with him were alarmed by war whoops and scattered shots, and then stunned when they discovered that the Cherokee had attacked the Creek and Yamassee envoys, quickly dispatching all of them. Moore had no idea why until a Cherokee chieftain explained that the Creek and Yamassee believed they had convinced the Cherokee to massacre Moore and his men. Even now there were three hundred Creek in the nearby woods ready to fall upon his troops. Moore and his officers were shocked by the turn of events, but when the Cherokee suggested that they move quickly to ensnare the nearby Creek war party, the colonel called his men to arms and moved forward to close the trap. Creek scouts, however, had warned the detachment of what had transpired, and they hastily withdrew. The English and Cherokee followed for a week but finally called off the pursuit.

For the citizens of South Carolina, it appeared a "wonderful Deliverance." With the intervention of the Cherokee and a recently arrived Chickasaw delegation who confirmed their alliance with the colony, the war seemed to be reaching a conclusion. In late February 1716 Governor Craven expressed this sentiment to the South Carolina Assembly. "The clouds that then threatened ruine and destruction to this Colony are now blowne over and dissipated, our enemies for the most parte defeated and fled away, and the war itself in a manner extinguish'd."[11]

In fact, the colony would soon discover that there were still many flames left to be put out.

CHAPTER TEN

Proprietors and Pirates

With the end of large-scale encounters, the war shifted toward the pattern of the border wars of New England. "They have already begun to make incursions amongst us in small parties," the South Carolina Assembly informed London on August 6, 1716, "having by that means destroy'd several of our inhabitants very lately." Given that the Yamassee were now operating from the safe haven of Florida, the assembly suspected Spanish collusion. A report from a captured Englishman, who had been taken to one of these villages near St. Augustine, seemed to confirm these suspicions. It was reported that the former captive "has heard the Indians telling one another oftentimes that the Spanish perswaded them what they could, to kill the English, provided they did not let them see it done, and he has all along been an eyewitness to the Spanish furnishing ye Yamassees with whatever they wanted to carry on the war against us." The informant also pointed out that, when he was taken to a Creek village, he saw ammunition arriving from Mobile and Pensacola.

By the spring of 1717 there was some good news when the Creek sent envoys seeking a peace conference, but the sporadic attacks still continued on isolated homesteads and those looking to travel the byways of the colony. With the collapse of the colony's economy, and the inflation that followed, money was becoming nearly worthless. With the raiders still present, many had yet to return to their homes and were still in Charleston, which was running out of supplies to cope with this influx. It had become so bad that one colonist noted, "At Charles Towne we are ready to eat up one another for want of provisions."[1]

In June 1717 unsettling news arrived that the expected Creek peace delegation would not be coming. Rumors abounded that the Seneca, supplied by the French, would intervene on the Creek's side, which suddenly cast a doubt over any arrangement, not only with the Creek but with the Cherokee as well. Anxiety was further heightened when reports arrived that the Cherokee and Creek had concluded a peace, one that, through the urgings of the French and the Spanish, called for them to unite and drive the colonists into the sea. While such tales imparted great powers upon the French and Spanish, they were diffused when a Creek delegation arrived at Charleston in February 1718 to meet with newly arrived Governor Robert Johnson. While the deliberations proved slower than most would have liked, by June Johnson announced to the Board of Trade that he had made peace with the "great nation of the Creeks."[2]

During this long negotiation process the dire circumstances faced by the citizenry and the lack of aid from the lord proprietors had set off a political firestorm within the colony. Although the opening salvos of the war had been brief, they had been nothing short of devastating to South Carolina. Hundreds of plantations and homesteads had been destroyed, and perhaps three hundred to four hundred inhabitants had been killed or carried off with another fifty or so militia slain in the fighting. While these losses were significant, it was the economic devastation that threatened to accomplish what Yamassee and Creek war parties could not. The food crops were damaged, and the colony's livestock herds had been decimated. The funds and time required to reestablish this trade would take years, but there was yet another component to this recovery: manpower. The profit crops such as tobacco were labor intensive. The Indian slave trade, which was behind the conflict and made up a sizable portion of this manpower, was over. The importation of more African slaves was viewed as an answer, but they were far more expensive, and for a cash-strapped colony it would prove difficult to obtain the numbers required. When combined with the threat of famine and an enemy that was pursuing a war of a thousand cuts, it would lead to a slow return to pre-war levels.

The answer seemed obvious to the citizens of the colony and their representatives. In June 1716 the assembly sent a letter to their agents in London, "being now fully convinced that the Lord Proprietors are neither able or willing to afford that assistance to this providence as is absolutely necessary to preserve it from ruin and desolation." They asked that their petition, which outlined this case, be laid before the king and for his intervention in the matter. The letter led to a request by the Board of Trade for the lord proprietors to provide a report on the state of the colony and the measures they had taken regarding its defense. The lord proprietors pointed to the arms and ammunition shipments made to the colony, Craven's speech, the alliance with the Cherokee, and the renewed treaty with the Chickasaw, which was more than sufficient to bring the Creek to their senses and restore the peace.[3]

The matter was hardly settled with this response, and after another round of letters from the colony detailing their plight, in May 1717 the Board of Trade returned with more questions for the proprietors. The response was in the same vein as before; the crisis had passed, and the war was almost over. An appeal arrived in London in early May 1718 signed by the colony's assembly and 568 citizens. It pleaded with the king, convinced that ruin awaited the colony unless the king took "them into his immediate protection and care." Unconvinced by the answers provided by the lord proprietors of the colony, the Board of Trade agreed with the colony, informing the court that "the proper methods should be taken for resuming of this and all other Proprietary Governmts into the hands of H.M., since it is evident they cannot support or protect themselves, and that any misfortune happening to them must in consequence affect the rest of H.M. Dominions on the Continent of America."[4]

While the merits of such a move were being discussed in London, another threat emerged, this time from the sea. The king had offered a pardon for any pirate who would surrender, most of whom were privateers from Queen Anne's War who for one reason or another had simply continued their trade after the Treaty of Utrecht. Some had taken advantage of this clemency, sailing into colonial ports and receiving their official pardon from the governor, and many of these same pirates, bored by their limited economic opportunities, returned to their old trade. Others rejected the pardon because it meant that they would have to give up their ships and their spoils. With relations between Britain and Spain rapidly deteriorating, piracy, which had been a long-term problem for the governors of the American colonies, began to accelerate. "The King's gracious Proclamation has not produced the hoped for effects," Governor Shute of Massachusetts informed the Board of Trade in late June 1718, "for the pirates still continue to rove on these seas; and if a sufficient force is not sent to drive them off our Trade must stop." Governor Hunter of New York agreed, choosing to wait for a warship before returning to England because of pirate activity off the coast.

For Charleston, no stranger to pirates, June 1718 would prove to be one

A portion of a 1729 map of South Carolina. (*Norman B. Leventhal Map Collection, Boston Public Library*)

of the more memorable months. Governor Johnson had seen numerous occurrences of piracy since arriving at Charleston in October 1717. Several pirate vessels would lay off the Charleston Bar, "taking and plundering all ships that either go out or come into this port." Without a Royal Navy presence in the harbor there was little Johnson could do but arrange lookouts and a warning system. On June 4, four pirate vessels, a large 40-gun vessel, a 10-gun sloop, and two smaller sloops descended on the Charleston Bar. In sight of the town, they quickly chased down and captured nine vessels, "with several of the best inhabitants of this place on board."[5]

One of the captured vessels, flying a white flag, later anchored near Charleston. Three men came ashore and met with Johnson and his staff. One was a captured inhabitant, another was a sailing master of one of the sloops, and the spokesman was a Lt. Thomas Richards, commander of the 10-gun sloop *Revenge*. The demand was for a chest of medicines, otherwise the prisoners would be put to death. Johnson asked who he was dealing with and was informed that "This company was commanded by one Teach (Thatch) alias Blackbeard." With little choice, the governor sent a chest of medicines. Teach and his men celebrated and then complied with their part of the agreement but not before robbing all of their captives and sending them ashore "almost naked." Teach soon departed north, but with reports of a score of pirates in the area, Johnson pleaded with London to send a frigate to cruise the coast. Otherwise, the colony's trade, still recovering from the Yamassee conflict, would be utterly destroyed as "hardly a ship goes to sea but fails to fall into their hands."[6]

After a visit by veteran buccaneer Charles Vane in August, which resulted in the capture of over half-a-dozen vessels, Johnson and the merchants of Charleston had a pair of sloops in the harbor fitted out as warships. The first, the 8-gun *Henry*, carried seventy men and was commanded by Captain John Masters, while the 8-gun *Sea Nymph* carried sixty men and was commanded by Captain Fayrer Hall. The former vice admiral of Charleston, Colonel William Rhett, who had defended the town against a Spanish attack during Queen Anne's War, commanded the flotilla. By mid-September Rhett had put out to sea. Initially the two vessels steered south along the coast, searching for signs or news of Vane. With the trail cold, Rhett reversed course, and after sunset on September 26, he spied three vessels in the Cape Fear River. In the fading light the *Henry* and *Sea Nymph* entered the tricky waterway and, without a pilot, soon went aground. It would not be until later that evening that Rhett and his men freed their vessels and took up station at the mouth of the river.

As Rhett suspected the three vessels were indeed pirates, but they were not Vane's ships but those of Captain Stede Bonnet. Known as the Gentleman Pirate, Bonnet was an unlikely participant in such activities. He was a fairly wealthy, refined, and well-educated citizen of Barbados who had served the colony on several occasions, obtaining the rank of major before retiring to his estate on the island. While this alone would appear to be a disqualifying background, his complete lack of maritime knowledge would seem to have excluded his participation. Such, however, was not the case, and in early 1717 he outfitted and manned a 10-gun sloop named the *Revenge* and took to the open sea. Bonnet's crew quickly discovered their captain's ignorance of naval affairs, but while lacking in this area Bonnet knew how to handle men, and with frequent threats and personal courage, he suppressed any attempts at a mutiny. Morale improved after making a number of captures off the Capes of Virginia and several more a few weeks later in New York and New England waters. In August 1717 Bonnet turned south, making a pair of captures off the Charleston Bar before refitting his ship and setting sail for the Bay of Honduras, one of the great pirate haunts of the day.

Here the Gentleman Pirate met a real pirate, Edward Teach, better known as Blackbeard. The two men decided upon a cruise together, but like Bonnet's crew, Teach quickly realized that the *Revenge* required a new captain. With the backing of the two crews, Teach transferred Bonnet onto his ship, and after assigning him a trivial position, placed his trusted lieutenant, Thomas Richards, in command of the *Revenge*. Bonnet was outraged, but under the circumstances there was little he could do but comply.

Bonnet would serve with Teach on several successful cruises and was present when Blackbeard arrived before Charleston in June 1718 making demands on the town for a chest of medicines. After the completion of this successful venture, Teach had sailed north with his four ships looking for a location on the North Carolina coast to refit the flotilla and scrape the hulls of barnacles. Topsail Inlet (Beaufort, NC) was chosen, but with little knowledge of the inlet, Teach ran his flagship, the *Queen Anne's Revenge*, hard aground on a sandbank. Another sloop, the *Adventure*, also went aground. Both vessels were considered a loss and abandoned.[7]

The nature of the event has led to a number of claims that it was intentional on the part of Teach. Certainly, without charts and unfamiliar with the shifting sandbars near the inlet, the accident scenario is understandable. Vessels long after the Civil War armed with charts and navigation aids still fell prey to these obstacles, so it is not unreasonable to conclude that the event was nothing more than this and that the events that followed were *ad hoc* plans. Another explanation put forth claimed that Teach intentionally wrecked the vessels to gain a larger portion of the spoils by leaving Bonnet and many others behind. One of the most plausible explanations for the wrecks being intentional claimed that both Bonnet and Teach were seeking a pardon. The pair had spoken to the crews of the vessels they had captured and realized that, with relations between Spain and Britain on the verge of war, a royal pardon would soon put them back out to sea with a letter of marque. After all, why sail as a pirate when you can sail under the banner of the Crown and accomplish the same thing?

Bonnet and Teach would receive a pardon from Governor Charles Eden of North Carolina not long after the incident. Teach would live up to the terms of the agreement for two months, but Bonnet would not even wait that long. Now pardoned he announced that he was taking the *Revenge* to St. Thomas Island to apply for a letter of marque to operate against the Spanish, and by July he had put together a crew and set out to sea. A more seasoned captain now, Bonnet heard a rumor that Blackbeard had set out to sea again. The rumor did not prove to be true, and thus Bonnet wasted time looking to track down Teach. At this point Bonnet decided to return to his old ways. He changed his name to Captain Thomas and the *Revenge*'s name to the *Royal James* in a feeble attempt to disguise his identity and maintain his pardon.

The new Captain Bonnet was a much-improved pirate, although several of his crew objected to the change of plans when he announced his intentions to them. Moving up the coast he made several captures before entering Delaware Bay. Here he found a rich environment, robbing several vessels and seizing a pair of sloops: the *Francis* and the *Fortune*. After departing with the two sloops the *Royal James* developed a serious leak. The trio of vessels slipped into the Cape Fear River in late July to makes repairs and wait out the hurricane season.

On the evening of September 26 several of Bonnet's scouts reported a pair of sloops aground near the mouth of the river. The pirate captain dispatched three armed longboats to ascertain if they were merchantmen, and if they were, to board the unsuspecting vessels in the darkness. The three longboats crept forward, but after examining the stranded craft from a distance they returned with news that they were warships. Bonnet shrugged at the report and ordered his men to make the ship ready for battle. At first light they would attack.[8]

After the tide freed his vessels, Rhett maintained his position, as it was too dark to risk proceeding upriver. As with Bonnet's men, the evening was spent preparing for what appeared to be a morning battle. At daylight Rhett ordered his ships forward only to encounter the *Royal James*, now flying the Jolly Roger, proceeding downriver. Seeing that the pirate ship was looking to run past the sloops, Rhett ordered the vessels to either side of the *Royal James*, hoping to place it in a crossfire. Bonnet, with no knowledge of the waterway, shifted to starboard, looking to avoid the pincer movement, and as a result went aground near the west bank of the river. In maneuvering toward the *Royal James*, Rhett's flagship, the *Henry*, also went aground a musket shot from the pirate ship, and soon the *Sea Nymph* was stuck fast a few hundred yards away.

For Bonnet it was a stroke of luck. The *Henry* had come to a rest at an angle, which exposed the warship's deck, while the *Royal James* was situated on a more level keel, offering the crew better protection than the Carolinian vessel. It would not be until noon that the tide would offer a chance to refloat the ships. In the meantime, if he could destroy the *Henry*, he could then turn on the *Sea Nymph* once he was free. The cannon on the *Royal James* flared to life, followed by dozens of muskets that peppered the English warship's decks. Although exposed, Rhett's men stood their stations and returned fire, their cannon strikes creating bursts of debris along the length of Bonnet's hull.

At first Bonnet and his men believed they would make short work of the tilted *Henry*, but as the morning wore on it became clear that the Carolinians, who had already suffered over a score of casualties, were not going to yield. As the tide began to creep in, the pirates became more desperate with their fire until the waters lifted the smaller *Henry* and the nearby *Sea Nymph*. With the English vessels firing and preparing to move forward to board, Bonnet declared he would fight to the end, and if need be, he would ignite the ship's magazine to prevent capture. The crew, however, deciding their chances were better in front of a judge than surviving such an explosion, seized Bonnet before replacing their current banner with a white flag.

It had been a hard battle for Rhett's men. Twelve had been killed and ten wounded aboard the *Henry*, with another two killed and six wounded on the *Sea Nymph*, which had only been closely engaged toward the end of the battle. Rhett would spend the next several days repairing the *Royal James* and the *Henry* before returning to Charleston with the three captured vessels, Bonnet, and thirty-nine of his crew.[9]

The church bells rang throughout Charleston as news of the vice admiral's success spread through the war-weary town. A trial was ordered for Bonnet and his men, but before it could get underway another pirate threat appeared. A 50-gun ship reputed to be commanded by pirate scourge Thomas Moody had appeared off the bar seizing a pair of New England vessels looking to enter the harbor. Johnson shook his head at the news and called together his council. Although he had pleaded with London about a frigate to patrol the coastal waters, it had become clear that even if such help arrived it would be too late to prevent catastrophic economic damage. It was agreed that a flotilla of four vessels should be outfitted to protect the town's economic lifeline. After surveying the vessels in the harbor Johnson impressed the merchantmen *King William* and *Mediterranean*. He then added the *Sea Nymph* as well as the captured *Royal James* now under the command of Captain Masters. Work quickly commenced on outfitting this fleet. The larger *King William* and the *Mediterranean* were braced and outfitted with thirty and twenty-four cannons respectively while the sloop *Sea Nymph* was refitted with six guns, and the reworked *Royal James*, once again renamed the *Revenge*, was armed with eight.

Most expected Colonel Rhett to command the fleet, but he and Johnson did not often see eye to eye on matters, leading Johnson to take command. With provisions onboard and three hundred recruits manning the fleet, Johnson suddenly found himself stopped by a legal matter. The captains and many of the crew of the impressed vessels had freely volunteered their services to the expedition, but they did not own the vessels. The owners, who stood to lose their vessels, asked for relief from the government should the craft be damaged or lost. Johnson agreed, and the assembly quickly passed a bill indemnifying the owners against any loss.

With this matter attended to Johnson was surprised by a messenger who informed him that Bonnet and his sailing master David Herriot had escaped. Both had been held at the sheriff's home, and, not closely guarded, they had rode off in a carriage dressed as women. The alarm was sounded and a reward offered for their capture. As it turned out, the fugitives had headed for Sullivan's Island in hopes of rendezvousing with Moody's vessels rumored to be offshore, but after a week of seeing nothing, the pair were hungry and exhausted. On November 4, with his fleet ready to sail, Johnson received intelligence that Bonnet and Herriot were on Sullivan's Island. He asked Rhett to put together a detachment and capture the duo. Rhett arrived on the island the next day, and after forming a skirmish line, he encountered the pirates a few hours later. There was a flurry of shouts, a brief exchange of gunfire that killed Herriot, and a few moments later a cheer as the Gentleman Pirate was once again in custody.[10]

Johnson spent the evening of the fourth anchored near Fort Johnson. Reports had arrived of a pair of pirate vessels lying off the bar. The plan was to sail out the next morning with the appearance of merchantmen, and when the pirates approached to intercept them, unmask their guns, hopefully catching the enemy off guard. At dawn Johnson's flagship, the *Mediterranean*, raised sail and steered for the main channel through the breaking autumn mists. Behind him at regular intervals were the rest of his fleet, their guns covered and their crews anxiously waiting below deck. The governor steered toward the two vessels near the bar. Finally, around eight o'clock he saw the intruders weigh anchor and set sail for the mouth of the harbor, looking to cut the four merchantmen off from Charleston. With the trap set the two unidentified vessels closed on the fleet from behind and made their intentions clear by raising the Jolly Roger and calling on the *King William* to surrender.

Johnson responded by wheeling his flagship, raising the Union Jack, and unleashing a broadside upon the nearest pirate ship. The other three vessels did likewise as their crews rushed up onto their decks with a resounding cheer. Soon the volleys of cannon and musket fire engulfed all of the craft. While caught off guard the pirate sloop, under the command of another well-known pirate, Richard Worley, not Moody, returned a furious fire as the more numerous Carolinians moved to pin the two pirate vessels against the shore. Seeing the circumstance, the larger of the two pirate ships dashed for the sea. Johnson ordered the *Sea Nymph* and the *Revenge* to engage Worley's sloop while the *Mediterranean* and the *King William* chased down the larger craft.

Johnson's task proved the easier of the two, albeit longer. The *Eagle*, recently captured by Worley and his men, was not a fast sailor, and its head start was quickly disappearing. The crew threw items overboard to lighten the vessel, discarding the lifeboats and even the six cannons on deck. It would only buy them another hour, as around mid-afternoon, Johnson came within range and signaled the *King William* to fire. The broadside of chain and shot rippled across the *Eagle*'s deck, killing and wounding a number of the crew. Without guns, the vessel immediately surrendered. To the surprise of Johnson and his men, the hold of the *Eagle* held 106 convicts, thirty-six of whom were women. The vessel had left London bound for Virginia with the indentured servants onboard.

The *Sea Nymph* and the *Revenge* had a much tougher time. Worley and his crew in the 6-gun *New York's Revenge* refused to give in. For four hours the vessels exchanged broadsides and musketry within pistol shot of one another. Some of Worley's crew broke and took shelter below deck, but the rest, facing a hangman's noose, fought until the end. The *Revenge* and *Sea Nymph* finally closed to board, which set off a violent struggle on the decks of the pirate ship with pistol, cutlass, and pike. Worley and twenty-five of his forty-man crew were cut down in the battle and the concluding melee, while those in the hold surrendered once Captains Hall and Masters had cleared the deck of any resistance. While it was not Moody, Johnson and all involved were pleased with the results. Bonnet, most of his crew, and Worley's men were convicted shortly thereafter, hung, and buried at White Point.[11]

Johnson would hold onto the impressed vessels while he continued to press for Royal Navy support, but the next few months brought more pressing concerns than pirates. In April 1719 word of war with Spain arrived, and not long after reports followed of a frightening Spanish plan. Reinforced by troops from Mexico, the Spanish governors at St. Augustine and

Pensacola, Florida, would raise what native forces they could recruit and march on the South Carolina frontier. Were this not bad enough, a squadron of Spanish warships assembling at Havana would at the same time attack Charleston by sea.[12]

Once again, the alarm was raised among the weary colonists, although this time, given the state of the colony and the strength of the enemy, few held out any hope of success.

CHAPTER ELEVEN

Louisiana and Florida

For Spanish Florida Queen Anne's War had been a bitter defeat. At the end of the conflict only Castle San Marcos at St. Augustine and Fort San Carlos at Pensacola offered any semblance of safety. The extensive Spanish mission system in Florida and Georgia had been ravaged and destroyed by Anglo-Creek war parties who ranged as far south as St. Augustine. An outpost of New Spain, Florida lacked not only the resources to defend this network of missions but the trust to arm its denizens as well. It was a formula for disaster, and the scars at the end of the conflict spoke to the tale. Failure to supply the colony from Mexico led to a shortage of hard currency, inflation, and an uncertain food supply. Colonial credit often had to be employed to purchase provisions in Cuba as a stop-gap measure, which only compounded many of the existing problems.

In 1715 a number of Yamassee chieftains appeared at St. Augustine. With the Yamassee conflict raging in South Carolina these chieftains had expressed an interest in relocating their villages to Florida. Governor Juan de Ayala y Escovar was delighted to accommodate these requests, which he considered a major step toward improving the colony's shattered defenses and reestablishing its influence in the region. More villages would follow as the war shifted in the favor of the South Carolinians. By early 1717, Ayala was able to report that he had established over 160 Indian settlements near St. Augustine and in Apalachee and that trade delegations from the Creek had begun to arrive. The trend was so positive that the governor began considering reestablishing the Apalachee province and planned to send a detachment of soldiers to the province that summer to negotiate with the villages that had shifted their allegiance back to the Spanish. Although the governor's superiors were delighted with the news, and even expressed sentiments about recapturing the colony's lost territories, they were slow to finance the effort.[1]

Even so, by 1718 the fort at San Marcos de Apalachee had been reconstructed, and within a few years the Yamassee and Apalachee villages erected nearby had reestablished a Spanish presence in the area. Efforts were also made to exploit the English rupture with the Creek by sending delegations to these nations, but here the Spanish found little success, as the divided Creek either returned to their trade relations with the English or refused to be single sourced, preferring instead to trade with all the colonial powers in the region.

The attempt to expand Spanish influence was not well received by either the French at Mobile or by the English in South Carolina. In something of an ironic turn of events, the latter pointed to the Spanish harboring and supplying Yamassee war parties who were still raiding the colony's countryside. Rumors of an attack on St. Augustine followed and were serious enough that Ayala released funds to repair the weather-beaten Castle San Marcos and its outlying works.

When Governor Antonio de Benavides arrived to replace Ayala in late 1718, he was pleased with the new Native alliances but aghast at the logistical nightmare before him. Funds were slow in arriving from Mexico, and their new allies placed an additional monetary strain on a resource-strapped colony that could barely care for its own citizens. English and French pirates often intercepted supply vessels and discouraged maritime trade, and many shipments, when they did arrive, were less than stated with portions being diverted to more important posts within New Spain. Even the garrison was not immune to such actions. In early 1718 one hundred troops were sent to St. Augustine, but along the way detachments were drawn from this by order of New Spain's viceroy, leaving only thirty-seven men for St. Augustine. The situation had created a demoralized populace and a vibrant contraband trade with the English. Benavides condemned this last behavior, but at the same time he realized that the driving force behind the problem was the failure of his superiors in Mexico to properly maintain the colony.

Ultimately, the answer was to populate the colony such that it could at least agriculturally sustain itself. The governor urged the settling of poor Spanish families in the country, and to see to their protection he suggested

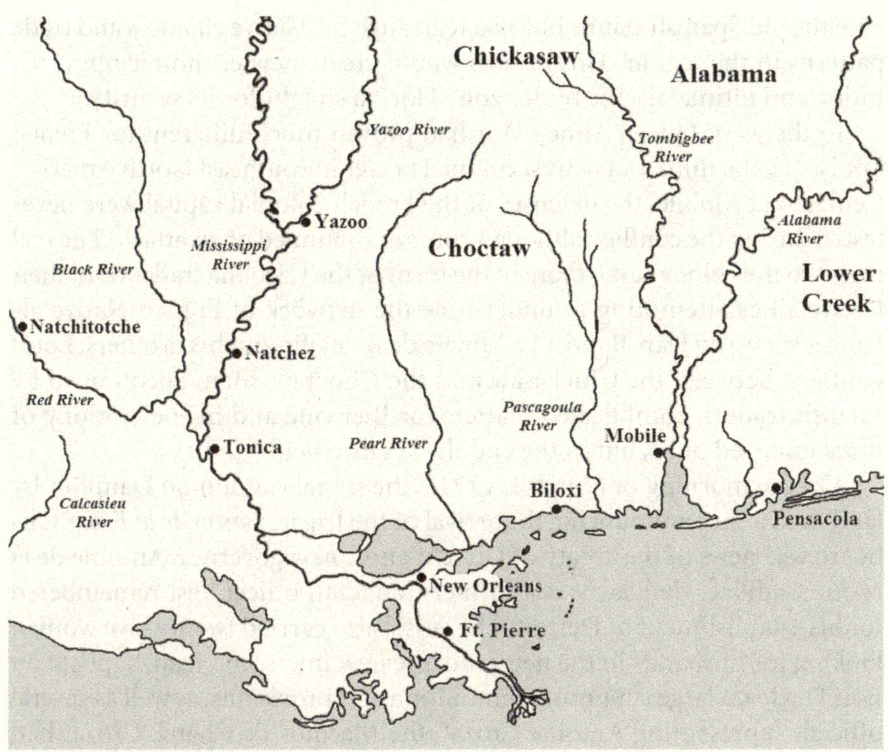

French Louisiana, c.1730.

that another five hundred soldiers be sent, which would effectively double the number of Spanish troops in Florida. Little would come of either idea. Most potential colonists were not interested, stating that it would be better to starve to death in Spain rather than Florida. In addition, the cost of the additional troops was deemed too high. As it had always been with Florida, opportunities abounded, but money to exploit these was nowhere to be found.

In early 1719 this suddenly changed with news of the War of the Quadruple Alliance (1718-1720), which pitted Spain against a coalition of France, Britain, Austria, and the Dutch Republic. While the vast majority of fighting would take place in Europe, in the New World it was viewed as an opportunity to retake lost Spanish territory. The plan called for a Spanish-Native force to strike along the southern frontier of South Carolina while a fleet of warships and transports was assembled at Havana to launch an attack on Charleston. The belief was that this strike would not only secure the old Spanish claims but also rearrange the Native alliances and trade patterns in the region. This in turn would create new economic opportunities, and ultimately, the buffer zone Florida sought for its security.[2]

To the west, Queen Anne's War had proven much different for French Louisiana, the third and newest colonial power in southeast North America. Centered at Mobile, the defenses of the French colonial capital were never tested during the conflict, although rumors abounded of an attack. The real threat to the colony came more in the form of the Carolina traders and their Native allies attempting to undermine the network of Franco-Native alliances set up by Jean-Baptist Le Moyne de Bienville and his brothers. Local conflicts between the Chickasaw and the Choctaw, often encouraged by English traders, complicated matters for Bienville and his new colony of three hundred or so, but in the end the alliance held.

On the morning of March 17, 1713, the signal cannon on Dauphin Island fired a shot announcing the arrival of the frigate *Baron de la Fosse*. Onboard was news of the Treaty of Utrecht and a new governor, Antoine de la Motte Cadillac. Cadillac was a former Canadian officer best remembered for his establishment of Detroit. The vessel also carried twenty-five women looking for husbands in the new land, the new intendent, Jean-Baptiste du Bois Duclos, a large supply of ammunition and provisions, as well as several officials representing Antoine Crozat, the Marquis de Chatel. Crozat had obtained a patent for Louisiana from the king in 1712, which gave him exclusive trade rights in return for populating and advancing the colony.[3]

Cadillac informed Bienville that he would retain the post of lieutenant governor, which was perhaps fortunate, as Cadillac spent little time overseeing the colony. During what time the two were together, they argued. Part of this was the product of two legendary and headstrong Canadian frontiersman meeting, and part of this was Cadillac's jealousy, perhaps understandable for someone looking to replace a governor who had seen the vulnerable colony through Queen Anne's War and not only held the loyalty of inhabitants but the respect of the nearby Native nations as well.

In August a large Choctaw delegation arrived at Mobile to meet with Cadillac. They pledged to uphold the treaty between the two parties and informed Cadillac that the Chickasaw and Alabama, along with a number of English traders, had visited them seeking peace. It was good news, as the general peace that had been the backbone of the French colony's diplomacy looked to be returning, although news of the English traders, mostly Carolinians, was a troublesome complication.

For Crozat it was about profits, and as such, he directed that an expedition be sent west to open trade with the Spanish settlements in this region.

Another would be sent to the Illinois, and several representatives from the colony would travel to Vera Cruz, looking to open trade with this port and obtain the livestock the colony desperately needed. This would be followed by additional delegations with the thought of creating a depot at Dauphin Island that traded with all the Spanish ports in the area now that peace existed between all parties. Most of the efforts would fail, as the Spanish were not interested in opening their ports, and the delegation that went to Vera Cruz was told to pay cash for the livestock, which were delivered to them at the docks to hasten their departure.

In early 1715 after hearing rumors of silver mines to the north, Cadillac left Mobile on an expedition in search of their origins. A few months later Bienville, who was now in charge, questioned the Choctaw when he discovered that they were still harboring English traders in the villages. The chieftains admitted that this was the case but claimed they would drive them off soon. It proved to be somewhat prophetic, as the Choctaw carried through with their promise in the opening weeks of the Yamassee War, slaying the traders and pillaging their trading houses. It would not be until July that news reached Mobile of the devastation wrought on South Carolina and reports arrived that many of the western nations had killed or deposed the Carolina traders in their villages. For Bienville it was good news that opened new avenues for the colony and spoke to its current security. In fact, security would soon improve. The previous December a frigate had arrived ladened with provisions and Indian gifts, and on August 15, 1715, the brig *Dauphine* arrived at Mobile with provisions and two companies of infantry. Shortly thereafter Cadillac returned to France in the *Dauphine*, leaving Bienville once again in command.[4]

One of the issues before Bienville concerned the Natchez. Reports of the death of several French traders and the pillaging of others strained the colony's relations with this nation. Bienville employed a heavy hand until the culprit, a chieftain named Arrow, had been punished and his head delivered to the governor. Bienville then demanded that the Natchez help build a fort near their villages to provide for the safety of the French. Although sickness struck down the French detachment overseeing this work, the Natchez provided enough manpower that, by August 2, 1716, the palisade was enclosed, "and the Natchez covered the barracks, store-house, guardhouse, and magazine with bark, which was finished on the 5th." The stronghold, known as Fort Rosalie, was built on a bluff that overlooked the Mississippi and would soon be the center of not only a French settlement but an even greater crisis.

Cadillac's replacement, Jean Michiele de L'Epinay, arrived at Dauphin Island with two 30-gun frigates and a transport on March 9, 1717. The new governor brought with him supplies, three companies of infantry, and fifty settlers. He also brought something from the king, the Cross of St. Louis for Bienville. At first there was some hesitation, but L'Epinay and Bienville soon began working together. They both agreed that another portage was needed for vessels coming from France, given the shifting sand bars in Mobile Bay. The site selected, New Biloxi, was to be on the mainland a few miles west of the Old Biloxi settlement and opposite the sheltered anchorage at Ship Island. In something of a fortuitous event, a ship arrived not long after with a large detachment of carpenters and masons aboard. L'Epinay and Bienville quickly dispatched them to the location to begin work.[5]

On February 9, 1718, three ships entered the Dauphin Island anchorage. On board was a letter from the king recalling L'Epinay and appointing Bienville governor. While Bienville had acted as governor for much of the colony's existence, the official acknowledgment must have been satisfying. One of Bienville's first acts was to establish a new colonial capitol. Scores of failed homesteads pointed out that the barren coastal lands were not sufficient to create an agricultural base that would lead to self-sufficiency. The new settlement should be placed inland. In addition, it should guard the Mississippi, the true prize of the region. The founding of New Orleans, the arrival of eight hundred settlers with land grants from the Western Company, a Royal entity formed when Crozat relinquished his Louisiana patent in 1717, the building of Fort Crevecouer at St. Joseph's Bay, Florida, and shortly thereafter the abandonment of this post occupied much of Bienville's year.

Spring brought the resupply vessels from France. The first to arrive was the frigate *le Comte de Toulouse* on March 17. Carrying supplies and a hundred passengers, the ship also brought rumors of war in Europe. A little over a month later Bienville's brother, Joseph Le Moyne de Serigny, navigated three vessels into the Dauphin Island anchorage. There were 130 colonists onboard, including thirty who were planning on starting a tobacco plantation. There were more troops as well as skilled workmen, 250 Black slaves, and sizable amounts of ammunition and provisions. The last was important, as Serigny informed Bienville that war had been declared against Spain by a quadruple alliance of France, Britain, Austria, and the Dutch Republic.

Bienville summoned a council of war after reading the letter Serigny delivered to him. The dispatch had called for an attack on Pensacola, which would then be used as the new headquarters for the Western Company. Bi-

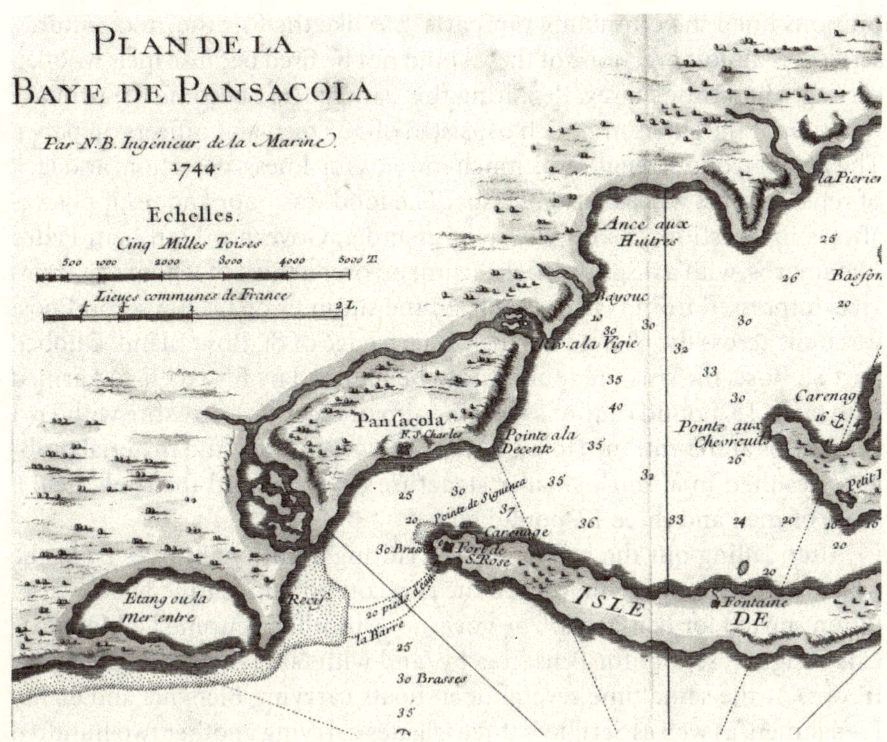

A 1744 plan of Pensacola. (*Norman B. Leventhal Map Collection, Boston Public Library*)

enville was in favor of the plan. Having witnessed Spanish influence returning to western Florida and looking to strike before the English, he agreed that Pensacola was the logical target. The timing was also good. The French colony now numbered close to two thousand souls, making it more populace than Spanish Florida, and with English influence waning after the Yamassee War, the Franco-Native alliances in the region had been strengthened. There was also his brother's flotilla of three 20-gun frigates, which could be used to launch a combined attack from land and sea.[6]

Bienville's target, Fort San Carlos at Pensacola, had been the scene of several engagements during Queen Anne's War. Anglo-Creek war parties had pressed on the key post but had failed to seize the stronghold. The strength of the fort was a function of its construction and the state of its garrison. Built of earth and faced with pine logs, the four-bastion structure continually leaked sand through the wooden containment as the ravages of wind and rain slowly reduced its form. An impressive array of twenty-eight cannons lined the crumbling ramparts, but like the fort they too required service, as almost every one of these could not be fired because their wooden carriages had rotted away. Repairing this damage had become the primary function of the garrison, which consisted of 307 men and officers on paper. The actual troop strength was much lower, as sickness, desertion, and lack of replacements was a constant issue. The food was poor and resupply was always in question, leaving their commander, Governor Don Juan Pedro Matamoros, with a disgruntled detachment, over a third of whom were convicts impressed from Havana's jails. In the summer of 1717, a second post was built across the channel on the western edge of St. Rose Island. Dubbed Fort St. Rose, the small redoubt was to be manned by fifty men and armed with eight 18-pound cannons with the aim of creating a crossfire with Fort San Carlos at the entrance to the harbor. However, labor and material problems resulted in a much smaller structure being erected that only held a score of men and three 12-pound guns.[7]

After calling out the militia and recruiting additional forces from the nearby native nations, on May 12 the two components of Bienville's expedition started for Pensacola. The governor's brother, Antoine Le Moyne de Chateauguay, set out for Pensacola by land with 60 French and 350 Native troops. At the same time several open boats carrying Bienville and eighty Frenchmen, as well as Serigny's three frigates carrying another two hundred soldiers and militia, set sail from Dauphin Island. That evening Bienville landed on St. Rose Island east of the small fort. After a short march, the detachment burst upon the unsuspecting Spaniards, capturing Fort St. Rose without firing a shot. As a bonus, Bienville also captured another detachment of twenty men the next morning when they arrived as part of the normal rotation of the garrison. Exposed to the guns of Fort San Carlos, Bienville ordered the three cannons in the post spiked and returned to his brother's flotilla still anchored outside the harbor because of the winds.

Although Chateauguay had yet to arrive, the next morning Serigny positioned his three warships before the fort and opened fire. The French vessels and the Spanish stronghold dueled for a few hours while troops were landed and took positions on the high ground near the structure. For Matamoros, who claimed to be unaware of the state of war between the two nations, there was little to do but surrender. He was short on both powder and provisions and was clearly outnumbered and outgunned.

Chateauguay's detachment arrived the next day to find a French flag flying over the fort. During a council of war that day the question became how to hold the captured post. As support from France was expected soon, the plan had been to send Matamoros and his garrison back to France on

Serigny's ships, so as to not alarm the Spanish. A shortage of provisions in the flotilla, however, necessitated a change. Instead, the prisoners would be put on two smaller company vessels and returned to Havana.

When the French ships *Comte de Toulouse* and *Marechal de Villars* arrived at Havana, Governor Gregorio Guazo Calderon was shocked to hear what had transpired given that no news of the war had reached him. He immediately confiscated the French vessels and imprisoned their crews. In the harbor Admiral Alfonso Carrascosa de la Torre had assembled a fleet of thirteen small vessels for a potential assault on Charleston. Led by a pair of 16- and 14-gun brigs, the makeup of the fleet had been chosen to operate in the shallow waters around Charleston. Now, with news of the French capture of Pensacola, Calderon changed Torre's mission. Replacing two of the smaller vessels with the captured French 20-gun frigates, on July 19 he ordered the admiral to proceed to Pensacola and retake Fort San Carlos.[8]

Bienville had left Chateauguay in charge of Pensacola with 250 troops. Accompanying Chateauguay were forty clerks and traders and a pair of vessels from the Western Company that had already begun transferring their headquarters from Dauphin Island to this location. In something of a repeat of its initial capture, on the morning of August 6, Torre landed a hundred men on St. Rose Island and quickly seized the small post there. He then entered the harbor with several warships and opened fire on the fort as well as the Western Company vessels *Dauphine* and *St. Louis* that had been pulled ashore for repairs. Chateauguay responded with the fort's guns, and a furious exchange took hold until six o'clock that evening. As the *Dauphine* burned on the beach, Torre delivered a surrender demand. A truce was declared until ten o'clock to give the French commander time to consider. Chateauguay was surrounded, outnumbered, and outgunned. In addition, forty of his men had deserted in the opening exchange, and it was clear that many others would do so soon. Out of options, he surrendered the next morning with full honors of war.[9]

Pensacola was once again Spanish. A few days later the Spanish took the offensive as Torre's small boats descended on Dauphin Island. For the next few weeks, the light draft vessels and the captured French frigates fired on the island's defenders and entered Mobile Bay, looking to seize the French frigate *Phillip* at anchor. It was more a harassing action than a concerted attack, and Bienville and Serigny knew why. With restored Governor Matamoros's permission, their younger brother had written them with news that a squadron of Spanish ships-of-the-line at Vera Cruz would soon join the attackers. When five sails were seen approaching Dauphin Island on September 1, it appeared to the French defenders, who numbered a few hundred at most, that the end would come soon. Convinced that their reinforcements had arrived, the Spanish sailors and soldiers cheered at the sight, that is until French colors were seen atop their masts. Suddenly it was the defenders cheering and launching insults at the rapidly retreating Spanish.

The 54-gun *Mars*, the 54-gun *Hercule*, and the 52-gun *Triton*, along with a pair of craft from the Western Company, dropped anchor not long after. Admiral Desnos de Champmeslin came ashore and met with a relieved Bienville and Serigny. The pair informed Champmeslin of what had transpired at Pensacola as the 250 troops, 300 colonists, and a large supply of stores were unloaded. The trio agreed to launch another attack on the Spanish port once the troops had spent some time ashore and all the supplies had been unloaded.[10]

By mid-September the French force was on the move. Bienville with a hundred French and five hundred Native allies marched by land, while Champmeslin's warships, further reinforced by the 20-gun *Phillips* and the 36-gun *Union*, approached along the coast. The admiral dropped anchor outside of the harbor on the sixteenth. In the distance he could see Bienville's signal fires a few miles from the fort. The next morning Bienville's detachment moved forward and began a harassing fire on the defenders of Fort San Carlos. Champmeslin responded by moving forward with his five vessels and taking a position in front of the fort. Matamoros, however, had been busy in the interim, erecting a new battery of twenty-four heavy guns at Fort St. Rose. Combined with the guns of San Carlos and those aboard a handful of Spanish vessels in the harbor, it placed the French squadron in a severe crossfire. With over two hundred cannons on his ships the French admiral accepted the challenge, and a two-and-a-half-hour artillery duel shook the serene Florida port. After an hour the Spanish battery on St. Rose Island fell silent, leaving Champmeslin to focus on San Carlos and the Spanish vessels anchored a little over a musket shot away. Within an hour the Spanish flotilla had hauled down their colors and the fire from Fort San Carlos had become sporadic. Shortly thereafter, Matamoros requested a parley. The Spanish governor sent a small boat out to the flagship *Hercule* to seek terms, but Champmeslin offered none. With over a hundred casualties and no prospects of relief, Matamoros unconditionally surrendered.[11]

A few days later a Spanish supply ship from Havana carrying provisions was seized when it entered the harbor, and a few weeks after this, a relief force of a hundred men aboard two small vessels also found themselves taken when they entered the harbor. It proved an impressive victory. In addition to the three vessels that were captured after the battle, Bienville and Champmeslin had taken a small privateer, a 16-gun frigate, and had retaken the French ships *St. Louis, Comte de Toulouse*, and *Marechal de Villiers*. They had also captured over sixty cannons, and although a few small privateers had escaped to the east side of the bay where their crews abandoned them and fled on foot, the French leaders still had close to 1,300 prisoners.

Matamoros, his officers, and many of the professional troops were kept aboard Champmeslin's warships, while the rest, save a handful of French deserters who were hung or thrown in chains, were sent back to Havana. The question then became what to do with Pensacola? While the French hoped to use Pensacola as a new trading center, it was clear that the position required too great a force to secure it from the Spanish, and as such, it would not work as the Western Company's new headquarters. The events had even raised concerns regarding the security of Dauphin Island, and it was agreed that the company's current headquarters would be moved to Ship Island. As for the fortifications of Pensacola, Champmeslin left a sergeant's guard, who razed both Fort St. Rose and Fort San Carlos, before eventually abandoning the post altogether.

The War of the Quadruple Alliance would end with the signing of the Treaty of Hague on February 17, 1720, although it would take months for the news to arrive in the New World. During this time a few raids and privateering in the Caribbean were the only American components, and even these were pursued in a limited fashion. While both New Spain and French Louisiana had failed to achieve their goals, there was one big winner from the contest: South Carolina.[12]

CHAPTER TWELVE

The Natchez and Chickasaw Wars

It is perhaps ironic that Bienville had inadvertently saved Charleston from possible destruction, but with the attack on Pensacola, this is exactly what transpired. The people of Charleston would not understand why the Spanish attack on the town failed to materialize but were relieved nonetheless. It would prove a long road to recovery for the colony, but at least the lord proprietors would not be involved. In 1720 the series of appeals to the king were finally rewarded, and South Carolina became a royal colony.

This did not come easy. With the lack of assistance from the proprietary government during the Yamassee War, and the existing threat from a Spanish fleet assembling in Havana, combined with arbitrary rulings regarding the rights of the inhabitants, a new assembly headed by Colonel James Moore looked to accelerate the question of royal rule and the removal of the lord proprietors from colonial affairs. On November 28, 1719, they delivered the following letter to Governor Johnson:

> Sir, we doubt not but you have heard of the whole province entering into an association to stand bv their rights and their privileges, and to get rid of the oppression and arbitrary dealings of the Lords

Proprietors. As we always bore you the greatest deference and respect imaginable, we take this opportunity to let you know, that the committe of the people's representatives were last night appointed to wait on you this morning, to acquaint you, that they have come to a resolution to have no regard to the Proprietors officers, nor their administration: and withal to beg, that your honour will hold the reigns of government for the King, till his Majesty's pleasure be known.[1]

If the hope had been to convince Johnson of the justness of their cause, it did not work. At first Johnson, who was no friend of the proprietors, addressed the uprising in a calm manner, asking the assembly to be more specific in their intentions. While such a moderated approach might have worked in the past, it now failed miserably. The colony's militia refused to obey his orders, and Moore was made the new governor by popular demand. Johnson informed the proprietors and the Board of Trade of the state of affairs. The latter, against proprietary governments in America, put the matter before the Crown. On August 11, 1720, the lord justices ruled in the favor of the Board of Trade and directed that "the Governmt. of said Province be forthwith taken provisionally into the hands of the Crown." They also ruled that a governor be appointed by the king and that measures be taken to ensure the safety of the colony. It only took a few days to nominate Francis Nicholson and arm him with a royal commission. It would take far longer for the new governor to reach the colony.[2]

While events were occurring in London that would place the colony under royal rule, matters in South Carolina had reached a boiling point. With the Spanish threat to the Bahamas having subsided, a pair of British warships, the 24-gun H.M.S. *Flamborough* and the 20-gun H.M.S. *Phoenix*, sailed into Charleston in early 1721. While the primary mission was to patrol against pirates and intercept any Spanish efforts along the South Carolina coast, the captain of the *Flamborough*, John Hildesley, and Captain Vincent Pearce of the *Phoenix* became embroiled in the local politics. Both men declared for Johnson, but Hildesley did not leave the matter at this. Hildesley actively organized those opposed to the assembly's actions and offered his services to Johnson, who appointed him colonel of militia. With the backing of Hildesley and a number of disaffected recruits, Johnson and his council looked to take control of the government again. On May 9 Johnson and Hildesley at the head of 120 men, most of whom were sailors from the *Flamborough*, marched on the town. Johnson sent two envoys ahead to deliver a summons to Colonel Moore to surrender the government. "Two of H.M. ships or war as being now in harbour," he informed Moore, "and the Commanders sensible of the difficulties I have laboured under as well as the whole country by your unjust usurpation of the Government, have therefore resolved to assist me with all their force to resume the same."[3]

Moore and his allies were not swayed, and when Hildesley advanced toward the town to enforce the summons, the order was given to fire three of the city's cannons on the column. The action had the desired effect, and Johnson's forces retreated to the cheers of the town's defenders. Hildesley was captured and arrested by an angry populace, based in part on rumors that he had promised the sailors that joined him that they would be allowed to plunder the town. Seeing that the attempt had failed, Johnson disbanded the remaining troops and asked Captain Pearce to negotiate Hildesley's release.[4]

Nicholson's arrival did not solve all of the colony's problems, but it did put it back on the track of recovery and expansion. One of the issues that persisted was Spanish depredations at sea. Under the Treaty of Utrecht Spanish ports were opened to British trade. While this traffic was limited, many Spanish colonial governors refused to allow any British vessel from calling on their ports. Matters were even worse, as these governors employed a *guarda-costas* to enforce their mandates and intercept illegal traffic. The captains of these vessels often operated more as privateers and pirates than customs enforcement. The Dutch governor of Curacao complained of one of these Spanish vessels seizing nine sloops near Caracas, plundering the craft and killing most of their crews. British and French vessels reported similar instances not only in the Caribbean but along the coast of North America. The matter finally reached the point that in May 1726 a group of London merchants, after having suffered a loss of nearly £300,000 in what they viewed as a violation of the Treaty of Utrecht, demanded that the government launch a reprisal against such behavior.

The response was to send a squadron to the Caribbean under Admiral Francis Hosier to blockade the Spanish treasure fleet coming out of Porto Bello and Cartagena. The thought was that this demonstration would bring Spanish authorities to the bargaining table, but illness decimated Hosier's crews and undermined the effectiveness of the operation. Rumors of war began to take hold among the British colonies, and several Spanish governors began to issue letters of marque for ships to operate against the English. While an actual state of war was not declared in Europe until February 1727, Spanish forces in the Caribbean did not wait for the official declaration and attacked St. Christophers on February 12. A pair of Spanish sloops descended on the harbor and seized half-a-dozen merchantmen before re-

Jean-Baptiste Le Moyne de Bienville. Another of the famous Le Moyne brothers. Although never officially made Governor of early Louisiana, Bienville acted as such and would successfully guide the infant colony through the perils of Queen Anne's War. After the conflict he would go on to found the city of New Orleans and oversee a period of expansion, before becoming embroiled in a series of conflicts with the Natchez and Chickasaw nations. (*Albert Ferland, 1905*)

turning back to sea with their prizes. There were also reports that a sizable Spanish fleet was expected at Havana to assist in these efforts.

The Anglo-Spanish War of 1727-1729 was more notable for a failed Spanish siege of Gibraltar than any events that occurred in North America or the Caribbean. For the governors along the American coast, the increased activity of Spanish privateers occupied most of their concerns during the short-lived conflict. Captured vessels were reported from South Carolina to New Hampshire, and matters had become so intolerable in Virginia that a convoy system was implemented to protect their trade. While a truce was negotiated in the summer of 1728, and the Treaty of Seville in November of the following year officially brought an end to the conflict, in the New World it had little effect. Incidents of privateering and piracy would continue on all sides.[5]

For French Louisiana the years following the War of the Quadruple Alliance were marked by a rapid expansion of the colony. From 1720 to Bienville's departure for France in 1725, immigrants, soldiers, and Black slaves increased the population of the colony to over six thousand. The shift of the colonial capital to New Orleans and the fertile lands in the area had led to a growth in agriculture with numerous rice, indigo, and tobacco plantations soon taking hold. The effort was not without its challenges. Still not self-sufficient, food shortages occurred, and in September 1723, a hurricane struck, badly damaging New Orleans and plantations in the region.

The year was also marked by troubles with the Natchez, who had launched an attack on Fort Rosalie and the nearby French settlers. The matter became serious enough that, in October, Bienville organized a force of seven hundred French, Tonicas, Yazoo, and Choctaw and marched to the relief of the fort. From here the governor's plan was to attack each of the five Natchez villages: the Great Village, the Corn Village, the White Apple Village, Jenzenaque, and the Grey Village. On Halloween, Bienville left Fort Rosalie in two columns. He soon encountered Stung-Serpent, the chieftain of the Great Village, who informed him that the attacks had come from the White Apple, Jenzenaque, and Grey Villages. The inhabitants of the Great Village and the Corn Village had done nothing to bother the French, and as such, he asked that they be spared. Bienville agreed and the next day set out for the other three towns. For over a week the column marched and countermarched, burning the three villages in question but only finding a handful of Natchez.

Unsatisfied with the punitive effort, Bienville returned to Fort Rosalie and summoned Stung-Serpent. He informed the chieftain that, while he had agreed not to attack the Corn and Great Villages, he had changed his mind. Stung-Serpent, who had been a friend of the French, pleaded for peace, which Bienville agreed to under the condition that he bring him the head of the war chief of the White Apple Village, Old Hair, who he suspected was behind the attacks. Stung-Serpent accepted the terms and two days later returned with the requested trophy. Satisfied that the conflict was at an end, Bienville returned to New Orleans.[6]

The First Natchez War, as this campaign was referred to by French authorities, was just the precursor to a much larger and wider confrontation. For the next several years the French colony around Fort Rosalie grew. The land was fertile, some of the best in the colony, and being elevated, it was not subject to the ravages of the nearby Mississippi River. There were a few isolated incidents, but in general, the new settlement lived in peace with the five Natchez villages. This situation would change when Captain Etienne de Chepart was appointed commandant of Fort Rosalie.

Much like with the Carolina traders before the Yamassee War, Chepart began to dictate to the nearby Natchez. He summoned the new chieftain of the Great Village, and after extorting tribute from him, ordered the town to be moved, as he planned to use the current location for a plantation. The Natchez were visibly taken aback by the demand and asked for time to discuss the matter. The next day they returned and agreed to the terms, asking for two moons to carry out the operation. While Chepart was delighted by the news, among the Natchez there was no plan on moving anything. Instead, the time was used to send envoys to nearby nations in order to plan a coordinated strike against the French. The fruit of this effort was an alliance between the Natchez, Yazoo, and Choctaw to expel the French from the region. Rumors of the impending attack reached Chepart and his officers, but the commandant dismissed these and punished those who attempted to propagate them. It proved a fateful decision. On the morning of November 28, 1729, a Natchez delegation arrived at Fort Rosalie with the requested tribute while hosts of Natchez visited the local settlements and homesteads on what appeared to be routine matters.

Around 9:00 a.m. the atmosphere changed dramatically as war whoops and muskets shattered the calm. Caught completely unaware, a slaughter commenced for the next hour, leaving Chepart, the fort's garrison, and some three hundred settlers either dead or prisoner. A few days later the Yazoo carried out their end of the arrangement and fell upon the unsuspecting Fort St. Claude located about a dozen miles from the confluence of the Yazoo and Mississippi Rivers. Before the garrison of twenty or so realized what was happening, the Yazoo war party was over the walls and within a few minutes had slain every Frenchman within the structure.

The Choctaw were to launch an attack on the French settlements downriver on the same day as the Natchez attack, but a confusion in the timing between the two nations resulted in the Choctaw moving forward on December 1. Six hundred Choctaw advanced on New Orleans. When they reached Lake Pontchartrain, they sent a pair of envoys forward asking permission to enter the town. Governor Etienne Perier, who had arrived in the colony in 1726, was suspicious of such a large party and responded that, if the Choctaw wanted to smoke the peace pipe, their chieftain and an escort of thirty should suffice. Believing that the French had discovered their plans, the war party turned back.[7]

A few days later the Choctaw sent a large delegation to the Natchez, where they discovered the timing error. The Natchez offered a number of gifts to the Choctaw ambassadors, but the latter were unimpressed and accused the Natchez of purposely starting the attack early so they could keep the choice prisoners and booty for themselves. Another delegation followed, but they were also convinced that the Natchez had deceived them and threatened to retaliate against the Natchez for their duplicity.

Thus, when small groups of survivors reached New Orleans with news of the massacre, and the French reached out to the Choctaw to join a punitive expedition against the Natchez, the latter quickly agreed "to serve the

French in the campaign with all their forces." Several hundred troops and settlers were organized under the command of the mayor of New Orleans Chevalier de Loubois and advanced upriver to the Tonica villages. Here they recruited more men and built a small fort. Not believing himself strong enough to move forward without his Choctaw allies, Loubois could do little but wait.

It was not until late February that close to nine hundred Choctaw arrived. Now almost two thousand strong, the French commander pushed onto the Natchez villages. Slowed by his five cannons, which had to be dragged by hand, the Choctaw arrived first. Most of the Natchez had fled into a small palisade fort, but many had left their women and French slaves behind. Regardless of their alliance with the French, the Choctaw took these women and slaves, seemingly as a fulfillment of the original plan. The war party then advanced on the fort, but after a brief skirmish with the defenders, they moved off to encamp.[8]

Loubois appeared a few days later and opened siege trenches. The next day the Natchez sallied out of the fort and drove the sappers out of their trenches. Once the war party returned to the fort, and the wounded were tended to, the siegeworks continued. The Natchez fired on the advancing sap with muskets and a small cannon taken from Fort Rosalie, although the latter appears to have only been used once. When Loubois's troops were within a hundred yards of the fort, a firing parallel was dug and platforms for the cannons were laid out. That night the guns were dragged into place as the occasional shot from a nervous sentry echoed over the landscape. The next morning the main sap was continued toward the fort under the fire of four small cannons. In the midst of this a French officer advanced to a point halfway between the fort and the French lines. He planted the fleur-de-lis in the ground and shouted out in Natchez for the defenders to lay down their arms and become friends of the French. The response was several musket blasts and a rush of Natchez through the gate looking to seize the officer. When the latter fled, the goal shifted to capturing the flag, but one young French soldier who darted forward proved fast enough and returned with the banner under the cover fire and cheers of his comrades.

When the trenches came close enough that the French could storm the walls, and the 4-pound cannons could do serious damage to the palisade, the Natchez lowered their banner and asked for a parley. The Natchez agreed to release all hostages under the condition that neither the French nor the Choctaw entered the fort for twenty-four hours. After receiving the prisoners, Loubois held up his end of the agreement. If he thought that meant the Natchez would surrender after the twenty-four-hour period, he was

Fort Rosalie, pictured in "View of the Fort of the Natchez," from Georges Henri Victor Collot's *Voyage dans l'Amérique Septentrionale, ou Description des pays arrosés par le Mississipi, l'Ohio, le Missouri*, published in 1826.

mistaken. The next morning it was discovered that the defenders had fled under the cover of darkness. Already encountering difficulties with the Choctaw over the prisoners they held, Loubois did not pursue. Instead, he burned the fort and returned to the site of Fort Rosalie. Here he raised and provisioned a new fort, and after leaving a garrison of 120 men, he returned to New Orleans with the remaining French forces.[9]

The Natchez, who had reestablished a village near the junction of the Red and Black Rivers, were hardly defeated by the loss of their villages. Soon they were attacking work parties from the new Fort Rosalie, and in one instance, half a dozen convinced the garrison that they were Choctaw. The small party seized one of the guard towers and opened fire on the surprised French. The battle raged for several hours before the intruders were slain. A larger expedition against Fort Natchitotche on the Red River followed. When the war party of 150 arrived near the fort, they dispatched three emissaries to speak with the fort's commander, the Chevalier Louis Juchereau de St. Denis, Bienville's cousin and one of the founders of the colony. The Natchez ambassadors asked for permission for the war party to enter the fort. They wished to smoke and make peace. They even pointed out that they had brought a French woman with them as a gesture of good will. St. Denis was not fooled by the talk and informed them if ten returned with the women he would let them in; otherwise he was not interested.

Frustrated at their failed attempt, the French captive was burned in sight of the fort. The Natchez then busied themselves by constructing an earth redoubt in front of the fort. The plan was to intercept the fort's supplies and hopefully starve the garrison into submission. Seeing the Natchez entrenching, St. Denis sent a runner to the chief of the Natchitotche. The commandant asked for forty of the chief's best men. This detachment was brought into the fort after dark and mustered together with the bulk of the garrison. Just before daybreak the gates of the fort were quietly opened, and St. Denis's men crept forward in the twilight. When they were only a few dozen yards from the Natchez redoubt a chorus of war whoops and shouts shattered the dawn. The Natchez seemingly did not consider a sally by the garrison and were caught completely off guard. Many were still asleep as the howling charge rolled through their encampment. Dozens of Natchez fell in the opening minutes of the attack. Most bolted, but St. Denis pressed his advantage and extracted a heavy toll on the retreating enemy. When it was over, almost half of the Natchez war party was slain, and the siege of Fort Natchitotche was lifted.[10]

While the success had lifted the colony's morale, Perier looked to strike another blow that would bring the Natchez to the peace table. In August reinforcements arrived from France. The numbers were less than had been hoped, but when combined with the troops on hand it was deemed a sufficient force. The governor, after discovering the Choctaw's role in the initial attack, had spent months in conference with representatives of the nation. Diplomatic efforts had proven successful, and the Choctaw pledged their commitment to the alliance, but even with this Perier had no intention of involving them in the ongoing Natchez conflict.

The French expedition departed New Orleans on December 9, 1730. The vanguard, under Perier's brother, M. de Salverte, captain of the recently arrived *Somme*, consisted of three companies of marines and a company of sailors, some two hundred men in all. Perier followed a few days later with another two hundred men, and two days after this the rearguard, another 150 men under Captain Etienne de Benac, pushed out onto the Mississippi. When they reached Bayagoulas, a war party of forty Acolapissa joined the expedition.

Sleet and thick fog slowed the detachment's progress, but by the twenty-seventh, Perier was at Tonica. Here he waited for more of his native allies. Some, like the Arkansas, tired of waiting for the governor's detachment, had departed, while others followed their lead. Even so, Perier was able to recruit another hundred men for the campaign. Having sailed into the Black River in search of the Natchez, on January 20, 1731, the governor's scouts found their villages. The poor weather, which had delayed the expedition, now proved of help, as the surprised Natchez withdrew to a palisade fort when the French force began appearing out of the fog and started landing. The fort was quickly invested and siege operations began. When the defenders saw the trench work advancing, they sallied out of the fort to initiate a sharp skirmish before returning to their stronghold. It did little to stop Perier. The musketry continued, but by January 22 a parallel had been started for a few pieces of artillery and a small mortar. The latter, once positioned, proved particularly effective as it lobbed explosive rounds into the stronghold.

Two days later, as the last of the cannons were being dragged into position, the Natchez asked for a parley. The Natchez ambassador agreed to return nineteen Black slaves they had captured and vowed that they would never again make war on the French. In return, they asked the governor to retire. Perier told the envoy to return with the Black slaves and the Sun Chief or he would open fire with his battery of cannons and reduce the fort to ashes. It took several attempts, but the Sun Chief finally appeared before Perier. With bands of rain pelting the encampment the conference was held in a small cabin. The governor asked the Sun Chief why the Natchez had made war on the French. The Sun Chief claimed that, as he was young, the older chieftains had ignored his opinion and organized the attack. He then shrugged. "I am well aware that it will always be ascribed to me," he concluded, "because I was the sovereign of my nation, yet I am quite innocent." When the governor questioned one of the chieftains that had accompanied the Sun Chief, he simply shook his head and responded, "We had no sense, but hereafter we shall have."[11]

As it was late, Perier held the Sun Chief and the two chieftains that had accompanied him under guard for the night. The plan had been to resume the negotiations in the morning, but that evening the one of the chieftains escaped and made his way back into the fort. Unclear on how to proceed, the next morning a Natchez envoy appeared before the French lines. The messenger claimed that the chieftan had convinced many of the older warriors to abandon the fort and seek refuge among friendly nations, but before they could accomplish this it was light. After continued negotiations some 350 Natchez, mostly women and children, surrendered. The rest, close to three hundred in all, escaped under the cover of darkness and a torrential downpour. A few days later the governor returned to New Orleans with his prisoners, which included the Sun Chief, his wife, and a number of chieftains.

The remaining Natchez, hearing that the Sun Chief and those captured with him had been sold into slavery on St. Domingo, continued to fight. Claiming that they were in search of peace, they entered a Tonica village and launched a surprise attack. While they managed to slay a score including the Tonica chief, a counterattack by the Tonica killed or captured thirty-six Natchez. Other Natchez efforts scored some success but at a cost in manpower that the Natchez could ill afford. While the Natchez were still capable of launching small raids, at this point they ceased to pose a serious threat to the colony. Instead, this position was slowly being assumed by the Chickasaw, among whom many of the remaining Natchez had found refuge. News of Chickasaw overtures to win over the Choctaw, Illinois, Arkansas, and Miami reached Perier, as well as reports that another group of Natchez were now seen among the Chickasaw. The governor proposed a military expedition against the Chickasaw in 1732, but he never carried through with the plan.[12]

In 1733 Bienville, who had been in France for eight years, returned as governor of Louisiana. He found the colony in much worse condition than he had thought, not just because "of the want of provisions, of merchandise and of money, or because of the considerable decrease in the number of colonists," but specifically in terms of relations with the Native nations around them. "Since the slackness with which they saw that the French carried on the war with the Natchez, they have conceived a sovereign contempt for the nation." The British traders had solidified their alliance with the Chickasaw, who were now not only sheltering the remaining Natchez but had started exerting influence on the Choctaw, Alabama, and a number of smaller nations in the region. In the governor's mind the Natchez were not the issue but the pro-English Chickasaw. It was clear that the British and Chickasaw were attempting to break the Franco-Native alliances in the region, not only to expand the domains of the Carolinas and secure trade but to cut French communications between Louisiana and the Illinois country. This last element was too important to the young French colony, and France's overall approach in North America to contain British settlements east of Mobile and the Appalachian Mountains, to ignore.[13]

As he read through the reports and spoke with his officers, Bienville concluded that to secure the Mississippi Valley, the Chickasaw had to be shown the consequences of their actions and convinced that the English could not protect them. "If we cannot gain over this nation, it will be necessary to drive it away from the territory of the colony," the governor informed the French court. While he might have wanted to destroy the Chickasaw, Bienville had seen far too many campaigns in the south to believe that this would be the result, especially with a feared nation like the Chickasaw who could put a thousand men in the field. The goal was to weaken the Chickasaw and then bring them back into the Peace Treaty of Mobile to act as a buffer against British expansion.

To accomplish the reduction of the Chickasaw, Bienville applied a familiar formula. First, he needed justification for the plan. Second, he would use this justification not only to launch his Choctaw and southern allies at the Chickasaw, but the Illinois and French-allied nations among the Great Lakes as well. Third, under the screen of these attacks he would assemble a large expedition and march on the Chickasaw villages.

Bienville did not need much to push forward with his plan. Sporadic raids on the frontier, regardless of actual origin, he attributed to the Chickasaw or the Natchez that they harbored, and diplomatic efforts built for failure, such as his demand that the Chickasaw turn over the Natchez among them, provided the foundations required for his response. In late 1733 he turned to the Choctaw and the Canadian nations for assistance. For the next two years these and other allied tribes raided the Chickasaw. Given their proximity and long-held animosity toward the Chickasaw, the Choctaw struck first and conducted several raids in 1734, one in the fall against the village of Chatelaw. The Choctaw war party, led by Red Shoe, burst upon the village only to find it abandoned. The inhabitants, fearing an attack, had retired to a pair of palisade forts in the village. It appeared that the raid had failed until a stratagem was devised to lure the Chickasaw out of their strongholds. Red Shoe ordered the war party to lay in ambush while a dozen Choctaw appeared before the forts. This group fired upon the wooden structures and taunted the defenders with insults. It worked. The enraged Chickasaw poured out of the gates and set off in pursuit of the enemy war party, which led them to Red Shoe and a disaster that would cost them forty-five of their number.[14]

Attacks by the Illinois, Ottawa, and Seneca had also cost the Chickasaw another seventy-six killed or taken prisoner by the end of 1734. When a pair of Chickasaw envoys arrived at Mobile in 1735 seeking peace, Bienville believed that these raids had accomplished what he sought. However, whatever opportunities came from the meeting were soon undone when the governor received news that English traders among the Chickasaw had appeared in some of the Choctaw villages. Having seen enough, Bienville moved to the third phase and prepared for an expedition against the Chickasaw in the spring.

The plan called for Bienville with a force of six hundred French and a like number of Choctaw to ascend the Tombigbee River as far as possible, approaching the Chickasaw villages from the south, while the commander of Fort Chartes, Pierre D'Artaguette, was to raise a force of French, Illinois, Arkansas, Ottawa, Miami, and Iroquois and descend the Mississippi River, rendezvousing with Bienville in March 1736. Sensing the urgency

D'Artaguette, a decorated soldier from the Natchez Wars, pushed forward to the rendezvous with an advanced guard of 130 French, 100 Illinois, and another 130 Ottawa and Iroquois. As directed, he appeared at the northern edge of Chickasaw country on March 4 only to discover that there were no signs of Bienville and his army. Here he waited for several weeks until a letter arrived from Bienville announcing his delay and informing him that he would not be in position until late April at the earliest.[15]

D'Artaguette called together a council of war to discuss the news. Most agreed that they did not have enough supplies to wait and would be forced to depart. One option presented was to capture the nearby Chickasaw village recently discovered by their scouts. If successful they would not only find more than enough provisions to sustain them, but they would also secure a good defensive position where they could wait for Bienville's forces. If the French commander wished to attack, now was the time; otherwise the war party would disband. In keeping with his character D'Artaguette was in favor of attacking. On the morning of March 25, he left his supplies and baggage under the guard of a lieutenant and thirty men about a quarter of a mile from the start of a prairie, at the end of which was a cluster of thirty to forty Chickasaw cabins and a hill fort. After a short march along the trail to the village, D'Artaguette and his troops emerged out of the dimly lit woods. From there they pressed forward in a skirmish line across a long field before entering the village of Ougoula Tchetoka. War whoops and shouts in French rang out as the detachment surged forward, but if they thought they had taken the Chickasaw by surprise they were badly mistaken. Well aware of D'Artaguette's presence, a reinforcement of five hundred Chickasaw from a nearby village was positioned near the town. In a chorus that quickly drowned out the attackers, these reinforcements charged D'Artaguette's flank.

Fearing an even larger trap, the Illinois, Miami, and a number of others fled after a few shots. With over half his force retreating, D'Artaguette ordered the rest to fall back. The Chickasaw pursued, and a desperate battle took hold around the baggage train. The French, abandoned by all their allies except a detachment of sixty Iroquois and Arkansas, put up a furious defense, but it was clearly a losing cause. D'Artaguette was wounded twice, the second proving fatal, and a number of his senior officers had either fallen beside him or were wounded as well. Resistance finally collapsed, and what was left of the detachment abandoned their position and retreated under the cover of an Iroquois-Arkansas rearguard. The Chickasaw pursued for a time, but having already been fighting for hours, they were not interested in falling into an ambush, and the effort was soon abandoned. It

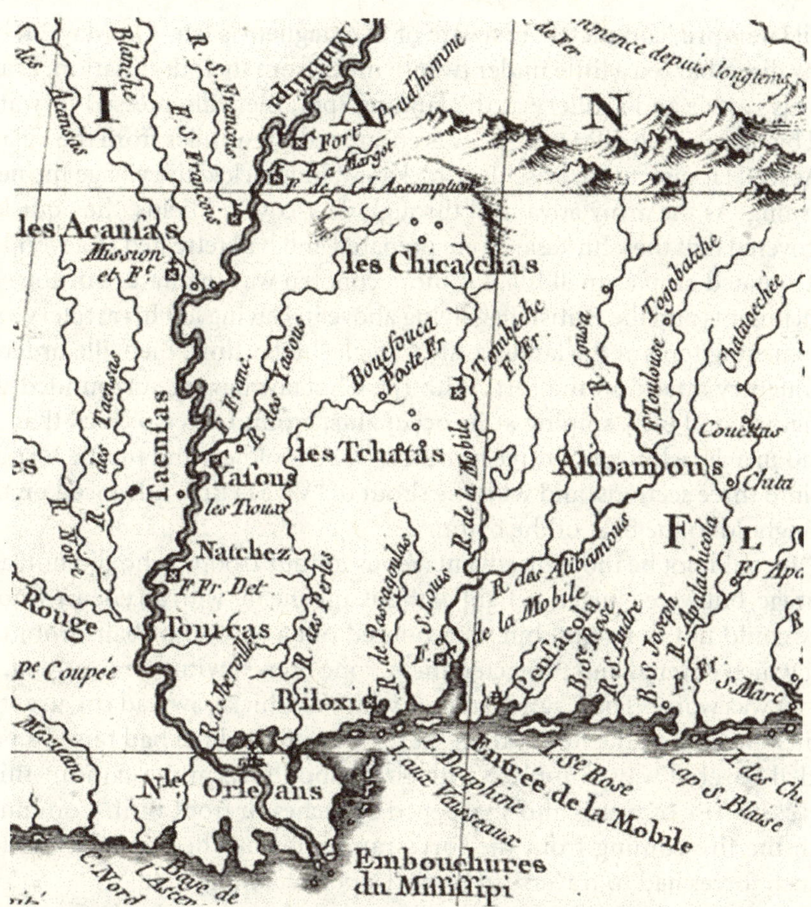

A period French map showing the locations of the Tonica, Alabama, Natchez, Yazoo, Choctaw, and Chickasaw nations, as well as the French posts in the region. Note that the Tombigbee River, often called the Chickasaw River at this time, is referred to as the Mobile River. (*Norman B. Leventhal Map Collection, Boston Public Library*)

proved to be a great victory for the Chickasaw. The French had lost forty men, including their commander, and there were likely just as many wounded who had escaped. D'Artaguette's entire supply train was now in their hands, as were several French prisoners, including a French Jesuit who had stayed behind to tend to the wounded, a task the victors quickly made a moot point when they dispatched his charges.[16]

Bienville, who had been delayed by the late arrival of the king's ships, heavy rains, and a lack of vessels to carry his men, would not move forward until late April, completely unaware of D'Artaguette's fate. On May 24, his army disembarked a little under twenty miles from their destination. Leaving his vessels and artillery at the landing spot, Bienville pressed forward, and by the evening of May 25 he was encamped a few miles from the village of Aekeia. Hoping to surprise the Chickasaw, he attacked the village the next morning. As the army advanced through dew-covered fields, they quickly discovered that the Chickasaw were prepared and had retreated to a wooden fort situated atop a small hill. Of more concern was the nature of the entrenchments and the British flag flying above it. Having left his artillery and entrenching tools at the landing site to make better time, Bienville ordered an infantry attack on the fort. With the Choctaw having surrounded the structure, and busy sniping at its occupants, around three o'clock that afternoon a detachment of three hundred French soldiers and militia formed up into three sections, and with the shout of "Vive le Roi," advanced on the stronghold to the beat of the drum.

"It could not be more disadvantageous for our troops, who did not lack courage, but were obliged to fight without any shelter with an enemy whom they could not draw out, but who poured out a shower of balls from the fort which covered and protected them," one French witness recounted. In fact, it was worse. The English traders with the Chickasaw had constructed a ditch in front of the fort and on the far side of the ditch had raised a palisaded covered way, complete with firing loopholes and a fathom-thick *chevel-de-frise* of brush and sharpened branches in front of it. Combined with the fire coming from the fort's ramparts and the open incline the French forces had to traverse, it proved a perfect killing field.

When the colorful French formations, their flags fluttering before them, came within range, the defenders loosened a deafening volley that opened holes in their ranks. Undeterred, the columns pressed forward and secured a small cabin on the slope of the hill. To the calls of their officers, and another cry of "Vive le Roi," the troops surged forward toward a second cabin along their route and even secured this post, but the volume of fire coming from the Chickasaw made any further advance impossible. For several hours, the French fired on the defenders and searched for a weak spot in the Chickasaw defenses, but they found none. In fact, even the second cabin, caught in a crossfire, was proving untenable. With their losses mounting this cabin was put to the torch and a retreat ordered to the first cabin. With most of the detachment's officers either killed or wounded, Bienville sounded the recall around five o'clock and sent forward a second force to cover the withdrawal. The fort was simply too strong to be taken by storm.[17]

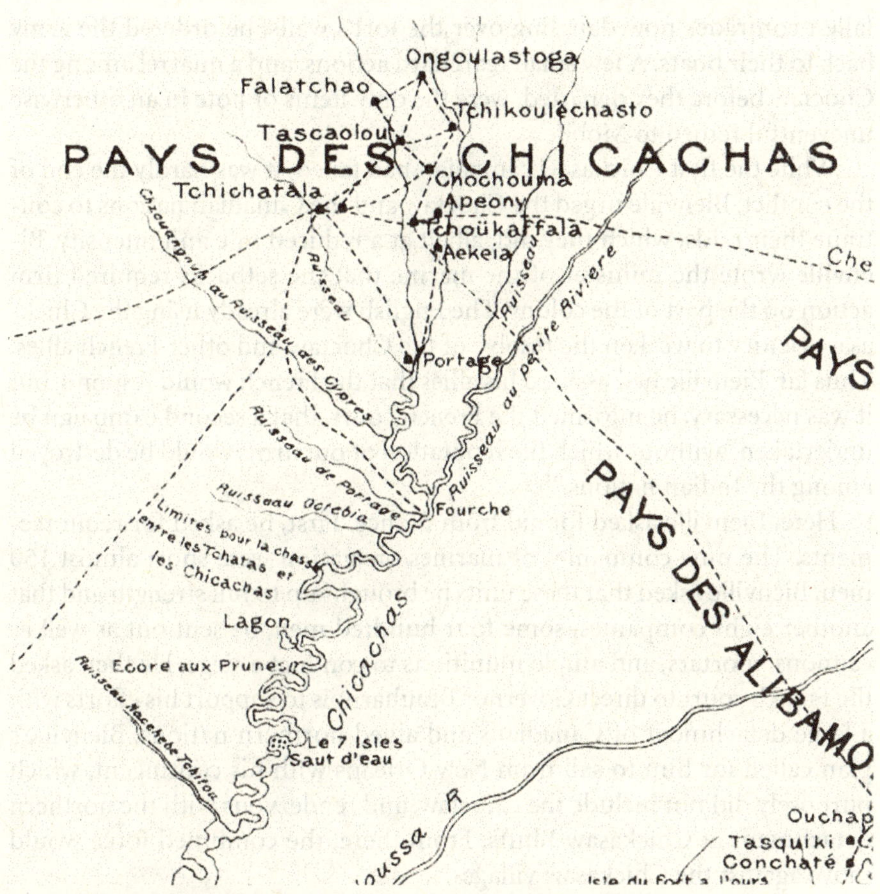

The Chickasaw villages near the headwaters of the Tombigbee, or Chickasaw, River. (*Birmingham Public Library*)

The attack had cost Bienville twenty-four killed and fifty-two wounded and had accomplished nothing but to alarm the other Chickasaw villages. While the army entrenched for the evening, the governor considered his next steps. It would take several days to move the artillery forward and reduce the fort by siege, and during that time the Chickasaw from the other villages would march to Aekeia's relief. If D'Artaguette's forces were present, he could divide the Chickasaw forces by having D'Artaguette strike at the villages to the north, but there had been no word of the French commander and his men since they arrived. Given the circumstances, Bienville called off the expedition, and the next morning, with the sight of their mutilated fallen comrades now dangling over the fort's walls, he ordered the army back to their boats. A few small rearguard actions, and a quarrel among the Choctaw before they departed, were the only items of note in an otherwise uneventful return to Mobile.

While the first Chickasaw campaign had failed, it was hardly the end of the conflict. Bienville urged the Choctaw and the Canadian nations to continue their raids, which they did, albeit at a reduced rate and intensity. Bienville wrote the minister of the marine that the setbacks required firm action on the part of the colony. The English were already using the Chickasaw victory to weaken the resolve of the Choctaw and other French allies. Thus far, Bienville had assured his allies that the French would respond, but it was necessary, he informed the French court, that a second campaign be undertaken "without which the reputation of our arms would be destroyed among the Indian nations."[18]

Here, Bienville asked for aid from France. First, he asked for reinforcements. The nine companies of marines on station were short almost 150 men. Bienville asked that these units be brought up to full strength and that another eight companies, some four hundred men, be sent out as well as cannons, mortars, and ample munitions to conduct a siege. He then asked the French court to direct Governor Beauharnois to support his efforts with a large detachment of Canadians and allied northern nations. Bienville's plan called for him to sail from New Orleans with his contingent, which purposely did not include the Choctaw, and rendezvous with the northern detachment at Chickasaw Bluffs. From there, the combined force would move against the Chickasaw villages.

It would not be until 1739 that Bienville's second campaign against the Chickasaw was put into motion. By summer the governor had landed at the Wolf River, near modern-day Memphis, and erected a stronghold named Fort Assumption. In August the governor was joined by the Canadian contingent under Captain Pierre-Joseph Céloron de Blainville, consisting of thirty Marine cadets, 170 Canadians, and a sizable detachment of three hundred Huron, Ottawa, Seneca, and a handful of other allied nations. Captain Alphonse de la Buissonniere, the new commander of Fort Chartes, and commandant of the Illinois country, also arrived with several hundred Illinois and a handful of French traders. While Bienville now had well over 2,500 men at his disposal, shortages, transportation delays, and illness quickly decimated his ranks. Winter and the new year soon arrived, with nothing to show for the effort but full hospitals and daily burials.

With his army incapable of conducting a campaign, Bienville turned to Celeron and the Canadian contingent to launch a winter attack against the

Chickasaw. Bienville, looking to end the campaign, made it clear to Celeron that he was looking for peace, and if any Chickasaw envoys appeared seeking this, he was to call off the attack. After a brief exchange of musket fire, the Chickasaw pursued just this path, asking Celeron for a truce. They too had tired of the war and wished to negotiate a settlement. By April 1740 the terms of a treaty had been agreed upon, leading Bienville to dismiss his forces.[19]

With a level of stability returned to the colony in June, the sixty-one-year-old Bienville, now in failing health, asked to return to France. The minister of the marine agreed to the request in October, but it would not be until May of 1743 that his replacement, Pierre de Riguad de Vaudreuil, the son of the former governor of Canada, arrived to replace him. In August, Bienville said his goodbyes, and after almost forty years of service to the colony, returned to France.

Part Three

War Drums in the South

CHAPTER THIRTEEN

Georgia and Jenkins' Ear

In South Carolina the summer of 1732 would bring a pandemic, supposedly via a vessel from the Leeward Islands. The "violent malignant feaver, which few have escaped," carried off several hundred in Charleston, according to Governor Johnson. Some retreated from the town to the countryside, while most in the latter stayed away from the port. Given the disruption, it was not until early November that the colonial assembly could meet. During this time Johnson received news that the king had granted a charter and a board of trustees for the colony of Georgia, which was to stretch from the Savannah River south to the Altamaha River and west to the source of these waters. Lord John Percival, who had promoted the project, was named the first president of the board. James Oglethorpe, a member of the board and another driving force behind the charter, would accompany the first colonists. Johnson was directed to help these settlers in any manner he could.

The official origins of Georgia concerned opportunities for "numbers of indigent persons who are reduced to such necessity as to become burthensome to the publick." These individuals, the petition claimed, would prefer to settle in His Majesty's plantations in America. More importantly, the new colony would provide a buffer between South Carolina and Spanish Florida, although there were still questions as to the location of the border between Spanish Florida and South Carolina. British claims extended far into Florida and even included St. Augustine, while the older Spanish claims reached as far north as Cape Hatteras. When viewing such dueling titles one English diplomat pointed out that Spanish Florida only had one settlement in its entire bounds: St. Augustine. If Georgia were settled by the English, it would only strengthen their claims through occupation.[1]

Oglethorpe, carrying the powers of governor, and some eighty colonists arrived at Charleston on January 13, 1733. Here they were met by Johnson, who had compiled a number of measures in support of the new colony. Given that the new settlement would act as a barrier against any threat posed by Spanish Florida or French Louisiana, the South Carolina Assembly had voted to provide Oglethorpe's party with over a hundred head of cattle and twenty-five hogs to stock the new settlers' herds. Twenty barrels of rice were also provided as well as a detachment of rangers in small boats that would protect the settlement until it had raised its own defenses.

Oglethorpe raised Georgia's first settlement at Savannah on the river of the same name. By the summer of 1733 a small fort had been erected, and most of the settlers had built homes. Oglethorpe had also met with the Creek and negotiated a peace treaty, which was essential for the safety of the colony. By 1735 Augusta had been laid out, and it would be garrisoned the next year. Several other smaller hamlets had sprung up as well, allowing Oglethorpe to report to the Board of Trade in August that he now had eight hundred men in the colony who could bear arms.

The Spanish and British did host talks to address the Florida-South Carolina border problem, but nothing came of the effort. With the erection of Savannah, Governor Francisco del Moral y Sanchez complained to the Spanish court that the English were in violation of the Treaty of Utrecht. Matters would get worse for Sanchez. The rapid growth of the British colony coupled with sporadic raids on the Florida frontier proved cause for alarm, as did the construction of Fort Frederica on St. Simon's Island near the mouth of the Altamaha River. Only seventy-five miles from St. Augustine, reports were that heavy cannons had arrived for this fort, as well as the forts at Savannah and Augusta.

While Sanchez was correct in regard to the provisions of the Treaty of Utrecht, it made little difference. Spanish power in Florida was simply too weak to oppose the growth of Georgia, and there was little interest on the part of the Spanish Crown to change this balance of power. This lack of resistance led the Georgians to push their claims to the northern bank of the St. John's River in Florida. With his hands tied, Sanchez negotiated with Oglethorpe in late 1736 to make this waterway the border between the two colonies, while the Spanish and British Crowns resolved the matter. In ad-

General James Oglethorpe, c. 1744. One of the founders of Georgia, and colonel of the first British regiments stationed in North America, Oglethorpe proved to be a tale of two generals. (*State Library and Achives of Florida, PR07725*)

dition, the treaty between the two governors pledged that each side would prevent their Native allies from conducting attacks on the other.[2]

Although the negotiations on the Georgia-Florida frontier were a source of tension between Britain and Spain, a larger issue was accelerating a conflict in the New World. Under the Treaty of Utrecht, the British had secured a number of rights to trade at Spanish ports in the Caribbean. One of these concessions was the *Asiento de Negros*, which allowed English traders to sell five thousand slaves a year to the Spanish colonies. Another was the *Navio de Permiso*, which allowed British vessels to call on the ports of Porto Bello and Vera Cruz. While neither of these activities proved particularly profitable, they did provide a thin veil for the real moneymaking enterprise: smuggling. A black market for British goods had formed among the Spanish colonies, which drew participants into the lucrative trade.

Spain had addressed this problem in the 1729 Treaty of Seville, which had ended the Anglo-Spanish War of 1727. Under the treaty Spanish governors were given the right to stop and inspect any vessels attempting to enter a Spanish port or appearing to be involved in contraband trade. The *guarda costas* employed by the various Spanish governors to fulfill this task and protect Spanish trade from pirates had carried several of their encounters to the extreme. One such instance in 1731 would bring a name to the upcoming conflict. Captain Robert Jenkins of the brig *Rebecca* was stopped and boarded off the Florida coast. The Spanish captain accused Jenkins of smuggling, seized his cargo, and reputedly cut off Jenkins' ear with his sword while insulting the British king.

Jenkins was hardly alone in this experience. By March 1735 attacks on British shipping near St. Kitts by Spanish privateers and the *guarda costa* had "begun an open war with H.M. subjects in these islands," Governor William Mathew informed the Duke of Newcastle. Mathew provided a long list of depositions to support his claim and asked the duke for Royal Navy support to enforce free navigation. Newcastle responded by requesting that the Board of Trade prepare a report, and any supporting papers, regarding losses suffered by British subjects from Spanish depredation in Europe and North America from the date of March 25, 1725.[3]

In the fall of 1736 this activity increased and carried through 1737 with fifteen reported encounters, most being captured. Some of the crews were whipped and carried to Havana where they were thrown into irons. Petitions of aid were sent to the king, and fear of war with Spain began to take hold among the British colonies in the Caribbean and in North America, particularly Georgia and South Carolina. These fears seemed well founded when rumors began to circulate that five hundred Spanish reinforcements had arrived at St. Augustine and that a fleet was outfitting at Havana. The Spanish plan was to launch a campaign with their Native allies against the Georgia frontier from St. Augustine while a Spanish fleet attacked by sea. While not all believed that the Spanish were planning an attack, with one observer concluding that, "it seems very unlikely that the Spaniards should bring a war in those parts," some were convinced. James Oglethorpe, who had returned to England in November 1736, informed Newcastle that the Spanish were planning to march on the Georgia frontier with five hundred soldiers and two thousand Native allies. In addition, the French who were currently fighting with the British-allied Chickasaw might join them. There was another problem as well. The citizens of South Carolina were encouraging the Creek to fall on the Florida frontier in a preemptive strike, and Oglethorpe was having a difficult time restraining them. If this should happen, counter to the agreement he had signed with the governor of St. Augustine, it would justify Spanish reprisals and might well trigger a large-scale expedition against Georgia or Charleston.

In Oglethorpe's mind it became a question of projecting strength, and to this end he requested a regiment of seven hundred men be raised in England for service in Georgia. He also asked for a trio of 20-gun frigates to secure the Georgia and South Carolina coast. The king agreed with Oglethorpe's suggestions and in June 1737 made him captain general of the militia of Georgia and South Carolina. In addition, Oglethorpe was appointed colonel

The southern coast from St. Augustine to Savannah showing the barrier islands and an expanded view of St. Simon's Island. (*Collections of the Georgia Historical Society*, VII [1913])

of a regiment of six hundred men, ordered to be raised for duty in the new colony.[4]

It proved anything but a speedy process, as it would not be until September 1738 that Oglethorpe returned to Georgia with his new regiment, the 42nd. The influx of manpower altered the dynamic on the Georgia-Florida frontier, although the troops selected proved troublesome. In November some of the troops drawn from the Gibraltar garrison mutinied at St. Andrew's. In the effort to suppress this act Oglethorpe was shot at twice, one time from so close that it singed his uniform with powder burns. "I am here in one of the most delightful situations as any man could wish to be," he wrote a friend after the incident. "A great number of debts, empty magazines, no money to supply them, numbers of people to be fed, mutinous soldiers to command, and a Spanish claim and a large body of their troops not far from us."[5]

Of just as much concern as Spanish military threats were the efforts made by Spanish emissaries with the Creek nations. During Oglethorpe's absence there had been repeated rumors that the French and Spanish were "very busy among the Creek and other neighboring nations of Indians in making presents, forming treaties and stirring them up against us." These rumors occasionally flared into alarms, but there were no serious indications that the Creek had considered such offers. To defuse any possibility of Spanish or French influence, Oglethorpe met with several Creek chieftains at Savannah in late October 1738. The Creek spoke to the efforts made by the Spanish to win over their allegiance, but they had refused and reconfirmed their alliance with the colony. "I am persuaded the nation will continue fixed in their fidelity to H.M.," Oglethorpe wrote Newcastle after the conference, "notwithstanding all the endeavors the Spanish have used, both by gifts and threats, to animate them against the English."[6]

While Oglethorpe saw to matters in Georgia, there were talks between Spain and Britain seeking to resolve a number of maritime and border issues between the two in the New World. In January 1739 there appeared to be some headway in these matters. Spanish and English envoys met at the El Pardo Palace in Madrid and signed the Convention of Pardo. Under the agreement the British accepted the Spanish offer to pay £95,000 in compensation for Spanish maritime acts, and in return Spain eventually agreed to only search vessels in territorial waters. The last major element of the agreement called for the British South Sea Company to pay the Spanish Crown £68,000, its share of the proceeds from the *Asiento de Negros*. Nothing substantive was accomplished in regard to the border between Florida and Georgia, but the representatives did agree to set up a commission to address this matter.

The Convention of Pardo was deeply unpopular when it reached London. The envoys had only managed to get about half of the £200,000 merchants had claimed in damages, and many thought that it did little to address the search and seizure of British vessels on the high seas. Prime Minister Horace Walpole did manage to get the convention ratified but only at the constant clamoring of the opposition party led by the Duke of Newcastle. At the urging of Newcastle, the South Seas Company refused to pay the agreed-upon sum. The Spanish responded that they would target the company's vessels to collect, which did little to calm the situation. The previous year the one-eared Captain Jenkins was paraded before Parliament, and although the story that he brought his severed ear to the proceedings in a glass jar was not true, the shouting and outrage toward Spain his presence spawned did not need any embellishment. The populace called for war, and on October 19, 1739, Parliament declared war on Spain. Walpole had been against the conflict, which might well bring France in on the side of Spain, but it was not enough. When the church bells began ringing through London announcing the news, Walpole shook his head. "They are ringing their bells now," he commented to a friend. "They will be wringing their hands soon." A few days later Newcastle would send a circular letter to the governors of the North American and Caribbean colonies informing them of the declaration of hostilities and authorizing them to issue letters of marque against Spanish shipping.[7]

Oglethorpe had spent the summer of 1739 negotiating a new treaty with his Creek and Cherokee allies while seeing to the defenses of Georgia. A number of settlements had sprung up along the river near Savannah. Forts and palisades protected these hamlets with First Fort and Fort Argyle on the Ogechee River providing a screen to the south. To the northwest the farthest post on the Savannah River was Fort Augusta while the rest of the colony lay along the coast farther south. At the mouth of the Altamaha River the Scottish Highland settlement of Darien had risen near the ruins of old Fort George, and not far away on Great St. Simon's Island Oglethorpe erected several forts. The first, called Fort St. Simon's, was located on the southern end of the island. The four-bastioned structure was built of earth faced with one-foot-thick timber and mounted a battery of heavy cannons to guard access to Jekyl Sound and thus the Altamaha River. Ten miles to the north, on the west side of the island, Oglethorpe raised Fort Frederica. The four-bastioned structure was built in the same manner as Fort St. Simon's and was supported by a second battery of cannons in a redout near the shoreline. A town was planted near the fort and encircled with a wooden palisade. Oglethorpe would use Frederica as his headquarters for much of the time he spent in Georgia. Farther south Fort St. Andrew's was erected on the northwest end of Cumberland Island, and several smaller posts were raised on Amelia Island, the closest point in the colony to St. Augustine. Oglethorpe's regiment garrisoned these island posts, with the majority of the troops stationed on St. Simon's Island.

Matters with the Spanish deteriorated further when a slave rebellion along the banks of the Stono River broke out on September 9, 1739. Led by an Angolan slave by the name of Jemmy, the score of escapees raided a nearby store and armed themselves before marching south, attacking homesteads and freeing other slaves along the way. This act delayed their march, allowing a detachment of militia to arrange an ambush near the Edisto River that resulted in the death of all but two or three of the group. There were ample explanations for the revolt and its timing, but given the political temperament of the moment, the finger was quickly pointed at Spanish Florida. One contemporary writer claimed that the insurrection would not have happened "had they not Depended on St. Augustine for a place of Reception afterwards was very certain, and that the Spaniards had a hand in prompting them to this particular Action, there was but little Room to Doubt."[8]

In late September Oglethorpe received a letter from the Crown ordering him to "annoy the Subjects of Spain" in whatever manner he could. The general would carry through with this directive. Sending envoys among the Creek, Chickasaw, and Cherokee he was able to recruit a sizable force. Just as importantly, he revoked the agreement made with Governor Sanchez in 1736 concerning restraining each side's Native allies and reported that some two hundred Creek had already marched toward Florida. "I hope the people of Carolina," Oglethorpe wrote the governor and Assembly of South Carolina, "will give the Necessary assistance, that we may begin with the Siege of Augustine before more Troops arrive there from Cuba."[9]

The response in South Carolina was as expected. St. Augustine had long been a threat to the colony, but just as in the opening days of Queen Anne's War, the question had once again become whether or not to launch an expedition against Castle San Marcos. With the memories of Governor James Moore's failed attempt to seize the fortress in 1702 once again brought to the forefront, the South Carolina Assembly agreed to the idea but asked for three things: a plan or scheme from General Oglethorpe, the probability of success, and what would be required from the colony to execute this design.

On November 13 a Spanish-Native war party landed on Amelia Island. The raid was in retaliation for an Anglo-Creek attack a few weeks before and at first appeared successful when the war party overwhelmed three sentries. They then attempted to surprise the fort but were quickly discovered and retreated back to their boats to the occasional discharge of the garrison's cannons. For Oglethorpe the attack only furthered his resolve to strike at St. Augustine. Given this, he asked the Georgia trustees to send powder, artillery, and some gunners. "The best expedient I can think of is to strike first," he informed the trustees.

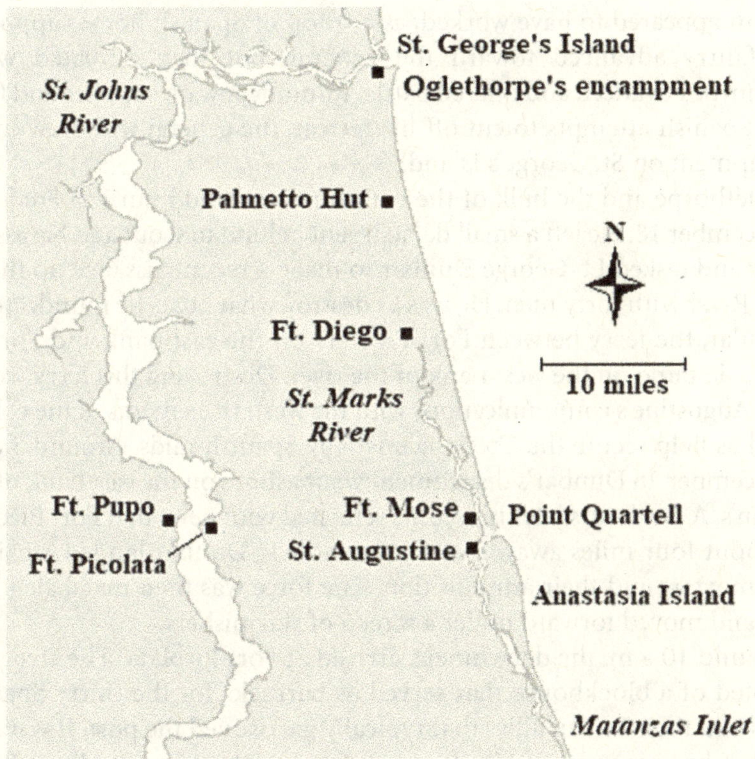

Spanish outposts to the north and west of St. Augustine.

> And as our strength consists in men and that the people of the colony as well as the soldiers handle their arms well and are desirous of action, I think the best way is to make use of our strength and beat them out of the field and destroy their plantations and outsettlements (in which the Indians who are very faithful can assist us) and to form the siege of Augustine if I can get artillery.[10]

Responding to what he believed was a clear breach of the peace, Oglethorpe raised a detachment of two hundred rangers, soldiers, Chickasaw, Yuchi, and Creek and set sail for Florida on December 1. He landed on St. George's Island and made camp. Crossing the St. John's River, Oglethorpe pushed south toward the outskirts of St. Augustine. He chased a small Spanish garrison out of a newly built outpost before spending the rest of his time killing cattle and destroying crops. With too few men to attack St. Augustine Oglethorpe hoped to draw the Spanish out into the open. For a moment the plan appeared to have worked, as a troop of Spanish horse supported by infantry advanced toward the general, but they retreated when Oglethorpe advanced and offered battle. Running low on supplies and fearful of Spanish attempts to cut off his retreat, the general withdrew to his encampment on St. George's Island.

Oglethorpe and the bulk of the detachment would return to Frederica on December 18. He left a small detachment behind to scout and harass the enemy and tasked Lt. George Dunbar to make a reconnaissance up the St. John's River with forty men. He was to destroy what boats he found, and in particular, the ferry between Fort Picolata on the east bank and Fort St. Francis de Pupo on the west bank of the river. Destroying this ferry would cut St. Augustine's communications with the western elements of the colony as well as help secure the Creek against any Spanish raids. Around 3 a.m. on December 28 Dunbar's detachment went ashore on the east bank of the St. John's. A few hours later his scouts returned with news that Fort Picolata was about four miles away. Deciding to attack, Dunbar landed a pair of small mortars and their ammunition. The force was then marshaled into ranks and moved forward under a screen of skirmishers.

Around 10 a.m. the detachment arrived at Fort Picolata. The structure consisted of a blockhouse that served as barracks for the thirty Spanish troops and their Indian allies that typically garrisoned the post. It was surrounded by a wooden palisade and armed with a few small cannons. Oglethorpe had given Dunbar permission to attack the fort if he thought it was weak, and believing that this was the case, the lieutenant ordered his men forward. The open terrain about the fort created problems for Dunbar's troops. "We were within fifty yards of the fort without the least shelter," one soldier recalled. The two sides exchanged musketry, and the bark of swivel guns from the fort sprayed grapeshot among the attackers. Dunbar's gun crews finally positioned their mortars, adding the deep thump of these guns to the din.

The two sides skirmished for a few hours before Dunbar, who had suffered a handful of casualties, withdrew and returned to Frederica. For the exhausted seven-man Spanish garrison it was a relief. They had lost one of their number but somehow managed to keep up enough of a fire upon the enemy that they never realized the weak state of the garrison. This latter part was complicated when the small cannon in the blockhouse jumped off its mounts after the first discharge, leaving only a few swivel guns to assist the defenders. While Dunbar believed that the mortar rounds had not produced any effect on the stronghold, the two that burst within the compound nearly ended the engagement, structurally damaging the blockhouse and

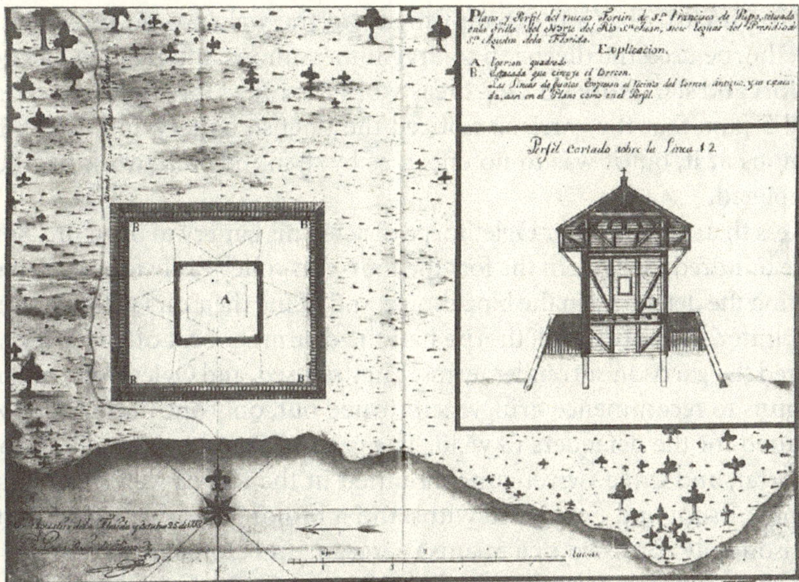

A 1738 plan of Fort St. Francisco de Pupo on the west bank of the St. Johns River. The post was essentially a large blockhouse surrounded by a wooden stockade. Fort Picolata located across the river on the east bank was laid out in a similar fashion. (*Castillo de San Marcos National Monument*)

palisade walls to the point they had to be braced to prevent their falling down. In fact, once Dunbar retreated, the garrison agreed that the fort was too badly damaged to defend and abandoned the structure.[11]

Oglethorpe returned to Frederica and began assembling a much larger force with the aim of destroying both Fort St. Francis and Fort Picolata. Leading a force of militia, regulars, and Native allies, several hundred in all, on New Years' Day 1740 he landed in Florida near the St. John's River. After a number of difficulties, Oglethorpe split his forces. On the morning of January 7, he sent a party of Creek and Chickasaw ahead to scout Fort Picolata. After watching the structure in the morning mists and seeing no signs of sentries, the war party rushed the walls and with a shout were inside, only to find that the stronghold was deserted. After searching the location for anything of value they put it to the torch and returned to their boats.

To the north Oglethorpe landed with the main body of his forces and quickly invested Fort St. Francis. The area about the fort was generally open with the exception of a few clusters of trees that approached the walls. The Yuchi, Creek, and Chickasaw quickly found this cover and began a fusillade on the fort. The garrison returned fire with muskets and small cannon, making it clear that any attempt to storm the walls would prove costly. Oglethorpe used the diversion to drag four cannons into the tree line near the fort and start work on a log breastwork to protect these guns. It was not until 5 p.m. that the garrison noticed the English battery and fired a few cannons at it, but it was to no effect, as by then the breastwork had been completed.

Less than an hour later Oglethorpe ordered his battery to open fire. Some three hundred yards from the fort the four-gun volley easily found its mark, shaking the defenders in the blockhouse and filling their ears with the sound of splintering timber. Oglethorpe had the drummer beat out a parley and offered the garrison surrender terms. They refused, and Oglethorpe ordered his guns to recommence firing. As it turned out, only one more volley was required for the defenders to yield. The general found two small cannons, a mortar, and three swivel guns mounted in the fort as well as an ample supply of shot and powder to withstand a prolonged siege. However, the garrison only consisted of a Spanish sergeant and eleven men. It was typically three times this size, but the Spanish governor had withdrawn the rest back to St. Augustine after the general's first foray into Florida in December.

Oglethorpe repaired the fort and assigned a forty-man garrison. The location was well suited to prevent Spanish forces from moving north against the Creek or Georgia. It also provided a possible invasion path for the English. The landing at Picolata, the general noted, "is within 21 miles of Augustine, and the Countrey between is full & Stocked with Cattle and Horses." Of even more interest was the testimony of some of the prisoners. Oglethorpe and his officers were able to obtain a good description of Castle San Marcos and eyed each other when the prisoners noted that it was constructed of soft stone. There were fifty cannons mounted in the Castle, some of which were 24-pounders. The nearby town was surrounded by an extensive set of outworks supported by small cannons at key points. What interested Oglethorpe the most was the prisoners' estimation of the garrison at Castle San Marcos. The consensus was that there were 565 Spanish troops and perhaps as many militia, freed slaves, convicts, and Indian allies that would be raised to support this force.[12]

Armed with this intelligence, as well as letters from captured Spanish vessels speaking to supply shortages and discontent among the garrison, Oglethorpe traveled to Frederica in late January to organize an expedition against the Spanish stronghold.

CHAPTER FOURTEEN

Oglethorpe's Campaign

When he reached Frederica, Oglethorpe wrote Lt. Governor William Bull of South Carolina about his exploits and the need to strike at St. Augustine before it was reinforced. "If we do not attack, we shall be attacked," he emphasized. This was followed by an estimate of what the general would require: 1,000 militia, 105 Rangers, 800 Black slaves acting as pioneers, and 58 officers and translators for the estimated 2,000 Cherokee, Chickasaw, and Creek he would raise for the effort. To this he would add 400 men of his 42nd Regiment and whatever artillery he could lay his hands on. Six months of provisions were to be supplied to the colonial force and three for the allied nations accompanying the expedition. In addition, these latter forces were to be outfitted with a gun, hatchet, and blanket.

A committee assembled to consider Oglethorpe's proposal calculated the total expense at £209,492 and gave their opinion that it was "too great for this Province to Bear." Instead, the committee proposed an alternate solution. They would agree to raise £120,000 if the general was convinced that the task could be accomplished within these financial bounds. In keeping with this reduction, the committee suggested a new force which would consist of a 480-man South Carolina regiment, a troop of 50 horses, 300 militia, 400 Black slaves, and 1,000 Native allies. When the 400 men in the general's regiment were added in, it tallied to a little over 2,600 men.

With news of war between Spain and Britian having arrived in the interim, Oglethorpe informed the committee in late March that the endeavor could be accomplished for this amount or, in the case of instant success, for far less. He then asked for the half of the South Carolina regiment to be raised from Charleston to speed up the assembling of his forces. The rest would come from Georgia and the southern sections of South Carolina. He dismissed the militia and Black slaves, as they would take too long to organize, and now only asked for five hundred Native allies but insisted on equipping this force as in his first estimates. He would raise two companies of rangers and equip them with horses, two independent companies of a hundred Highlanders from the Darien militia, and another independent company from the settlers in Georgia. He required a battery of eight 6-pound cannons on field carriages, a large mortar, a number of Coehorns, and ample ammunition for the artillery train. Of more importance was transport. Dozens of small vessels would be required to carry his regiment and the colonial troops to the rendezvous point at Port Royal. Here, after combining with his allies, and filling out a pair of ranger companies, the force would set sail for a sudden descent on St. Augustine.

Money, Oglethorpe informed the committee, he could manage, but time and circumstances he could not. He needed a decision quickly for a number of reasons. First, reports were arriving that the Spanish stronghold was desperately short on provisions, pointing to now being the time to strike. Second, he still had to notify Commodore Vincent Pearce to have his squadron rendezvous with the attacking forces to blockade the Spanish port. Even here time was critical, as Pearce would only be able to stay on station until the seasonal storms appeared. Third, the Cherokee, Creek, and Chickasaw were assembling and ready for the campaign, as was his regiment, but if the forces called up in Georgia and South Carolina could not be assembled in fourteen days, the general would have to abort the campaign and shift to protecting the frontier from Spanish raids. As with Moore two generations before, Oglethorpe pressed for speed not to surprise the garrison, which would be difficult to resolve given that he had spent the last several months attacking positions near St. Augustine, but in order to invest and hopefully overwhelm the defenders before a relief force could reach them.[1]

For Florida Governor Don Manuel de Montiano the loss of Forts St. Francis and Picolata, only a half day's march away, had not only given the English control over the St. John's River but left St. Augustine isolated from Apalachee. Montiano's scouts had warned him of a large English force in the St. John's and of Oglethorpe's capture of Fort St. Francis, but there was little the governor could do except monitor the situation. He lacked the resources to challenge for control of the river, without which he could neither establish a fort farther downriver to isolate the English post or even launch an effort to take back Fort St. Francis. "Lacking such forces," he wrote of his plight, "there is no remedy, and that is precisely why I have not sent out by land, a large detachment, for it would require at the same time, a strong expedition by sea." He pleaded with his superiors in Cuba to send half a dozen shallow draft galleys, "well manned with good crews, under a mariner of proved valor and skill." These shallow draft vessels could be fitted with cannons and used to assert naval control over the St. John's as well as secure St. Augustine's harbor. "For without this help," Montiano continued, "it is a physical impossibility for me to carry out my plans, and as a matter of fact we shall see ourselves shut up in a corner, without a single man that dares leave the place for any purpose whatever." Not that it would matter, as the provisions would soon run out unless relief was sent.[2]

Looking to erect a new post downriver of Fort St. Francis on March 9, 1740, Montiano sent engineer Don Pedro Ruiz de Olano and a detachment of cavalry to select a location. The scouting party returned a few days later having chosen the narrows of San Nicholas. The bluffs on either shore and the narrow waterway, which could be obstructed with a wooden boom or a chain, made it an ideal location. A pair of forts, one on either bank, would catch any vessel attempting to navigate the obstacles in a crossfire, and if the requested galleys appeared, they could seek shelter in the river under the guns of these strongholds.

On April 14, the governor's incessant pleas for ships paid off. Six galleys led by Captains Don Juan Fandino and Don Francisco del Castillo arrived at St. Augustine. The vessels not only gave Montiano the naval forces he sought, but their crews added another 122 men to the garrison, raising his overall numbers to 735. The arrival was also well timed in that a pair of English frigates appeared off the bar a few days later. On the twentieth only a single frigate could be seen, leading the galley commanders to consider an attack. Supported by a pair of armed launches and fifty soldiers, the plan had been to cross the bar under the cover of darkness and attack at first light, but a sloop was spotted to the north at sunset, delaying the flotilla's departure until dawn.

On the morning of the twenty-first, the Spanish vessels cleared the bar, and as the mists began breaking up, they spotted a British warship, alone and becalmed. Fandino and Castillo ordered their men to pull on their oars as the galleys looked to board the warship. The enemy vessel turned out to be the 20-gun H.M.S. *Squirrel*, which launched a volley of grape and chain shot at the approaching Spanish warships. Any thoughts of boarding were quickly dismissed as this was followed by 12-pound cannonballs that skipped past on the surface of the water before disappearing in an arching spray. The 9-pound cannons on the galleys responded for over two hours as the craft maneuvered until Fandino and Castillo were able to achieve the weather gauge and break off the engagement. The flotilla returned to St. Augustine with nothing to show for the effort but a few holes in their vessels. There was some good news, as a few days later a vessel loaded with provisions arrived from Cuba. It was nowhere near enough to meet the governor's projected needs, but he was grateful nonetheless.[3]

With the South Carolina Assembly and Oglethorpe agreeing on the proposed plans and allocated monies, on April 5, 1740, an act was passed by the house calling for a military expedition against St. Augustine. Oglethorpe had successfully made his case with one member of the South Carolina Assembly, recalling that, "It Readily occurred to the Committee what Glorious Success had often Crowned attempts of such a nature merely from their Suddenness and a vigorous Execution of them." Any opposition to the effort had rapidly vanished when news of Britain's declaration of war against Spain arrived, and along with this, a letter from Newcastle directing Oglethorpe to attack St. Augustine. To support this endeavor a squadron of Royal Navy warships under the command of Commodore Pearce had been dispatched to cruise the colonial coast. Oglethorpe was directed to call upon these forces whenever he felt ready to advance on the Spanish stronghold.

As the provisions were being procured and the troops recruited, Oglethorpe met with Commodore Pearce and Colonel Alexander Vander Dussen, who would command the South Carolina regiment. The trio first decided to shift the rendezvous point to St. George's Island on the north side of the St. John's River, much closer to their intended target than Port Royal. The commodore would use several of his warships to transport the artillery from Frederica while the H.M.S. *Squirrel* took up station off the St. Augustine bar to blockade the port. In addition, Lt. Governor Bull had purchased a schooner and equipped it with fourteen guns. Pearce had placed one of his lieutenants in command and intended to employ the craft in the shallow waters about St. Augustine.

The agreed-upon plan called for Pearce to blockade the harbor while Oglethorpe attacked the fort and the nearby town from the landside. The general proposed moving on the town first. This would lead many of the 2,500 or so inhabitants to seek shelter within Castle San Marcos. If an opportunity presented itself in the chaos, he would attempt to storm the fort; otherwise he would call upon the commander of the garrison, now overwhelmed with logistical issues, to surrender. If he refused, Oglethorpe would bombard the structure with mortar fire. With the panicked citizens confined within the structure this alone might force a surrender. If not, he would ask South Carolina to forward pioneers and heavy artillery. Once these arrived, he would open siege trenches and systematically reduce the fortress.[4]

With a number of his forces yet to be raised or furnished transport, Oglethorpe put together a mosquito fleet of small sloops, schooners, pirogues, and scout boats and set sail with an advanced guard in mid-May. By the twentieth, he was encamped on St. George's Island with 220 men of his own regiment, 125 South Carolinians, and 103 Native allies, almost all of whom were Cherokee. The latter brought in a Spanish prisoner that evening. The scouting party reported a fort they had seen halfway between St. George's Island and St. Augustine while the prisoner informed the general that four Spanish galleys had arrived from Cuba and were to operate on the St. John's River.

Oglethorpe crossed the St. John's and established a camp on the south bank of the river the next morning. He then gathered together the bulk of his forces and marched south toward the reported fort. The sandy trail along the coast slowed his column and forced him to abandon a 4-pound cannon, which, without horses, was being dragged by hand. While the column made camp that evening, Oglethorpe sent Captain-Lieutenant Primrose Maxwell ahead with a detachment of regulars, Carolinians, and Cherokee to invest the Spanish stronghold. Maxwell arrived around midnight and surrounded Fort Diego, a fifteen-foot-tall palisade structure with bastions at two corners. Inside was the living quarters for Don Diego Espinosa's cattle ranch. Espinosa had originally built the structure to protect himself and his workers from raiders, but as the ranch grew in importance the Spanish governor had sent several small cannons as well as a garrison to the location.

Positioning his men about the fort, Maxwell attacked at dawn. However, the defenders proved alert, and with the terrain around the fort cleared for several hundred yards, they soon halted Maxwell's advance. Oglethorpe and the rest of the army arrived a few hours later to sporadic sniping between the participants. The general encamped near the fort and the next morning sent a Spanish prisoner forward with a surrender demand. Outnumbered and with no likelihood of relief, the garrison agreed and marched out of the fort.[5]

Oglethorpe was pleased with the location, which was a four-hour march from St. Augustine, and planned to use the post as a staging point for his advance on the town. He ordered a ditch dug about the fort and garrisoned the post with fifty men before returning to the St. John's encampment with his troops. For the next several weeks the general would be occupied in shuttling men and supplies from the encampments on the St. John's to this location. In one instance the column was ambushed by a Spanish-Native war party, which resulted in a running skirmish and several holes being shot through Oglethorpe's cloak. There were also a number of false alarms resulting in exhausting sun-scorched marches and the expedition's first casualties when several men died of heat stroke. The good news was that Pearce arrived at St. George's on May 29 with the *Flamborough* and *Phoenix*. Onboard was Colonel Vander Dussen, a number of Carolina troops, and the expedition's artillery.

After a few long-range scouts of the Spanish town, Oglethorpe decided to send a pair of Spanish prisoners taken at Fort Diego to St. Augustine with promises of good terms for those who would desert. There was disagreement concerning the idea, which one of the general's officers claimed would only alert the Spanish as to "our real Strength and Numbers, and also our Situation." Oglethorpe ignored the advice and sent the men.[6]

Governor Montiano was shocked when Espinosa's foreman appeared before him with news of Oglethorpe's Cherokee scouts having taken a prisoner near Fort Diego on the evening of May 20. Although the incident occurred almost two weeks prior, the governor had received no other reports regarding the status of the fort. He immediately sent a twelve-man detachment north to answer this question, and two days later, when they failed to return, he sent a cavalry detachment in search of the first detachment. This party returned not long after with news that they could not approach the fort because of heavy enemy patrols. This seemed to answer the governor's question, and a few days later he summoned a council of war.

After a lengthy discussion it was agreed to dispatch a force of three hundred men and retake Fort Diego. It proved a short march, as Spanish scouts reported a strong detachment of English drawn up near the fort ready to meet them, enough so as to convince the officers in charge to return to Castle San Marcos. For Montiano it was clear that an attack was imminent. The English were "establishing storehouses at San Diego for food and stores, in preparation for the siege of this place," he wrote the Cuban Governor Don Juan Francisco de Guemas y Horcasitas. "I am persuaded of this too from their having shown to-day five vessels in addition to the two that have now been watching this bar and that of Matanzas for a long time." Short on provisions and with a near panicked populace on his hands, Montiano pleaded with his superior to send a powerful fleet to drive away the British warships. "I doubt very much if help can be got in in any other way, or if we can exist much longer without supplies, shut in by the enemy on sea and land."[7]

As dismal as the situation appeared to Montiano, indecision, poor planning, and flagging morale within Oglethorpe's army would still give him some time. After three weeks of patrols, scouts, and incremental movements the Creek contingent threatened to go home unless they attacked St. Augustine. The Cherokee were also tired of the maneuvering, and when scolded by the general for killing Spanish cattle, they threatened to leave. Their war chief Caesar noted that, "it was a strange thing that they were permitted to Kill the Spaniards, but not their Cattle." There was also discontent concerning Oglethorpe's behavior. The general refused to let the Carolina troops requisition horses from local livestock, and houses encountered were not to be burned or plundered, being potentially useful to the advance the general claimed.

By June 10 Oglethorpe was prepared to advance on St. Augustine. The vanguard, consisting of a hundred Creek, Cherokee, and rangers departed Fort Diego at sunset. They were followed shortly thereafter by Oglethorpe with three hundred volunteers and soldiers of his own regiment, while the four hundred men of Colonel Vander Dussen's regiment formed the rear guard. It proved a perilous march. Swamps, creeks, and tangles of brush impeded progress. Oglethorpe rested his troops through the day and resumed the march that evening. It proved far worse than the first night as thunderstorms pelted the troops with rain and made it so dark that they could only see a few yards ahead of them. The storm would subside, exposing the rising moon, and a few hours before sunrise on June 13, the column halted at a fork in the road two miles from St. Augustine.

Colonel William Palmer, who had led raids in the area during the Anglo-Spanish conflict of 1727-1729, knew where they were. The road to the left led to Fort Mose, a four-bastioned earth and wood fort that acted as shelter against raiders for several plantations run by freed Black slaves. The road ahead led to St. Augustine. With several hours of darkness still before them Palmer asked Oglethorpe for two hundred Carolinians and a party of Creek and Cherokee to attack and burn the town. Oglethorpe denied the request, calling it too hazardous an undertaking. A few words passed between Palmer and the general, but the latter was adamant that the town would not be burned. Instead, he informed the colonel, "That it was the Custom of Armies, always to shew themselves to the Enemy first, and to make a feint."[8]

With that the general motioned for the column to take the road to Fort Mose. Oglethorpe arrived at the post around daylight to find that it had been abandoned. Here he halted the army and made camp. Around 8:00 a.m. Oglethorpe departed with Colonel Vander Dussen and a mounted escort to scout Castle San Marcos. The party approached close enough to the structure that Oglethorpe had a drummer and a line of soldiers advance toward the stronghold to the beat of the "Grenadier's March." The act was responded to by a discharge of a cannon from the fort, which seemed to delight Oglethorpe who quickly recalled his troops and returned to camp.

Both Oglethorpe and Vander Dussen agreed that the Spanish fort was a strongly built, regular work with a number of recent outworks having been erected. More importantly, it would be impractical to attack the fort from the landside. There were no roads to bring up the siege guns, some of which weighed up to three tons, and once established here, the supply lines would be difficult to secure, particularly if the town was not to be taken. However, after surveying the area, both men agreed that Point Quartell near the north entrance to the harbor would make a good site for a battery, as would the northern point of Anastasia Island. It would require the army to fall back to Fort Diego in order to reach the new positions, but from these locations they could bombard the fort and maintain communications with Commodore Pearce's squadron.

As Oglethorpe was returning to his tent, he encountered Lt. Jonathan Bryan of the Carolina volunteers who had just returned from scouting the town. Bryan reported that everything there was in chaos and confusion. He then asked the general if they should not take advantage of this and strike at the town. There would be no better time to do it. Oglethorpe shook his head and informed the lieutenant that it would cost the army three hundred men to storm the town, and that was a risk he was not willing to take.[9]

CHAPTER FIFTEEN

The Siege of St. Augustine

On the morning of June 14, Oglethorpe's troops formed up outside Fort Mose. The general then ordered the main gate destroyed, the walls breached, and the structures in the compound put to the torch before marching back to Fort Diego to the sound of fife and drum. A number of men collapsed under the blazing sun and high humidity, but the bulk of the column arrived at the stronghold before sunset. A few days later Oglethorpe received good news. A Chickasaw and Yuchi war party had arrived at the camp on the St. John's. They, along with a detachment of South Carolinians, were on their way to Fort Diego. In addition, the H.M.S. *Tartar* had anchored off of Palmetto Hut, an outpost along the coast between Fort Diego and the camp on the south bank of the St. John's River. The warship put ashore some supplies and reinforcements, as well as several letters from Commodore Pearce. While the influx of troops and supplies brought about a few happy reunions and a wave of activity, morale problems were beginning to surface within Oglethorpe's camp. All but two of the company of South Carolina volunteers marched off to the St. John's camp, tired of the "perpetual Marches" and "disappointed in their Expectations of Attacking the Town of St. Augustine." Given their status there was little Oglethorpe could do, but as it turned out, they made it no farther than the St. John's where they encountered a number of volunteers just arriving and were convinced to join their ranks.[1]

That evening the general ordered Colonel Vander Dussen to march the South Carolina regiment to Point Quartell. Short on provisions and without horses to carry their supplies, it proved an arduous trek, but the following morning Vander Dussen's men were encamped on the east side of Point Quartell. Arrayed before them was the welcome sight of four British warships stationed off the main bar. The colonel sent runners back to the camp on the St. John's with orders for boats to bring provisions to the point and a letter for the captain of the H.M.S. *Tartar* requesting that he sail to Point Quartell and begin landing the 18-pound cannons and their carriages.

While the Carolina troops waited, Vander Dussen and several of his officers surveyed the Spanish fort and town from the top of the sandbank that dominated the point. Castle San Marcos proved farther away than originally thought, close to 2,200 yards with the center of the town several hundred yards beyond this. What was of more immediate concern was the six galleys anchored before the fort. Vander Dussen and his officers returned to camp believing they had found a good location for a battery of guns on the western side of the point. A few hours later the cry of a sentry informed the colonel that three of the enemy galleys were moving toward their position. Believing that the Spanish might attempt a landing he formed up the regiment and marched down to the beach. The galleys, taken back by the sudden appearance of over three hundred men, fired a score of cannonballs at the Carolinians, but none came close. Seeing that the Spanish were not prepared to attack, Vander Dussen marched his men back from the shore, and after monitoring the enemy's withdrawal, the vessels returned to St. Augustine.

Not long after three British longboats pulled ashore near Vander Dussen's encampment. The fire from the Spanish galleys had alerted Commodore Pearce to Vander Dussen's position, giving him the opportunity to establish communications and deliver a letter to Oglethorpe. The letter held the results and recommendations of a council of war held by Pearce and his captains. The first point behind this gathering was to answer a question posed by Oglethorpe: How long could the fleet stay? It was the unanimous opinion of the council that July 16 was the latest, and it might well be earlier if indications of the seasonal storms appeared. There was also agreement that the squadron could provide two hundred men to help secure Anastasia Island and erect batteries within a mile of Castle San Marcos and the town.

Oglethorpe, who was at Palmetto Hut, received the letter the next day and remarked that it was precisely what he wanted to do. He then countermanded Vander Dussen's request for artillery and only sent him a few boats with provisions and a handful of troops. The general then dispatched 132

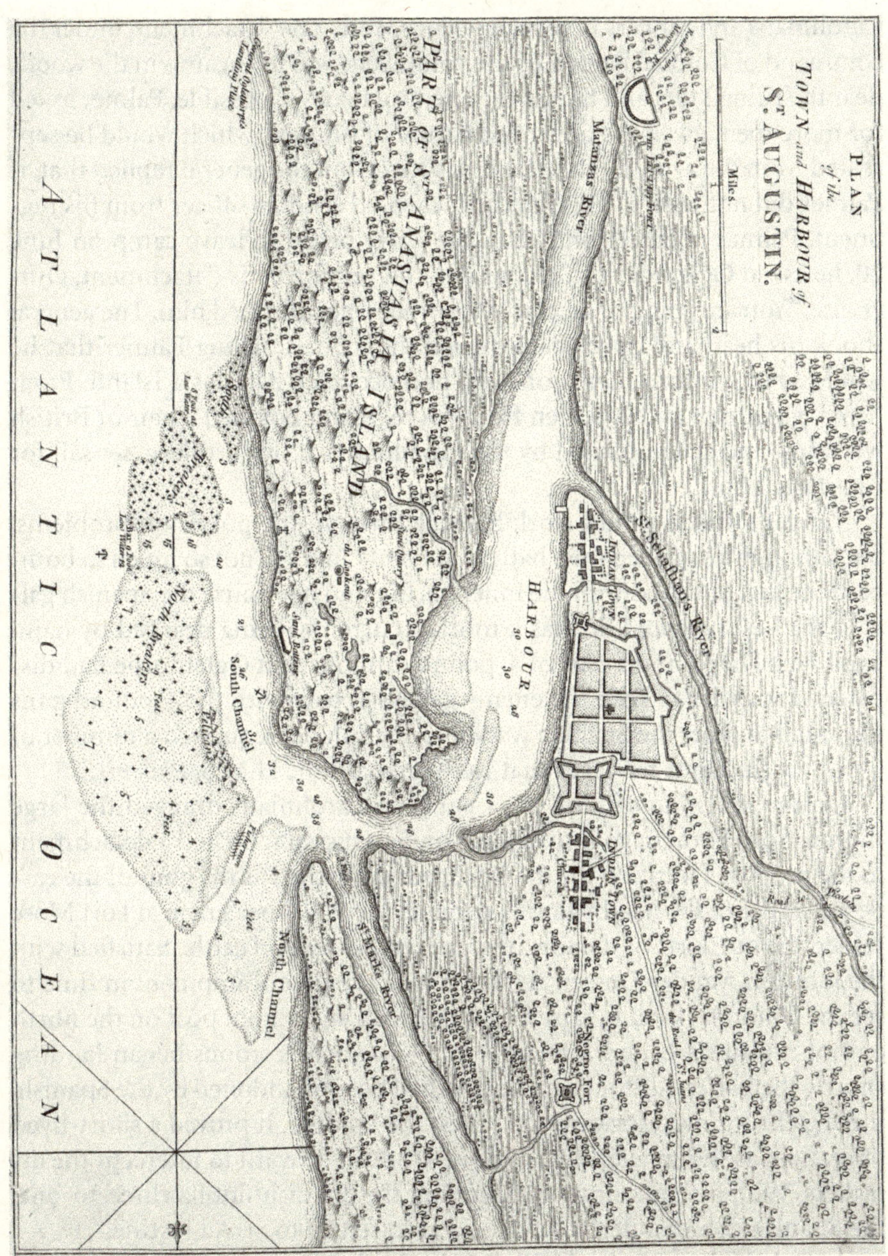

A view of St. Augustine, c.1740. (*Norman B. Leventhal Map Collection, Boston Public Library*)

Carolinians and rangers to reoccupy Fort Mose. The detachment, under the command of Colonel Palmer of the volunteers, was to encamp in the woods near the ruined fort and harass the enemy whenever possible. Palmer asked for more men, given the advanced nature of his post, which would be separated from the army by the St. Mark's River, but the general replied that, if Palmer did not wish to go, Oglethorpe would send an officer from his regiment. Palmer relented, but when the party began to leave camp on June 20, he asked Oglethorpe to reconsider and reinforce his detachment. Otherwise, "You are going to sacrifice these men," he informed him. The general shook his head and once again denied the request, telling Palmer that he would send reinforcements once he had occupied Anastasia Island. From here Oglethorpe and 275 men from his regiment boarded a pair of British warships, and accompanied by the expedition's heavy artillery, set sail for Anastasia Island.[2]

Vander Dussen would work his way through the provision problems, but although he pressed for a battery at Point Quartell, not so much to bombard the fort but to control the inner harbor and neutralize the Spanish galleys, the best he could do was a mortar, currently being dragged by hand from Fort Diego, and a pair of 4-pound cannons that Oglethorpe had dispatched in order to keep the enemy galleys at bay. With the 4-pound guns too small to deter the Spanish warships, the colonel requested a number of 6-pound guns and carriages that were onboard the H.M.S. *Phoenix*.

On the morning of June 23, a party of Carolinians dragged the large mortar from Fort Diego into camp. Vander Dussen marched a detachment to the proposed location for the battery and watched as the guns of the castle and those of the nearby flotilla flared to life as Palmer's men at Fort Mose raided the outskirts of the fort in search of horses and cattle. Satisfied with the location, Vander Dussen returned to the main encampment in time to see the Union Jack being raised over the Spanish lookout post on the north end of Anastasia Island. The bulk of Oglethorpe's troops began landing shortly thereafter. Although the island had been abandoned by the Spanish, three galleys moved forward to contest the landing. It proved a short-lived operation, as the smaller British sloops moved forward to intercept the attackers. With a single sloop outgunning the Spanish flotilla three-to-one, the Spanish commander wisely decided to return to St. Augustine.

As Oglethorpe secured the island, Vander Dussen brought three 6-pound cannons and a pair of carriages ashore from the *Phoenix*. Although the carriage for the mortar had not been landed, the next morning the colonel ordered the mortar and a pair of 6-pound guns dragged to a position on the west side of the point. Lacking a carriage for the mortar and the carriages for the 6-pounders proving worthless, the decision was made to mount the guns in the sand. That is to say, the guns were positioned on a sand bank and aimed by muscling them into place. After discharge they would drive themselves into the sand and had to be dug out and repositioned all over again. While Vander Dussen's men prepared the new battery, a handful of Spanish galleys advanced and fired on Oglethorpe's position.

Around 8 a.m. Vander Dussen was able to distract the enemy vessels when he ordered the mortar fired. The hollow thump echoed over the harbor as the bomb arched toward its destination, exploding over the fort a few seconds later. There was a cheer from the Carolinian gunners and surprise among the Spanish warships. The latter advanced on Point Quartell, firing their bow guns, but Vander Dussen's 6-pounders returned fire, dropping a pair of shots among the attackers who, content with their work, broke off the engagement and returned to St. Augustine. Their departure was fortunate for Vander Dussen and his men, as it would take close to an hour to dig the guns out of the sand and prepare them to fire again.[3]

Governor Montiano noted that a few splinters had landed in the fort, but most of the bombs from Point Quartell passed over the structure. The fort occasionally returned fire, but for Montiano there were more pressing concerns. The handful of shots that went over Castle San Marcos had gone off in or near the northern part of the town. Combined with signs of an English encampment on Anastasia Island, even closer to the town and fort, it had set off a panicked flight among the settlers. "The families have abandoned their houses," the governor wrote of the situation, "and come to put themselves under protection of the guns, which is pitiable, though nothing gives me anxiety but the want of provisions." Now several weeks into the siege, rationing food, under fire, and with enemy batteries being erected even closer, Montiano made it clear to the governor of Cuba that if he could not send relief, "we must all indubitably perish."[4]

Oddly, it was Vander Dussen's determination to bring the fort and the Spanish flotilla under fire that had fulfilled Oglethorpe's original plan to force the inhabitants into the fort in order to strain the garrison's provisions. Pleased with the effects of his guns, Vander Dussen took a small boat over to Anastasia Island to confer with Oglethorpe about expanding his battery with heavy cannons. Here the colonel found a battery of 18-pound cannons, but the general informed him these were to be moved to the west side of the island. Oglethorpe and Vander Dussen then advanced with a small detachment to view the proposed location for the new battery, a little under a mile from the fort. The Spanish gunners at Castle San Marcos fired on the scouting party, at which point they returned to the landing area. Both men agreed that the battery should go forward, and Oglethorpe agreed to send more provisions to Vander Dussen, as well as any artillery he could spare. He approved of the cannons being taken from Fort Diego to support the colonel's efforts, which would provide cover fire against the galleys while the siege batteries were erected on the island. With a path settled upon, Vander Dussen returned to Quartell Point before sunset.

Noting the enemy's shift of focus to Point Quartell and Anastasia Island, Montiano's officers began to eye the English outpost at Fort Mose. This Anglo-Indian force had made frequent raids about the town and fort, but now with the bulk of the English forces having shifted to the other side of the St. Mark's River, this position was isolated. It appeared that the enemy had given them a chance to strike back, and the governor agreed that the garrison should attack. On the evening of June 25, three hundred Spanish and a number of their Native allies, under the command of Captain Antonio Salgado, crept out of Castle San Marcos and advanced on Fort Mose. Here they found many of Palmer's men encamped in and about the ruins of the fort, with little in the way of sentries. Still undiscovered, Salgado arranged his forces in hushed movements and waited for daylight to launch an attack.

It would turn out Oglethorpe made a more serious mistake than just sending too few men to repel a sally from the Spanish garrison. He also failed to notify the other officers in the detachment of his decision to place Palmer in command, in particular Captain Hugh MacKay and Captain John MacKintosh. When the detachment reached Fort Mose, these two captains and over half the force casually encamped within the ruined fort. Palmer scolded both officers, pointing out that his rangers were purposely encamping outside the "mousetrap," where they could face an attacker in the open. Both MacKay and MacKintosh ignored the comments, and without written orders from Oglethorpe to the contrary, there was little Palmer could do, as MacKay, a captain in the 42nd, was technically senior officer via his regular army commission. As such, both MacKay and MacKintosh, who commanded an independent company from Georgia, dismissed Palmer's advice. Without authority, Palmer turned to passion and persuasion, making his case over and over again, "Particularly, that they should all rise at four every morning, and Stand to their Arms, because the Indians are constantly used to make an Attack, just before Break of day." Many would soon wish they had paid more attention.[5]

Around 4:30 the next morning Salgado's troops, divided into four parties, surged forward. The attackers were well within a hundred yards before the sentries in the fort began to shout out warnings. Sporadic shots followed

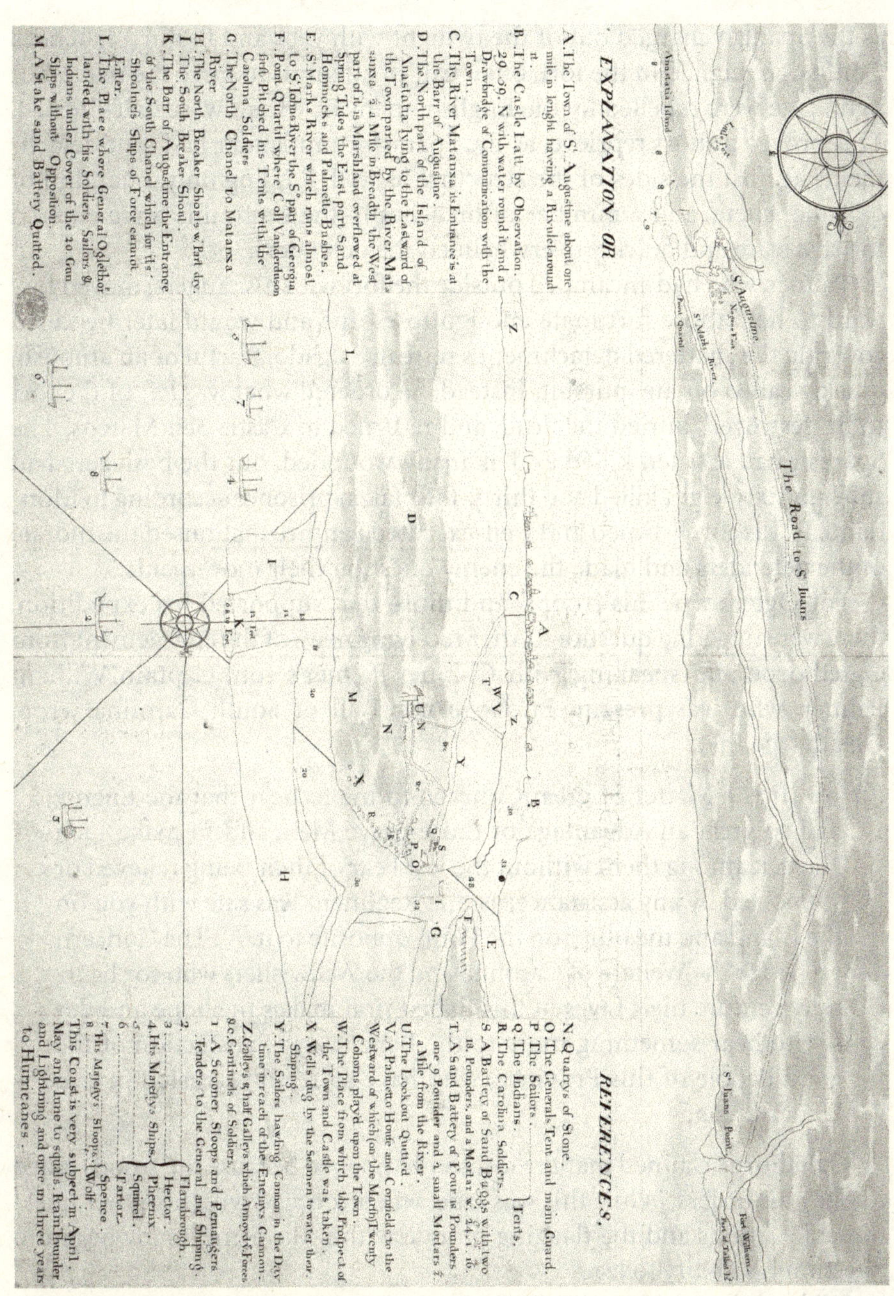

The siege of St. Augustine, 1740. (*Norman B. Leventhal Map Collection, Boston Public Library*)

as the Spanish charged out of the twilight with yells and flashing hatchets. Confusion reigned in the fort, but a pair of attempts to force the makeshift main gate were repelled by the English, many of whom were half-dressed. This proved a short reprieve, as the Spanish commander had sent detachments against the sides of the structure as well. Finding only a handful of defenders here, and a number of breaches in the walls, this force entered the structure and quickly overwhelmed the defenders.

Palmer, who had encamped outside the fort with his rangers, moved forward to help those fortunate enough to escape and would later be killed covering the shattered detachment's retreat. Salgado, fearful of an ambush, quickly called off any pursuit. Instead, he ordered what was left of the fort to be destroyed, buried the dead, and returned to Castle San Marcos. The Spanish had lost ten killed and as many wounded, but the besiegers had suffered sixty-eight killed and thirty-four taken prisoner according to Montiano. It was a well-timed and well-executed venture that raised the morale of the defenders and made the enemy question their movements.[6]

For Oglethorpe, his troops, and those that supported his expedition, there were lingering questions. After receiving news of the engagement from Oglethorpe and speaking with Colonel Palmer's son, Captain William Palmer, who was present, Lt. Governor Bull of South Carolina wrote Oglethorpe that,

> It is a Matter of great Concern to me to hear that the Enemy had so great an Advantage of those brave Men, and to make such Havock among them without the lest Fear of their being relieved or supported by any assistance, as one Regiment was safe with you on the Island and the other on the Point opposite to it.... The Concern I have for the Welfare of Carolina and the Wellwishers who so chearfully venture their Lives in this Expedition makes me hope and desire to hear something more to the Benefit and Satisfaction of the good People of this Province, who have so readily assisted in this Undertaking.[7]

Oglethorpe claimed that the disaster happened because the troops failed to obey his orders. While this was true, when coupled with his other questionable actions and the flagging morale within the army, many began to question his ability to lead.

With a firing platform having been obtained, the mortar on Point Quartell announced the morning of June 27 with a shell that burst over the fort. Both the English and Spanish only fired a handful of shots through the day, with no tangible results. Vander Dussen and his lieutenant colonel, William

Cook, returned to Anastasia Island and found confusion. Only one gun had been moved forward to the proposed battery. Captain Peter Warren, in charge of the naval contingent, complained that Oglethorpe had landed the detachment with nothing more than the shirts on their backs. There were no provisions, water was short, and more tools were needed. In addition, in his haste to land, the general had not even brought ammunition for the guns. Warren and his men had seen enough. Vander Dussen begged the Royal Navy captain to push forward the battery. These guns were the key to destroying the Spanish flotilla and securing the inner harbor. Vander Dussen then informed Warren that, if the new battery did not neutralize the Spanish galleys, he would lead a nighttime small boat attack on them as long as the navy would provide the vessels. Warren, perhaps simply happy that a plan now existed, agreed and offered to join Vander Dussen if they were forced to take such measures.

When he heard of the plan Oglethorpe took the matter one step further and ordered Vander Dussen to conduct the boat attack as soon as possible. This, the colonel informed Oglethorpe after holding a council of war with his officers at Point Quartell, was not advisable. With most of the regiment committed to this operation the encampment at Point Quartell would be vulnerable to a Spanish sortie. The 6-pound guns at the point were not properly mounted and would prove of little use in an actual duel with the Spanish galleys. Not that it would matter, as there would not be enough troops left on the point to repel a landing, nor was there a place to retreat if the enemy also put ashore a detachment farther up the point. Oglethorpe seemed more concerned that Vander Dussen's troops were disobeying orders, but the colonel shrugged and said that these were simply opinions and that, if the general wanted, he would bring the troops over to the island and press forward with the attack. Oglethorpe, satisfied with the reasoning, told him that would not be necessary and dropped the matter.[8]

Halting the small boat attack did little to clarify the path forward and the outstanding issues between Warren and Oglethorpe. As such, it was agreed to have an *ad hoc* council of war, although it was not recorded as such. In one of the few instances during the campaign, Oglethorpe, Commodore Pearce, Vander Dussen, Captain Warren, and Captain William Laws of the H.M.S. *Spence* met in Warren's tent on Anastasia Island. Oglethorpe opened the meeting by asking "the Commodore what was to be done in the Present Situation of affairs, as they had declared that they would stay no Longer than the 16th of next month?" Pearce deferred, pointing out that siege matters fell into the general's domain and not his own. However, as he had stated before, he would lend whatever assistance he could to further the project. Vander Dussen was then asked his opinion. Consistent in his approach, the colonel suggested that the battery on Anastasia be completed as quickly as possible and that its first focus should be on the Spanish galleys. If these guns could not neutralize the enemy fleet, a small boat attack should follow. He then suggested that one half of the army be transferred to Fort Mose and that the Chickasaw, who had already spoke about leaving after a run-in with Oglethorpe, go with these troops. This force would threaten the Spanish on the landside and cut their communications to the west. After a bombardment of both the fort and the town, a force from the island would cross to the mainland and attack the town from the south while the forces at Fort Mose attacked from the north. The plan met no opposition, and it was agreed that Oglethorpe should lead the troops at Fort Mose while Vander Dussen and his men forwarded the operations on the island. A small detachment would safeguard the encampment and battery at Point Quartell.[9]

It would take several days to shuffle the troops about and erect batteries on the island, but late on the afternoon of June 30, Vander Dussen gave the order to fire. A siege mortar firing from what was called the lower battery thundered to life, followed by a thump from the mortar at Quartell Point. The fort occasionally responded to the methodical bombardment, but near sunset the pace quickened when over a dozen small Coehorn mortars began firing in strings of flashes from the closer advanced battery. Targeting the Spanish galleys anchored near the fort, the gunners burst several bombs over the vessels, but just as many fell short.

The firing continued until about 10 p.m. when the guns on both sides fell silent. The next morning was quiet. Around 8:00 a.m. Oglethorpe sent a small boat forward under a white flag. A Spanish vessel soon arrived to meet it. The British officer delivered a letter from Oglethorpe calling upon the commander of Castle San Carlos to immediately surrender. The Spanish vessel returned to the fort and a short time later returned with news that the governor would reply to the summons tomorrow morning. A pair of deserters had arrived as well. Sailors from the Spanish flotilla, they informed Vander Dussen that the mortar attack on the fleet the previous evening had forced them to anchor closer to the fort. The duo spoke to what they knew regarding the attack on Fort Mose and the status of English prisoners and noted that although the successful Spanish counterattack had raised the spirits of some, "a Great many would Desert if they could find an opportunity."[10]

With a ceasefire in place until the next morning, Vander Dussen and his men busied themselves improving their batteries. A supply ship had arrived from Frederica with wood planks for the gun platforms, 250 cannon and mortar rounds, and 116 barrels of powder. Three 18-pound cannons were dragged forward, one being placed at the advanced battery and two at the lower battery. That evening Captain Richard Wright and a detachment of men worked feverishly on the advanced battery, and "did more this one night than had been done ever since the force had been upon the Island." The work, however, was interrupted by reports that a Spanish force was landing in the marsh in front of the advanced battery. Drums beat out the assembly, and Vander Dussen lead the regiment down to the shore in what turned out to be a false alarm.

The Spanish vessel carrying Governor Montiano's response did not appear until the next afternoon. Unsurprisingly, the governor refused and informed Oglethorpe that he would defend the fort to the "Last drop of his Blood." To the rhythmic rumble of the British guns, which had resumed their bombardment, Pearce, Warren, Law, Oglethorpe, and Vander Dussen met that afternoon to discuss their current plans. The council agreed on two matters. First, given the time restraints imposed by the departure of the fleet, Oglethorpe needed to assemble his forces and take command at Fort Mose as soon as possible. Second, the remaining artillery should be landed and the batteries pushed forward with all vigor.

By the morning of July 3 Wright had finished the advanced battery, which consisted of a breastwork of sandbags and a number of wooden firing platforms. Now mounting four 18-pounders, a pair of mortars, and a number of Coehorns the battery opened fire on the fort and the nearby Spanish fleet at sunrise. Although the fort and the galleys responded, it appeared that the British gunners were accomplishing their task when the galleys raised anchor and began to move south, away from thc fort. They were mistaken. It was in fact a deliberate move to strike back. The vessels soon took up a position where they were able to enfilade the advance battery, causing a number of casualties and briefly halting the bombardment as efforts were made to raise a breastwork and mount a 9-pound gun to counter the flanking fire. By late afternoon the British guns were back in action, and the two sides traded fire until sunset.

The daily exchanges of cannon fire continued for the next few days as Oglethorpe struggled to move his regiment to Fort Mose. While Castle San Marcos did not differ greatly from other stone forts of the day, there was one important exception. Technically, it was not built of stone. The coquina block used in the structure was actually small seashells that had fused together in a porous network under the weight of the earth and water above them. Quarried on nearby Anastasia Island, it was much lighter than stone and could easily be fashioned into blocks. Since there was no limestone to be found, oyster shells were burned and mixed with sand and water to make the mortar to bind these blocks together. The choice of this building material was dictated by economics. The only other option was to import the stone from Cuba, which would have bankrupted the project from the onset. Even with this compromise it would take close to thirty years to finish the stronghold.

Little did the architects of this venture realize, but they had inadvertently created a ballistic-resistant fortification. The coquina's cellular structure gave it deformational properties that not only absorbed the impact of a cannonball but allowed this energy to dissipate through the interconnecting pathways, thereby minimizing any cracking in the fort's walls. "It will not splinter but will give way to cannonball as though you would stick a knife into cheese," one British gunner noted of his efforts. Cannonballs either dented the near twenty-foot-thick harbor walls and fell to the wayside or buried themselves within the wall where they still remain today.

With the batteries in action, and the Spanish galleys proving one of the primary obstacles, Vander Dussen proposed to launch the small boat attack that had been discussed earlier. He soon ran into problems. Several captains had agreed to provide the small boats and accompany the attack, but after discussing the plan with Commodore Pearce, Warren was now against the attempt. When word reached him of these objections Vander Dussen met with Pearce and his captains aboard the *Flamborough*. It was initially agreed that the navy would command the expedition, but when the number of small boats available was tallied and found to only be able to hold a little over two hundred sailors and soldiers, Pearce began to express his doubts. The force was too small in his consideration, and he pointed to the fact that they would have to face the fire of the fort and the galleys before attempting to board the latter. Given the manpower shortages throughout the fleet, he viewed the venture as questionable, but he ultimately left the decision in Warren's and Vander Dussen's hands. "I hope your and their prudence will Lead you to Undertake Nothing but where there is a possibility of Success," he informed the colonel. The matter was discussed again the next day, but by then Pearce had made up his mind and ruled the attack as too risky, bringing an end to the idea.[11]

For Montiano the bombardment was not as severe a threat as his dwindling provisions. Fortunately, after the strike on Fort Mose, he had been able to drive some cattle into the fort, but if the English returned to Fort Mose in numbers, he would lose this resource. On the evening of July 6, a small boat pulled ashore near the fort. Its occupants quickly made their way to the governor and informed him that six small vessels ladened with provisions had arrived from Cuba and were currently anchored at the Matanzas Inlet. This good news was suddenly dampened when an English deserter came into camp claiming that Oglethorpe was planning to launch a land and sea attack on the fort at any moment. Montiano had originally planned to slowly funnel these newly arrived supplies into St. Augustine, but given the circumstances and the peril the vessels found themselves in with a British fleet nearby, he decided to make a concerted effort to unload the craft. Three of the smaller vessels were able to cross the bar and continue onto the town, while a flotilla of small boats was dispatched to the location to unload the others. Even though a number of smaller British vessels appeared to contest the operation, the supplies were successfully transferred to the fort with minimal losses. With his greatest fear addressed and the enemy guns, while active, doing little damage to the fort or the galleys, Montiano realized that the contest had now shifted in his favor.

On July 8 Oglethorpe arrived at Fort Mose. The next day he advanced toward the fort and made camp. News reached him from Vander Dussen that the attack on the galleys had been suspended by Pearce but that there was hope that some of the smaller British sloops could enter St. Augustine Harbor via the Matanzas Inlet. These armed vessels would be more than a match for the enemy galleys and would open a path for a landing to the south of the town as part of the planned combined assault. It was not to be. After scouting the bar, the sloop's pilots claimed they could not cross. In addition to this setback, on July 12 Captain Wright and most of the South Carolinian volunteers declared that they had seen enough and departed. An act that "produced a great uneasiness in the minds of those that were Left upon the Island."[12]

With Pearce planning on departing within a few days, Vander Dussen proposed a new plan to continue the siege. He would construct a battery farther south on the island on a bluff across from the mouth of the St. Sebastien River. From here the battery could limit all galley and boat traffic to the south of the town while the upper battery and the guns of Point Quartell blocked all Spanish traffic to the north. Combined with Oglethorpe investing St. Augustine from the landside, the British guns could then reduce the isolated post. However, in order to carry through with the plan, Vander Dussen needed Pearce to agree to leave two hundred men to man one of the batteries, as the colonel did not have the manpower to staff and protect all the post on the island and Point Quartell.

Had Vander Dussen's plan been implemented from the start of operations the siege of St. Augustine might have produced some success, but by now it was too late. After months in the Florida heat, marching and counter marching, lashed by rain and cooked under a relentless sun, morale was collapsing. Nor was Pearce interested in leaving two hundred men behind for the same reason he had given concerning the small boats' attack. He could not spare them. Sickness had drained his already depleted ranks to the point that it was about to affect his operational abilities. He then noted that, even if he did provide the men, he did not have the provisions aboard to leave them or the clothing they would need for such an operation.

It was over. The next day, July 15, the naval landing parties returned to their vessels. Oglethorpe passed orders to Vander Dussen to withdraw, saving whatever he could and destroying the rest. The colonel responded that it would take some time to move his forces, for lack of small boats. He then attempted to persuade the general to continue the effort. "I cannot apprehend our Case is so bad as to Leave our affairs in such a Manner," he wrote Oglethorpe, "for if nothing else can be done, I am sure, if your Excellency comes over to this Island, we may still keep them Blockaded till we can get more assistance."[13]

While Oglethorpe thanked Vander Dussen for his opinion, there were greater matters to consider at this stage. He found it unlikely that they could stop water traffic into the town, when Pearce's squadron could not. Given the odds of success, it was not worth the risk of losing more of his troops or their guns. "Whilst they are preserved," he reasoned, "we may keep the Spaniards within Bounds, but if they are Lost, the Damage to the Province of Carolina will be very great."[14]

It would take almost two weeks to withdraw the army to the encampment on the south side of the St. John's River. In the end, Vander Dussen managed to save all of the cannons on Anastasia Island except one 18-pounder that had split during firing. He also saved the mortar at Point Quartell, but the three 6-pound guns were buried by Oglethorpe's men, who in their haste to carry out the general's order to withdraw burned a damaged vessel near the shore, drank the surplus liquor, and started a raging bonfire to consume anything else they could not carry. Unfortunately, one of these items was a loaded musket, which discharged after being tossed in the fire, wounding one of their officers in the leg. At Fort Mose Oglethorpe skirmished with Spanish patrols until he too withdrew to the St. John's. There were discussions regarding burning Fort Diego, but strangely it was spared. When Spanish patrols later occupied the structure they admired the newly crafted ditch, the extensive repairs, and the well-made wooden breastwork now erected about the stronghold.

Oglethorpe would only stay in Florida for a few more weeks while transportation was being arranged. A handful of patrols were sent out, one for instance to burn Fort St. Francis, but these started proving costly when a number of soldiers from Oglethorpe's regiment began deserting during the operations. What remained of the army boarded transports on July 25, but it would not be until the next day that the last English vessel had cleared the bar at St. John's carrying Oglethorpe and Vander Dussen's men aboard along with their artillery. For some, there was reluctance in having come so close to their goal only to abandon it, but for most who had survived the brutal marches, packs of mosquitoes, and the guns of the Spanish, it was relief, not remorse, they were feeling.[15]

CHAPTER SIXTEEN

The Invasion of Georgia

"I ASSURE Your Excellency, that I cannot arrive at a comprehension of the conduct, or rules of this General," Montiano wrote the governor of Cuba a few days after his scouts confirmed Oglethorpe's departure from the St. John's. "My wonder is inexpressible," he continued, "that this gentleman should make his retreat with such precipitation, as to leave abandoned, four 6-pounders on the battery on the point of San Mateo (Point Quartell), one schooner, two kegs of gunpowder, several muskets and escopettes, and to set fire to a quantity of provisions, such as boxes of bacon, cheese, lard, dried beef, rice and beans, to a schooner, and to an excellent mortar carriage."[1]

The siege itself had done little damage either to Castle San Marcos or the town, and the governor reported only two killed and two wounded by the bombardment. He saluted the garrison and the militia for their steadfast efforts, particularly at the battle of Fort Mose, and commended the crews and captains of the galleys that had proven so instrumental during the siege. As for Montiano, his conduct proved steadfast. He wisely refrained from committing large numbers of troops to defend the outlying posts and exploited the opportunities presented, such as the attack on Fort Mose. In many ways his actions can be viewed as what would be expected from an experienced professional soldier and one versed in the art of siege craft.[2]

Far more questions arise when viewing Oglethorpe's actions. The general's conduct in the first part of the siege is odd. First, he deviated from his original plan of striking the town to force the inhabitants into the fort, thereby taxing the garrison's provisions and resources. On several occasions Carolinian troops offered to carry through with this plan, and each time he rejected the idea. Even the Chickasaw volunteered to burn down the town, but they too were rejected. The general, who was reputed to have learned his trade from the legendary Prince Eugene of Savoy, seems to have concluded that an operation against the town would be too costly, although his scouts were routinely reporting on the panicked state of the inhabitants and their vulnerable defenses. This hesitancy would have a ripple effect on the remainder of the operations. With a siege now the only path before the attackers, Oglethorpe appeared more interested in custom than actual siege craft, to the extent that one begins to wonder if he actually understood the latter. The weeks of marches, scouts, and indecision regarding attacking the town leaves one with the distinct impression that Oglethorpe was attempting to bluff the garrison into surrender, which in itself is puzzling given that, under the customs of siege craft, a fort's commander would never surrender until fired upon. This aside, it is even more difficult to understand the general's behavior given the limited time Commodore Pearce could remain on station.

Along with the failure to attack the town, the decision not to besiege the fort from the landside is difficult to reconcile. With Pearce's squadron blockading the harbor the only way to truly invest Castle San Marcos was to occupy the landside of the fort, as Moore had done in 1702. The latter had been able to establish a firing position from which to bombard the fort on the landside; he just lacked the artillery to effectively do so. While batteries at Point Quartell and on Anastasia Island would provide useful cover fire, especially against the Spanish galleys, they were simply too far away to breach the fort's walls and too few to bombard it into submission. The only way to reduce Castle San Marcos, short of a costly and questionable attempt to storm its walls, was from the landside where siege trenches could approach to within a few hundred yards, well within breaching distance of 18-pound siege guns, regardless of the unique qualities of the structure's coquina construction. With a fort filled with civilians, coupled with an effective blockade and a legitimate threat to beach the structure's walls, Montiano would have been forced to surrender to prevent a catastrophe.

When the siege shifted to erecting batteries on Anastasia Island and Point Quartell, Oglethorpe made another mistake by leaving too few men at Fort Mose to counter a sally from the garrison, even though he had been warned of such a possibility. This was not exclusively his fault, as the troops failed to undertake necessary precautions, but what perhaps is just as puzzling is that the numbers assigned to this detachment were not only too few to ward off a sally by the garrison but were also too few to invest the landside of the fort and prevent supplies from reaching the stronghold.

After this event the general's influence seemed to have waned, and he turned to his fellow commanders for guidance, at times seemingly handing operations over to Vander Dussen. Whether this was because, having failed to convince the garrison to surrender, the general was unsure what to do next or some other matter is not clear. What is clear is that Pearce and Vander Dussen began to assert control over the expedition at this point. Had this new approach been implemented from the start of operations, and supplemented by a battery of guns on the landside of Castle San Marcos, Montiano might have been forced to surrender before reinforcements reached him. Thus, although the British ring around the fort and town proved too porous to maintain a siege of attrition, as demonstrated by the success of the relief flotilla from Cuba, the real window of opportunity to capture the stronghold was wasted through inaction and indecision. It was here that the general's critics took aim. One South Carolina officer compared the string of marches and countermarches more "to Squirrel Hunting rather than War," while another South Carolina writer concluded, "In short, to characterize such extraordinary Conduct with the strictest Propriety, we must admit, it has more the air of a Farce than of a Siege."[3]

Recriminations and booklets would be exchanged between Oglethorpe's political supporters and his opponents over the next few years, but as for the other two British commanders, Pearce and Vander Dussen, there was far less controversy. The former supported the operation in a manner expected of a British squadron commander and at times pressed Oglethorpe for action. The lack of shallow draft vessels would haunt his effort as, technically, it was the Spanish penetration of the naval blockade at Matanzas Inlet that collapsed the expedition, but even so, by then Pearce could not remain on station, and most had already concluded that the opportunity had been lost. As for Vander Dussen, he had proven an active and aggressive commander, and much of what was actually accomplished was via his and the Carolina troops' hands. His attempts to launch a nighttime small boat attack on the Spanish galleys was one of the few solutions given the circumstances. Although Warren and Pearce ultimately failed to support the effort, it was more for logistical reasons and not for a lack of agreement that it was the correct move to break the stalemate and further isolate the Spanish post. In fact, after viewing the South Carolinian colonel's conduct, one is left with the impression that, if he had been given command of the expedition to start with, St. Augustine would have faced far more perilous days.

Montiano, still badly outnumbered, did nothing to interfere with Oglethorpe's departure from the St. John's, but as he pointed out in his report, the triumph might only be temporary, as a large number of English deserters claimed that Oglethorpe planned to return in the spring with two additional regiments from England. The governor doubted that South Carolina would assist Oglethorpe given the costs and vexations of the failed venture. Still, if the British Crown supported Oglethorpe with men, guns, and money, he might well convince the colony to support another attack. Such possibilities prompted Montiano to ask for more troops, having suffered most of his casualties, well over a hundred, defending the outlying forts such as Fort Mose, Fort Diego, and Fort St. Francis. Beyond these losses, disease, desertion, and sickness had reduced the fort's garrison to 356 men, only 116 of whom were presently fit for duty. The garrison should consist of 750 men: 350 of the old establishment and eight companies of reinforcements. As such, he asked for 394 men to return the garrison to full strength, two dozen of whom should be artillerymen. He then suggested that, in addition to this, three hundred Cuban militia should be sent to augment the garrison's numbers.

Late summer and early fall of 1740 proved a trying time for St. Augustine, as the promised supply convoy from Cuba was lost in transit. Circumstances forced Montiano into the privateering business. The results were the capture of a pair of ships, one of which was loaded with rice that helped alleviate the food shortages. British and colonial privateers began to appear as well, lurking off the bar and capturing the occasional small craft before departing, only to be replaced by another vessel not long after. It would prove a constant source of irritation to St. Augustine, but the real fear, another attack, did not materialize as the calendar turned to 1741. Rumors of Oglethorpe's return made for an anxious spring and summer, but with the onset of hurricane season Montiano was able to breathe a sigh of relief.[4]

There were other reasons behind this inactivity. Much of the fighting in the War of Jenkins' Ear, at least in its early stages, would occur in the Caribbean, and while this theater falls outside the scope of this work, a few words regarding these operations are in order. One of the first major efforts occurred in November 1739, when Admiral Edward Vernon left Jamaica with a small fleet and struck a stunning blow by capturing Portobello, Panama. Without the manpower to occupy the valuable port, Vernon destroyed the fortifications and anything of military value before abandoning the town a few weeks later. News of this success would inspire the British public and lead to the planning of an even greater effort in the region. The following spring Vernon focused his efforts against the Spanish stronghold of Cartagena. The admiral would test the Spanish defenses for almost a month in March 1740 before withdrawing and launching a successful attack on Fortress de San Lorenzo el Real Chagres near Portobello. Vernon would test Cartagena again in May, but the action resulted in nothing more than a long-range artillery duel. The admiral had expected a large fleet from Britain to support his efforts and began to worry when a French fleet arrived in the Caribbean instead. Although the French were technically neutral, fear that they might combine with a Spanish fleet for an attack on Jamaica put the admiral on the defensive for the rest of the year. An attack never materialized, but as the new year approached, neither had Vernon's reinforcements.

Storms and bad weather had delayed the British fleet, and it would not be until January 9, 1741, that Admiral Chaloner Ogle dropped anchor at Jamaica. Aboard Ogle's fleet were the 15th and 24th Regiments of Foot and six regiments of marines. Combined with artillery and a brigade of colonials from Virginia, it gave Vernon over ten thousand men. In addition, his fleet now consisted of twenty-nine ships of fifty to eighty guns each, twenty-one frigates, bomb ships, and tenders manned by over eleven thousand sailors. Together it was the largest military force ever assembled in the Caribbean. Most, including London, believed that Havana was the target, as its capture would collapse Spanish Cuba. Vernon, however, had the authority to modify the plan, and after discovering that the French fleet at Port Louis, Haiti, had already returned to France, in late February 1741 he did just that when he ordered the fleet to set sail for Cartagena.[5]

Things initially went well for Vernon and the army's commander Brigadier General Thomas Wentworth, although the two were already beginning to disagree. The troops landed near the entrance to the harbor on March 9 and by the twenty-sixth had demolished or captured the Spanish forts and batteries guarding the channel. The Spanish warships *Africa*, *San Carlos*, and *San Felipe*, damaged by the British fleet and a battery of siege guns dragged ashore, were put to the torch. The 70-gun *Galicia*, however, was seized by a detachment led by Captain Charles Knowles of the *Weymouth* and towed away as a prize. A few days later Vernon pressed forward to the inner anchorage. The enemy abandoned a pair of forts at the mouth of the anchorage and did not contest a British landing at the northeastern end of the harbor. Facing little in the way of opposition, within a few days Wentworth's troops were before Fort St. Lazar, which overlooked the city.

Here what appeared to be a successful venture came to a halt. While disease and illness had already claimed a thousand of Wentworth's and Ver-

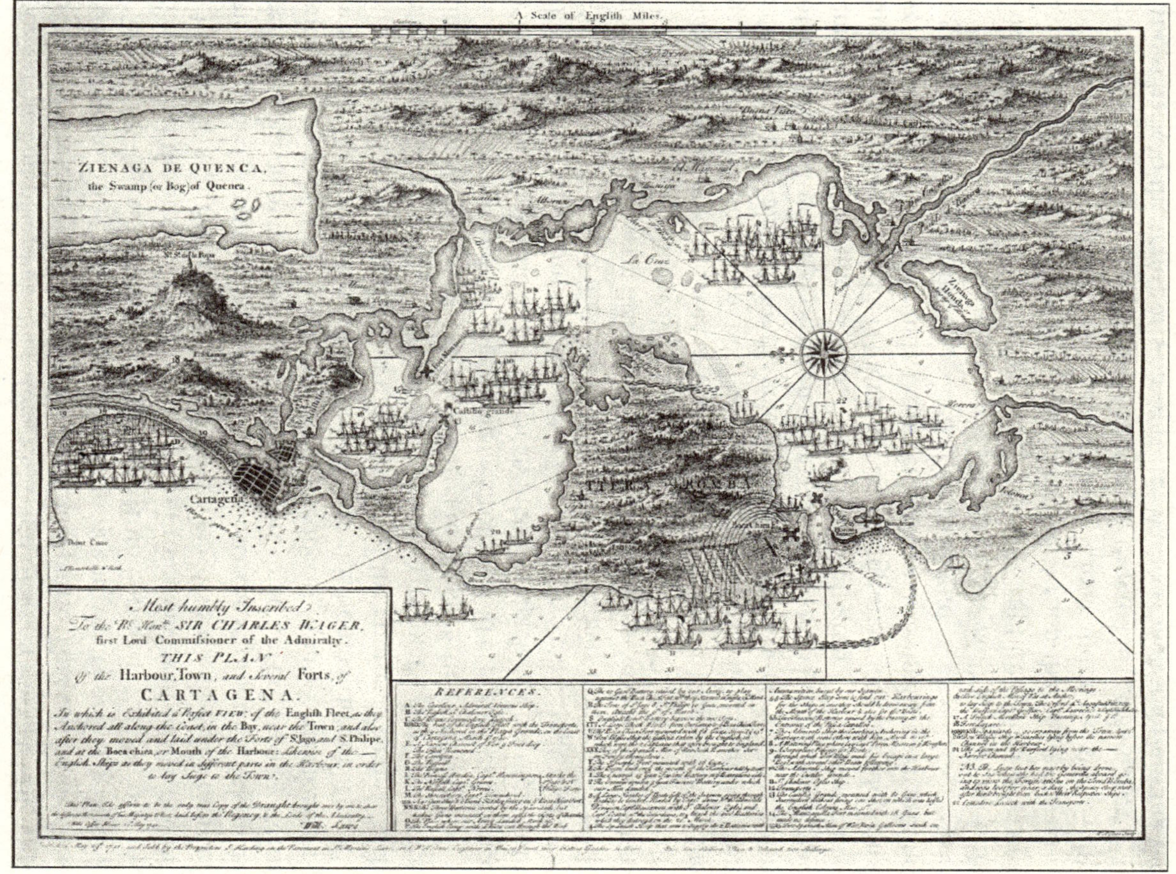

The Siege of Cartagena, 1741, William Toms, engraver.

non's men, and placed another three thousand or so on the sick rolls, this was not the underlying cause behind the deadly pause. That can be ascribed to the deteriorating relations between Vernon and Wentworth. By April 7 Wentworth's forces were encamped a mile from Fort St. Lazar. Reports indicated that the stone structure was heavily armed and well positioned on a hill with a clear field of fire. To make matters worse, the slow assembly of his forces had given the Spanish time to reinforce the stronghold. Taken together, a council of war had agreed that the fort could not be taken by storm and that a siege battery should be raised to reduce it. Wentworth asked Vernon to use his three bomb ketches to assist in this bombardment. The admiral scoffed at the request and disapproved of the approach against such a weak fortification. More importantly, this disagreement also came with no commitment on the part of the admiral to support the venture.[6]

Vernon's stance and the increasing sick rolls would eventually convince Wentworth and his officers to launch an infantry attack against the fort in the early-morning hours of April 9, 1741. At four o'clock that morning Colonel John Grant led the advanced guard of grenadiers into the ditch before the fort. It was soon discovered that the Spanish had recently deepened the ditch, meaning that scaling ladders would now have to be used. Grant sent a messenger to the rear to bring the ladders forward, but by now the garrison had begun to respond. The troops behind Grant held their position and fired at the walls, but for the colonel and his men dawn brought a storm of musket and grape shot upon them. Grant soon fell, and while the grenadiers and detachments behind them held their ground, it was a deadly limbo where a lack of ladders prevented advancing and a lack of orders prevented withdrawing. Mercifully, the order to retreat was finally given around eight o'clock, bringing the one-sided affair to an end.

The poorly organized and hastily constructed assault would not only cost Wentworth 179 killed, 459 wounded, and 16 captured, but Cartagena as well. On the eleventh Wentworth informed Vernon that, without reinforcements from the fleet, the army would have to abandon the siege. With no aid coming from the admiral, Wentworth ordered his remaining 3,500 troops back to the transports on April 15. With sickness still thinning the expedition's ranks, and morale at its lowest point, Vernon realized that the campaign was about to slip away. In one last effort he reinforced the captured *Galicia* and then outfitted it as a 16-gun floating battery. The vessel was anchored in front of the city on the night of the fifteenth and at first light opened fire. It proved to be a long day for the crew of the *Galicia*. They worked their guns tirelessly for seven hours under a hail of heavy shot that fractured the craft's side and slowly started disabling the ship's guns. By early afternoon the vessel's commander, Captain Daniel Hore, had seen enough. Stuck twenty times near the waterline, and with his casualties mounting, he ordered the anchor cables cut and slowly drifted away. At this point it was not a question of if the *Galicia* would sink but when. With over fifty wounded onboard, such an event would prove to be a disaster, but fortunately, the vessel grounded near shore, allowing for the rescue of the crew. It now became clear to all that the siege was over. After stopping to destroy the captured Spanish fortifications, the fleet set sail for Jamaica, arriving there on May 19.

While Vernon's advocates blamed the army for the failure, and Wentworth's advocates blamed the navy, both appear to have been correct. More important was the missed opportunity and devastation brought about by their disagreements. While the expedition had suffered some nine hundred or so combat casualties, over ten times this number succumbed or were incapacitated by yellow fever, dysentery, and a host of other tropical aliments. Skeleton crews manned ships, and many units were decimated, such as the American brigade of which only three hundred returned home. Even the Spanish fell prey to disease from the unburied bodies after the campaign, with the Spanish commander to be counted among these losses.

The siege of Cartagena proved to be the climax of the War of Jenkins' Ear in the Caribbean. Vernon and Wentworth would launch an abortive campaign against Santiago del Cuba in July but abandoned the effort in late November, and the following spring Commodore Knowles would briefly besiege La Guaira. These incidents aside, the conflict was slowing down as both sides delt with the attrition of manpower that came with operating in the theater. Vernon would return to England with his fleet in 1742, and with war clouds building over Europe, the Caribbean theater took on a secondary importance. The conflict did not stop; it just now became more focused on privateers and cruisers.[7]

In St. Augustine, Governor Montiano had received reports of the British repulse at Cartagena and Santiago. It was welcomed news, made even better by his own report stating that, beyond privateers and small scouting parties, the enemy had made no attempt against his position. The governor continued to ask for supplies and reinforcements, although he had all but given up on seeing the latter. In February 1742, the captain of a vessel from Spain handed Montiano a dispatch. The governor expected another letter expressing sympathy for his plight and a well-crafted reason why he could not be sent additional supplies or reinforcements. Instead, he was startled. The idea of a putative expedition against Georgia had been discussed off and on for years, but now, as he read the letter before him, Montiano suddenly realized that this plan was to go forward. The king had directed that the governor of Cuba, Don Juan Francisco de Guemas, provide three thousand men and see to the military details of the expedition with the support of the fleet in Havana, if they could be spared for the operation. Montiano was to assist de Guemas with troops from St. Augustine and see to the operational details. The goal was nothing short of the "destruction of Carolina and of its dependencies." Were this not enough, the orders were more specific as to what was expected. "Devastate it by sacking and Burning all the towns, posts, plantations and settlements of the enemy, for the purpose of this invasion must be solely to press hostilities until the effort shall have gone home, and success be achieved."[8]

Montiano, who had been in favor of such a plan, was delighted by the news, seeing the expedition as more than just punitive in nature. If it was successful, it would garner large numbers of freed Black slaves who would settle in Florida. These in turn would boost agricultural efforts and act as a militia in case of an English attack. In addition, a devastating blow to Georgia and South Carolina had the potential to rearrange Native American trade and alliances. If the two colonies were badly injured and could not fulfill their normal trade with the Cherokee, Chickasaw, or Creek, it opened avenues for Spanish traders or even French traders. In either case, the shift in supply lines combined with the damaged prestige of the English, already weakened by the failed siege of St. Augustine, offered fertile ground to create new alliances that would further secure Spanish Florida.

For de Guemas, the timing was fortunate. The British had just lifted a four-month siege of Santiago, meaning any near-term attempt on Havana was unlikely. The governor was unable to secure much in the way of warships, with a British fleet still active in the Caribbean, although for what he was considering he would not necessarily need them. It was also clear to de Guemas that he did not have the three thousand men required to make a direct assault on the two colonies, even if he could find transportation for them. Instead, he viewed the operation in two stages. First, as a bold stroke against Oglethorpe's headquarters at Frederica, and then one of opportunity once the general and his men were captured or destroyed.

On June 2, 1742, de Guemas wrote Montiano placing him in command and informing him that he had sent six hundred regulars and seven hundred militia on thirty small transports that could operate in the shallow waterways of the Georgia barrier islands. These would be escorted by a 24-gun French frigate, a 14-gun packet ship, and an armed galley. Montiano was to contribute three hundred men from the garrison of Castle San Marcos and two hundred others from recent reinforcements sent to the post. These

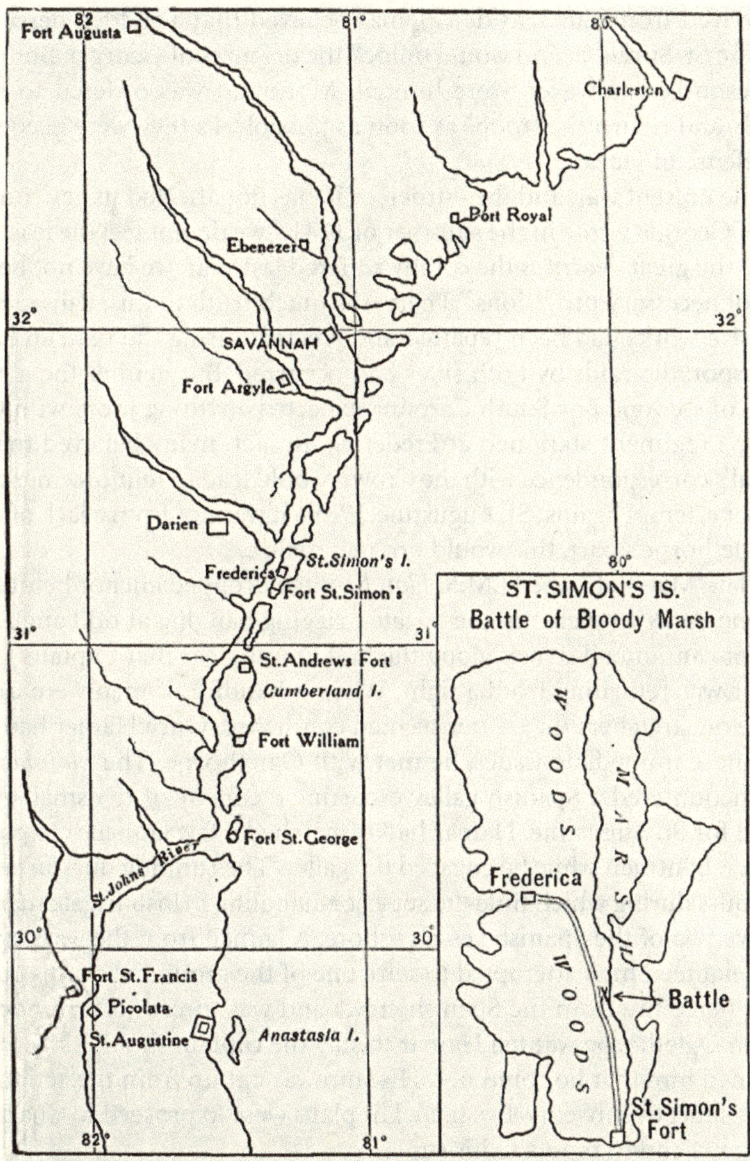

The southeast coast from St. Augustine to Charleston with an inset showing St. Simon's Island. (*Robert Preston,* History of Georgia, *1913*)

troops were to board the six galleys under his command and as many small craft as he could muster. They were to be ready to sail the moment the convoy arrived from Cuba, as de Guemas believed that a sudden descent by water on St. Simon Island would unlock the defenses of Georgia. Both time and resources, however, were limited. Montiano was ordered to strike quickly and return the troops as soon as possible, as they were needed for the defense of Havana.[9]

"The present war, and the burden of it, has not affected us yet," one citizen of Georgia wrote in the summer of 1741, "we do not feel the least of it; and in the great dearness the colony suffered last year, we have not been in want of necessary provisions." There was much truth to this. Palisades and defensive works had been repaired and erected during the year, and a few small sporadic raids by both sides had occurred, but neither the governments of Georgia nor South Carolina expected anything more with Oglethorpe's regiment stationed at Frederica. In fact, many believed that the general's correspondence with the Crown would lead to reinforcements and another attempt against St. Augustine. While it was not from a lack of effort on Oglethorpe's part, this would not materialize.

In late May 1742, the H.M.S. *Flamborough* dropped anchor before Fort St. Simon's. With pieces of the frigate's rigging hanging at odd angles and signs of cannonball strikes along the hull, it was clear that Captain Joseph Hamar was returning from a fight. When a handful of men were carried ashore on stretchers the matter seemed confirmed. Once Hamar had dealt with these immediate issues, he met with Oglethorpe. The *Flamborough* had encountered a Spanish galley escorting a convoy of ten small vessels bound for St. Augustine. Hamar had dispatched a few launches to go after the merchantmen while he engaged the galley. The running duel lasted several hours during which time the superior-handling British frigate managed to drive two of the Spanish vessels ashore. A launch from the warship carrying eighteen men attempted to seize one of the grounded sloops but ran into a fierce fire from the Spanish crews and was forced to surrender. Although Oglethorpe wanted Hamar to stay the captain shook his head and informed him that he could not. His ship was cut up from the action, and he was short over twenty-five men. His plans were to proceed to Charleston for repairs and to report to his superior.

Oglethorpe immediately sent a dispatch to the governor of South Carolina and sent envoys to the Cherokee and Creek asking for their assistance. Although the Georgia guard schooner had sighted fifteen Spanish ships near St. Augustine a few days later, the government of South Carolina was not convinced of the threat. Nor was Captain Thomas Frankland, the Royal Navy commander at Charleston. At first, he agreed to send the frigates *Rose* and *Flamborough* to Oglethorpe, but this never materialized.[10]

On June 8 Oglethorpe wrote Governor Bull to press his point. The general had dispatched several vessels to the south to gather intelligence, but in the meantime, "You would be in the right to have the militia immediately reviewed and ready for service.," he advised Bull. "I expect the Spaniards will attack us; and, if they do, doubt not to give them a warm reception and make them sick of it, but, if they should get the better of us, they will immediately follow their advantage, and you may expect a visit." The South Carolina Assembly released some military supplies, but they were not interested in placing their troops under Oglethorpe's command given what had transpired at St. Augustine a few years before. Instead, the colony called out its militia and focused on safeguarding Charleston, which was used as an excuse as to why troops were not being dispatched to the general. Even so, by mid-June Oglethorpe had managed to gather together some seven hundred men consisting of Georgia militia, Creek, Cherokee, and the troops of his regiment at Fort St. Simon's. From here he appealed for assistance and anxiously awaited news of reinforcements from Governor Bull.[11]

On June 21, it became clear that time was up when nine Spanish vessels entered Amelia Sound and approached Fort William on the southern end of Cumberland Island. The 18-pound cannons on the ramparts roared to life as the squadron of Spanish vessels closed and responded with their own guns. Fortunately for the sixty defenders in the fort, Lt. George Dunbar, who commanded Oglethorpe's 14-gun schooner, was nearby and soon added his guns to the fight. The Spanish maintained a respectable distance and departed after an hour. When news reached Oglethorpe at Frederica, he put together a detachment of reinforcements and set sail for Fort William in three vessels. In Cumberland Sound the general's ships encountered the Spanish flotilla. The largest of the British ships fled, leaving Oglethorpe to fight his way through with the remaining two vessels. The discharge of cannons interlaced with musketry and the shouts of the gun captains echoed over the waters, but by now the Spanish warships, some with clear storm damage, were running low on ammunition and did not press home their numerical advantage. After a brief exchange where both sides scored hits, the Spanish turned south and disappeared behind Amelia Island.

After leaving the reinforcements at Fort William, Oglethorpe withdrew the garrison at St. Andrew's and returned to St. Simon's Island aboard his schooner on the twenty-fourth. One of the general's first acts was to send an envoy to Charleston to plead for men. He then seized all shipping in St. Simon's Harbor. This yielded the 20-gun sloop *Success*, which had just arrived from England, and a number of smaller unarmed vessels. Combined with Oglethorpe's 14-gun schooner, the 14-gun sloop *St. Phillip*, and a few small craft from New York, it provided Oglethorpe with a naval component with which to challenge the nearby waters. The general also held out hope that the frigates *Rose* and *Flamborough* would appear soon. There were additions in manpower as well. Two companies from Georgia had arrived, and a new company of rangers had been raised. The batteries at Fort St. Simon's and Frederica were reinforced, trenches dug, and ammunition for the cannons and mortars dispensed. Mounted scouts were sent to the coast, and the guard was doubled as the troops spent anxious days toiling away at the defenses in anticipation of what most believed would be an attack by five to six thousand Spanish.[12]

Of course, Montiano never had anything close to these numbers. Beyond the vessels run ashore by the *Flamborough* and a few forced to turn back from storm damage, the bulk of the Spanish fleet under the command of Colonel Don Francisco Rubiani arrived off the St. Augustine bar on July 15. The fleet was in desperate need of fresh water, but the storms and strong winds played havoc with the resupply operation, sinking a launch with all hands during one attempt. Weather now determined the start of operations, and it was not until July 1 that Montiano gave the order for the fleet of fifty-two vessels, carrying close to three thousand soldiers and sailors, to set sail for St. Simon's Island.

The next day, "a furious storm beyond any human power to resist, overtook us from the southwest and scattered us all," Montiano wrote. One detachment, seeking refuge from the sea, sparred with Fort William and Oglethorpe before moving off, while others sought shelter where they could find it. It took several days to collect the fleet, and it was not until the afternoon of July 10 that the Spanish flotilla, now thirty-three strong, dropped anchor outside the St. Simon's bar. The warning cannons were fired both at the fort and the blockhouse to the west, while Oglethorpe's little fleet sailed forth and dropped anchor under the umbrella of Fort St. Simon's guns.

A pair of stragglers appeared the next day, but it was not additional forces that Montiano was waiting for but a break in the weather. The high winds and rough seas would make it difficult to conduct a landing. This was further compounded by the missing shallow draft galleys and pirogues from St. Augustine. The next morning the weather appeared to calm, leading Montiano to order a landing, but a sudden squall nearly drowned the occupants of the small boats, leading to the operation being called off. It was then decided that, given the shallow waters, the uncertain weather, and the lack of sufficient landing craft, a landing on the east shore of the island was out of the question. Instead, it was agreed to attack Fort St. Simon's and look for a potential landing area near the port. After marching on and seizing the latter, the captured docks and wharfs would allow the army's supplies and its artillery to be quickly landed.

On the evening of July 15, the rainstorms and westerly winds subsided. With an opportunity finally before him, the next morning Montiano ordered the fleet to raise anchor and make for the channel. Most of the vessels had to wait here for the tide, while three galleys sounded the channel before them. After deploying a number of buoys, the galleys returned as Fort St. Simon's fired a few long-range shots. The weather was calm, and when the tide began rising shortly before one o'clock, the signal to advance was given.[13]

The Spanish entered the channel and began exchanging shots with both Fort St. Simon's and Oglethorpe's warships anchored nearby. With the range closing, the 24-gun Spanish flagship unleashed a broadside against the stronghold. The other armed vessels fired on both the fort and the English ships as the flotilla passed into the harbor. Both sides scored hits, one cannonball cutting the mainmast of a Spanish pink in half and another wounding three in a cloud of wooden debris when it struck a galley. While bombs fired from the fort's mortars plunged into the waters about the fleet, Spanish guns also found their mark, disabling an 18-pound cannon in the fort and peppering the vessels in Oglethorpe's navy with grapeshot and musketry.

The firing became general for several hours, and twice Spanish boats tried to board the *Success* but both times were driven away. They then turned their efforts against Oglethorpe's schooner, but meeting a sustained fire they aborted this attack as well. For the Spanish pink *Parreno*, the battle started off poorly. Advancing near the front of the flotilla the vessel had gone aground. The British gunners soon discovered this fact and pelted the motionless target with grapeshot and ball for half an hour, hulling the vessel twice. Fortunately for the beleaguered crew the rising tide freed the vessel, which limped past the fort to the rendezvous point in the harbor.

By a quarter past five Montiano's fleet had assembled in the northwestern end of the harbor out of sight of Fort St. Simon's and only a few miles downriver from Frederica. The governor met with Colonel Rubiani and his senior officers. The ground before them appeared unsuitable for a landing, and it was agreed that the fleet could not spend the night here for fear that the enemy might erect a battery nearby over the course of the evening. With the waters and channel to Frederica unknown, it was agreed to follow through with the original plan and force a landing at Fort St. Simon's.[14]

In this task the Spanish were greatly aided by Oglethorpe. The fort was not damaged, and the general had only suffered a score of casualties, but with the Spanish having run past the guns of Fort St. Simon's, and now within striking distance of Frederica, he ordered the fortifications abandoned. The troops stationed on the warships were withdrawn as the guns were spiked and storehouses put to the torch. The general thanked the crewmen of the *Success*, his own schooner, and the *St. Phillip* for their bravery and then ordered their captains to make good their escape. Detachments of Oglethorpe's army were already on the march to Frederica in a race against the Spanish fleet when around 10:00 p.m. the rearguard put a number of buildings and a few small boats to the torch before lighting the fuse to the magazine in the fort and departing for Frederica.[15]

CHAPTER SEVENTEEN

The General's Finest Hour

A LITTLE AFTER sunset eighteen boats from the Spanish fleet watched as the galleys and other armed craft swept a portion of beach to the west of Fort St. Simon's with grapeshot. Satisfied with their work, the warships moved off, and the signal to land was given. Wind and waves combined with the failing light to make the landing a little more confused than would have been liked, but by 7:00 p.m. an advance guard of fifty men had secured the beachhead and sent scouts in the direction of the British fort. Lt. Colonel Don Antonio Salgado, in charge of the first division of five hundred men, followed over the next hour. At 10:00 p.m. the grenadiers came ashore in three barges, having had difficulties with the rough seas. More troops and supplies followed, and an hour later Montiano, Rubiani, and the general's chief engineer, Don Antonio Arredondo, landed. As the boats returned for more men and materials, the thousand men ashore pointed and spoke among one another as fires consumed several enemy vessels near the docks. A few smaller fires could also be seen near the town before a much brighter flame appeared near the fort. "From the great blaze which arose," one Spanish officer wrote, "we thought this last must be some powder magazine which they had blown up."[1]

With hours of landing operations still ahead Montiano arranged the troops to protect the landing area while several Native scouts reported that both the town and the fort were deserted. With the grenadiers in the lead, at daylight the army formed up and marched down the beach. The fort was indeed abandoned as were large amounts of stores and provisions that could not be carried away. Three smoldering vessels lay near the burning docks, their cargo of caved-in barrels of flour and meat now washing up along the beach. The four-bastioned earth fort proved well-constructed, with a ditch, glacis, and outer wooden palisade to break up an infantry attack. Inside several buildings had been burned, including what appeared to be a magazine. After a quick search, three scorched 18-pounders, and six 6-pounders were discovered, the latter being "imperfectly spiked." There were also a large number of tools and several crates of grenades. At the blockhouse near the entrance to the harbor, the Spanish found even more. The earth and tabby structure contained a mortar, and nearby was an operational battery of four 6-pounders and two 4-pounders. The artillery and the handfuls of small arms were a welcomed addition, but provisions were what most desired. "These, which had been all burnt, might have been very useful for our maintenance."[2]

More importantly, Montiano had taken a wounded English sailor. The man had just arrived, so he had no knowledge of the terrain, but he did know that Oglethorpe had retreated up the road to Frederica with five hundred men. With this the general ordered the fort and the blockhouse manned while the army made camp in the open ground between the two. Pickets were placed outside the encampment, and the troops spent the remainder of the day bringing forward their supplies.

On the morning of the eighteenth Montiano dispatched a pair of scouts. The first was composed of a company of the St. Augustine garrison and forty militia. Under the command of Captain Sebastian Sanchez, this group was to scout the ground to the west for a place to land artillery. The second detachment, under Captain Nicholas Hernandez, consisted of twenty-five rangers and forty Yamassee. Hernandez was to scout the road to Frederica and, if possible, ascertain the best approach by which to attack the town.

Early in his march Sanchez became lost, made a wrong turn, and ended up joining Hernanadez. Together the two detachments pushed down the trail, which wound through tangled brush and cypress-filled woods, occasionally revealing glimpses of the broad swamp that skirted the path on their right. The trail was broken by a few narrow causeways that passed through swampy clearings before once again plunging into the dark wood line. With knee-deep mud and water on either side of the path, it soon became clear to both commanders that "no formation whatever was possible nor any manner of march other than single file." The two companies came within a mile of Frederica when, after negotiating a narrow defile near Gully

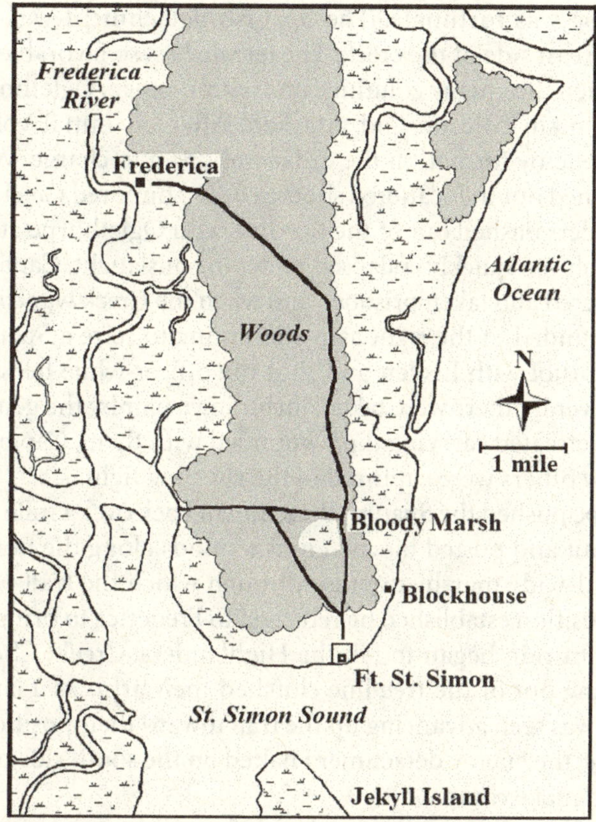

The Spanish invasion of St. Simon's Island and the Battle of Bloody Marsh.

Hole Creek to the south of the town, they spied a partially covered log redoubt laying across the trail. Hernandez halted the column and had barely sent scouts ahead when the forest around him erupted in flashes and tongues of flame.[3]

The day of Oglethorpe's arrival at Frederica a party of Creek brought in five Spanish prisoners. The captives gave the general an idea of the numbers he was facing but no insight into the enemy's plans. Early the next morning Oglethorpe had been apprised of the advancing Spanish detachment by a party of rangers. Wasting no time, he shouted out a series of orders, mounted a horse, and raced down the trail with the Creek and Cherokee detachments as well as a company of Highlanders and a detachment of rangers. After a cascade of hoarse calls, sixty men from the 42nd were quickly mustered together and proceeded down the path after them.

Oglethorpe was fortunate. The Spanish detachment was still in the woods on the east side of the creek. The terrain was so favorable for an ambush that, when the enemy column came within range, Oglethorpe did not wait for the main column and attacked. After an initial volley ripped through the enemy formation the order was given to charge. War whoops quickly drowned out the scattered shots as over a hundred Creek, Cherokee, and Highlanders dashed out of the tree line with Oglethorpe at their head. The enemy column quickly collapsed under the onslaught. Captain Sanchez was overpowered and taken prisoner, and when the Creek war chief Tooanahowi was wounded in the right arm attempting to seize a Spanish ensign, he drew his pistol with his left and shot the officer while he was drawing his sword. Several others were taken, including a pair by the general, and as the Spanish retreated carrying their wounded with them, Captain Hernandez and a few others were captured in the running fight.

Oglethorpe pushed the Spanish detachment back over a mile before halting the pursuit and posted his men in the woods along the northern edge of a fifty-yard-wide marshy expanse through which the trail passed. With this strong position established he returned to Frederica to bring up his regiment. As light rain began to fall the Highlanders, Creek, Cherokee, and rangers staring out of the tree line clutched their arms as a large Spanish detachment was seen advancing up the trail toward their position. Then, to their surprise, the enemy detachment halted on the south side of the marsh and began to make camp.

A runner from Captain Sanchez had informed Montiano that morning of the detachment's ambush and retreat. The general responded by ordering three companies of grenadiers and a detachment of militia to advance up the trail to support Sanchez and Hernandez. These troops, having encountered the remnants of the fleeing detachment, halted at the southern edge of the marsh, stacked their arms, and began to prepare cooking fires while waiting for any additional refugees. A spooked Spanish horse gave away the British position, but it was too late. As the enemy raced for their guns Lt. Hugh McKay of the Highlanders ordered his line to open fire. The initial volley tore through the Spanish encampment. The Spanish officers struggled to form up their men but soon returned fire, the weight of which was enough to send a number of Georgian troops running to the rear. McKay, however, moving up and down the length of the firing line, called on his men to hold their positions and maintain a steady fire on the encampment. With a sizable portion of the Spanish troops having fled at the start of the engagement, and casualties mounting among those that remained, when the Spanish commander toppled off his horse mortally wounded, the order was given to retreat.

Oglethorpe, riding forward with part of his regiment, listened to the flurry of gunfire ahead. He soon encountered a large part of the original detachment in full retreat. The general rallied these men and pushed forward with all speed fearing the collapse of Lt. McKay and those who had remained with him. The firing had come to a stop when Oglethorpe encountered McKay who informed him that no reinforcements were required, as the enemy had already retreated.[4]

For Montiano, the morning had resulted in close to a hundred men killed, captured, or wounded. Just as importantly, it pointed to the need to find another way to advance on Frederica. The general sent out frequent scouts, but none could find another path through the woods. As stragglers appeared in the camp, including Captain Hernandez, who had escaped after slaying his captors, Montiano ordered several galleys to advance up the Frederica River to gauge the depth of the channel and examine the shoreline for a suitable landing spot. Late on the afternoon of the twenty-first, Ensign Don Francisco Pineda returned from his naval reconnaissance of the river. The good news was that he found the water deep enough for the entire fleet and the channel broad enough that three vessels could operate abreast. He had approached close enough that a battery of 18-pound guns and small mortars fired on his ships without incident, but he could not ascertain if the shoreline was capable of supporting a landing as it was covered in tall grass.

Unconvinced, the next morning Montiano sent another flotilla to confirm Pineda's discoveries while the army began destroying the British fortifications. Early on the morning of the twenty-fourth an English deserter came into camp claiming that Oglethorpe was preparing to attack the Spanish lines. The army was put under arms, but beyond a few shots and the occasional distant rattle of drums nothing materialized. The deserter claimed that Oglethorpe had close to nine hundred men and a set of batteries, backed by a firing trench, which commanded the Frederica River just below the town. The general, the deserter informed Montiano and his officers, was expecting reinforcements from South Carolina at any moment, and ships and men were coming from as far away as New England to deal with the Spanish threat. Around noon the deserter's testimony took on more importance when the lookouts near the entrance to the harbor reported five warships under sail a few miles to the northeast, at least one of which was identified as a 30-gun frigate.

With an enemy fleet nearby, and no practical way before them to advance on Frederica by either land or sea, Montiano and his officers agreed that the best course of action was to withdraw. Creek and Chickasaw war parties had made securing fresh water difficult, and several Spanish parties looking to obtain this precious resource were ambushed and driven away. "The woods," one Spanish sergeant pointed out, "were so full of Indians that the devil could not get through them." With his provisions already running low and the bulk of troops still needed for the defense of St. Augustine and Havana, Montiano ordered the army to cross over to Jekyl Island that evening. The next day the fleet passed out to sea. The plan had been to engage the five English warships sighted the day before, but when these could not be located, the convoy set sail for Fort William in Cumberland Sound. Here they rendezvoused with Montiano and four galleys that took the inside channel to the stronghold. The combined Spanish force sparred with the fort for several hours, looking for an opportunity to land, but gave up on the idea and set sail for St. Augustine when reinforcements sent by Oglethorpe began to appear.

For Montiano the expedition to Frederica was hardly a disaster. Fort St. Simon's was destroyed, as were parts of the nearby village and several vessels in the harbor. Overall, casualties had been low, with sickness taking a much larger toll on his forces. Terrain and weather had been the true enemies of the campaign. The storm on July 2, the day after the flotilla had set out from St. Augustine, severely undermined the approach of employing a suddenly overwhelming stroke that would destroy Oglethorpe's forces as a prelude to attacking the settlements of Georgia and South Carolina. Strong winds and tides also delayed Montiano's fleet from entering St. Simon's Sound, giving ample warning to the British. Yet even with these sizable obstacles, it was a lack of knowledge of St. Simon's Island that would have even more bearing on the campaign's outcome.[5]

Although Oglethorpe would have liked to pursue the retreating Spanish, he was in no position to do so. Nor did he need to. The general, who had performed so poorly at the siege of St. Augustine a few years before, had repelled a major Spanish attack with only a handful of casualties. Oglethorpe's and Georgia's fortunes were both buoyed by the experience, but perhaps the most rewarding accolades came from South Carolina, which had chosen not to support the general in his hour of need. "That 5,000 men with so good an officer as the Governor of St. Augustine should fly before 600 or 700 men and about 100 Indians," one Charleston writer noted, "was a matter of just astonishment to all."[6]

Oglethorpe wrote London with news of the victory, ascribing it to divine providence and requesting additional troops. "I hope his Majesty will approve of the measures I have taken," he wrote Newcastle.

> I must entreat your Grace to lay my humble request before his Majesty that he would be graciously pleased to order troops, artillery, and other necessaries sufficient for the defence of this frontier and the neighbouring provinces, or give such directions as his Majesty shall think proper; and I do not doubt, with a moderate support, not only to be able to defend these provinces, but also to dislodge the enemy from St. Augustine if I had but the same numbers they had in this expedition.[7]

The general came close to receiving his request before the letter even reached the secretary of state. In late August a squadron of twelve warships under Captain Frankland of the H.M.S. *Rose* arrived from the Caribbean. The general accompanied the vessels as they patrolled the bar off St. Augustine and the Matanza Inlet, but he did not have enough men to use the opportunity to launch another attack on Castle San Marcos. A month later a detachment of five hundred British marines arrived at Charleston. The governor of Jamaica had sent these troops to cooperate with Oglethorpe and the governor of South Carolina in dealing with any Spanish threat to the two colonies. If there was none, the detachment was to immediately return to Jamaica. The colonel in command of the marines sent a dispatch to Oglethorpe in Frederica and spoke with Governor Bull. The latter expressed his thanks to the governor of Jamaica, but at the moment the borders of South Carolina were secure. Oglethorpe shook his head at the news. He now had the manpower to attack St. Augustine but no fleet to blockade it. The general responded a few days later. While the troops would be welcomed at Frederica, with no immediate threat before him Oglethorpe left the decision in the colonel's hands. With no clear need of their services the marines returned to Jamaica.[8]

For both Oglethorpe and Montiano, without a major influx of resources the war would become one of raids and counter raids. Oglethorpe's Creek and Chickasaw allies started this campaign, but Montiano, having organized a company of dragoons, had managed to intercept several of these war parties. With his raiding parties unable to provide him intelligence, and rumors abounding that St. Augustine was to be reinforced from Cuba to make another descent on Georgia, Oglethorpe organized a force of over five hundred Creek, Chickasaw, Highlanders, rangers, and troops from his regiment. On the evening of March 20, 1743, this force crossed the St. John's River into Florida.

Advancing through the night the war party struck the outer Spanish posts and Yamassee villages before dawn and quickly routed whatever defense was offered. The next morning the detachment pushed on to St. Augustine, scattering a few small Spanish detachments along the way. Here Oglethorpe stopped. Over the next few weeks, he would do everything he could to draw the Spanish out of Castle San Marcos and the fortified town, but to no avail. With the town invested the general's schooner and the 20-gun sloop *Success* patrolled the waters off St. Augustine. Oglethorpe went aboard his own schooner for one of these patrols and was almost killed when a cannon burst near him. With blood running out of his nose and ears he assured everyone he was fine after they lifted him to his feet.

Although the general had pushed in all the Spanish outposts, at this point, with Montiano unwilling to leave his fortifications, there was little to do but withdraw. By April the English forces had returned to Frederica and their native contingents to their villages. Oglethorpe also received a letter granting him leave to return to England to tend to financial matters. The general was over £12,000 in debt, having used his own credit to address his troops and the colony's needs. On July 12, 1743, Oglethorpe boarded the *Success*, and while he did not realize it at the time, departed Georgia for the last time.[9]

Part Four

Delenda est Canada

CHAPTER EIGHTEEN

King George's War

In the summer of 1743 Britain militarily entered the ongoing War of Austrian Succession on the side of Empress Maria Theresa of Austria. King George II's presence at the Battle of Dettingen on June 27, 1743, where a British, Hanoverian, and Austrian force defeated a French army, left few doubts in the matter. Even so, it was not until March 1744 that an official declaration of war between France and Britain took place. In North America the war, which was referred to as King George's War, combined with the current Anglo-Spanish struggle to recreate the scenario of Queen Anne's War: the British colonies and their Native allies against a Franco-Spanish alliance and their Native allies.

One of the first individuals to receive this news was the governor of Louisbourg, Jean-Baptiste Duquesnel. On May 3, 1744, the master of a merchant vessel sent from France handed the governor a pair of letters. The first announced the official declaration of war, while the second was from the minister of the marine, Jean-Frederic Phelypeaux, the Count Maurepas. The minister informed Duquesnel that a pair of French warships and several provision ships would arrive soon. In the meantime, he was authorized to issue letters of marque. An attack on the long-disputed British post of Canso was also authorized, and the king expected that the governor would encourage the Micmac and Maliseet to launch attacks against the English.[1]

An attack was not foremost in Duquesnel's mind. The seasonal fishing fleet had not come out from France, meaning that the town was short on provisions and men. Worse yet, news of war had caused the local fishing fleets to stay in port for lack of French warships to guard them. A handful of vessels arrived with some supplies, but within a few weeks the port was on the verge of famine, forcing the governor to hand out provisions. Fortunately, relief would come from Quebec, averting a disaster. With the sudden influx of supplies Duquesnel felt strong enough to attack Canso, which most thought would offer little resistance. The expedition would consist of 139 French and Swiss soldiers from the garrison and 218 sailors. To carry these troops the governor gathered together fourteen fishing vessels, a French privateer, the schooner *Succes*, and a sloop. These transports would be under the watchful eye of the 50-gun French warship *Caribou*, launched at Quebec only a few weeks before.

By May 24 the French flotilla was before Canso. The fort consisted of a wooden blockhouse and a number of dilapidated barracks and storehouses. The forgotten garrison of 120 men of the 40th Regiment were supported by a small sloop under the command of Lt. George Ryall, who was assigned to protect the fishing fleet. The garrison's commander, Captain Patrick Heron, was shocked when Captain Francois Duvivier of the French Marines demanded the fort and the town's surrender. Heron, like the rest of the British colonies, was unaware of the declaration of war. Caught completely by surprise, and with a French 50-gun warship anchored before him, he capitulated. It was agreed that the women and children would be sent to Boston while the men would be imprisoned at Louisbourg for a year.[2]

On May 16 unofficial news arrived at Boston that war had been declared on France. For Governor William Shirley it was not unexpected, and rumors of such actions had been circulating for some time. Without official news, however, there was little the governor could do but to dispatch a courier to the Wabanaki reminding them of their agreement under treaty to act as British subjects should a declaration of war arrive. On the thirty-first, the governor met with the Massachusetts Assembly to discuss the state of the colony and its preparedness for a conflict. Shirley spoke to the need to repair Castle William and the seaboard forts. Measures also needed to be taken to secure the colony's western frontier, which was now within easy striking range of the French fort at Crown Point. Shirley had previously issued a proclamation restricting trade with the French, particularly French Canada, and he now asked that the assembly pass a law to support this measure.

These matters aside, a pressing issue needed to be addressed. Lt. Governor Mascarene of Nova Scotia had written Shirley with an urgent request

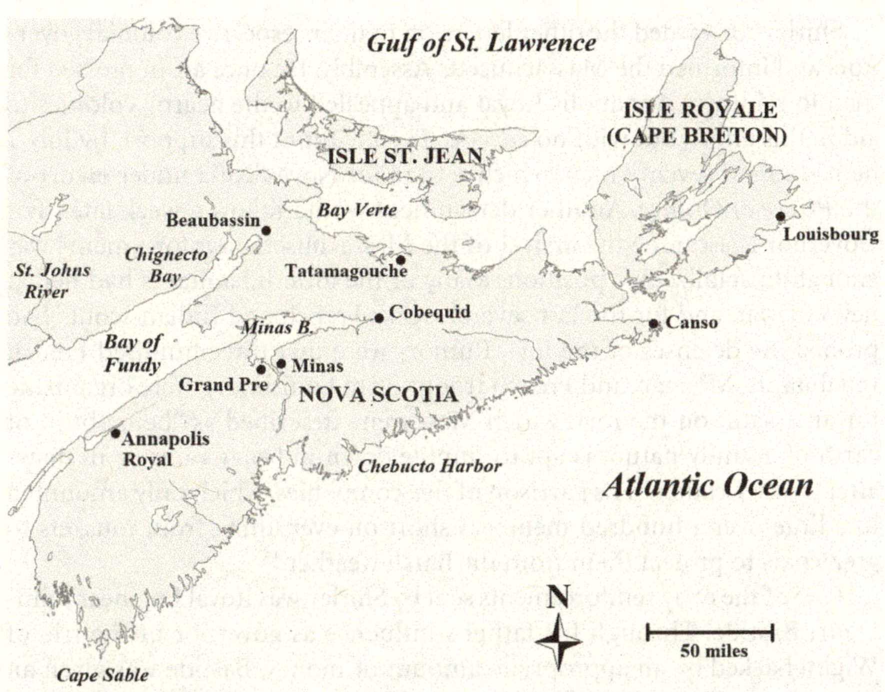

Nova Scotia and Îsle Royale.

to send two hundred men to bolster the hundred or so troops that now made up the garrison of Annapolis Royal. Shirley was for safeguarding Annapolis Royal and had already dispatched the 16-gun provincial snow *Prince of Orange* to Nova Scotia. He now asked that the assembly raise the requested troops, pointing out that it was in their own interest to do so. The expense involved in raising, equipping, and supplying two hundred men was deemed too costly, but the assembly did agree to raise two companies of sixty men each to reinforce Mascarene.

On the afternoon of June 2, the H.M.S. *Swallow* came to dock in Boston. Its captain left his first officer to see to the details of the arrival and soon found himself before the governor with a packet of letters. After a brief exchange of pleasantries, Shirley broke the seal on a letter addressed to him. It proved to be from Secretary of State Newcastle informing him of the declaration of war against France. Shirley was to encourage privateering, issue letters of marque, and "take all Opportunities, as far as depends upon you, to distress and annoy the French in their Settlements, Trade and Commerce."[3]

Shirley forwarded the other letters on to their respective colonial governors and informed the Massachusetts Assembly. He once again pressed for men to reinforce Annapolis Royal and appealed to the nearby colonies to aid in this effort, but with no success. Even without this support, by July 1 he had raised seventy men, which set sail for Nova Scotia under escort of the *Prince of Orange*. Another detachment would follow a week later. For Governor Mascarene the arrival of the Massachusetts reinforcements was enough to stabilize his position. Many of the local inhabitants had fled at news of war, and for the last several weeks French and Indian scouts had probed the defenses of the fort. Rumors were that three hundred French inhabitants, Micmac, and French troops from Louisbourg were organizing for an assault on the fort, which Mascarene described as "being built of earth of a sandy nature is apt to tumble down in heavy rains or in thaws after frosty weather." His garrison of five companies, which only amounted to a little over a hundred men, was short on everything from muskets to greatcoats to protect them from the harsh weather.[4]

One of the early reinforcements sent by Shirley was Royal Engineer John-Henri Bastide. Through his father's influence as governor of the Isle of Wight, backed by an appropriate amount of money, Bastide was given an ensign's commission in Hill's regiment of foot at the age of eleven. Although uncommon, such arrangements were not unheard of in the British Army of the day in which rank was obtained by purchase. In early 1718 Bastide purchased a lieutenancy, and not long after, he and his regiment were dispatched to Scotland to quell a potential Jacobite uprising. For two years Bastide spent his time creating maps and battle plans. His regiment was involved in the Battle of Glenshiel in June 1719, and Bastide later drew one of the principal plans of the engagement. The works generated by Bastide belied a natural talent, which was soon recognized, as we find him a few years later working for the Ordinance Board "in the Drawing Room in the White Tower." The next year Bastide, a practitioner engineer, was assigned to "the works and fortifications at Jersey and Guernsey." Repeated wars with France, and the likely possibility of another, coupled with the deteriorating defenses on the Channel Islands, had convinced the Ordinance Board to repair and rebuild the island's fortifications. This task was to occupy Bastide's time for the next thirteen years. The engineer, promoted again in 1733, worked on St. Aubin's Fort on the island of Jersey but spent most of his time modifying and repairing Elizabeth Castle across St. Aubin's Bay. The changes to the sprawling defensive structure, which occupied a small island at the east end of St. Aubin's Bay, along with the topography of the islands, were frequent subjects of Bastide's continuing map work.

In 1740 Bastide was assigned to Annapolis Royal as chief engineer in Nova Scotia. When the engineer arrived at the town, he informed Mascarene that he had orders to construct a new fort. After a quick survey of Fort Anne, which was essentially the same structure that French Governor Daniel Subercase had surrendered to General Francis Nicholson in Queen Anne's War thirty years ago, he began to appreciate why Mascarene, who would soon hold an engineering warrant of his own, had called for a new stone structure. Although the two men were of a like mind in this matter, executing the plan proved problematic. For over a generation governors and military officers in Nova Scotia called for a new fort to replace the decaying French structure, but funds, resources, and desire dried up within the confines of the peacetime environment. This attempt was no different. Funding, material delays, and the lack of a proper dock to land the stone, as well as the funds to build one, left the project in limbo.

With the onset of war between Spain and Britain in 1739, and the threat of a widening conflict with the Spanish attack on Georgia in 1742, Mascarene warned Whitehall of the dire position the colony would find itself in should France enter the war. There were simply not enough troops to protect the outlying towns, so they by default would fall. And as for Annapolis Royal itself, Mascarene painted a dismal picture.

> The Fort being built of earth of a sandy nature is apt to tumble down in heavy rains or in thaws after frosty weather. To prevent this, a revestment of Timbers has been made use of which soon decaying remedies the evil but for a short space of time, so that for these many years past there has been only continual patching. The Board of Ordnance has sent Engineers and Artificers in order to build the Fort with Brick and Stone, but little could be done for these two summers past than providing part of the materials and making conveniences for landing them, so that when I received the above mentioned directions there were several breaches of easy access to an enemy, which I immediately ordered to be repair'd in which the season has favored us beyond Expectation.[5]

With work on the new fort stalled, in the summer of 1743 Bastide was ordered to examine the coastal fortifications of New Hampshire and Massachusetts. Starting with the former, he inspected Fort William and Mary at Newcastle. He conducted a survey of the cannons within the fortification, and although a large number were found unserviceable, there were more than enough to meet the needs of the fort. The engineer found the river and harbor side defenses of the fort adequate, and with some minor changes, the landside defenses could be brought up to the same level. Bastide continued on to Massachusetts where he visited Castle William in Boston Harbor and drew up the necessary changes to mount an additional battery of cannons on the island. At Marblehead, Cape Ann, and Falmouth, he surveyed the ground and drew out plans for new gun batteries at each location. The engineer's work had brought him into contact with Governor Shirley and Governor Benjamin Wentworth of New Hampshire, both of whom were impressed with his talents, which no doubt had bearing on Bastide being promoted twice within the royal engineers from June 1742 to March 1744.[6]

When Shirley received reports in early May 1744 of an impending war between France and Great Britain, he sent Bastide back to Nova Scotia to help oversee the current defenses. When the engineer arrived at Annapolis Royal in mid-May, his first decision was purely practical in nature. All work on the new fortifications would stop. An attack seemed imminent, and any effort at this point would be better spent putting the old fort in its best state of repair. There were other issues as well. The fort was too large for the current garrison to effectively man the ramparts. In addition, shot, powder, and small arms were in short supply. About the only good news was that Governor Shirley had promised to dispatch two detachments of seventy and forty men to aid in the defense of the fort. Assisted by a hundred workmen, many of whom were local French tradesmen, Bastide set to repairing the fort. The engineer was able to make good progress, spurred on in part by news that a French detachment from Louisbourg had seized Canso. French and Indian raids in July chased away the engineer's local labor, slowing the work on the fort, and in one instance, forcing the fort's cannons to clear the marauders from the edge of the stronghold's glacis. The attacks stopped when Shirley's promised reinforcements arrived, even though most were without arms, because the Massachusetts Assembly did not wish to pay for these.

Rumors of a large French and Indian war party gathering in the countryside dominated the summer as the garrison, eventually reinforced by 170 Massachusetts militia, including a detachment of rangers, toiled away at their earth and wooden works. More alarming were reports that a pair of French warships from Louisbourg were to support this enemy force. For Mascarene there was little he could do but cling to his weatherworn stronghold, now decorated with recent repairs and wooden patchworks. "I must say they are already masters of the whole province," he wrote the Board of Trade, "except this Fort."[7]

There was a good deal of truth behind the rumors of a French attack. On May 29, a panic seized the lower town where many of Mascarene's men

Lt. Governor Paul Mascarene. (*Los Angeles County Museum of Art*)

and their families were quartered. The inhabitants, hearing news that a French privateer by the name of Morpin (Morpain) and five hundred men were about to fall upon the town, abandoned their homes and took shelter in the fort. While Morpain did not appear, on July 12 a war party of three hundred French, Micmac, and Maliseet under the leadership of Abbe Jean-Louis Le Loutre did appear. In May Loutre was at Louisbourg and had spoken with Governor Duquesnel about launching an attack on Annapolis Royal. The abbe could raise several hundred Micmac and Maliseet for the cause, and the governor, expecting a pair of French warships in the next few weeks, agreed to support the effort with these vessels and a detachment of marines. For the next four days Loutre's forces probed the fort and skirmished with the outer guards, but waiting for Duquesnel's warships to arrive, there was no real interest in storming the structure, which occasionally fired a round of grapeshot to remind the war party of the consequences of such an act. When Loutre saw the convoy sent by Shirley enter the Annapolis Royal Basin, he alerted his detachment, thinking it was the promised reinforcements, but instead he was greeted by the sight of British flags and the first of the Massachusetts troops disembarking. Convinced that something had gone seriously wrong, Loutre lifted the brief siege and retreated toward Minas. In fact, something had gone wrong. Duquesnel's promised warships, the 64-gun *Ardent* and the 50-gun *Caribou*, were late. He had sent a messenger to warn the abbe, but he had arrived too late.

While Mascarene and Bastide used the resulting interlude to improve the fort, a larger French effort was being formulated. The approach called for a company of marines, led by Captain Duvivier, to be transported on the *Succes* and four smaller craft to Bay Verte. From here they would march to Minas gathering together local militia and whatever Micmac and Maliseet support Abbe Loutre could raise. After organizing their ranks, the detachment would advance on Annapolis Royal collecting any Acadian volunteers they encountered along the way. Once in position, if Duvivier felt that he could not take the fort by surprise, he was to invest the stronghold and notify Duquesnel to send the naval component of the plan. The *Caribou*, which had just arrived at Louisbourg, and the shortly expected *Ardent*, would be sent along with artillery and several hundred troops to assist Duvivier in the assault on the British fort.

In early August, Duvivier landed at Bay Verte in eastern Nova Scotia with a company of a little over fifty regular troops. From here he marched to Minas where he rendezvoused with Loutre and began recruiting volunteers. Looking to resecure the area for France and boost his recruitment efforts, on August 27 Duvivier issued a decree to the French inhabitants of Nova Scotia. "The inhabitants of Mines comprising the parishes of Grand Pre, River Canard, Piziquid and Cobequid, are ordered to acknowledge the obedience they owe to the King of France," the dictum began. It called for military support from this populace in the form of horses, men, provisions, and powder horns. To make matters worse for the Acadians, those who did not comply with the oath of fidelity to the French king would be viewed as British and have their homes visited by French and Indian war parties. Duvivier did not spend long following up on these orders, which did little to augment his numbers. Duquesnel had given him until September 15 to seize the British fort. This he was to attempt only if he could surprise the garrison. If this could not be done but after a reconnaissance of the structure he believed that the fort could be taken, Duquesnel would send several vessels to assist him. Otherwise, Duvivier was to leave a few handpicked French and Indian detachments in the countryside and return to Louisbourg. Just as importantly, the governor made it clear that the inhabitants were not to be molested, as it was harvest.[8]

The French detachment consisting of fifty marines, a hundred Micmac and Maliseet, and a like number of Acadian volunteers did not reach Annapolis Royal until early September. With thoughts of surprise dismissed, Duvivier attempted to magnify his numbers and approached the fort with his men marching in a line-abreast formation and their flags fluttering in the cool morning breeze. On the ramparts Mascarene watched as the French ranks broke to filter through a hedgerow or over a fence only to reform again and continue their advance. When still several hundred yards from the fort the British commander motioned to a nearby cannon to fire. The resulting shot, aimed at the French colors in the center of the line, struck the ground in front of the French formation and skipped past Duvivier. With several more guns lining the wall, the French captain ordered a halt and withdrew to make camp about a mile away.

For the next several days French and Indian war parties harassed the defenders, particularly at night when they could easily approach unseen to within musket range. Sporadic shots from nervous sentries and sniping intruders were occasionally broken by the bark of small cannons as Duvivier's scouts collected their information. On September 14 he reported to Duquesnel that he should send the warships. With the fort before him invested and reinforcements on the way, Duvivier focused on making scaling ladders in preparation for an attack.

As custom, Duvivier informed Mascarene of the expected warships and offered him generous surrender terms. A brief truce resulted but soon broke down, and both sides began to snipe at each other once again. With the arrival of another fifty rangers, Mascarene began contemplating a sally. He was beginning to organize this effort when a scout arrived with news that the French had left. The governor was delighted but puzzled by his good fortune. The answer was not in Duvivier's actions but those of marine captain Michel De Gannes. De Gannes had arrived on Nova Scotia with a detachment that was selected to spend the winter. Outranking Duvivier, De Gannes took command of the operation on October 2, and two days later, when the promised French vessels had not arrived, he abandoned the siege and withdrew the army to Minas. The promised French flotilla appeared near Annapolis Royal three weeks later, but when Duvivier's troops could not be found, it returned to Louisbourg.

At Minas, De Gannes's combined war parties taxed the resources of the local residents to the point that they could not possibly provide the provisions the French leader sought without devastating the community. "We live under a mild and tranquil government," they wrote De Gannes of their plight, "and we have all good reason to be faithful to it. We hope therefore, that you will have the goodness not to separate us from it and that you will grant us the favour not to plunge us into utter misery." It was hardly the response the marine captain was looking for, but with their provisions failing and orders not to disturb the inhabitants, both war parties returned to Louisbourg having accomplished nothing from their combined efforts.

For the French, the prize had slipped away. Not because the enemy had defied them but from self-inflicted causes. Given the disparity in forces and the dilapidated state of the British fort, it is unlikely that Mascarene would have been able to repel a land-sea assault by Duvivier. The reinforcements sent by Massachusetts were mostly unarmed, and many in the garrison, including a good number of officers, were for surrendering the fort, Mascarene later confided to Shirley. For one French journalist in Louisbourg the lost opportunity was easy to explain.

> M. du Vivier was relieved of the command by M. de Ganas [Gannes], another captain of a free company [of marines], who had left Louisbourg later. This second commander maneuvered badly. Out of patience because the ships for which he was waiting did not come, he imprudently abandoned the investment and retired more than fifty leagues inland. It was this that caused the expedition to fail.[9]

The question that would later be raised was, why hadn't Duquesnel started with an attack on Annapolis Royal? Had the forces committed to Duvivier for the attack on Canso been combined with Loutre's forces and employed against Annapolis Royal, the chances were good that the British fort would have fallen. More importantly, the seizure of this weak post would have collapsed British power in Nova Scotia. At that point, the isolated and far weaker Canso would not offer much resistance. While certainly considered, here Duquesnel faced a pair of obstacles. First was that Canso had been at the heart of several Anglo-French disputes, and its capture was explicitly mentioned in his orders from France. The second problem was one of resources, primarily provisions and arms. Both were in such short supply that a number of the sailors in the Canso expedition were without pistols and cutlasses. He had pleaded with the minister for arms, men, and supplies and considered himself fortunate that an appeal to Governor Beauharnois at Quebec had at least procured some of his immediate needs. An attack on Fort Annapolis Royal was envisioned, but given the circumstances, it was too risky as a first effort.

For the moment Annapolis Royal appeared safe, an important first step in Shirley's mind, as he was convinced that if Nova Scotia had not been held the French population and the Wabanaki would have returned to their old alliance. A general attack on the New England frontier would have followed, which given its unprepared state would have been a disaster. The situation was stable but still needed to be addressed. After taking Canso the French held free reign throughout the countryside, leaving Fort Annapolis Royal as the only British foothold in the colony. With such advantages, it seemed unlikely that they would not return. Shirley expressed his concern for Mascarene's position to London and wrote Admiral Peter Warren in the Caribbean asking if some of his squadron could cruise the Gulf of Maine in support of the Nova Scotian port. Doing so would also help safeguard the New England coast given that, at the moment, Shirley only had a few small craft to see to this task. If a French 40-gun frigate appeared out of Louisbourg it would shut down traffic to Boston and terrorize the already hesitant fishing fleet. Given the state of his ships Warren was unable to comply, leaving Shirley to bolster the defenders of Annapolis Royal with his colonial flotilla.[10]

Turning to the Massachusetts frontier Shirley had raised several companies to garrison the small posts and conduct patrols throughout the winter. He had also warned the settlers who now filled the garrison houses at night or had moved to a more secure location. However, the biggest efforts toward securing the frontier came from Shirley's approach toward the Wabanaki, traditional French allies. He cautioned the Eastern Indians, as they were called by New Englanders, to remain neutral and reminded them of the consequences of not doing so by pointing to a recently signed treaty with the Iroquois, which would bring these British allies down upon any nation foolish enough to fracture the peace. There were some successes from this approach. The Iroquois had convinced their Christianized brothers in French Canada to remain neutral in any upcoming conflict. A representative from these missions arrived before Shirley and pledged that his people had informed the governor of Canada that they would not take up the hatchet as in former times. When Pequawket sagamores arrived, pledging their allegiance to the colony, Shirley held out hope that he could prevent another Anglo-Wabanaki War. "These Events seem to afford a fair Prospect of a Neutrality among all the Indians, which is a new thing here in time of a French Warr," he wrote the Board of Trade. "But I must at the same time observe to your Lordships that I don't flatter myself with much dependance upon the Present Disposition of the Eastern Indians, who are many ways liable to be drawn into a Rupture with us by the artifices of the French, their own Weakness & the Influence which the French Missionary Priests have over them."[11]

While efforts to protect the frontier proceeded slowly, Shirley's work toward outfitting privateers was already providing dividends. By the end of the year nine craft had been outfitted for this work, with the early participants having already begun to return with enemy prizes. The governor had also added two more vessels to the small colonial navy: the eighty-man, 6-

gun sloop *Orphan* and a brigantine. This growing guard fleet would sail the shallow coastal waters and watch over the fishing fleet.

Another unexpected task that occupied Shirley's time was a proposed prisoner exchange. A number of English prisoners from the capture of Canso had arrived at Boston in a pair of small vessels. Consisting mostly of women and children along with a handful of sick soldiers, the two vessels were commanded by Ensign John Bradstreet who carried a letter from Governor Duquesnel. At first Duquesnel had been reluctant to exchange his prisoners who would be able to report on the conditions at Louisbourg, but forced to ration provisions, he was not interested in feeding a large number of captives. The French governor suggested a general exchange, and in the meantime, he requested provisions for the British prisoners now being held at Louisbourg until such an agreement could be reached. He also proposed a compact of neutrality concerning the French and English fishing fleets. If agreed upon, both fleets would be left unmolested and free to carry out their commerce. Shirley was in favor of a prisoner exchange, which would go forward, but he frowned at the request for provisions and only sent a small amount for fear that the French might confiscate it for their own use. He dismissed the proposed fishing neutrality out of hand, pointing out that such an arrangement would certainly benefit the French now that Canso had been seized.

More importantly, after speaking with Bradstreet, Shirley was anxious to speak with the returning captives, who amounted to 340 over the course of the summer and early fall. Many were women and children who professed no knowledge of the fortress, yet even here Shirley was able to extract useful information regarding the garrison and French inhabitants they had encountered. The returning soldiers offered more direct military data regarding the nature of the fortifications, their positioning, and the number of cannons and men at each. Taken as a whole they painted a surprising picture of the state of Louisbourg. Enough so that Shirley began to piece together the skeleton of a risky plan.[12]

CHAPTER NINETEEN

A Mad Scheme

FEAR OF PRIVATEERS and elements of the French Navy operating from a safe haven near the New England coast had been a recurring theme since King William's War. This challenge to the New England fishing and maritime trade had culminated in the capture of Port Royal, Nova Scotia, during Queen Anne's War and its incorporation as a British holding at the subsequent Treaty of Utrecht. With the construction of Louisbourg, these matters had only become magnified. Louisbourg was vastly more fortified than Port Royal, and being built as a French naval base from the onset, it was equipped to do exactly what New England feared. Privateers operating out of this port could collapse the maritime industries of New England, and French expeditions from this fortress, bolstered by the sudden arrival of naval elements from Europe or the Caribbean, would imperil British holdings in Nova Scotia. Should this province be taken the French would be in a position to win over the population and reignite the animosities of the pro-French Wabanaki Confederacy, who would undoubtably fall upon the northern New England frontier. Coupled to these more immediate issues there remained another that would have an influence on upcoming events: the commercial rivalry of the French fishing trade.

Several colonial officials had previously illuminated the threat posed by the French naval fortress. Lt. Governor George Clarke of New York, for instance, wrote the Board of Trade in 1743 with his thoughts on these matters. Clarke suggested that a fleet be sent to winter in Boston, so as to be ready to strike the French stronghold in the spring, when it was at its weakest. As for assistance from the colonies, the lieutenant governor assured London that the place "is such a Thorn in the sides of the New England people, that it's very probable a large body of men may be raised there to assist in any such design." Christopher Kilby, a Massachusetts agent in London, expressed similar views when news of war reached him in England. He urged an attack on Louisbourg, informing the Board of Trade "that the reduction of the island (Cape Breton) is not only practicable but easy, and that in the present conjuncture which brings the war upon them in the midst of a famine, a well-conducted and vigorous attempt, would entirely subdue all their possessions on the continent." This was followed a few days later by a paper from Massachusetts Judge Robert Auchmuty, which detailed yet another plan to seize the French fortress via an Anglo-American attack in the spring.[1]

Shirley was familiar with a number of these thoughts and many that predated the ones mentioned. Certainly, the governor discussed the mechanics of such an operation with Bastide while the latter surveyed the forts along the Massachusetts coast. At the time, such thoughts were nothing more than speculation and opportune conversation with the royal engineer, but after speaking with several individuals returning from Louisbourg Shirley began to form a clearer picture of the fortress. In particular, two of these men, Captain Joshua Loring, whose privateer had been captured and carried into Louisbourg by a French warship, and Ensign John Bradstreet, who had been captured at Canso, cast doubts upon the reputation of the French stronghold. Both men were talented, dynamic young officers who would go on to make names for themselves in the last French and Indian War, and at the moment, were slowly gaining the governor's trust. While the works themselves were solid, they informed Shirley, those who backed them were not. Everything was lacking from food to ammunition. The city relied on convoys from France for almost everything, and the fishing fleet not arriving had only worsened the situation. There were too few men to man all the fortifications, a general lack of artillery skill, and a major morale problem among the garrison.

There was a good deal of truth behind these statements, especially concerning the mood of the garrison, but it would still be several months before this openly manifested itself. On the morning of December 27, 1744, the Swiss companies assembled with their arms against orders. The officer on duty ordered them to disperse and return to their quarters. They did dis-

Massachusetts Governor William Shirley, c. 1750. An able servant of the Crown, Shirley embodied attributes that made him not only a popular colonial governor, but at the same time a respected authority on North America in Britain. The governor's belief that the ongoing disputes between France and England in North America could only be settled by the elimination of New France often put him at odds with London, even though this ultimately turned out to be the policy adopted. (*William Johnson Papers*)

perse, but they did not return to their quarters. Instead, they marched to the French barracks and berated these troops for not joining them as they had previously agreed. The scolding worked, and soon the entire garrison, minus its sergeants and officers, had formed up on the parade ground. These soon arrived when drummers beat out the call to arms, although there was also a great deal of confusion when these individuals arrived and found their men already assembled. With some sense of order restored, Governor Du Chambon addressed the leaders of the mutiny, asking them why they were acting contrary to their officer's orders. The response was a list of complaints ranging from being six months in arrears with their pay to the quantity and quality of rations and the need for more firewood, as well as the issuance of proper clothing. Du Chambon agreed to the demands, as there was really little else he could do, and for the moment this seemed to work, although there was still a good deal of fear among the governor and his staff that the troops might raid the city's treasury and turn the fortification over to the enemy. This fear soon faded when the garrison behaved well over the winter, leaving Du Chambon with hope that he could replace some of the troops with the fall convoys from France.

Although Governor Shirley would not know of this event for months, it would only confirm his thoughts on the matter. After lengthy conversations with the returning Louisbourg prisoners he became convinced that circumstances had presented a narrow window of opportunity to seize the fortress. The governor pressed the Admiralty for naval support, not only to help secure Annapolis Royal but the Gulf of Maine as well. He then wrote Newcastle in November 1744 on the intelligence he had gathered and the idea of a joint Anglo-British expedition against the stronghold in the spring before the first convoys from France. If successful the plan would eliminate problems in Nova Scotia and secure the New England coast from French vessels operating out of the port—a problem he currently could do little about without Royal Navy support. In addition, seizing Louisbourg would also place New France's lifeline through the Gulf of St. Lawrence in jeopardy. A few weeks later he clarified the thought, informing Newcastle that the garrison was on the verge of revolt and that a scarcity of basic supplies haunted the French seaport. In the governor's estimation half a dozen warships could force the entrance to the harbor and land two thousand men, which would be sufficient to subdue the garrison.[2]

It was not just Newcastle and the Board of Trade that were on the receiving end of the governor's correspondence. When Shirley discovered that a French East Indies fleet had sought refuge at Louisbourg he informed the Admiralty in hopes that they might be able to intercept this valuable convoy when it departed for France. He then used the opportunity to press his need for Royal Navy support. If Louisbourg was to provide safe haven for such valuable fleets, he argued, it only followed that a small detachment of French warships could wreak havoc along the colonial coastline and disrupt maritime activity for weeks, if not months. He asked the Admiralty for several 40- to 50-gun ships to patrol the coast of New England and secure the king's foothold in Nova Scotia or help retake it should it be captured during the approaching winter months.

Shirley and a number of leading citizens pressed London for an Anglo-American expedition against the fortress, but little in the way of results had come from these proceedings. The official response to the governor's requests had proven lukewarm, in part given the conditions in Great Britain at the time, but in late fall a dispatch containing a letter from Newcastle's private secretary presented more promise. Understanding the repercussions of not acting, the duke promised to dispatch naval forces in the spring to support any attempt Shirley might make against the French. While unofficial, it was enough to set the governor into motion.

Armed with this knowledge Shirley and a small group of supporters, which included Loring, Bradstreet, and William Vaughan, began to formulate an attack on the French fortress. Two elements quickly came to the forefront. First, the attack had to come in the spring of 1745 before the supply fleets arrived from France. This left little time to organize and put together the resources required for such an operation. Second, they needed the Royal Navy. Troops and artillery Shirley could raise in New England, but warships he could not. Perhaps a handful of small frigates and a number of armed schooners and sloops could be outfitted in New England ports, but without Royal Navy support a single French man-o-war could lift the blockade and end the attempt on the stronghold in a complete disaster.

Satisfied with the preliminary details, the governor addressed the Massachusetts Assembly on January 9, 1745, and proposed that the colony organize an expedition against Louisbourg. The governor detailed his knowledge of the French stronghold, the importance of the timing, and the need to act. If nothing was done, the war would soon come to the New England frontier, but if they acted swiftly, they could capture Louisbourg and remove the threat to New England and its maritime trade. Yes, it would be expensive, and yes, it had many challenges, but the circumstances were such that "Nothing would more effectually promote the interests of this province at this juncture," he concluded, "than a reduction of that place."[3]

It was an aggressive and extremely risky plan, especially for the financially strapped colony. The first reactions were astonishment followed by questions of whether the other New England colonies would participate and what forces London would send to support this. The latter Shirley maneuvered around, as he had no official guarantees of support from Britain, but he did inform the assembly that he would write Admiral Peter Warren in the West Indies seeking Royal Navy assistance. As to aid from the other colonies, from his personal correspondence the governor already knew that New Hampshire and Rhode Island had shown interest, and he would press the other colonies to contribute men, guns, and money to the effort.

The proposal set off a two-day debate in the assembly, but in the end, without direct aid from Britain or a concerted combined effort by several colonies, the venture was deemed too risky for Massachusetts to attempt on its own. The matter, however, was hardly put aside. There was a general feeling that the operation was, as Shirley pointed out, necessary to secure the borders and interests of New England. The question was really about assuming the bulk of the risk. The assembly pressed Shirley to ascertain what the Crown's wishes were in such matters, pointing out that the colony stood ready to assist as soon as a force was sent out from England.

Shirley complied and sent another letter to Newcastle informing him that he had presented his plan to the assembly and asked for resources to assist in the venture. This was a symbolic gesture in Shirley's mind, as the reply would arrive too late to be of use. Fortunately for the governor, Vaughan, who would claim to have originated part of the plan, took to changing the assembly's mind. The eldest son of a former lieutenant governor of New Hampshire, Vaughan had amassed a sizable fishing business along the coast of Maine before later shifting his business interests toward lumbering in the Damariscotta area. He now utilized his business connections in the fishing, timber, and maritime industries. The message was simple. Not only would capturing Louisbourg remove the threat to the English fishing fleets but it would also remove French competition to the financial benefit of all. Vaughan, busy pushing forward the plan, informed Shirley that he could raise a thousand men and offered to lead the expedition if called upon or follow with the same diligence if Shirley found another more suitable. Within a few weeks over three hundred businessmen from Boston and Marblehead called upon the assembly to reconsider their decision.[4]

In late January 1745 these petitions were presented to the assembly along with a message from Shirley that urged a committee of both houses to conduct a formal inquiry into the matter. While a closed session of the assembly followed, Shirley looked to lessen expectations by pointing out that, although it was highly unlikely they would take Louisbourg by surprise, as some had suggested, this did not rule out success. Even if the New England troops could not force the French works, they could invest the fortifications in anticipation of a force arriving from Britain. And even if this should fail, the contingent was strong enough to shift its efforts again the French fishing ports along the coast of Cape Breton and Prince Edward Island. In this scenario the threat posed to Louisbourg, coupled with the economic damage to the smaller French fishing ports, would likely prevent an attack on Annapolis Royal and safeguard Nova Scotia for another year. The governor concluded his message by advocating "in the strongest terms, to lay hold on the present favorable opportunity, which Providence seems to have put into our hands, of securing the province, by the single reduction of Cape Breton."[5]

The inclusion of William Pepperrell, a prominent merchantman from Kittery, Maine, who had been absent at the initial vote on the plan, as head of the joint committee was exactly what Vaughan had hoped for. Pepperrell knew most of the petitioners and had already spoken with Shirley in regard to his support. The committee gave a positive recommendation, and on January 25, 1745, the assembly approved the project and voted the money for three thousand men to be raised along with their transportation. They

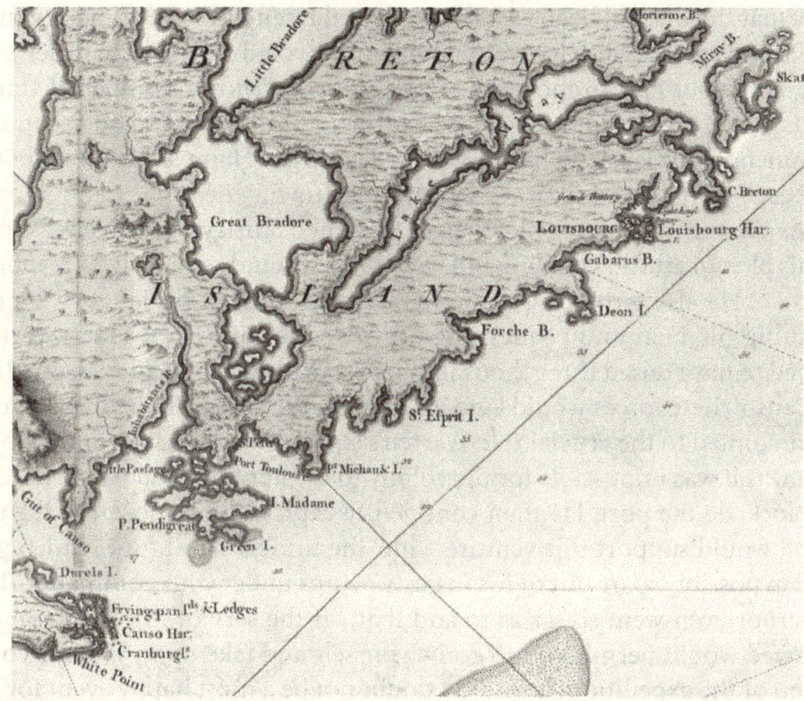

The coast of Cape Breton from Canso, Nova Scotia, to Louisbourg. (*Norman B. Leventhal Map Collection, Boston Public Library*)

also formally asked Shirley to seek the participation of the New England colonies as well as New York and Pennsylvania. While Shirley would find some material aid from New Hampshire and Rhode Island, he did not press the issue, fearing that the time required to organize and equip a large contingent from several colonies would undermine the overall approach. Along these lines the governor was able to accelerate the raising of Massachusetts troops by appointing Pepperrell, who held the rank of colonel in the militia, as lieutenant general and commander of the expedition's land forces. While Pepperrell lacked any significant military experience for this posting, so did every other potential candidate in the colonies. More importantly, he was quite popular, which would soon translate into a successful recruiting effort.

A flurry of contracts were signed as drums beat out the prelude to the recruiter's call. In Boston Harbor and along the docks teams of men worked on vessels while a cluster of small craft went ashore on Castle Island in the distance, having been tasked with selecting the artillery for the siege train. Like Sir William Phipps's campaign against Quebec over fifty years before, now that the die had been cast the spirit at the center of the effort began to ignite and spread. The Connecticut Assembly voted to support Shirley's effort, contributing 516 men, the armed sloop *Defence*, a number of transports, and Lt. Governor Roger Wolcott who Shirley appointed second in command. Rhode Island raised 150 men and New Hampshire another 500, and each contributed several vessels to the growing fleet.[6]

As the transports and men began to gather, Shirley wrote Newcastle as to his plan to attack, knowing full well that he would not receive a response in time. He also wrote to Admiral Warren in Antigua on January 29, explaining his plan and requesting aid from his squadron. The governor hoped to have raised three thousand men by March 1, and after assembling at Canso, these forces would land at Cape Breton shortly thereafter. Shirley then pointed to the crucial role Warren's squadron would play in the operation, as it was impossible for the colony to muster the naval might needed to blockade the port. He then confidently expressed his view that the admiral would support this venture with "the utmost naval force which you sir can possibly spare out of his majesty's ships under your command." The governor even went so far as to add that, "If the service in which you are engaged would permit you to come yourself and take upon you the command of the expedition, it would I doubt not be a most happy event for his Majesty's service and your own honor."[7]

While Shirley rightly believed, via personal correspondence with his patron, the Duke of Newcastle, that Warren would have been issued orders to assist in his campaign, the problem was that Warren had yet to receive these directives when Shirley's letter reached him on February 22. Warren shrugged at the request. He had no orders to leave station with his squadron, and although he was told to cooperate with the colonial governors regarding naval defenses along the coast, this went beyond that. After meeting with his captains, it was agreed to dispatch the *Launceston* to Boston and the *Mermaid* to New York. With the recent loss of the *Weymouth*, it was the best he could do at the moment.

It would be several weeks before Shirley received Warren's response. In the meantime, formations of men drilled in open areas as the transports began taking on provisions and the siege artillery. The latter consisted of eight 24-pound and twelve 9-pound cannons, two 12-inch mortars, one 11-inch mortar, and one 9-inch mortar. New York would send an additional ten 18-pounders, but this was all that could be had on such short notice without seriously weakening the seaboard defenses of either colony.

While this activity moved to a conclusion, Shirley dispatched his colonial fleet to Louisbourg in mid-March. The flotilla was led by the newly completed 22-gun frigate *Massachusetts*, which would act as Commodore Edward Tyng's flagship. Alongside this was the contracted 24-gun frigate *Molineux*, the 16-gun snow *Prince of Orange*, and the 12-gun *Boston Packet*. A pair of privateers were commissioned from Rhode Island as well. The first, the *Fame*, was a 250-ton, 24-gun frigate while the second, the *Caesar*, was a smaller 14-gun snow. A pair of 10- and 6-gun Massachusetts sloops, the *Resolute* and the *Bonetta*, would also move forward to scout the rendezvous point at Canso. Icy weather and the staggered departures brought Tyng's flotilla before Louisbourg in piecemeal fashion, but by March 20 the colonial vessels began to patrol off the harbor. The *Resolute* and the *Bonetta* cruising along the coast of Nova Scotia reached Canso on March 25. The site was abandoned, and there were no indications of the enemy.[8]

With the colonial fleet deployed along the southwest coast of Cape Breton, the troops began filing onto their transports. On March 21 Shirley was informed that the New Hampshire contingent had set sail for Canso in eleven transports under the protection of the 10-gun sloop *Abigail*. A few days later on March 24 a much grander version of this event took place at Boston. At 4:00 p.m. the first detachment, some 2,800 men, departed in fifty-one vessels under the watchful eye of a few armed sloops and Captain Rous in the 24-gun frigate *Shirley*.

While the second detachment, which was scheduled to depart on the twenty-eighth, tended to its final preparations, Shirley received Admiral Warren's disappointing response. It was hardly the level of commitment the governor had hoped for, and although even one or two Royal Navy warships might well make the difference, it added an unexpected risk that cast a cloud over the entire venture. A few days after the second contingent set sail, this anxiety would suddenly dissipate when Shirley was handed another letter from Warren on March 30. Newcastle had made good his promise to the governor and sent orders for Warren to proceed to New England with his squadron. When Warren received these orders a few weeks after Shirley's initial request, he sent Shirley a dispatch and ordered his vessels out to sea.[9]

The New Hampshire troops arrived at Canso on March 31, but the Massachusetts vessels were scattered by a series of storms and arrived at the rendezvous over the first week of April. Ice flows blocked the harbor so the army sat at anchor, waiting for the remainder of the force to arrive. The troops went ashore a few days later, and not long after word reached Pepperrell that brought a cheer from the encampment; Admiral Warren was on the way. Although several of his officers pushed him to move on Cape Breton, Pepperrell wisely waited for Warren. The general erected temporary quarters and spent the next few weeks under overcast skies that occasionally produced periods of freezing rain. Weather permitting, he drilled his raw troops and constructed a blockhouse on a nearby hill to mount a battery of eight 9-pounders. A pair of vessels were dispatched through the Gut of Canso to intercept any enemy vessels in Bay Vert that might be looking to reinforce Louisbourg, and a detachment was sent to scout the French village of St. Peters at Port Toulouse. News also arrived that Captain Tyng and the Massachusetts fleet had engaged the 36-gun French frigate *Renommee* near the harbor's entrance. After a running battle of several hours the French warship escaped in the bands of fog and fading light. The best news, however, came from a pair of French prizes brought into port. Both were loaded with molasses and rum, items quickly being depleted within the idle colonial army.[10]

On April 22 signal flags sent alarms throughout Pepperrell's fleet as a large warship was seen approaching. If it were French, the transports would be captured and the expedition brought to a quick conclusion. There was a scramble to arms when suddenly the flags switched to blue, meaning all clear. It was the 40-gun H.M.S. *Eltham* with news that Admiral Warren in the 60-gun *Superb* and the 40-gun frigates *Launceston* and *Mermaid* would arrive tomorrow. Fearing for the colonial force Warren had intercepted a local vessel headed for Boston, taken its pilot, and sailed straight for Canso. Spirits soared as many who had grumbled over the last month questioning the hastily organized expedition were suddenly eager to press forward now that they possessed naval superiority.

Warren was not to be counted among these. An old friend of Pepperrell from his time stationed in Boston, the admiral was in favor of an attack on Louisbourg, but by British regulars. Given his experience at the siege of St. Augustine and the myriad logistical problems that came with an attempt on the much stronger fortress of Louisbourg, which he believed could not be surprised, and thus, would have to be reduced by a professional siege, he thought the venture outside the capabilities of the colonies. In fact, the latter attempting this feat without British support could easily lead to a disaster. Warren wrote the Secretary of the Admiralty, Lord George Anson, and the Secretary of the Navy, Thomas Corbett, that in his opinion, "to undertake an affair of such consequence and Expence, too rashly, that must, if they fail in it, Involve both England and the Colonies, in a large debt to no purpose, I think wou'd be madness, both in the Advisers, and the Executors, of such an attempt."[11]

Now, as he shook hands with his old friend William Pepperrell, the admiral realized that he was about to play a prominent role in just such a scheme.

CHAPTER TWENTY

The Dunkirk of the West

SPEAKING WITH Pepperrell brought little in the way of comfort to Warren. Clearly the senior officer present, the admiral was offered command of the expedition, but he declined, preferring instead to conduct a customary joint operation. He would command the naval forces, and Pepperrell would command the land forces. The general then briefed Warren concerning the plan of attack, and when the admiral asked about the troops, Pepperrell shrugged. The idleness had led to a few disciplinary problems and a general disinterest had fallen over most. However, the army's mood had changed dramatically with Warren's arrival. Of more importance, he confided, was the army's supplies. There was not enough powder or shot for the cannons, and many of the troops' muskets, which had been stored in the armories for years, were bad. Nonetheless the army was ready to move. Warren offered to give Pepperrell some powder from his vessels, and it was agreed that the admiral would move to immediately block the harbor while the transports would follow and conduct landing operations at Gabarus Bay once the winds shifted and drove the ice clinging to the shores out to sea.

The next day seven Connecticut troop transports arrived at Canso under the escort of the sloop *Defence*. The convoy had encountered the 36-gun French *Renommee* and had narrowly avoided capture when one of the escorts, the 14-gun Rhode Island sloop *Tartar*, charged the warship. The ploy worked, and as the *Tartar* dueled with the *Renommee* the convoy made good its escape. After an hour the outgunned Rhode Island sloop broke off the engagement and, after a long chase, made good its escape.[1]

On April 29[2] the winds cooperated and Pepperrell's army set sail. Over a hundred vessels arranged in four divisions proceeded to Gabarus Bay under the watchful eye of three armed Massachusetts vessels. As the flotilla advanced up the Cape Breton coast, shadowed for some time by a pod of whales, several vessels carrying 270 men from the New Hampshire contingent sheared off and set a course for the French village of St. Peters at Port Toulouse. Their orders were to seize and burn the town as well as the nearby fort. Pepperrell's fleet pressed forward and by sunset found themselves half a dozen miles from the landing site. As it was too late to do anything, orders were issued that the army would land in the morning.

After a failed attempt to seize Nova Scotia that summer, in November 1744, Du Chambon and Intendent Francios Bigot proposed a plan that would safeguard Louisbourg by retaking Annapolis Royal and Placentia. The operation would require two ships-of-the-line and a pair of frigates. The eight hundred troops being transported on the fleet from France would rendezvous with 350 French and Indians sent by Du Chambon before Annapolis Royal on April 15. The crumbling fort would certainly fall before such a force, which could then move on Canso or Placentia. By seizing Nova Scotia, the governor argued, any attack planned against Louisbourg in the spring would be redirected to recover Annapolis Royal. Minister of the Marine Maurepas agreed with the analysis and brought the effort before King Louis XV. Louis did not like the cost of the project, so Maurepas, looking to save money while still providing some sort of aid for Louisbourg, suggested that three warships be sent to protect the fishing fleet and the approaches to the harbor. When the minister informed Louis that it would prove half the cost of the original project, the king accepted the compromise and ordered the vessels to be sent.

The first of the three warships, the *Renommee*, departed for Louisbourg on February 7, 1745. Winter storms damaged the ship and forced it back into port for repairs. Thus, it was not until mid-March that the French frigate restarted its voyage to Louisbourg. The second vessel, the *Castor*, was being built at Quebec, but Maurepas believed that it would be ready by March, although it would not be until May 16 that the vessel was launched. The last ship, the *Mars*, had been delayed with repairs, so on April 25 the minister ordered the 64-gun *Vigilant* to take its place.

The *Renommee*, carrying a message from the minister of the marine as to the cancellation of Du Chambon and Bigot's plan to attack Nova Scotia,

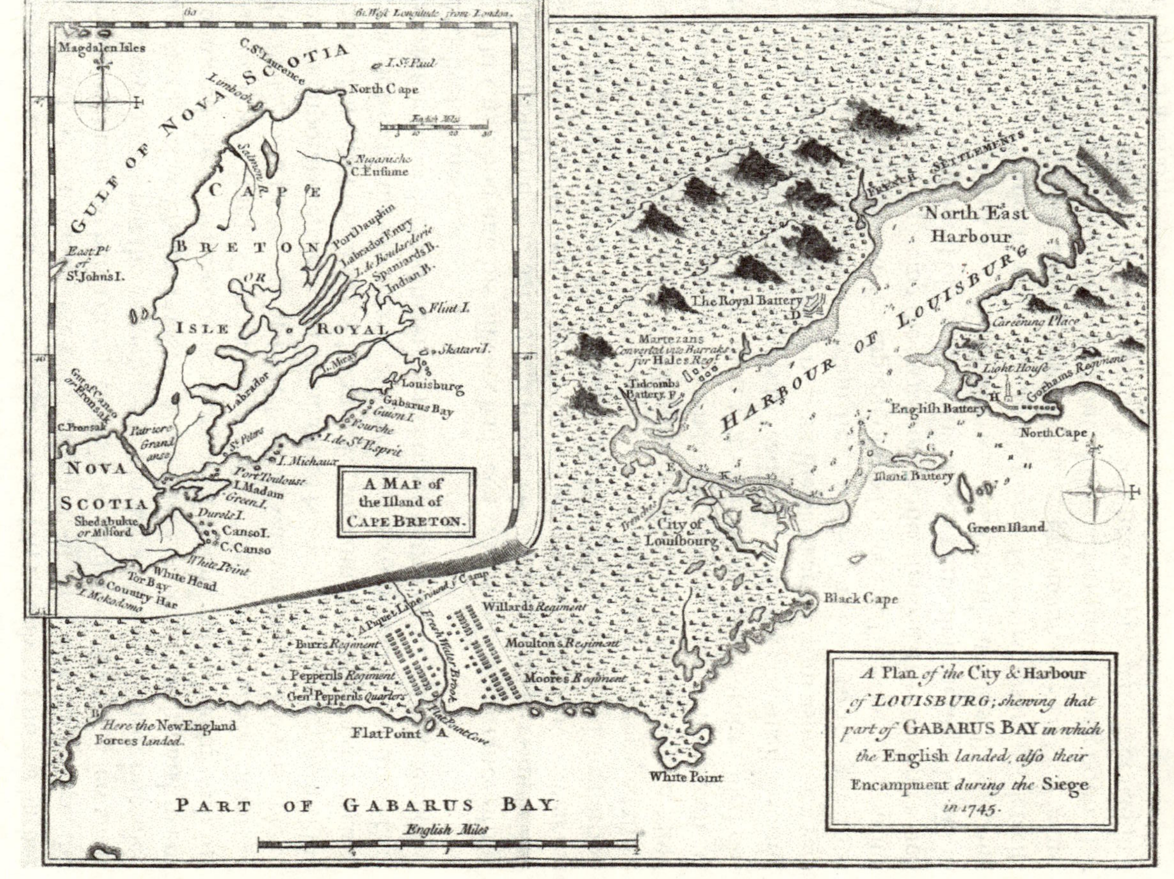

A map of Gabarus Bay and Pepperrell's landing and encampment at Flat Point, *Gentleman's Magazine*, 1758.

arrived before Louisbourg on the last days of April only to find the harbor icebound. Moving down the coast in search of a possible anchorage, the frigate encountered half a dozen colonial warships near Canso. A few shots were exchanged, but the *Renommee*, not looking for a fight, easily outsailed the smaller New England vessels. A few days later the French warship encountered the *Tartar* escorting a convoy of troops. After dueling with the *Tartar*, it was clear to Captain Alexandre Boisdescourt de la Maisonfort of the *Renommee* that a major British effort was underway. He was able to make temporary repairs in an uninhabited Nova Scotian bay before making another attempt to reach Louisbourg. Facing contrary winds, a shortage of provisions, and the presence of enemy warships off the entrance to the harbor, Masionfort decided to return to France with a damaged frigate and his undelivered message.[3]

Du Chambon and his officers had seen vessels off the entrance of the harbor from mid to late April, but most believed they were just supply vessels waiting for the ice to clear. This belief was shattered on May 7 when the 18-gun *St. Jean du Luz* cleared the coastal ice field and entered the harbor. The captain of the vessel informed Du Chambon that he had engaged three enemy warships outside the harbor, one of which was a 24-gun frigate. More importantly, they were not alone. There were half a dozen of these craft attempting to blockade the harbor. With this news the governor called out the militia, ordered the batteries to readiness, and sent out small scouting parties toward Gabarus Bay to prevent the blockaders from using the rivers and creeks in this area to obtain fresh water. On May 10 the governor handed his dispatches to the captain of the *La Societe*. They spoke to routine matters, such as replacing the Swiss companies in the garrison with French ones, and the handful of small enemy vessels patrolling the approaches to the harbor, but this was of little worry, as Du Chambon was still expecting a force from France to attack Annapolis Royal. The warships in this detachment would quickly chase away the Yankee privateers. The *La Societe* cast off its mooring lines and slipped out of the harbor that evening bound for France, while half a dozen miles to the southeast Pepperrell's fleet had just dropped anchor.

At dawn cannons on the city's ramparts sounded the alarm, which was followed by the ringing of church bells throughout the town. Du Chambon raced to the ramparts just in time to watch Pepperrell's fleet enter Gabarus Bay. The governor was stunned by what he saw. He was aware of enemy activity along the coast, as news from one of the arriving ships spoke of a British naval presence at Canso. In response to this information, Du Chambon had ordered the French commander at Port Toulouse to send out a scouting party. The four-man detachment found immediate success, capturing four Englishmen near the post. Unfortunately, the captives soon turned the tables and captured the detachment.

With no news from Port Toulouse of enemy activities at Canso, Du Chambon viewed the reports reaching him as the work of English privateers, which was hardly unexpected. While the governor had called out the militia and sent out patrols, little else had been done to prepare the town for a siege, even though this was precisely the time of year to expect an attack. This is perhaps even more surprising, given that a British landing at Gabarus Bay is precisely what the French expected. No one believed that the enemy would challenge the heavy guns of the Island and Royal Batteries and attempt a landing in the harbor, leaving them with the logical option of nearby Gabarus Bay. True, there were other locations where the enemy could land, but these were distant enough to impose a major logistical penalty on the attackers and would allow time for French forces to prepare to meet them. Yet, while this obvious scenario lay before the defenders, nothing had been done to secure the potential landing zone along the north shore of Gabarus Bay. Part of this thinking was clearly based on the information reaching the governor, part on a lack of resources to execute the required defenses, but a portion may be blamed on the interim governor's lack of wartime experience. Although he began his military career in 1730, Du Chambon had spent his entire service in peacetime operations on Cape Breton, Isle St. Jean, and as commander of Port Dauphin.

At this point two men approached the governor. The first was a retired officer of the Regiment de Richelieu by the name of Le Poupet de la Boularderie, while the second was Louisbourg's longtime port captain, Pierre Morpain. Both men urged the governor to oppose the British landing. Boularderie called upon Du Chambon to march half the garrison to the shores of Gabarus Bay and push the enemy back into the sea while they were coming ashore. Morpain's approach was more palatable. The senior officer asked Du Chambon to allow him to advance on the enemy with what civilian volunteers he could muster. The governor, who was reluctant to risk his garrison, agreed and added another twenty-four men to the fifty Morpain had assembled.[4]

By 10 a.m. Pepperrell's fleet was at anchor and busy filling small boats with green-, blue-, and red-coated New Englanders. The vanguard of the landing force was given the signal to advance and steered for Flat Point. Lookouts perched in the ships' masts soon called out and pointed to Morpain and Boularderie's force advancing toward the landing area near Flat Rock Cove. For a moment it looked as if Morpain and Boularderie's plan might come to fruition. The small French force braced itself behind whatever cover it could find and prepared to fire once the boats came within range. Suddenly there was a flurry of signal flags, and the small craft turned back toward the fleet. Here they were joined by a second detachment of landing craft, and the combined force began to proceed toward a cove about halfway between Flat Point and White Point.

When Boularderie saw the numbers arrayed before them he viewed the matter as hopeless and was in favor of returning, but Morpain ordered the column to march toward the landing area. The problem was that Pepperrell's escorts knew of Morpain's presence, and sliding toward shore the *Massachusetts*, *Boston Packet*, and *Lady Montigue* began firing grapeshot and ball at the French troops. By the time this small force reached the British landing area over a hundred men were already ashore. This, however, was not as much of an issue as the terrain before the French detachment, which led into a depression. Morpain had originally taken this route, but thinking better of it, he was busy withdrawing his troops when a detachment advancing from the landing area appeared. The New England troops launched a sharp fire on the French column, which, when combined with the unfavorable terrain, quickly broke their ranks. A wounded Morpain and most of the detachment fled, leaving Boularderie and a dozen others to cover the retreat. The detachment fought the growing number of British muskets for another fifteen minutes before a twice-wounded Boularderie, seeing the folly of further resistance, surrendered.

With the threat removed the English advanced guard pushed forward and established a skirmish line along a row of wooded hills seven hundred yards to the southwest of the town. Behind them some two thousand men went ashore, and a camp was established at Flat Point. A few shots from nervous sentries interrupted the night, but at daylight Pepperrell and the rest of his men went ashore. The artillery and provisions followed, but without proper harbor facilities everything had to be brought across the beach from open boats. The strong surf hampered these operations and often forced men into freezing waste-deep water to accomplish their task. Some days the weather made it impossible to conduct this work, meaning that it would be several weeks before all the supplies and munitions were ashore.[5]

For Du Chambon, who spoke with the refugees of Morpain and Boularderie's detachment, it was clear that it was too late to oppose the English landing. The hastily organized effort had resulted in almost fifty casualties, and by now the enemy was ashore in such numbers that it ruled out a sally against their position without risking the entire garrison of the fortress. For the moment, all he could do was send out small scouting parties to monitor the enemy's progress and prepare the town for a siege. What proved just as alarming was a message that evening from Captain Chassin de Thierry, the commander of the Royal Battery. With the landward defenses of the Royal Battery under repair, in his opinion the position was untenable against a land assault. He recommended that the garrison be withdrawn and the structure blown up. The governor summoned a council of war where the chief engineer Etienne Verrier agreed with Thierry's opinion, although he did not find it necessary to destroy the battery given the powder it would take and its already weather-damaged condition.

Several junior officers disagreed, but with the council of war in favor of abandoning the Royal Battery, Du Chambon ordered Thierry to spike the guns and carry away whatever food and ammunition he could. Thierry and his men spent the evening carrying out this task, and by midnight they had returned to the town. As there were still a number of salvageable items that had been left behind, the next morning the governor dispatched a pair of officers and twenty men to finish the task. By the afternoon of May 1, they had returned, and thus, without a shot being fired, Du Chambon had already lost a key piece of the harbor's defenses. One French journalist during the siege was at a loss to explain the action: "Unless it was from a panicked fear which never left us again during the whole siege, it would be difficult to give any reason for such an extraordinary action."[6]

Late that evening a detachment of four hundred men was assembled at Flat Point. Their orders were to march around the outskirts of the harbor and fall upon the French posts along the northeastern shore. This was easily accomplished, and several homes and storehouses were put to the torch. With their work complete, and the main column starting its return march, Colonel William Vaughan decided to lead a small detachment forward to conduct a reconnaissance of the Royal Battery a little less than a mile away. After watching the darkened form through sunrise and seeing no signs of life, Vaughan's detachment crept forward and found the stone fortress abandoned. Delighted, the colonel dispatched a message to Pepperrell asking for reinforcements and a flag, as he had used his red jacket as a temporary solution.

Du Chambon noted the English capture of the Royal Battery, and not long after sunrise he ordered a detachment of the town's militia and eighty soldiers of the garrison to burn a number of homes along the southwest shore, from the Dauphin Gate to a shallow lagoon half a mile away where the inhabitants put up their boats in the winter. After this was accomplished, the detachment traded a few shots with English patrols before returning to the fortress. Fearing that the enemy might seize several vessels moored in the northeast harbor and at the town's docks, the governor also sent a pair of detachments to burn these vessels.

A handful of New England troops arrived at the Royal Battery not long after Vaughan. Their presence, while welcomed by Vaughan and his men, spoke to the nature of the colonial army. Numbering a few dozen in all, the group was not a patrol per se but more a collection of idle soldiers who "had a Great Mind to see the Grand Battery." Whatever the case, Vaughan was thankful for their curiosity when several French boats that Du Chambon had sent to the northeastern harbor approached the Royal Battery. While cannon and mortar rounds from the city and the Island Battery supported their approach, Vaughan's firepower was enough to dissuade any landing, and the vessels soon moved off.

Around noon Vaughan's request for reinforcements was answered when Pepperrell's second in command, General Samuel Waldo, arrived with three companies from his regiment and Lt. Colonel John Bradstreet with Pepperrell's regiment. As the occasional mortar round fell near the stone structure, Waldo and Bradstreet examined the army's first conquest. The two men agreed that the stronghold was in poor condition, and after examining the cannons left behind, they discovered twenty-eight 42-pounders and a pair of 18-pounders. All the guns had been spiked, but their carriages were intact and there was an ample supply of shot still in the magazines. Upon closer inspection the pair were delighted to see that the retreating French had done a poor job of spiking the guns. Both men were convinced that most of the guns could be quickly put back into action. "I beg you'l send smiths & armerores as soon as possible to drill open the vents of the cannons," Bradstreet wrote Pepperrell. They would need powder and artillery implements as well, but if these were dispatched immediately, Bradstreet was convinced that they could have four 42-pounders in action against the city by the next afternoon.[7]

Pepperrell was encouraged by the news and sent powder, food, and armorers. In the meantime, he and his staff had spent time visiting Green Hill about 1,600 yards from the city's main citadel. Here colonial engineer Richard Gridley, whom many consider the father of the U.S. Army Corps of Engineers, had begun clearing the ground and laying a firing platform for a 13-inch mortar. It seems that Shirley originally planned to hand the siege over to Bastide, but as we shall see the royal engineer was delayed by a French move against Annapolis Royal. In his absence Gridley, who had studied briefly under Bastide when the latter toured the New England coastal forts, laid out an approach to force the Dauphin's Bastion, which protected the town's main gate. The battery at Green Hill was but the first

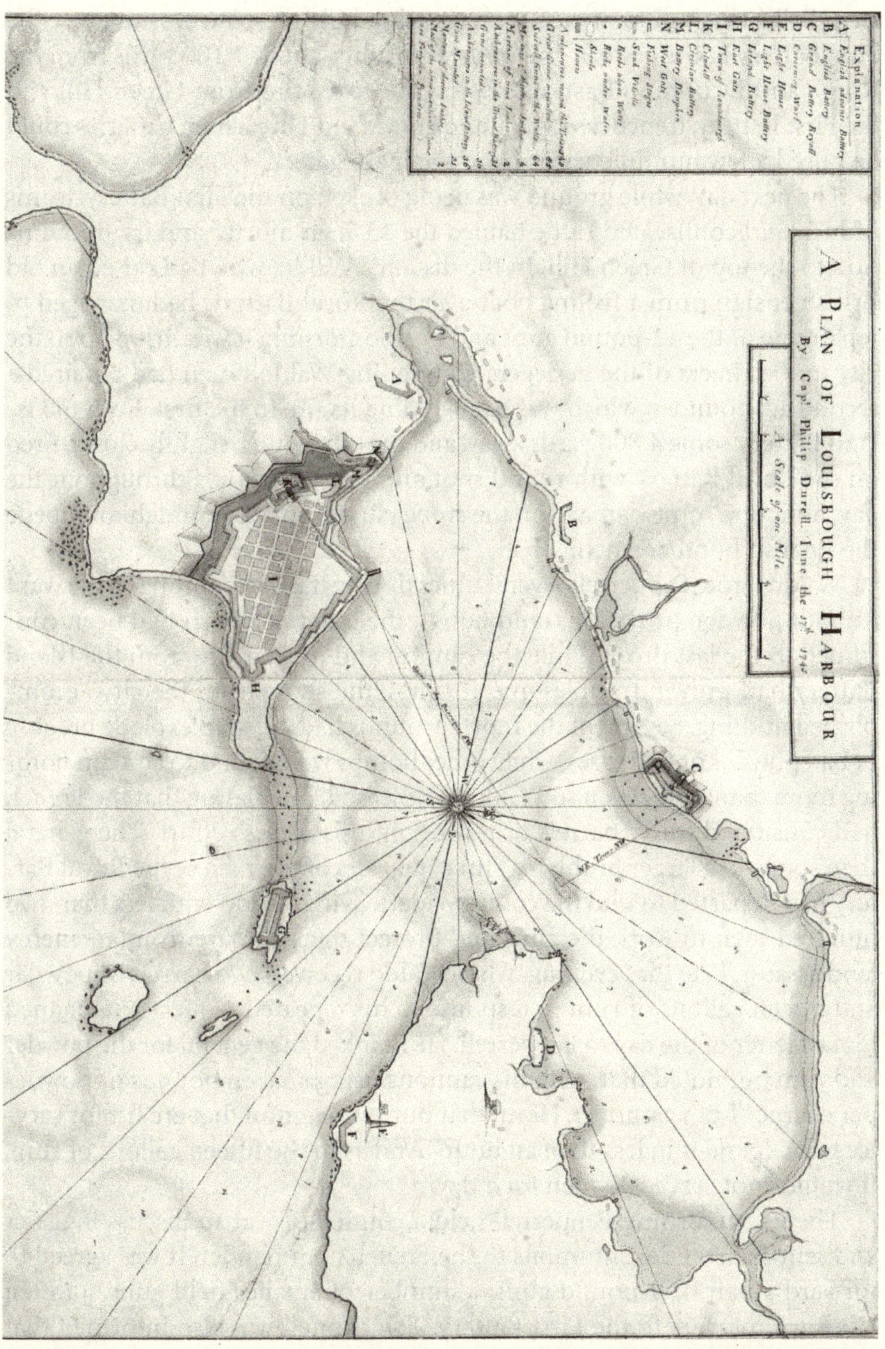

A plan of Louisbourg, June 1746. (*Norman B. Leventhal Map Collection, Boston Public Library*)

step. Following a line of east-west running hills the plan was to erect the First Battery at the eastern end of these heights, about 1,100 yards from the King's and Dauphin's Bastions. Using the cover fire from Green Hill and the First Battery, trenches would be advanced until breaching batteries could be raised a few hundred yards from the main gate.

The next day, while ground was being broken on the First Battery, teams of men and confiscated cattle hauled the 13-inch mortar and its ammunition to the top of Green Hill. In the distance Waldo, who had raised an old British ensign from a fishing boat over the Royal Battery, had managed to repair one of the 42-pound guns and by midmorning it was firing upon the city to the cheers of the besiegers. By evening Waldo's men had repaired a second 42-pounder, which was soon adding its fire to the first. Both the Island Battery some 4,800 yards away, and the city's guns, slightly closer, fired on the Royal Battery with round shot and mortar rounds throughout the day, inflicting some damage on the stone citadel but not enough to impede the English bombardment.

Waldo wrote Pepperrell several times during the day pointing to the want of both powder, provisions, and liquor, the latter of which had been consumed to the last drop. While the cannon and mortar fire from the Island Battery had proven troublesome at times, the shots from the city accomplished nothing. Several of the mortar rounds had failed to explode because of bad powder or bad fuses, while other bombs were found to contain nothing more than sand. Even so Waldo was pleased, calculating that the French had consumed thirty barrels of powder in this useless effort. The general then spoke to a larger problem. Three quarters of the men at the Royal Battery had departed to raid the countryside, leaving Waldo with less than two hundred men to work the guns and protect the structure from an enemy land assault. Late that evening, when Waldo received two barrels of powder and fifteen gallons of rum in response to his repeated requests, he penned his last letter of the day to Pepperrell. He thanked the general for the powder and rum but noted that, with his cannons using sixteen pounds of powder per charge "I can assure yr. Honr. that our two cannon that are fitt for service will expend it in less than an hour." And as to the fifteen gallons of rum, it would "not serve 300 men for a day."[8]

The next morning Pepperrell held a council of war to discuss logistics and sent a surrender summons to the French commander. It was agreed to forward a pair of 9-pound guns, a number of smaller field guns, and ten Coehorn mortars to the First Battery. The council was also informed that the mortar battery on Green Hill would be prepared to fire in a few hours. The matter of sending a formal summons to the French was then considered. It appeared that the council would agree, but a number of members, including Waldo and Bradstreet, who were still at the Royal Battery and had written Pepperrell with their views, expressed the need to finish the batteries before issuing a summons. The idea was to present an overwhelming presence, so as to give the French commander a reason to capitulate. Given that this work was not finished, it was agreed to table the matter for the moment.

The 13-inch mortar on Green Hill flared to life late that afternoon, dropping several explosive rounds into the fortress. The Coehorns in the First Battery followed a short time later, while in the background the Royal Battery, now with three operational cannons, continued its bombardment of the city. The combined effect drew a response from the fortress's guns and the Island Battery, but ultimately it created more confusion and panic among the populace than actual damage. Fire and church bells sounded throughout the afternoon as a few columns of smoke began to emanate from the town. By nightfall Waldo had fired at the city more than ninety times, with the mortar batteries to the west of the fortress having nearly matched this number.

Pepperrell had spent part of the day corresponding with Warren. The admiral had encountered a few French vessels but not as many as he would have expected. Suspicious, he wanted to look in on a number of small harbors along the coast for fear that Louisbourg was being reinforced with men and materials from these locations. He was planning on sending the 40-gun H.M.S. *Eltham*, Captain Tyng's 22-gun frigate *Massachusetts*, the Rhode Island sloop *Tartar,* and the Connecticut sloop *Defence* to investigate rumors of this activity some forty miles to the east. If the general could add a few shallow draft colonial schooners to this detachment, it would prove helpful. Warren then spoke to communications between the general and himself. Several colonial vessels had been flying flags that had been reserved to signify that Pepperrell wished to speak with Warren. He asked that this be stopped and then arranged an "all is well" and "we need to speak" signal between the two commands. Realizing that this would not be enough, Warren then asked Pepperrell to exchange aides to further communications and that a schooner be assigned to carry dispatches between the two commanders.

Pepperrell agreed with Warren's approach toward the blockade and promised to send him the requested vessels. Just as importantly, he also transmitted his approval of a plan Warren had proposed to attack the Island Battery. The operation called for a joint army-navy small boat attack on the French battery, supported by an artillery bombardment and a feint against the Dauphin Gate. With the Royal Battery already in British hands, the capture of the Island Battery would give Pepperrell and Warren complete control of the harbor. From here they could bombard the city with over a hundred heavy naval guns and conduct a landing operation against the far less fortified harborside of the city. In reality, it would not likely go that far. Once the English possessed the harbor the French commander would have little choice but to yield to prevent a disaster. "I propose to lay your plan of operation before my Council of War to-morrow morning," Pepperrell wrote Warren, assuring him that "it will meet with universal approbation."[9]

In fact, the council of war met twice on May 5. Pepperrell started the first meeting by presenting Warren's plan to attack the Island Battery. The members discussed the matter but delayed any decision. Instead, most of the discussion centered on siege details. It was agreed to advance the trenchworks to within a few hundred yards of the Dauphin Gate and erect a Second Battery consisting of a pair of 42-pounders and a pair of 18-pounders captured at the Royal Battery. These would be supported by a battery of Coehorns located a short distance to the rear, as well as the 9-inch and 11-inch mortars now at Green Hill. It was also agreed to place eight 24-pound cannons in the First Battery and that they should commence firing on the fortress as soon as possible. Lastly, it was proposed that one of the colonial sloops, carrying a battery of cannons, attempt to run past the Island Battery into the harbor. These guns could then be erected near the lighthouse to bombard the Island Battery. The council sought Commodore Warren's approval of this last plan and agreed to leave operational control with him if the idea went forward.

The firing on both sides was subdued throughout the day and into the next. Part of this was the British guns near the city being moved, and the other part was the French limiting their fire to preserve their powder. There were also problems at the Royal Battery. It was difficult work, but Waldo's armorers had managed to repair a fourth cannon by May 5, however, gun platform issues limited the battery's fire for part of the day. That afternoon the four-gun battery was reduced to three when an inexperienced New England gunner double charged his piece, which burst upon firing, wounding five of the gun crew. The next morning two more cannons were added to Waldo's arsenal, and the colonials delivered a brisk fire on the city throughout the day. While Waldo did not know how many of the captured cannons could be repaired, he had no complaints as to the gun's performance, saying, "they are as good pieces as we could desire." Powder, however, was a continual problem. A hundred-pound barrel of powder translated to just six shots from a 42-pound gun. Although he now had five guns operational, and suspected that he could at least double or triple that number at the current pace, the question became whether or not the colonial supply lines

Brigadier General Samuel Waldo by Robert Feke, c. 1748. (*Bowdoin College Museum of Art*)

could sustain this level of consumption. "I fear the only badd quallity in them will be, in opinion of our principalls, that they devour too much powder," Waldo informed Pepperrell.[10]

Colonel Jeremiah Moulton and his New Hampshire detachment returned from St. Peters on the morning of the sixth. The French settlements and the fort had been burned, a few prisoners had been taken, and the livestock captured and sent to the encampment at Canso. Commodore Warren also came ashore and met with Pepperrell and his council of war. The meeting centered on the custom in a formal siege where the besieger demands the besieged to surrender. Such a request was typically only done after the fortress in question was invested and a demonstration of strength in the way of manpower and artillery had been presented to the garrison's commander. As both of these steps had been accomplished, it was agreed to present Du Chambon with a surrender summons signed by both Pepperrell and Warren. It was also agreed that, if the French declined, they would press forward with the attack on the Island Battery.

After a brisk exchange of cannon fire, around 11 a.m. the next morning the colonial guns fell silent. With a drummer beating out a parley a British envoy, Captain James Agnue, approached the town under a flag of truce and delivered the surrender demand to Du Chambon. The French commander's response was that he "could not listen to any such proposition until after a decisive attack." When the British envoy asked if that was his final response, the governor informed him that "my only other answer would come from the mouths of the cannons."[11]

Du Chambon's rejection of the English surrender demand was hardly surprising. Little damage had been done to the town and its defenses, he still had control over the entrance to the harbor with the Island Battery, the English blockade had yet to halt all traffic into the port, and he had ample means to hold out for several months until a French relief squadron arrived to lift the siege. It was clear to a number of British commanders that a bombardment was unlikely to alter the French governor's stance. What was needed was the decisive attack that Du Chambon had noted in his answer. Pepperrell, Warren, and the council of war agreed with the French commander and ordered the attack on the Island Battery to proceed that evening.

The confused attempt on the island was called off when the whaleboats arrived too late to attack under the cover of darkness. It was perhaps for the best, given the temperament of the ill-prepared detachment. The venture was tried again on the night of May 8 only to be called off once more. After these two failed attempts, a council of war met on the morning of May 9 and unanimously recommended to Pepperrell, "that the town of Louisbourg be attack'd by storm this night with all the force and vigour possible." As might be expected, when word spread of the attack, many bristled against what they viewed as a foolish idea. The breaching batteries outside the Dauphin Gate had not even been fired, and the enemy, expecting an attack from that quarter, could sweep the ground before the bastion for hundreds of yards with grapeshot. The Royal Battery, and those on Green Hill and the First Battery, had only been firing for a few days, yet now was the time for an infantry assault against the enemy's fortifications? One that had a questionable chance of success and could lead to hundreds of casualties? The idea smacked of desperation, and the troops let their officers know it. Later that afternoon Pepperrell met with several of his regiment commanders and their executive officers. They advised the general of the "great dissatisfaction in many of the officers & soldiers at the design'd attack of the town by storm this night," and worrying that an attack under such circumstances might lead to a disaster, they asked Pepperrell to cancel the operation for the time being.[12]

The general reluctantly conceded and called off the assault. As he was walking back to his tent an aide stopped him with news that a French cannonball had struck a mortar on Green Hill, badly wounding several of the gunners. Pepperrell thanked him for the news, shook his head, and continued on to write Warren of his decision.

CHAPTER TWENTY-ONE

The Fall of Louisbourg

With any hope of seizing Louisbourg via a quick strike having vanished, matters focused on tightening the siege. The eight 24-pounders in the First Battery, supplemented by a number of Coehorn mortars, would continue to fire on the town and attempt to suppress the cannon fire coming from the Royal Bastion, much of which was being directed at the advancing sap. Even after a few days of firing, the effect of the 24-pound cannonballs had begun to leave fractured pockmarks in the stone citadel. Mortar rounds that did not fall short burst on the ramparts or, as with the cannonballs, overshot their mark and landed in the town.

Work on the main sap would also press forward, with the aim of erecting a breaching battery a few hundred yards from the Dauphin Gate. These guns would be supported by a mortar battery, located farther behind, which could easily strike the town from this location and would prove particularly effective in dissuading French work parties from repairing any damage to the Dauphin Bastion or Gate. The New Englanders, under Captain Gridley's guidance, proved adept at the mechanics of siege work. Digging trenches behind a sap roller and harvesting the nearby trees to reinforce these earthworks and fashion firing platforms, Pepperrell's troops carved a six-foot-deep trench out of the ground, wide enough to move a 42-pounder forward on its carriage. The Royal Bastion launched bombs and grapeshot at the advancing earthworks, causing a handful of casualties, but such measures seldom halted a determined foe who followed the tenants of siege warfare. The real threat to a besieger at this point was a sally by the garrison. Here the New Englanders were prepared, with two regiments stationed nearby ready to intervene, not that Du Chambon ever seriously considered an attack.

Waldo's regiment at the Royal Battery was now employing five cannons and was firing into the town with more regularity. Here the issue was one of powder and rum. As for the first, it would prove a problem throughout the siege, one that was only magnified by the makeshift commissary and supply system. For those who manned the captured guns under fire from the Island Battery and the city, the second appeared to be of just as much concern. "The short supply of rum, the severall Captains till me, is of prejudice to the people," Waldo wrote Pepperrell. "Should one from the dead tell the soldiery anything in the prejudice of it 'twould have no weight." Combined with these two problems was a desperate need for trained gunners. On more than one occasion the novice New England gunners accidentally fired their pieces with a double charge of powder, which burst the gun, wounding those about it. "We are in great want of good gunners that have a disposition to be sober in the daytime," Waldo informed the general after two of his best gun commanders were injured in such incidents.[1]

With the bombardment of the fortress and the construction of the breaching batteries underway, attention shifted to another element of the siege. A promising venture put forward involved erecting a battery of cannons on the peninsula to the east of the Island Battery, where the lighthouse was currently located. From this location the Island Battery could be reduced as a prelude to a landing. The argument for moving the main body of the army to this quarter was made and agreed upon, but after surveying the logistics behind the work it was quickly abandoned. Instead, a regiment would be dispatched to this area to raise a battery once work on the breaching batteries near the Dauphin Gate was complete. To support these current and future endeavors Pepperrell would ask Shirley for a thousand reinforcements, another large mortar, as well as more provisions and munitions. The general would dispatch fourteen Massachusetts and four New Hampshire transports to Boston and Portsmouth to carry these men and the requested supplies.

While many were involved in these siege activities, a sizable portion of Pepperrell's army was involved in raiding and marauding activities. In order to prevent any relief from reaching the besieged fortress the general had ordered the local hamlets and homesteads burned and the occupant's taken prisoner. The plunder from such low-risk operations coupled with a general lack of discipline among the colonial troops attracted many to these activities, which drained manpower from siege operations. To make matters worse, on May 10 a party of twenty English raiders were near a small village about half a dozen miles from the Royal Battery when they were ambushed and decimated by a French and Micmac war party. Even so, it was not enough to stop English efforts to depopulate the island and its shores.

The lack of discipline was not just confined to these activities. Warren asked that liquor not be sold to his men when they were ashore. It had been the cause of a number of disciplinary problems and the loss of weapons among some of his men. On another occasion Pepperrell was forced to openly condemn attacks against Colonel Bradstreet's character by another member of the council of war, and although the issue appeared to have been satisfactorily resolved, it was yet another unfavorable sign. Sickness had begun to take hold as well, and when snow and blustering winds appeared on the morning of May 11, it did little to improve the morale of the army.[2]

Thus far, Warren and his makeshift fleet of colonial warships had struggled to maintain the blockade of the harbor. Weather, particularly fog, greatly limited the effectiveness of the fleet, as did the number of vessels available. Alongside the four warships in his squadron, Warren had another seven colonial warships and a few small schooners for shallow water work and dispatch service. The problem was that a number of these ships were employed in escort duty or were patrolling the smaller harbors along the coast for French blockade runners, while yet others would be off station resupplying. This left Warren with perhaps half a dozen vessels to enforce the blockade, and although he had made a few captures, he realized how porous the screen was and recommended that small colonial guard ships patrol near the entrance to the harbor at night to deter smaller enemy vessels from slipping into the harbor.

On the morning of May 13 Warren was reminded of the gaps in his naval barrier when a French snow appeared in the harbor. The vessel had hugged the shore near the lighthouse, and catching a fresh breeze once clear of the point, set course for the town's docks. The lookouts at the Royal Battery sounded the alarm and the gun captains ordered their men to shift their aim toward the intruder. Fifteen shots were fired at the 150-ton vessel, eliciting a fierce bombardment from the town and the Island Battery that killed one gunner and drove the rest from their guns for a short period of time. Waldo was stunned by his men's fire, which never came close to harming the French ship. In relating the affair to Pepperrell, he reiterated his need for experienced gunners and informed the general that, "This vessell's escape was not for want of powder, of which we had thirteen cartridges left, and had we been provided with all the ammunition in the fleet or army it could have made no alteration in this affair."[3]

With the French snow now anchored before the town it made an inviting target, and a few rounds were fired its way, but several members of Waldo's garrison wanted to burn the vessel and outfitted a pair of fireships. The attack did not go as envisioned. The first fireship went ashore 250 yards wide of the mark, while the second, a schooner, accidentally caught fire early, and abandoned by its crew, was badly damaged by cannon fire from the fortress before drifting away and slowly burning down to the waterline.

For Warren good news came when the 30-gun privateer *Bien Aime* arrived from Boston, but the schooner he sent to St. Johns, Newfoundland, had returned to report that neither the fishing fleet nor the squadron that escorted them had arrived. Warren had hoped to borrow several warships from the escorts, but it would have to wait. A few days later on May 16 news reached the commodore that the 60-gun H.M.S. *Princess Mary* and the 40-gun H.M.S. *Hector* had arrived at Boston and would join him in a few days. Warren was anxious to see the reinforcements, especially after the Rhode Island sloop *Tartar* captured a French brig on the nineteenth. The vessel's captain, having left France laden with wine, brandy, and provisions, claimed that "four sail of men of warr, one of seventy-two guns, the other three of fifty-six, and three Company ships of thirty guns each, may be daily expected here."[4]

It was the scenario that Warren had worried about, and one of the reasons he had been a strong advocate for an attack on the Island Battery or an attempt to storm the walls of the fortress. Time was not on the side of the besiegers. As the recent French snow had pointed out, the blockade was not impervious, and with a relief force from France likely, if just a few warships and supply vessels forced their way into the harbor it would end the siege.

While Warren and his squadron braced for a challenge to the blockade, on May 18 Pepperrell's men finished a battery of two 42-pound cannons and a pair of 18-pound cannons 250 yards from the main gate. The discharge of an 18-pound cannon that splintered the stone near the Dauphin Gate set off an exchange of fire between the two sides for most of the day. The mortar battery to the rear and these guns, and those of the First Battery joined in filling the sky with "Sulfer and Smoak." Captain Thomas Waldron of New Hampshire found himself and his company posted in the breaching or advanced battery this day and recorded his experience in his journal that evening.

> We lay much Expos'd and ye French kept a firing small armes and great guns the greatest part of ye Day we had Kild and wounded sundry men... it was such a day as new England men never see that is very few of them. The bullets flew in whole Showers as did bombs Cohorns and Cannon as well as from our enemies. May I have a proper sense of gods covering me in that day Engagement when whole showers of Death flew all about me and my company.[5]

Sunset brought all but the occasional discharge to an end. The next morning began in an odd fashion when one of the English gunners became confused in the morning mists and walked so close to the fortress walls that he drew a volley of musket fire. Although struck five times, none were serious, and the gunner dashed back to the English lines more concerned about the damage to the coat he had borrowed than anything else. It would prove another busy day for the British and French gunners. The pair of 42-pound naval guns in the advanced battery had now been supplied and announced their presence by continuing the demolition of the gate and the stone housing around it. Not that it proved to be an easy day in the advanced battery. One of the 42-pound cannons exploded, killing or wounding most of the gun crew. French grapeshot and cannonballs claimed a few others, and an accident that set off two barrels of gunpowder wounded several more.[6]

Late that afternoon the cannon fire slackened on both sides as a large warship could be seen approaching the harbor. It would prove to be the 64-gun French ship-of-the-line *Vigilant* and the only serious challenge Warren's blockade would face. The Frenchman first encountered the *Mermaid*, which raised sail and took flight, firing its guns in defiance. The *Vigilant* followed, looking to take the British frigate as a prize, until a lookout called out three sails. The commander of the *Vigilant*, realizing that the tables had been turned, reversed his course, but it was too late. By 8:00 p.m. the *Superb*, *Shirley*, *Eltham*, and *Mermaid* were firing on the French warship, which would not surrender until its rigging was so damaged that it had to be towed back to Gabarus Bay the next morning. All breathed a sigh of relief when they heard the news. Reports were that the French vessel was carrying four months of provisions for the garrison, three hundred reinforcements, a thousand barrels of powder, twenty brass cannons, and rigging for a 70-gun ship being built at Quebec.[7]

This news, along with the arrival of a supply convoy from Boston and the 60-gun *Princess Mary*, buoyed the spirits of Pepperrell's men. Waldo and Major Moses Titcomb of Hale's 5th Massachusetts regiment had scouted the north side of the lagoon where the inhabitants put up their boats. Here they selected a site for a battery of two 42-pound cannons. Some nine hundred yards away the guns would be able to bombard the anchorage and the Dauphin Bastion with any shot that traveled over these targets striking the town. There was also activity in the army's main encampment. With the siege batteries near the Dauphin Gate in action, Shubael Gorham's 7th Massachusetts regiment was transferred to the lighthouse peninsula, and according to the earlier plan, were tasked with raising a battery of guns to challenge the Island Battery. Detachments of this regiment occupying this ground soon discovered a cache of French cannons in shallow water. There were several dozen in all, but of those recovered, four were 18-pounders in serviceable condition. For the moment there were no carriages for the guns, and work on laying out a battery took second priority to dealing with probing French and Indian war parties.

News of the *Vigilant*'s capture soon faded, and morale and discipline problems returned. Forays by small French and Indian war parties that attacked wood-cutting parties, advanced encampments, and ambushed patrols resulted in sizable responses that more often than not proved futile and did nothing to improve the situation. Just as importantly, the sick rolls were starting to alarm Pepperrell. "Great numbers are now unfit for service," he confided in Warren. The admiral replied that he too was worried and had begun to feel this effect within the fleet.

Looking to break the growing stalemate Pepperrell ordered another small boat attack on the Island Battery on the night of May 22. The troops were to rendezvous at the Royal Battery and after nightfall proceed with their effort, but the timetable proved too optimistic. Several of the boats needed to be repaired, although at least thirty were ready. The real problem was the call for volunteers failed to raise a sufficient number of troops, and those that did assemble at the Royal Battery alarmed General Waldo. "The appearance of small detachments of men without officers was much less pleasing," he wrote Pepperrell, "many of which only under the conduct (not influence) of a sarjeant & many others only centinells without any officer of any kind, & not a few of them noisy & in liquor."[8]

Facing these logistical and communications issues, the attack was rescheduled for the night of the twenty-third. Warren had now agreed to support the effort with two hundred sailors and marines in the fleet's whaleboats and launches, but this attack was also called off. "This is ye 6th attempt," one witness noted, "To no Purpose." This time a council of war inquired into the reasons, holding Colonel Gorham's and Lt. Colonel Arthur Noble's conduct in question, but after examining a number of witnesses and reports of heavy fog, they laid the matter aside. The council did agree,

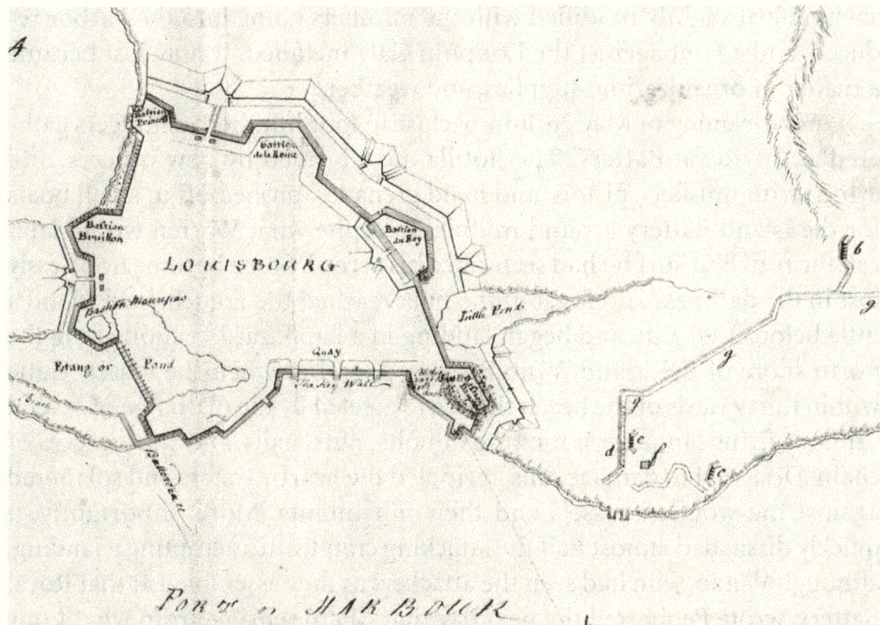

A sketch of the siege of Louisbourg by Royal Engineer John-Henry Bastide, 1745. A. ridge leading back to mortar battery at Green Hill, B. battery of eight 22-pounders, C. Mortar battery of ten Coehorns, one 9-inch, and one 11-inch mortar, D. Five gun breaching battery, E. Second breaching battery of four cannons and mortars, F. Powder magazine, G. main siege trench. (*Norman B. Leventhal Map Collection, Boston Public Library*)

however, that if three hundred to four hundred volunteers could be raised for an attack on the Island Battery they should be able to choose their own officers.

Warren had seen enough of the deteriorating mood of colonials and met with his captains aboard the *Superb* later that day. Here a council of war laid out an amphibious operation that called for running the guns of the Island Battery and landing troops in Louisbourg Harbor while the fleet and army bombarded the town and the Island Battery. Warren and his captains all agreed to the plan, which would be led by the admiral's squadron. What was required was 1,600 troops to be loaded onto these warships, the captured *Vigilant*, and a number of armed colonial vessels in order to execute the landing. When Pepperrell and his officers reviewed the plan the next day, they had a number of issues. It was simply too many men, and it would leave the land forces investing the town vulnerable to a sally. Besides, the *Vigilant* was not ready for such an operation. The plan was by no means shelved, just slightly modified with the numbers going into the harbor reduced, and a feint against the Dauphin Gate included. It now just became a matter of organization, supplies, and weather.[9]

On the evening of May 26/June 6, close to four hundred volunteers gathered at the Royal Battery. The flotilla, now headed by new officers, and armed with muskets, pistols, and hand grenades, pushed off in small boats for the Island Battery around midnight despite what Warren would later call the roughest surf he had seen since his arrival. Some became hopelessly lost in the darkness and fog, but the bulk reached the French-held island a little before 1:00 a.m. and began landing in a haphazard fashion along the north shore of the island. Visibility was poor, but when the vessels came within thirty yards of the beach they were greeted by the discharge of several cannons firing langrage, a mixture of bolts, nuts, nails, and small pieces of chain. Designed to damage sails, it rippled the nearby waters and splattered against the wooden vessels and their inhabitants. More importantly, it quickly dissuaded almost half the attacking craft from attempting a landing, although Waldo, who had seen the attackers as they assembled at that Royal Battery, wrote Pepperrell the next day that, "I am sensible from what I saw at the beginning of the attack that the greater part thereof never intended to land." The rest pushed forward in the face of several hundred French muskets that erupted from the ramparts. It was a difficult landing with the high surf toppling several boats and leaving many of those who made it to shore wet, along with their powder. Others disembarked with a "huzzah" and pressed forward with ladders to scale the ramparts.

The French commander, Captain Charles Joseph d'Aillebout, had been prepared for an attack and the 250 French Marines and militia in the garrison were quickly at their stations, but the staggered English landings had helped. The musketry, as well as some of the fort's cannons and a dozen swivel guns, soon stalled the enemy's advance. A few men under the expedition's commander Captain Edward Brooks managed to place a dozen ladders against the wall and appeared on the ramparts, but they were soon cut down by the garrison. For the rest, it was clear that they had underestimated the French defenses. Facing a concentrated fire, they found themselves pinned down on the beach and embroiled in a brisk firefight. After not being able to advance, a few of the attackers took to the handful of boats that had not been damaged by the surf or French fire and rowed away. For the rest, 120 or so, with no way off the beach and the freezing waters of the harbor out of the question, it was just a matter of time. They traded fire with the defenders in hopes that the vessels would return to evacuate them, but when no relief arrived, they surrendered at dawn.

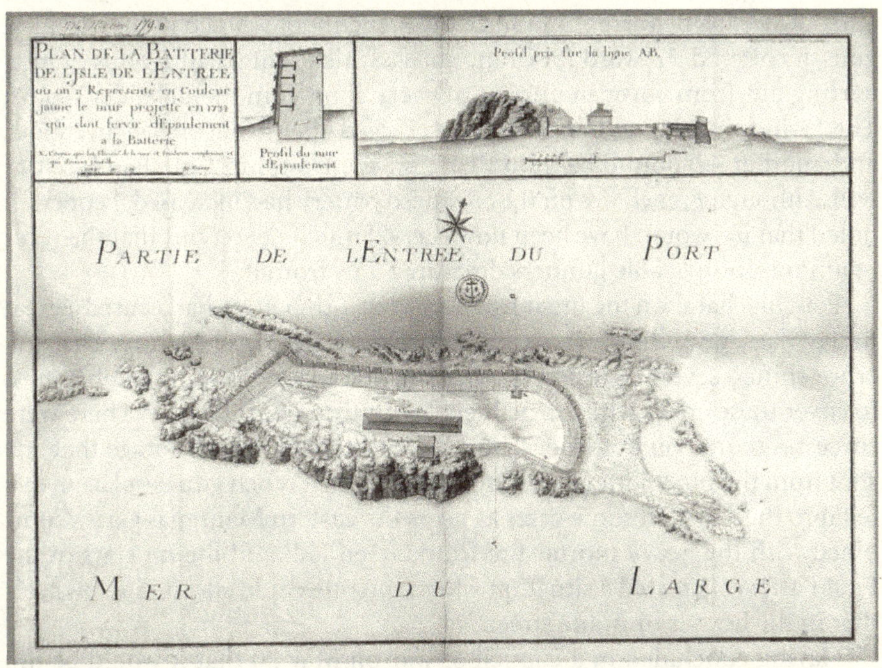

The Island Battery, c.1734-1738. (*Fortress of Louisbourg National Historic Site*)

Daylight also brought a better picture of the disaster, which would be the worst day of the siege for the New England army. Wrecked boats lined the shore or moved aimlessly with the tide, filled with stilled occupants. So too did many of the slain attackers who now drifted near the shore. Others were lying clustered in spots along the beach, but most, including a number of wounded, were now loaded into boats and transferred to the town under the eyes of the besiegers. In all, 119 men were taken prisoner, while another seventy were either killed or drowned.[10]

"Now things look't something dark," Pepperrell wrote of the affair. It was a blow to morale that was made worse in early June when the general reported that there were 1,500 sick and wounded in his camps, and the supply of powder and shot for the cannons was almost exhausted. "It is almost incredible to think what great quantities such a siege requires," he informed Shirley of his plight. On the good side, a hoard of French cannons was found sunk in a shallow inlet at the western edge of the bay. The guns were in good condition and required carriages, but without something to fire, and a means to do so, they would be of little use. Pepperrell borrowed shot and powder from Warren, and since the French shot worked in the captured guns, he offered a reward for cannonballs, which sent small groups of men darting out from cover in pursuit of every shot from the defender's guns. The 13-inch mortar on Green Hill had cracked after firing only eighty shots, and another 42-pound cannon firing on the Dauphin Gate had burst as well. Although French fire on the advanced battery had increased, Pepperrell noted that it, "would have been now carry'd much nearer but that the want of ammunition & able gunners discourag'd us from it."[11]

For Du Chambon the fire from the first British battery had caused a great deal of damage to the barracks and right side of the Royal Bastion. The governor shifted several guns on this bastion and made makeshift embrasures to cover these crews while they dueled with the enemy battery. There were successes scored on both sides, but the British held the advantage that any shot from the First Battery that traveled over the French gun emplacements fell into the town, in some cases as far as the eastern Maurepas Gate. Combined with the heavy mortar fire from Green Hill and the mortars in the First Battery it created a situation where "no one could stay in the town, either in the houses or in the streets."[12]

Having concluded in a council of war on May 20 that it would be too risky for the garrison to sally out of the fortress and attack the enemy's advancing trench work, there was little Du Chambon could do but focus on repairing the damage to the fortress, especially at the Dauphin Bastion and Gate. The advanced enemy battery supported by a number of nearby mortars had caused severe damage to these later positions. The governor blocked up the damaged gate and the walls next to it with an eighteen-foot-thick pile of stones and earth and reinforced the cannons on the bastion by repairing the damaged embrasures with earth and sod.

Although the English cannons carved fissures in the walls to either side of the main gate, and mortar rounds splintered the wood and stone buildings within the town, Du Chambon was more concerned with enemy movements toward the lighthouse across from the Island Battery. One of the garrison's artillery officers pointed out to the governor that a large number of cannons had been sunk near the point ten years ago, before efforts to fortify the position were abandoned. Some of these, 18- and 24-pounders, were likely still serviceable. Du Chambon frowned at the news. If the enemy, who had already raised a flag over the lighthouse, should discover these it would only be a matter of time before they constructed a battery to bombard the Island Battery and prevent any French vessel from entering the harbor.

In response to this serious threat the governor dispatched five hundred men under the command of M. de Beaubassin, a retired infantry officer, to surprise the British and drive them off the peninsula. The detachment departed on May 27 and by the following morning was advancing on the lighthouse when they were surprised by three hundred of the enemy. A brisk exchange took place, but Beaubassin, unclear of the enemy numbers, broke off the engagement. For many the command was unnecessary, as they had fled, tossing aside their arms and supplies to speed their departure. Beaubassin moved east to reorganize, but British scouts soon discovered his position, and after skirmishing with a large enemy detachment, the French war party scattered.

Beaubassin and the eighty men still with him traveled farther east to the town of Petite Lorembec (Little Lorraine) in search of a vessel to return to Louisbourg. Here the French commander encountered forty Micmac who had decimated a twenty-man English detachment they found in the town a few days ago. The Frenchmen were able to obtain a few shallops and were preparing to depart that afternoon when a large British detachment appeared. Beaubassin, aided by the Micmac, dueled with the enemy for four hours until the enemy retreated back into the forest. With their ammunition exhausted and facing the likelihood of a larger force the next morning, Beaubassin retreated north to the Mire River, ending any thoughts of offensive operations. According to one journalist of the siege, during this last engagement a memorable set of events occurred. One of the Micmac in the firefight, called Little John, had been struck in the chest by buckshot and collapsed. Not having time to bury the fallen warrior, his friends covered him with brush, and when the firing ended, they retreated north with Beaubassin. Three days later, while encamped near the Mire River, the French and Micmac war party was shocked into silence when Little John appeared around dinnertime complaining that he was hungry.[13]

Du Chambon listened intently on the night of June 6, as the sound of cannons and musketry could be heard coming from the direction of the Island Battery. Lookouts strained to see anything, but even the flashes were obscured in the thick mists that had descended over the area. A few hours later a courier arrived from d'Aillebout with news of an English defeat and the capture of a large number of prisoners. The news encouraged the defenders, but it also pointed to a problem. The enemy could attempt the same type of attack at the town's docks. To deter this the governor ordered a breakwater constructed of old masts and timbers. This would not be finished until June 11, and in the meantime the workers made a tempting target for the guns of the Royal Battery.

As the heavy guns of Pepperrell's advanced battery pummeled the Dauphine Bastion, Du Chambon sent repair crews out at night to patch the damage and remount damaged guns. Waldo's guns at the Royal Battery had taken a toll as well. "No one could stay behind the wall of the pier which had been riddled through and through." The flank of the Royal Bastion had been devastated by the 24-pound guns in Pepperrell's First Battery, and as for the town, which saw both solid shot and explosive rounds from the British mortars, Du Chambon reported that "All the houses in the town were demolished, riddled with holes, and not fit for habitation." With his powder running low and only a handful of bombs left for the mortars, the governor had rationed his return fire such that only a handful of cannons were fired throughout the day. Fortunately, the enemy guns had slowed as well, but the French commander realized this was but a lull. The enemy were masters of the waves and could resupply from Portsmouth, Boston, Providence, or New York at any point while, without relief, he and his garrison had perhaps a week of powder left in their magazines.

Du Chambon was correct; powder supplies were slowing Pepperrell's guns. "Our powder has been some days since expended," the general wrote Shirley on June 2/13. Commodore Warren had already lent the army 187 barrels and could be of no further help. There was also a shortage of shot, which when coupled with the lack of powder had created a situation where Pepperrell had been "oblig'd very much to keep silent our artillery." There was also the need for a replacement 13-inch mortar and recruits for the captured *Vigilant.*

The general, unaware of what had transpired at Annapolis Royal, used the opportunity presented by Commodore Warren sending Captain Rous in the *Shirley* to call upon the port to "take leave to ask of you the loan of a 13-inch mortar & a 7-inch brass mortar, with a number of shells for each, if you think it consistent with his Majestie's service at Annapolis to spare them." There was another matter as well. It seems clear that Shirley intended to use Bastide as chief engineer for the expedition and had pressed Mascarene to release him for this duty, leaving Bastide's assistant Royal Engineer William Cowley to address Fort Anne's needs. Pepperrell, either unaware of this or unaware of the nature of the delay, asked for the services of one of these men. "As we are in great want of engineers, which you are sensible it must be impossible to do without in our circumstances," he pointed out to Mascarene."[14]

Pepperrell had just dispatched this request when later in the day Bastide arrived in a small schooner. He handed the general a letter from Mascarene and offered to fill in any details. Mascarene explained that in early May a body of six hundred French and Indian troops under marine Lt. Paul Marin de la Malgue had moved against Annapolis Royal. Marin and his troops had spent the winter at the head of the Bay of Fundy to be in a position to conduct operations in early spring. Once he assembled his Native allies and any Acadian volunteers, he marched on Annapolis Royal.

For almost three weeks this large war party invested the fort and town. At night small bands of French and Micmac probed the fort's defenses, occasionally sparking a brief exchange of gunfire, while on other evenings volleys of flaming arrows arched through the darkness in an attempt to burn the fort and a number of nearby buildings. During the day bursts of muskets flashed from the nearby cover, testing the fort's defenses until a round of grapeshot silenced their activities. With the diligence of the garrison, the previous work done by Bastide and his assistant William Cowley, and an arsenal of thirty cannons lining the ramparts, it proved enough for Marin to put aside any thoughts of storming the structure. However, the raiders found success elsewhere. A pair of Boston schooners, the *Seaflower* and *Montague*, laden with trade goods were seized, a wood cutting party was ambushed and a few prisoners taken, and the harbor was now under Marin's control, meaning that if another colonial trading ship came into port, he would be able to capture it as well. Marin seemed content in pursuing this approach until a message reached him in early June from Du Chambon ordering him to come to the immediate aid of Louisbourg.

The marine lieutenant held a council of war after receiving the order and found that a third of his force was not interested in proceeding to Louisbourg. Undaunted, Marin loaded the rest in four sailing vessels and over sixty canoes and proceeded to Cobequid at the east end of Minas Bason. From here the war party marched along a well-worn portage road to Tatmagouche on the northern shore of the island. While the natives made canoes, the French busied themselves loading a pair of shallops, a sloop, and a small schooner that were awaiting their arrival. Proceeded by dozens of canoes, Marin's sailing vessels and some of the larger canoes put out to sea on June 14 and that evening encamped half a dozen miles down the coast in a sandy cove known as Ascamouse Bay.

Suspecting that the French might try to reinforce Louisbourg from northeastern Nova Scotia, Warren had dispatched Captain Daniel Fones of the *Tartar* along with the Massachusetts privateers *Resolution* and *Bonetta* to patrol Bay Verte and the nearby waters. After a week of seeing little, at 6:00 a.m. on June 15 Fones spotted smoke coming from an inlet to the southeast of his position. Believing this to be a possible French and Indian war party on its way to Louisbourg, Fones ordered the *Bonetta* to follow him and moved forward to investigate. Fones soon realized that he was correct when he encountered the vanguard of Marin's forces having just put back out to sea. Initially flying French flags, the two New England warships quickly replaced these with British flags and closed on the enemy. When within a few hundred yards the two vessels unleashed a pair of broadsides on Marin's men. Shot from the small cannons skipped past the clusters of canoes while grapeshot sprayed the waters around them. It then became a race for the shore, which Marin's men won as the New Englanders continued their fire. Dragging their canoes ashore and taking cover, the French realized that the enemy vessels were not finished when the *Tartar* and *Bonetta* dropped anchor nearby and began to bombard their positions.

Onboard the *Resolution*, Captain David Donahue watched as the *Tartar* and *Bonetta* slipped out of sight to the southeast. No sooner had this occurred when a lookout drew Donahue's attention to the main body of Marin's force now rounding a point to the west. Two schooners, two sloops, along with a slightly smaller craft, and over fifty canoes were now arrayed before him. Donahue steered for the enemy flotilla, and a little before ten o'clock opened fire with his 4-pound guns. Closing at times to within shouting range of one another, the *Resolution* launched grapeshot and cannonballs upon the French, who could only respond with musketry and the occasional bark of a swivel gun from one of the larger vessels. As long as Donahue held a maneuvering advantage, he could make passing attacks, limiting his exposure to the enemy's counterfire and preventing them from using their numerical advantage by trying to board the privateer. By noon, however, the wind was failing him, and not long after the enemy canoes easily surrounded the becalmed craft. The tables had now turned, and Marin's men pressed their attack from all angles. For the crew of the *Resolution* every cannon and swivel gun was in action, as were the marksmen in the rigging, but even with this they were forced to repel several boarding attempts with cutlass and pike. Riddled by musketry and having fired almost two hundred shots from his battery of 4-pounders and another fifty from his 3-pounders, only a return of the wind bringing with it the *Tartar* and *Bonetta* prevented Donahue's capture. Marin's forces quickly broke off the action and raced for shore.

Marin, fearing that the British would attempt a landing, spent the next several days fortifying their position at the mouth of a small creek. While this certainly improved their defensive posture, it did little to forward their objective. With the enemy now reinforced to six vessels, on the twentieth Marin suggested that the fleet sneak past the New Englander privateers after sunset. The Abenaki and some of the Mimac balked at the idea and informed Marin that they were returning to Canada, effectively ending the expedition.

Commodore Peter Warren, left, and General William Pepperrell, right.

Marin and a handful of others would eventually complete their journey but arrived too late and in too few numbers to be of any assistance.[15]

Pepperrell listened to Bastide's account of the siege of Annapolis Royal and asked a few additional questions regarding Governor Mascarene's current defenses, before briefing the royal engineer on the status of the siege works. Bastide was pleased to hear that the Royal Battery had been captured, and he did not have much in the way of criticism regarding the efforts at the Dauphin Gate, not that it mattered at the moment, with the shortage of shot and powder. He winced at the general's description of the attempt to storm the Island Battery and then nodded in agreement when Pepperrell pointed out that current efforts were focused on raising a battery near the lighthouse. After hearing Warren's plan to run into the harbor, Bastide urged the general to push forward the Lighthouse Battery, pointing out that once the Island Battery was neutralized the harbor and fortress would be theirs. With efforts in this direction revived, an earth redoubt was raised in front of the lighthouse about 1,200 yards from the barracks at the Island Battery. The sound of hammer and saw rang out as firing platforms were laid out and carriages constructed. When this was accomplished, work crews dragged the captured 18-pound cannons to the location and then mounted the two-ton guns on their recently fashioned carriages. Over three hundred men toiled at this work as the guns of the Island Battery attempted to dissuade their activities with the occasional cannonball or bursting mortar round.

On the morning of June 11/22, Captain de Gannes, who had relieved d'Aillebout and his men a few days before, realized that his limited efforts had not worked when a pair of 18-pound cannons opened fire on the island. Over the course of the next few days four more 18-pound guns would be added to the mix, although powder shortages still limited their fire. These frustrations would soon be set aside as two events quickly altered current operations. First was the arrival of the H.M.S. *Chester*, *Canterbury*, *Sunderland*, and *Lark* over the next few days. Second was the arrival of a convoy carrying a crew for the recently repaired *Vigilant* and a supply of powder and shot from Governor Shirley.

On the morning of June 15, a large mortar recently placed in the Lighthouse Battery announced the day by dropping a 13-inch explosive round onto the parade ground of the Island Battery. Solid shot followed, and after a few hours there was an explosion and then a larger one as a bomb found one of the fort's magazines. The barracks and a few interior buildings soon caught fire, obscuring the location in rolling black smoke. Pepperrell's batteries before the town opened fire, as did the Royal Battery, and with the French counterfire added to this chorus, the harbor echoed with bursts of thunder.

Against this background Pepperrell met with his officers at a council of war. The influx of warships, manpower, and powder meant that Warren's original plan to run past the Island Battery and conduct a landing on the harborside of the fortress could go forward. The colonial troops not participating in the landing or the bombardment would launch an attack on the Dauphin Gate. Although several large breaches, close to fifty feet wide had been opened in the walls of the bastion, it would be a harrowing 250-yard dash under the cover fire of their own guns to reach the walls of the fortress. Fortunately, it was to be a diversionary attack. If Warren was able to enter the harbor, there would not even be a need to land troops. With half a dozen 50- and 60-gun warships at his disposal, he could easily bombard the town and turn the harborside defenses of the fortress into ruins. The French would certainly see this and surrender. The council of war agreed to Warren's plan, and the attack was scheduled for the next morning.

It proved a restless night for those on land and those aboard Warren's rolling ships. For all, tomorrow held far more uncertainty than most days. However, it was not the sound of cannon fire that greeted the Anglo-American force the next morning but the sound of French drums beating out a parley. A loud cheer was the response from land and sea. A flag of truce was sent out by Du Chambon to discuss surrender terms. With no sign of relief, the governor had seen enough. One witness claimed that French internal discussions centering on the surrender of the fortresses abounded in panic and fear, but in reality, with even more enemy warships blockading the port, the Island Battery flanked and badly damaged, and down to their last forty-seven barrels of powder, surrender was a wise move. Envoys from both sides met, and after some negotiations, the French flag was replaced the next morning with the Union Jack.[16]

Fortunately, there were not a large number of casualties on either side. Pepperrell and Shirley reported a little over a hundred killed by enemy action or accidents, with another thirty dying of illness, and close to three hundred wounded. Du Chambon claimed that fifty French had been killed in the siege and a little under a hundred had been wounded badly enough that they required attention. Given the ruined state of the town and the fact that Pepperrell's artillery fired an estimated nine thousand cannonballs and six hundred bombs at the fortress, the French casualties were remarkably low. In fact, a number of British sources claimed that Du Chambon had not included the civilian casualties and as such doubled the number stated by the French commander. What was not in dispute was the scale of the victory. The fortress, the town, its garrison, and inhabitants, along with over 135 pieces of artillery, thousands of small arms, and a dozen captured French vessels, including the 64-gun *Vigilant*, were now in British hands. Like Port Royal, Nova Scotia, two generations before, the great maritime threat had been eliminated. No wonder when reports reached the shores of New England church bells rang for hours announcing the news.

While it would be convenient to lay blame for the French defeat at the feet of Governor Du Chambon it would be far from correct. Du Chambon did miss some opportunities and made a few mistakes. An example of the first was in not challenging the landing at Gabarus Bay, while the second was the strange abandonment of the Royal Battery. The key to Louisbourg was the Royal Battery and to a greater degree the Island Battery. The two worked together to bar the channel into the harbor. Once these were removed, there was nothing to stop a fleet from entering the harbor and attacking the weak shore defenses of the city. Thus, why give up one of these without a fight? While it was true the landside glacis and outer redan of the Royal Battery was not finished, it was not as if there were no defenses on the landward side of this fortress. The stone structure still had a ditch before it, a clear field of fire, and backed by a few cannons and a hundred muskets, it would only be able to be taken with artillery. This artillery would have to be dragged into position from Pepperrell's encampment on Garabus Bay. Thus, why the hasty withdrawal, which Du Chambon, the fort's engineer, and a council of war all agreed to? In fact, since a withdraw from the Royal

Battery would be conducted via boats, why withdraw until the structure was threatened with cannon? One argument was that the stone fortification was in poor condition. Waldo and his New Englanders agreed but were able to employ the position throughout the siege, even though they were frequently fired on by the city's guns and the Island Battery. More importantly, given the time it would take for the British to erect a battery to threaten the stronghold, why was such a poor job done in disabling the artillery left behind?

These two decisions aside, part of the defeat can be blamed on earlier problems. Unfinished works, a lack of preparations, and a poorly trained and dispirited garrison played a role in the fall of the fortress. The works to protect the landside of the Royal Battery should have been completed and the proposed battery near the lighthouse built and manned. With a larger, better motivated, and better led garrison, Louisbourg would have proven a much more difficult proposition. Some hope seems to have been placed on Marin arriving with four hundred reinforcements, but even if these troops had arrived in time, it is difficult to see how they would have changed the course of the siege, especially once the attackers realized that the Lighthouse Battery was the key to victory. Had the rumored French fleet arrived, matters might have turned out much differently, but the Dunkirk of the West fell before a major relief force could be assembled and dispatched.[17]

The siege of the fortress lasted forty-seven days, and during this time Warren's blockade managed to capture several smaller vessels, but given the foggy weather conditions, a number of others were able to run into the harbor. While these cargoes were certainly helpful, they would not be enough to lift the siege, as the pressing need was more for powder and munitions rather than the foodstuffs these vessels were carrying. Warren's fear of a French squadron as reported by a number of captured French vessels never materialized, and the only serious threat posed was the *Vigilant*, which had it entered port would have likely prolonged the siege long enough for a relief force to be sent. Fortunately for the admiral, who would be promoted and knighted for his role in the operation, his forces soon overwhelmed and captured the French man o' war. With the arrival of four more warships in late June, Warren was able to breathe easier, although the French Navy never appeared to challenge his barrier.

For Pepperrell it was an unlikely outcome given how the campaign had started, but with the quick capture of the Royal Battery and the investment of the city, he had been able to open his siege guns upon the town. Sickness, supply issues, and discipline problems haunted his efforts, and although slow to recognize and carry through with it, he finally focused the army's efforts toward erecting a battery near the lighthouse, which proved the key to entering the harbor and victory. Aided by the guidance of Warren, the businessman turned general found his frustrations and fortune rewarded when he was made a baronet and appointed colonel of a regiment that would garrison the captured stronghold.

The siege of Louisbourg, thought a wild gamble even by many directly involved, had paid off. In the span of a little less than two months the most powerful fortress in North America had surrendered to a handful of amateurs and a supporting cast of the Royal Navy. On the surface the achievement seems nothing less than remarkable. The planning, organization, and execution of the expedition was disorganized from the start. It was incredibly opportunistic and at the same time overly optimistic. The colonial force itself was unruly, untrained, and subject to emotional swings. Its leadership lacked command experience, and its logistics train was a patched together mess of hastily drawn up contracts, but luck favored the New Englanders, first with naval support provided by the Crown and second with a commander like Warren who, although he became impatient toward the end, displayed enough diplomatic skills to effectively cooperate with the colonial army.

For Governor Shirley, who was busy dictating a dozen letters speaking to the success, it was relief and a crowning moment. He knew that, although his forces were weak and untrained, the timing was right to land a decisive blow against an ill-prepared enemy. He had courted disaster based on this simple idea and succeeded against the odds.

CHAPTER TWENTY-TWO

The Raiders of Scalp Point

It was not until late 1745 that King George's War reached the Albany-Montreal corridor. Both sides had spent the previous year taking precautions. In New York, New England, and Canada militia companies were called out, citizens warned, and defensive works repaired, but beyond the quiet probing of a few scouting parties, neither side had breached the peace. All this changed with the fall of Louisburg. For Governor Beauharnois, it became a question of what to do. Outnumbered, facing an impending British thrust against Quebec, and with his limited supply line now subject to a British naval blockade of the Gulf of St. Lawrence, any major offensive action was out of the question. Oswego was a tempting target, but attacking the post would threaten Iroquois neutrality, and at the moment, Canada could not afford any new enemies.

Fortunately, history predicted his enemy's next move, and geography dictated where it would fall. The English would certainly revive the old invasion plan of King William's and Queen Anne's Wars: a simultaneous attack on Quebec and Montreal. As for Quebec there was little the governor could do but fortify the town and wait, but in regard to Montreal he could be a little more proactive. Of course, Fort St. Frederic and Fort Chambly would be reinforced, but neither of these actions would guarantee the security of the frontier. The only way to accomplish this was to dictate the terms of the conflict, and the best way to do this was to employ the proven strategy of *petite guerre*. A deluge of French and Indian war parties would strike at the New York and New England frontiers. If all went well, the British colonies would take the bait and switch to the defensive, allowing Beauharnois to hold each of them at arm's length with a minimum amount of effort and resources. The approach had its risks. There was always the chance that the raids might provoke a major English response, but given the turn of events it seemed likely that one was coming regardless of what approach was taken.

Beauharnois had recalled Lt. Marin and his detachment from Acadia after the fall of Louisbourg and ordered them to Montreal. After refitting his detachments and augmenting their numbers, the governor ordered Marin to proceed to Fort St. Frederic and from there launch a series of attacks on the settlements in the Connecticut Valley. Marin, accompanied by three hundred French and two hundred Indians, left Montreal on November 4, and by the seventeenth the war party was safely encamped beneath the ramparts of Fort St. Frederic. With the campfires crackling against the crisp autumn air, Marin called together his allies and informed them of his intentions. The sachems muttered amongst themselves at the news and shook their heads. The season was late, and the expedition was not equipped for winter, which would certainly take hold before their return. They would also have to cross the Connecticut River to reach their objective. If the river iced over there would be problems. The ice would not be thick enough to allow crossing by foot but would be enough of a hindrance to prevent crossing by canoe. Marin nodded at the arguments and then Father Francois Piquet, a French priest who had met the expedition at Fort St. Frederic, conferred with the chieftains and offered an alternative. The party could strike at Saratoga, an English settlement about thirty miles north of Albany. Marin, determined on a course of action against the enemy, quickly agreed.[1]

The next morning the detachment moved forward, a long line of canoes snaking its way up Lake Champlain and Wood Creek in the prevailing autumn mist. Near the overgrown remains of Fort Anne, the caravan hoisted their canoes out of the water and proceeded by land to the banks of the Hudson River. Here, along the northeast bank of the river, they found a lumber establishment, and apparently unconcerned with concealing their presence they set it ablaze before continuing south. By the evening of November 28, the detachment lay in the woods about Saratoga. The village was located along the west bank of the Hudson in the "flats" formed by the junction of this river with the Fishkill River. It consisted of some thirty families whose scattered dwellings were overlooked by a small wooden fort located on a hill at the center of the town. Marin had heard that the fort held a strong garrison, but any security the fort appeared to provide was an illusion. It was in such a ruinous condition that the governor had ordered its garrison of a dozen men withdrawn a few weeks before, not that it would have made much of a difference in the face of such overwhelming odds.

The French commander had planned to scale the fort's walls and overpower the garrison before turning on the town, but in the early morning hours of the twenty-ninth the overanxious war party sprang upon the populace before he was in place. It was over before it had begun. Doors were staved in and the occupants dragged into the bitter autumn night. Shots rang out and tomahawks flashed in the moonlight. There was almost no resistance. Some fifteen inhabitants fell before the onslaught, and another 109 were rounded up as prisoners, almost the entire town. Near the center of the village sat the brick manor of Saratoga's first citizen, Phillip Schuyler, the brother of Colonel Peter Schuyler. One of Marin's officers, a man named Beauvais, was acquainted with the elder Schuyler and raced to his house to protect him from the attack. Upon arriving, Beauvais called on Schuyler to surrender, assuring him that no harm would come to him and his own if he did so. Schuyler, however, like his brother, was not in the habit of trusting the word of French marauders. He returned the summons with a few choice words and the discharge of his musket. Exposing himself, Beauvais once more called upon him to yield, and once more Schuyler responded with gunfire. This time the shot passed too close to Beauvais, instinct took over, and he returned fire, instantly killing the elder Schuyler.

Undermined by his troops, Marin and a strong detachment quickly pushed up the hill toward the fort. All was strangely quiet, and within minutes the party was over the walls and realized why. The post was deserted. With the town firmly in his hands, Marin ordered it, along with the fort, to be put to the torch. The job was done so well that by morning it had become nothing more than a forest of chimneys and sizzling embers. The attackers then divided up their prisoners and began their trek home.[2]

News of the attack rippled through the frontier. Villagers retired to their forts and strong houses to spend uneasy nights while the government of New York scrambled to respond and assess the blame. For the French, Marin's attack was just the opening volley. In late December Beauharnois dispatched Lieutenant Jacques Legardeur de St. Pierre, a veteran of the Chickasaw Wars, to Fort St. Frederic with a detachment of 126 French and thirty-seven Iroquois and Nepissing. A few weeks later he augmented this force with another detachment of 140 French and Indians under the command of another veteran leader, Ensign Luc de La Corne, an officer who was fluent in four Native languages. Given the season and the addition of three hundred troops to the fort's garrison, there was little fear of an attack. This left the two commanders free to launch scouting parties onto the lake and dispatch small detachments toward the English settlements in order to gather intelligence, typically in the form of prisoners.[3]

St. Pierre and La Corne returned to Montreal with their forces in early April, but even with their departure Fort St. Frederic bustled with activity. From late April to the end of June no less than thirty-two French and Indian war parties struck at the New York, Massachusetts, and New Hampshire frontiers. The terse records of their journeys are tabulated within the official French dispatches, a few examples of which will suffice to illuminate their exploits.[4]

> April 20th. Thesaotin, chief of the Sault, left with 22 warriors, belonging to that village, to make war in the direction of Boston; they returned with some scalps; one Iroquois was killed and two wounded of the party.
>
> April 26th. A party of 35 Iroquois warriors, belonging to the Sault, set out; they have been in the neighborhood of Orange, and have made some prisoners, and taken some scalps.
>
> May 7th. Six Nepissings started to strike a blow in the direction of Boston, and returned with some scalps.
>
> May 12th. Six Iroquois Indians of the Sault set out towards Boston, and returned with some scalps.
>
> May 17th. 31 Iroquois belonging to the Lake of the Two Mountains, set out, and struck a blow in the neighborhood of Boston, and brought back some prisoners and scalps, and laid waste several settlements on their way back.
>
> May 25th. A party of 12 Nepissing who made an attack in the neighborhood of Boston, have brought away 4 scalps and one prisoner, whom they killed on the road, as he became furious and refused to march.
>
> June 3rd. Equipped a party of 18 Nepissing, who struck a blow at Orange and Colard.
>
> June 8th. Equipped a party of 8 Iroquois of the Lake, who have struck a blow near Guerrefille.[5]
>
> June 12th. Equipped a party of 10 Abenakis Indians, who struck a blow in the direction of Boston.
>
> June 17th. Equipped a party of 10 Abenakis, who went to make an attack at the River Kakecoute.[6]

In almost every case, Fort St. Frederic was either the starting point or a return stop for the raiders. War whoops and the shrieks of captives echoed through the stone parapets. The French often tried to buy back the captives, but in many cases their allies were not interested in parting with their human trophies. Insistence was useless and counterproductive. One could not foster such behavior on one hand and then condemn it on the other. So the war parties came and went with their bundles of scalp locks and their human cargo. "It is an abominable way to make war," one French officer would write of this experience a decade later. "The retaliation is frightening, and the air one breathes here is contagious of making one accustomed to callousness."[7]

Whatever its military merits and moral dilemmas, the French tactics were working and would continue to work so long as the British remained reactive instead of proactive. The former response was predominant primarily because it was the easiest to implement given the jealousies, internal strife, and lack of a centralized command among the colonies. As in the past, each colony would stand separate from the other, facing the enemy in its own fashion and with its own resources. It was the expedient solution that Beauharnois and his advisors sought.

To Governor Shirley of Massachusetts, nothing imperiled the colonies more than this approach. In his mind the only solution was a cohesive response, one that would bring all of Canada to its knees. Only then would the frontiers be truly secure. The governor was to spend the greater part of his career calling for the destruction of both Fort St. Frederic and Canada and, in the process, almost destroying his own career. At the moment, however, Shirley's star was ascending. With the capture of Louisbourg still fresh in the public eye, he turned to a more ambitious undertaking, the invasion of Canada. In October 1745 he informed the Duke of Newcastle that, with the spirit that now prevailed throughout the colonies, twenty thousand men could be raised to capture Canada, and all that was required to put this plan in motion was an order from the king. In December he followed this letter with another, pointing to the threat posed to the frontiers by Fort St. Frederic and the role played by this post in the destruction of Saratoga. Governor George Clinton of New York and Governor Benning Wentworth of New Hampshire supported this view with letters of their own.

Clinton, in particular, pressed on the duke the vulnerable state of his colony's northern frontier and the imminent threat posed to it by the French fortress at Crown Point. He informed the duke that he had already spoken with Shirley about launching a provincial expedition to reduce the fort and had gone so far as to send six pieces of heavy cannon and two of the independent companies to Albany in pursuit of the effort. He had even convinced a handful of Iroquois to join the expedition, but faced with a bickering assembly the plan seemed doomed. It was imperative that London intervene. Otherwise, he wrote Newcastle, "I can not answer for the safety of the province under the present circumstances."[8]

With the war going poorly in Europe, Newcastle and his supporters were in favor of intervention, but with the onset of winter any thoughts of a North American campaign would have to wait until spring. In a series of letters throughout the winter, Shirley worked out the basic plan with London. General John St. Clair would proceed from England to Louisbourg with a fleet of warships and eight British regiments. Here he would combine forces with the regulars in garrison and the colonial elements levied for the campaign before ascending the St. Lawrence to besiege Quebec. To the west, a colonial expedition would assemble at Albany and strike at Montreal via Lake Champlain. It was the old plan of King William's War and Queen Anne's War revived, with the only exception that this time the focus of the second effort was placed first on the capture of Fort St. Frederic. Once this was accomplished, only Fort Chambly, a structure never designed to withstand heavy cannons, would stand between the British Army and Montreal.[9]

In early April 1746 Newcastle dispatched a circular letter to the colonial governors, calling on them and their assemblies to levy as many men as possible to join the expedition. Shirley had been correct; a fervor for action still burned throughout the colonies, particularly in those most directly faced by the threat. Massachusetts, as it had with the previous years' campaign, took the lead. With Shirley standing at their head proclaiming, "*Delenda est Canada,*" the Massachusetts Assembly voted to raise three thousand men toward the effort in early June. The other colonies quickly followed suit. New Hampshire responded with five hundred men, Rhode Island three hundred, Connecticut one thousand, New York sixteen hundred, Maryland three hundred, New Jersey five hundred, and Virginia one hundred. Even the Quaker-dominated Pennsylvania could not block participation. Although the assembly refused to levy any troops, the governor raised four hundred men through private and public contributions.[10]

Major General Sir William Gooch, the lieutenant governor of Virginia and a veteran of the unsuccessful siege of Cartagena in 1740, was placed in charge of the Montreal element of the plan. The New York, New Jersey, Pennsylvania, Maryland, and Virginia contingents were assigned to his command. These troops were ordered to rendezvous at Albany in late July, where they would be joined by several hundred Iroquois volunteers. As with Nicholson's previous expeditions in Queen Anne's War, the entire force would then move forward once news reached them that the British fleet had set sail for Quebec. In the meantime, supplies were forwarded to Albany, and a detachment of shipwrights began constructing the vessels needed to carry the army and its artillery onto Wood Creek and Lake Champlain.[11]

Reports of the British effort reached Beauharnois and his staff through the capture of several prisoners along the New York and New England frontiers. At first he ignored the intelligence, treating it as rumor and gossip, but by late July the number of captives telling the same story convinced him otherwise. The reports were frightening. The British colonies were levying troops from as far away as Virginia. King George had ordered forty to fifty thousand provincials and several thousand British regulars to descend upon the borders of New France in late summer, and a fleet carrying British regulars and siege artillery would rendezvous with colonial forces at Louisbourg before setting sail for Quebec. Given that the latest information claimed there were currently forty warships, transports, and merchantmen at Louisbourg, at least nine of which were warships of forty guns or more, the French governor groaned at the thought of another fleet from England and the colonial fleet combining with this force.

In addition to this threat, thirteen thousand provincials, along with fifteen hundred Iroquois, were to rendezvous at Albany and attack Fort St. Frederic from both the direction of Lake George and of Wood Creek. The advanced elements of this army and their heavy cannons were already in position, and scouts reported half a dozen schooners plying the river between Albany and New York City transporting provisions and supplies. News of the twin attacks could not be contained and caused near panic in Canada. The militias of the various parishes were called out, detachments in the field were called in, and work on the fortifications about Quebec and Montreal intensified. "All the English on the continent must be under arms," the governor wrote the minister of the marine, "if all these rumors be true."[12]

While Beauharnois was not convinced that the British colonials could assemble a logistics train to support an army of thirteen thousand men in the Hudson and Champlain Valleys, even a third of that number would pose an overwhelming threat to Fort St. Frederic. In early July he dispatched Lt. De Muy to the scene with sixty-nine French and four hundred Native allies from the various missions and upper country posts. The lieutenant and his detachment spent the next few weeks scouting the lakes and felling trees along the narrow portions of Wood Creek to hinder any possible invasion along this route. In late July, with signs of a major British effort about to be launched against the fort, the governor wrote De Muy and ordered him not to scatter his forces. A detachment of four hundred French and Indians under the command of Major Rigaud de Vaudreuil was being outfitted at Montreal and would come to his aid shortly. To support these two detachments fifteen hundred militia were being levied at Montreal with orders to march to the fort's relief at the first sign of an attack.[13]

After a stormy ten-day journey, Rigaud and his forces made camp at Fort St. Frederic on the afternoon of August 13, 1746. Clusters of wigwams and rows of tents now surrounded the stone fortress, sheltering almost a thousand French and Indian reinforcements. On the morning of August 16 De Muy returned from a scout of the area around Albany. As his large war party filed off into the encampment, he met with Rigaud and informed him that all was quiet at Albany. It was true that there were signs of troops in the region, but nothing on the order of what they had been told. He had seen a few hundred at most, barely enough to secure the town, much less threaten Fort St. Frederic.

Rigaud was pleased with the news. With no indication of an British attack, talk quickly turned from defensive preparations to offensive action. The next day Rigaud held a council of war with the Indian sachems. Talk abounded about where to strike, but his allies could not agree on a target. The major finally intervened and told them that he planned to attack Schenectady. His allies seemed pleased with the decision and spent the evening singing and dancing in preparation for the coming campaign. But by the next morning they had changed their minds. The Caughnawaga, as the Christianized French Mohawks of that mission were called, had objected to the plan. They were afraid that the attack would bring them to blows with their Mohawk relatives known to be in the area.

The plan was off and the debate back on. After some time, the Abenaki in Rigaud's party offered a solution, an attack on the New England frontier. The French and Indian leaders gathered in a circle as one of the Abenaki sachems sketched out a crude map in the dirt. At its center was a British fort located on the Hoosac River, an easterly tributary of the Hudson. The Abenaki sachem pointed to Fort Massachusetts and addressed Rigaud. "My father, it will be easy to take this fort and make great havoc on the lands of the English. Deign to listen to your children and follow our advice." There was a momentary hush as the French leader studied the map. He knew that the Abenaki were keen to see this fort destroyed, having lost a chieftain in an attack on the place the previous spring, but as he glanced over the diagram, he saw nothing wrong with the plan. At length he nodded his approval, which set off a cascade of war whoops and shouts as the news spread throughout the camp.

The next morning 440 French and 300 Indians pushed their canoes onto the waters of Lake Champlain. Within the hour a few wanted to change the attack to Saratoga, but Rigaud would have nothing of it. They had made their decision, he informed them, and now must abide by it. There was a chorus of agreement, and the party continued on toward Fort Massachusetts. The detachment ascended the lake through the marshy expanse known as the "Drowned Lands" and on through the narrows of "Two Rocks," where the lake becomes a mere stream dominated by natural stone ramparts on either side. The party abandoned their canoes where Wood Creek joins Lake Champlain, today known as "The Elbow," just north of modern-day Whitehall. Thirty men under the command of De Muy's younger brother were left to guard the canoes while the rest proceeded forward on foot. Five days later they reached the Hoosac River. Here they split into two groups and ascended both banks of the river. Along the way they raided the abandoned farms of the area, killing whatever animals they could find to supply themselves, but to avoid detection the farms were not put to the torch. There would be time for that later.[14]

Fort Massachusetts was the most westerly of three forts recently built in the area. It was situated along the north bank of the Hoosac River in a rough clearing that had been hacked out of the forest. The clearing should have been extended, for the tree line was still too close to the fort's walls, particularly along the north side where the fort was dominated by the wooded slope of Saddleback Mountain. The fort's positioning was questionable, but no doubt it was placed with the idea of obtaining an abundant supply of water given that fire was the greatest enemy of such structures. As for the fort itself, it consisted of thick logs laid lengthwise one upon the other with their corners notched to form an interlocking arrangement, much like that of a modern-day log cabin. At the northwest corner of this wooden square was a blockhouse, slightly taller than the fort's walls and built in a similar fashion. This blockhouse had a watchtower placed upon its outer angle, and like the fort's walls, it was pierced with numerous firing ports. Within the compound there were several buildings, the most important of which was a large wooden structure, which rested along the interior of the southern wall and overlooked its ramparts.

The fort's garrison consisted of fifty-one men under the command of Captain Ephraim Williams, a respected and well-liked militia officer. At the time of the attack, however, Williams was at Albany where he and several of his men were preparing to take part in the campaign against Fort St. Frederic. In Williams's absence, command devolved to Sergeant John Hawks, a tall New Englander with bold features and a disposition to match.

Three days before the attack Hawks had sent Dr. Thomas Williams, Ephraim's brother, and fourteen men to Deerfield to obtain supplies for the fort, particularly powder and shot, both of which were in short supply. This left a garrison of only twenty-two men, half of whom, according to Sgt. Hawks, were sick when the attack came.[15]

On the afternoon of August 30 Rigaud's combined force was but a few miles from Fort Massachusetts. At a council of war that morning it was agreed that the army would move into the woods near the fort where they would spend the evening making the scaling ladders and battering rams needed for the attack the next morning. As they approached, however, several of the Canadians and younger Natives caught a glimpse of the watchtower through the tangled foliage. Unable to contain themselves, they rushed out of the woods howling and yelling "like lions." Had the brazen attack been carried forward and supported by even a fraction of Rigaud's troops, the fort would have certainly fallen right there. Inside were only a handful of surprised defenders, most of whom would have barely had time to reach their arms before the French were over the walls. But as brave as the "lions" might be, the tenets of bush fighting did not include storming forts. Instead, the attackers scattered themselves about the fort and began a useless fusillade on the structure from behind stumps and whatever other cover they could find.

The sudden ebb in the attack allowed the garrison enough time to reach their weapons and man the ramparts. Soon the defenders began firing back, and afforded with much better cover, they began inflicting a number of casualties on the attackers. It was by no means an easy task. The French and Indians exposed themselves only long enough to fire or shift positions. With the supply of powder and shot quickly being depleted, Hawks was forced to order the men to only fire when they had a clear shot. On several occasions the garrison watched as French officers, swords in hand, paced the battlefield in clear view, just far enough away that it was not deemed worth the price of a precious musket ball. Even with their diminished fire the defenders of Fort Massachusetts had by the end of the day killed an Abenaki chieftain and wounded sixteen others, including Rigaud, who, standing on a rise a few hundred yards away, had been hit in the arm by a chance shot early in the engagement.[16]

As darkness began to set in, Hawks took stock of the situation. The good news was that only two of the garrison had been injured, neither seriously. The bad news was that supply of shot had fallen so low that he was forced to order the women and the sick to make bullets. The supply of powder had fallen to a dangerous level as well, but there was nothing that could be done about that. As a cloudy humid night took hold, the garrison prepared for the worst. From the tree line Hawks heard the sound of axes and hatchets. At first, he thought that the French were making scaling ladders, but later when he realized they were making bundles of wood to burn against the fort's walls, he ordered every tub and bucket in the fort filled with water to douse the flames. It was a restless night for the defenders. The garrison could see the enemy campfires burning to the south and southwest, the numbers of which emphasized their predicament. Under the cover of darkness, the French and Indians crept closer, testing the fort's defenses and sniping at the garrison. Hawks and his men occasionally fired back at the murky shapes and musket flashes so as to keep the enemy at bay, but essentially, they moved and fired upon the defenders at will.[17]

Rigaud spent the night preparing for the next day's attack. His plans were "to open trenches two hours before sunrise, and push them to the foot of the palisade, so as to place fagots against it, set them on fire, and deliver the fort a prey to the fury of the flames." To even contemplate such a formal siege technique demonstrates beyond anything the determined resistance of the defenders. Clearly, Rigaud thought that he was dealing with a much larger force than a sergeant, a minister, and nine militiamen. When it began raining in the early morning hours, Rigaud put his plans on hold. With daylight the rain subsided and firing resumed on both sides but only briefly. During the exchange, however, one of Hawks's men, Thomas Knowlton, was killed while in the watchtower, the first and only of the defenders lost in the siege.[18]

The shooting slowly dissipated to sporadic musket shots, leaving the defenders to wonder what their enemy was planning. Around noon they found out. An Indian carrying a white flag approached the fort. The French commander wanted a parley, to which Hawks agreed. A few minutes later Hawks, Reverend Norton, and another of the fort's garrison met with Rigaud and several of his officers outside of the fort. The French commander was quick to come to the point: surrender and they would be well treated as prisoners of war, or resist and he would put everyone in the fort to the sword. Hawks nodded that he understood and asked for two hours to consider the terms. Rigaud agreed, and the two parties returned to their respective posts.[19]

Hawks called together the garrison and laid out the French terms. Their current position did not leave much room for compromise. There were only three pounds of powder left and about as much shot, the whole good for maybe a few minutes of firing. There were three women and five children within the fort, as well as a large number of sick. If they resisted, all would be killed or carried off. Reverend Norton, for one, claimed that if these individuals had not been present, the garrison would have chosen to resist to the end, but it is doubtful that this would have been the ultimate decision. Outnumbered seventy to one, with no relief in sight and only a few rounds left between them, any decision other than surrender would have been tantamount to suicide. After a few words it was agreed to surrender. Hawks sent a message to Rigaud asking the latter to list the specific terms of surrender. The major informed them that they would be French prisoners and would be exchanged at the first opportunity. They would be allowed to keep their personal possessions, and those who were too sick or too weak to travel would be provided for on the return trek to Canada.

Hawks agreed to the final terms and lowered the English flag around three o'clock that afternoon. Rigaud and several of his officers were admitted into the fort, and the French flag was run up the pole to signify the surrender. The Indians and Canadians, however, were not pleased with being shut out of the proceedings. They had been promised loot and scalps and planned to get them one way or another. Soon a few of these individuals had torn away a sufficient number of foundation stones at the base of one wall to create a hole. Someone wiggled through the opening, entered the compound, and opened the gates for all to enter. Before they could be stopped, the interior of the fort was filled with French and Indians eager for their spoils. Knowlton's body was dragged down from the watchtower, scalped, and dismembered by a group of howling Canadians and Indians. Wisely, Rigaud had the English prisoners led back to the main French camp while the Canadians and Indians plundered the fort. Satisfied with their work, they set the structure on fire a few hours later and returned to their encampments.[20]

The garrison's plight was by no means over. Contrary to the agreement, several of the New Englanders were handed over to the Indians. Rigaud had promised them their human trophies, and with nearly three hundred of them in his war party he found it a promise impossible to break. In general, the captives were well treated, even those taken by the Indians. Reverend Norton was allowed to nail a letter to the charred remains of the fort with a brief description of what had transpired. The reverend would spend several years in Canada before finally being exchanged. As for the rest of the garrison, at least half of them died in captivity, not through foul play but through the ravages of sickness and disease. Eventually, the remainder were either exchanged or chose to stay in Canada. The fort's commander, Sgt. Hawks, was initially criticized until the details of the siege were made public. At that point not enough could be said of his conduct. For nearly a day and a half he and ten others had held off a war party of seven hundred French and Indians. He had punished the enemy as much as possible and was wise enough to know when enough was enough. Little else could be said of his actions. He acted with courage and resolution, and in the end, he put the welfare of his charges before all else. He was a fine officer who would rise to the rank of lieutenant colonel in the last French and Indian War.[21]

With the destruction of Fort Massachusetts complete, Rigaud set out for Fort St. Frederic, but not before releasing numerous war parties upon the frontier. The first, some sixty in number, positioned themselves between Deerfield and Fort Massachusetts in hopes of ambushing a party of reinforcements they had heard was destined for the fort. The relief column, however, never materialized, so the war party moved east, attacking and killing a number of residents of Deerfield before finally being chased off. Other parties struck elsewhere. A band of seventeen struck at the settlements below Albany, and another war party consisting of three French and twenty-five Abenaki attacked a detachment of twenty soldiers from the newly built Fort Clinton at Saratoga. The English, escorting a wagonload of clay, were surprised within sight of the fort's gates. Four were killed and four more captured before the remainder were able to reach the safety of the fort. There were smaller detachments as well, but the main damage was done by Rigaud's returning column. They retraced their steps down the Hoosac River and revisited the abandoned homesteads they had plundered on their way to Fort Massachusetts. This time they left nothing standing for the space of forty miles. Crops were destroyed and livestock killed. Homes, barns, mills, stables, churches, and even a meetinghouse fell prey to the torch, two hundred establishments in all. The entire valley lay a smoldering ruin in the column's wake.[22]

As the frontier burned, the citizens of New England and New York pinned their hopes on the expedition being assembled at Albany, "hoping," as one contemporary writer stated, "the time was coming, that God would deliver us out of the hands of our enemies in Canada."[23]

CHAPTER TWENTY-THREE

Fleets, Forts, and Frustration

As the French raided the frontier, the English colonies busied themselves with larger plans. In New England over five thousand troops concentrated on Boston. Here they drilled and anxiously awaited word of General St. Clair's arrival. With the success of the previous year's endeavor, and the enticement of a handsome recruiting bounty, there was no lack of volunteers. In the southern colonies the effort moved more slowly. Monies were appropriated and troop quotas gradually filled. New York pushed forward with the energy of New England. Supply ships loaded with provisions and ammunition traced their way up the Hudson in steady streams. Building materials for the numerous boats and canoes followed, as did the carpenters and shipbuilders who would fashion them into their final form. Wagons, horses, tents, and whatever else thought needed was purchased or, when required, impressed. The four independent companies, already on station, prepared encampments for the fifteen hundred newly raised levies, which marched or sailed for Albany as soon as their companies filled out. There was a spirit of determination, a focused resolve that pushed the preparations forward, even though General Gooch had yet to issue a single command.

There was still one important task remaining: convincing the Iroquois to join the expedition. To this end Governor Clinton left for Albany in mid-July to meet with the representatives of the Five Nations. When he arrived, he did not find the reception he had hoped for; there were a total of three Iroquois in the town. The trio had just attacked a woodcutting party outside of Fort St. Frederic and proudly presented the scalps to the governor. After a brief conversation and the outlaying of gifts, the three departed, promising to carry the governor's request for a meeting to their respective castles.[1]

Unsure of his three messengers, Clinton turned to a young adventurer by the name of William Johnson for help. Born in Ireland, Johnson had come to the colonies in the late 1730s to take charge of his uncle's estate, Commodore Sir Peter Warren, on the southern Mohawk River. The close proximity of the estate to the Iroquois and the swelling population of the region offered Johnson several business opportunities. He established a lucrative trading post, frequented by the Mohawk and other Iroquois nations, and he eventually earned enough money to purchase a tract of land on the north side of the Mohawk River. Here he built a large stone manor, which from its appearance unofficially became known as Fort Johnson. The Mohawk, in particular, formed a close bond with the young adventurer who responded in kind, learning their language and customs.

Soon, Johnson was adopted into the Mohawk, and a short time later he was made a sachem. Although Johnson's initial affiliation with the Mohawk was motivated by commerce, the nature of this relationship slowly changed as the years progressed. Johnson had a wild curiosity that guided his soul, and before long he became comfortable in the world of the Iroquois. He changed mind frames as easily as another would shed apparel, thinking nothing of participating in Mohawk festivities one night and negotiating with agents of the Crown the next. In April 1745 Clinton, who had become familiar with Johnson and his unique qualifications, appointed him manager of Indian affairs for the colony. In doing so the governor had replaced a political rival, Colonel Schuyler, whose family had held the post for generations. The appointment was no doubt influenced by this and by Johnson's family connections, but it appears from their correspondence that Clinton was genuinely fond of the young man, perhaps finding a common bond in the zeal and dedication Johnson displayed toward his task.[2]

Johnson went to work immediately. He called upon the Iroquois chieftains and used his personal influence to convince the bulk of the nations to meet with the governor in early August. The council proved partially successful. The ill disposition of the Iroquois, blamed on the influence of the Jesuits and indirectly on the poor management of Schuyler, was amended, but the Iroquois were still in no hurry to break their policy of neutrality. One Jesuit had made a particularly convincing argument that stuck in their minds. "It is in your interest," he warned them, "not to suffer either the

French or the British to be absolute masters, for in that case, your slavery to one or the other will be inevitable." There was enough truth in the statement that the Iroquois sachems were hesitant to join the cause, but in the end, the influence of Johnson and their old ties to the British held the day. It was agreed that a few Iroquois would be left at Albany to join the cause while the rest, the chieftains decided, would be sent once the British were ready to launch their assault. The approach on the part of the Iroquois demonstrated their reluctance and was a repeat of their behavior during Nicholson's two expeditions down Lake Champlain in 1709 and 1711. The participation of a few Iroquois volunteers would not be construed as enough to break the peace of Montreal. The rest, the sachems would hold back. After all, the British had been unsuccessful in this plan three times before.[3]

Satisfied with the results of the meeting, which at the very least had secured a portion of the Iroquois to the British cause, Clinton turned his energies to the organization of the colonial forces. He had not expected to be involved in such affairs, but word had reached him that, due to his failing health, General Gooch had declined the appointment as the expedition's commander. Given that there was no news of Gooch's replacement, Clinton felt he had no choice but to assume temporary command. His first action was to put some order to the confusion about Albany. Several scouting companies had been formed to monitor French movements along the frontier, but they had refused to march without assurances from the governor that they would receive their pay. With their own homes and families in jeopardy, Clinton berated the men's conduct and then dismissed them from the service. A number of volunteers came forward, but unfamiliar with the task of scouting they proved nearly useless, as indicated by the fact that over seven hundred French and Indians were able to lay siege to Fort Massachusetts, a mere forty miles away, without a soul in Albany aware of their presence.[4]

In late August Clinton received a pair of letters from Governor Shirley and Admiral Warren informing him that General St. Clair had yet to arrive. The two considered it unlikely that he would arrive at all, and even if he did, it was too late in the year to attempt an assault on Quebec. Clinton understood the tone of the letter. It seemed the campaign was over, but as he read on, he found that the Massachusetts governor was not quite ready to give up. With the failure of St. Clair to show, Shirley proposed an alternate plan. The New England forces would join with those already at Albany for an effort against Fort St. Frederic. It was less than had been hoped for, but the seizure of the fort would at least curtail the French and Indian raids along the frontier. More importantly, it would provide the colonies with a jumping off point to continue the campaign next spring, "by making us masters of the Lake Champlain with the passes, defiles, and carrying places as far as the fort at Chambly." Shirley believed that, with the addition of five thousand New England troops to Clinton's forces, it was unlikely that the French could prevent the fort's capture, even if they shifted troops from Quebec to defend the fort. But with autumn taking hold, they must move without delay. If Clinton agreed with the plan the New England troops and the expedition's new commander, General Samuel Waldo, would begin their march to Albany next week. In the meantime, it was incumbent upon him that the transportation and artillery be in place to allow for a quick descent on the fort upon their arrival.[5]

Clinton and his officers agreed to Shirley's plan and pushed forward with their work. Anglo-Iroquois raiding parties were launched toward Montreal in an effort to divert French resources while detachments moved forward to secure the routes to Lake George and Wood Creek. In mid-September the New Jersey and Pennsylvania troops arrived, creating some supply issues but bolstering Clinton's numbers to 2,300 men. The artillery was forwarded to Saratoga, and boats ladened with provisions and munitions were hauled up the Hudson waterway. Elsewhere the troops toiled with hatchet, axe, and saw in a race against the autumn frosts. The preparations were hardly perfect, but as it turned out they did not need to be.[6]

A portion of the New England troops had already begun their trek to Albany when orders overtook them to return to Boston. News had reached Massachusetts that a large French and Indian force was assembling near Minas, Nova Scotia, with the intention of moving on Annapolis Royal and the other settlements of the area. With all Nova Scotia imperiled, Shirley had little choice but to recommend a reduction in the troops destined for Crown Point. Half of the five thousand men destined for the enterprise would be diverted to Nova Scotia, as the loss of the colony would have devastating consequences on New England.

The reduction of forces was quickly approved by the participating governments and in and of itself did not undermine the Crown Point campaign. As Shirley pointed out, there were still 2,500 men left to bolster Clinton's forces, which when added to the number of Iroquois prepared to join the effort, would amount to a force of over five thousand men, more than enough to overwhelm any defenses erected by the French. No sooner were the new troop dispositions agreed upon when even more threatening news arrived. A number of vessels sighted off the coast of Nova Scotia were reported to be the advanced elements of a large French fleet. Word of the armada spread quickly. Panic struck Boston and the coastal settlements as far south as Charleston. The fleet grew in size and scope with each rendition of the story, making it clear to the jittery citizens that it was bent on nothing less than the complete destruction of the eastern seaboard.

With reports of a French squadron operating off the coast of Nova Scotia, Shirley moved to counter the threat and harness the nervous energy of the populace. The militias were called out and the troops destined for Albany held in readiness. Within a week there were twelve thousand men under arms, building ramparts and repairing the fortifications along the New England coast. Connecticut held another six thousand men in reserve ready to respond the moment the French fleet actually appeared. By October Shirley was prepared to give the French squadron a "hot reception," but it soon became apparent that the strength of the fleet had been greatly exaggerated. Only a handful of vessels had actually landed in Nova Scotia; the rest had either returned to France or had been lost in a series of storms that had scattered the fleet.[7]

Although the French fleet did not prove to be a threat, had Shirley known the size and scope of the expedition, he would have redoubled his efforts. With France still electrified by Count Maurice de Saxe's victory at the Battle of Fontenoy, news of the fall of Louisbourg brought forth a defiant response from the French court. After little debate, it was agreed to form an expedition to recapture not only Louisbourg but Port Royal and Placentia as well. To accomplish this task the minister of the marine assembled ten ships-of-the-line, six frigates, two fireships, four armed schooners and brigantines, and forty-two transports and supply ships. The warships, to augment their firepower, would carry the two battalions of the Ponthieu Regiment, amounting to 1,440 men. Another 1,350 men forming two battalions of French militia drawn from the Saumur and Fontenay-le-Comte districts were carried on fourteen transports, while the French Marines, now augmented to over a thousand men, were dispersed among the fleet. It was an extraordinary commitment on the part of the French Crown, which had only once before sent a regiment of the line to New France. Over seven thousand men manning sixty-four vessels carrying 3,500 soldiers, marines, and an artillery train had been committed to a venture whose ultimate goal was nothing short of expelling the British from Cape Breton Island and Nova Scotia.

While some thought was put into the impressive flotilla and its mission, far less was put into the selection of a commander. The thirty-five-year-old Lt. General of the Galleys Jean-Baptiste d'Enville (D'Anville), the Duc d'Enville, who despite a line of impressive titles had no experience in naval warfare, was placed in charge of the expedition. D'Enville's second in command would be the captain of the 64-gun *Trident*, Rear Admiral Constantin-Louis D'Estourmel, a veteran who had served in several campaigns against the Barbary pirates and the British. Also accompanying the expedition would be Canada's new governor, Rear Admiral Jacques-Pierre Taffanel, the Marquis de La Jonquiere. Jonquiere, who like d'Estourmel, had a long record of naval service, would be third in command and captain of the fleet's flagship, the captured and refitted 60-gun *Northumberland*.

Governor Beauharnois received news of d'Enville's fleet and its intentions with the arrival of the *Letourneur* on May 7, 1746. The January 24 letter from the French court spoke to d'Enville's planned arrival in Nova Scotia, his targets, and orders for the governor to cooperate with the admiral. As part of this last directive Beauharnois was to dispatch a force of 1,200 French and Indians to rendezvous with the fleet at Chebucto Bay. Drawn from the militias of Quebec, Montreal, and Three Rivers the 680 troops under the command of Captain Roch de Ramezay boarded seven vessels and departed Quebec for Bay Verte on June 5. A pair of detachments made up of the three hundred Abenaki of the St. Francois and Becancour Missions and eighty Micmac who had wintered near Quebec, had departed a few days earlier in their canoes. Messengers were sent to the Wabanaki missionaries in the region, Father Pierre de l'Estage of the Restigouche Micmac, Father Charles Germain of the Maliseet, Father Maurice Lacorne of the Miramichi Micmac, and Captain Joseph Du Pont Duvivier, stationed at the St. Johns River, with orders to gather together as many men as they could and rendezvous at Beaubassin, Nova Scotia. Once the fleet arrived a decision would be made on how best to employ these combined forces.[8]

While Ramezay and his men slowly made their way to Bay Verte, unsettling reports began arriving. Several prisoners taken in raids on the New England frontier reported that three thousand troops from Old England had taken over garrison duties from the New Englanders at Louisbourg, and there were over half a dozen British warships in the harbor, several of which had been ordered to cruise the Gulf of St. Lawrence. Of more interest were comments about the martial activities in Boston, the stockpile of munitions, the raising of troops, and rumors that a fleet would arrive there to carry out an attack on Quebec. On the other hand, this news was counteracted by prisoners speaking to reports that a French fleet was on its way to attack Boston.

Although Ramezay's detachment was delayed by privateers and weather, Father Germain, one of the first to arrive at Beaubassin, immediately dispatched a small detachment to Chebucto Bay with orders to inform him of the fleet's arrival. On June 19 Germain wrote the governor that a courier had arrived with news that the 40-gun frigate *L'Aurore* and the 26-gun *Castor* were at anchor in the bay. The two vessels had left Brest in early April with orders to proceed to Chebucto Bay, and once there, await the arrival of the fleet.

Ramezay's detachment would not reach Bay Verte until mid-July. The captain's orders were to march to Beaubassin and rendezvous with his Wabanaki contingent. Once this was accomplished, he was to split his detachment in two with one part aimed at the village of Canso and the other proceeding toward Port Royal. However, Ramezay was still at Bay Verte when a local missionary passed a message onto him from the commander of the two frigates at Chebucto. Captain M. du Vignau of the *L'Aurore* proposed a move against Port Royal should the fleet not appear this month. Ramezay was receptive to the idea. Father Germain had referred to the route to Canso as "absolutely impracticable," and reports were that the British there had withdrawn to Louisbourg. Given the circumstances, Ramezay countermanded his earlier order and kept his detachment together. He then wrote Beauharnois of his decision and requested a mortar and ammunition to assist in the siege of the British stronghold.

While Ramezay's detachment spent the next few weeks moving their supplies and provisions to Beaubassin, Governor Beauharnois was beginning to have second thoughts concerning the detachment. Several prisoners reported a large build-up of troops and transports around Boston, while another noted that "there were at Louisbourg more than 40 men of war, transports and merchantmen." He then proceeded to name nine warships in harbor of forty guns or more. With British ships routinely being sighted in the Gulf of St. Lawrence, and every indication of a British move against Quebec, the governor sent a message to Ramazey, ordering his recall. He was to leave 250 of his force to cooperate with d'Enville's fleet when it arrived, but at the moment a siege of Port Royal was out of the question. He was to immediately march his men to Bay Verte and await the ships sent to carry them back to Quebec. Having spent the last month moving his men and their supplies toward Minas, Ramezay shook his head when he received the news, and after selecting a detachment to stay behind, ordered his troops and their supplies back to Bay Verte.

For Captain Vignau waiting for d'Enville at Chebucto Bay with a pair of frigates, it had proven to be a successful outward voyage. The *L'Aurore* had captured six small vessels while the *Castor* had seized two craft, one of which was laden with cattle and provisions bound for Louisbourg. A recent foray into the Gulf of Maine had led to the capture of a 10-gun British snow, but it was now the middle of August and Vignau began to worry. Both ships were running low on provisions, and rumors from captured crews were that the British had intercepted d'Enville. Given the circumstances, Vignau informed Beauharnois that both vessels would be returning to France.[9]

Vignau's departure was frustrating for Ramezay, given that three deserters from Annapolis Royal reported that "the garrison of that fort consisted of 300 men with 12 or 15 officers," and that there was "a frigate of 40 guns off Goat Island." His current force, coupled with Vignau's frigates and hopefully the arrival of a few of d'Enville's fleet, was more than enough to carry the British post. With Annapolis Royal in French hands, British power in Nova Scotia would collapse, bringing the bulk of the Acadians openly over to the French cause. With the recall letter in his hand, and the two frigates departing on August 12, Ramezay realized that it would be up to d'Enville to seize this important post and continued his withdrawal to Bay Verte.

Ramazey and his men waited at Bay Verte as the promised vessels and provisions were delayed by British privateers and warships, which in one case attacked the harbor at Cape Desrosiers, forcing the crew of a French brigantine to run their vessel aground and put it to the torch. Nor could Ramazey leave with the vessels on hand for fear of the same threat. More importantly, as August slipped into September, the question being asked in New France was similar to the one being asked in the American colonies: Where was the fleet? Or, in this specific case, where was d'Enville?[10]

After a series of delays, brought about in part by the British blockading fleet, d'Enville put out to sea in June, and choosing a path south of the Azores, soon became becalmed for twenty-two days. Water became an issue, as did dysentery and scurvy. The British posed another problem. Advanced elements of the French fleet sparred with enemy frigates near the islands for almost a week, nearly exhausting their ammunition before the weather shifted. Gales and headwinds followed as the food began to run low and sickness took hold of the fleet. A number of vessels turned back, and one transport was lost to fire while another disappeared in a storm with all hands.

D'Enville detached Captain Hubert de Brienne, the Chevalier de Conflans, with three ships-of-the-line and a frigate to act as escorts for the trade and supply convoy headed to the Caribbean with orders to rejoin the fleet in Nova Scotia when this task was complete. Running low on provisions and with the sick rolls increasing daily, d'Enville finally arrived at Chebucto Bay in the *Northumberland* on September 20, 1746, after a crossing of close to a hundred days. The frigate *Renomme* and four transports accompanied the flagship, which only found one vessel waiting in the harbor. The sick were quickly carried ashore, d'Enville now to be counted among them.

News of the battered 36-gun *Renommee*'s arrival at Beaver Harbor, about eighty miles to the east of Chebucto, in early September had instilled some hope, but it was not until news of d'Enville's arrival that Ramazey halted his detachment's departure, although part of his troops had already left. A week later, on the same day that d'Enville would die from his illness, three transports arrived, and that afternoon Admiral d'Estourmel in the *Trident*, two ships-of-the-line, and a frigate entered the harbor. Suddenly finding himself in command, d'Estourmel held a council of war abord the *Trident* the next day.

The new commander was in favor of returning to France. There was no news from Conflans' detachment, and several other warships had turned back or had yet to arrive. Only about a third of the army was ashore, and it was in a miserable state with dysentery and a scorbutic fever. Supplies were uncertain, and a British fleet was known to be in Louisbourg. Jonquiere and most of the officers in the meeting disagreed, believing that even with the limited force on hand, they should strike a blow against the British. Annapolis Royal was the most logical target. They still possessed five ships-of-the-line, a frigate, and seven armed transports. The crews of the vessels alone outnumbered the British defenders by five to one, and any guard ship reported would not stand long before such firepower. Cooperating with Ramezay's force they could not fail but to capture the British colonial capital.

The argument continued for the better part of the day before d'Estourmel, not feeling well, retired to his quarters. The fever that was ravaging the fleet had found the vice admiral, and in a delirium, he stabbed himself, leaving Governor Jonquiere to assume command. The flotilla would spend a month at Chebucto recovering its health and waiting for stragglers. Resupplied by sympathetic Acadians, Jonquiere took the fleet back out to sea on October 24 and set a course for Port Royal. Fog and storms quickly scattered the vessels. With his numbers decimated by scurvy and the season slipping away, Jonquiere finally concluded that "it was impossible to undertake any action," and ordered the fleet to return to France. Two warships and twenty-one transports along with close to seven hundred men were lost in the ill-fated expedition, and over 2,200 were listed on the sick roles. However, most suspected that the official casualty number was understated, particularly given how many of the sick later died or became invalids unfit for future service. Critics threw up their hands and pointed to the failure of the French Navy, which certainly was not the French Navy of King William's War. The fleet had suffered casualties expected from a major battle, yet not a single blow had been struck against the enemy. In fact, none were even attempted, nor had any of the intended goals been achieved. While this argument discounted the effects of weather, the enemy, and rushed planning, it was essentially true. However, what the critics would lose sight of was one important item; it would save Fort St. Frederic and French control over the Champlain Valley, which in turn safeguarded Montreal.[11]

Throughout this period the British colonies were also asking a similar question: Where was the British fleet? General St. Clair and his forces had assembled at Portsmouth mid-May, but contrary winds had delayed their departure. On June 15, the fleet finally put out to sea only to be immediately becalmed and then blown back into port by adverse winds. Had the weather cooperated, it seems likely that St. Clair would have reached Louisbourg, and perhaps it would be his name, and not Wolfe's, that would be forever linked with the fall of Quebec. At this point, however, the expedition faced problems beyond the weather. By late June the situation in Europe had changed to the point that many in the ministry questioned whether the Quebec expedition should go forward. It was clear that another campaign was brewing in Flanders, where St. Clair's five thousand men would be sorely needed. There was also talk of a French invasion of Scotland, perhaps coupled with another Jacobite uprising in the highlands. News of a French fleet's departure from Brest complicated matters. If St. Clair was to proceed, he would now require an additional escort, which again meant another delay while the necessary vessels were rounded up. In mid-July it was agreed to carry on with the American expedition, but as the season was too late to move against Quebec, St. Clair was ordered to winter at Louisbourg and launch his attack the following spring. On August 6 the English fleet put to sea and once again was blown back into port. At this point St. Clair's forces were too inviting a resource to be left idle. His troops were sent on an ill-fated expedition against the French coast, and upon his return in October it was agreed to put off any American expedition until the spring.[12]

All of this, of course, was unknown to Shirley and Warren, who felt there was no choice but to alter the focus of the campaign in late August to an attack of Fort St. Frederic when it became clear that St. Clair would not arrive in time. Threats to Nova Scotia and the presence of a French fleet had delayed this operation almost two months. It was now nearing the end of October, too late in the season to besiege the French stronghold. Clinton, unaware of the presence of the French fleet, had waited in vain for General Waldo and his New England contingent until Shirley informed him that he had held these troops in Boston to deal with the threat posed by the enemy fleet. While Clinton understood the change in plans, and was pleased to see the French fleet depart without having accomplished anything of note, as far as the New York governor was concerned the Crown Point campaign was over.

The question then became what to do with the forces already on the New York frontier. Technically, they should be dismissed, but neither Clinton nor his officers were interested in this course of action. A great deal of money had gone into their raising, and it seemed something should come from this effort. After a brief debate a compromise was struck. The troops would be posted so that they could defend the frontier over the course of the winter. By leaving these forces on station, the frontier could be secured while still presenting an opportunity to resurrect the campaign at a later date, perhaps in the spring. To facilitate both tasks, a palisade fort would be built and garrisoned at the Great Carrying Place. The military justification was sound. A fort at this location would not only deny the use of this important passage to French and Indian war parties, but it would provide a launching pad for future campaigns as well. The manpower to build and garrison the fort was available, but as desirable as it might have been, provisioning issues, costs, and arguments with the New York council forced Clinton to abandon the plan.[13]

By late November the threat posed by the French fleet had diminished to the point that Shirley once again turned his attention to the prosecution of the Crown Point campaign. Even at this late date the Massachusetts governor was still pushing for an attack. He wrote the governors involved that he was prepared to forward men, provisions, and artillery to Albany "to proceed in that part of winter as shall be judged most seasonable for this important expedition." His proposal reached the colonial governors in December and in its final form called for five hundred New Hampshire troops to make a diversionary attack on the Abenaki Mission on the St. Francois River while New York launched a second diversionary attack toward Fort Frontenac. Clinton showed some interest in the plan, but for the New York council it was out of the question. The thought of a winter campaign appealed to none of them. The supply issues were difficult enough in good weather and simply out of the question during the winter months. There were also concerns about a smallpox epidemic that had broken out at Albany, which was feared would pose a grave threat to the arriving New England troops. Nor could the Iroquois be counted upon at this point. The advanced season and the threat of smallpox would certainly keep them away. Governor Jonathan Law of Connecticut ended any hope Shirley might have held out. He and his council refused to furnish their quota of men, deeming it not "advisable at this season to proceed."[14]

The response was predictable. Although the French had shown the possibilities of a winter campaign on several occasions, the British colonies had always maintained a conventional campaign season, making their undertakings somewhat predictable. It was in this sense that Shirley's plan held promise. It would strike when the French felt most secure and when the fort was at its weakest, during the long winter months when its garrison was at its lowest, its supply lines tenuous, and its prospect of relief questionable. The diversionary attacks would be useful but were hardly required. A quick envelopment of the fort was all that was necessary. The stronghold would fall long before the French could organize a relief expedition, and even if they did manage to scrape together a response, such a feat would require them to drag cannons and supplies down the frozen length of Lake Champlain in order to retake the structure. It was a bold idea, and unlike many of Shirley's plans, which were typically short on details, this one was not. The troops, supplies, artillery, and transportation were in place. As with any military undertaking, there were risks involved. To Shirley, the prospects of success outweighed these risks, but Shirley did not have the final say in the matter, and in the end, he failed to convince others of its possibilities.[15]

And thus, the campaign of 1746, which captivated the hearts of so many colonists, concluded with a whimper. For large periods of the late summer, over eight thousand men were under arms, and at one point, during the scare from the French fleet, there were nearly fifteen thousand. How such a force could manage to accomplish so little was the question being bandied about in Boston, New York, and Philadelphia. St. Clair's failure to arrive, the ministry's failure to notify the colonies of his delay, French overtures in Nova Scotia, and the perceived threat posed by the French Navy all contributed to the campaign's failure. "Great numbers of men kept in pay and idleness 'till disbanded," one observer concluded, "to the ruin of many of them and the great hurt of the country."[16]

CHAPTER TWENTY-FOUR

Stalemate

For Ramezay and his men it had been a difficult and frustrating campaign, culminated by the dismal failure of the French Navy to carry out its role. If there was any consolation, rumors also arrived that the expected British fleet had been diverted and would no longer appear. Although enemy privateers and a handful of warships operating out of Louisbourg cruising the Gulf of St. Lawrence posed a long-term threat to Canada, by October the season had all but ruled out any attempt on Quebec, allowing Beauharnois and his troops a needed break from the uncertainty of the last few months.

In Nova Scotia Ramezay and seven hundred of his men had encamped within sight of Annapolis Royal since late September, but upon receiving news from Jonquiere that he was returning to France, the detachment fell back on Minas and then shortly thereafter returned to Beaubassin. For Governor Mascarene, the passing threat had pointed to the uncertain loyalty of the Acadians and French efforts to win over their allegiance. Looking to neutralize this latter effort, and prevent French forces at Beaubassin from using this area as a staging point for an attack on Annapolis Royal, Mascarene asked New England for a thousand men to secure the countryside.

While he would not receive the requested numbers, 470 men under Massachusetts Colonel Arthur Noble did arrive in early December. Mascarene advanced this detachment to Grand Pre on the Minas Bason. Major Erasmus Philipps and Edward Howe would accompany Noble and assume control of all civilian affairs in the region. After a grueling winter march, the detachment occupied Grand Pre without any opposition on December 24, 1746. With weather and supply issues threatening the New England forces, it was decided to quarter them among the populace. Although this was perhaps the only practical solution, it left Noble's forces scattered across the countryside.[1]

It was not until January 8 that a villager from Grand Pre informed Ramezay, who was still at Beaubassin with Captain Nicolas-Antoine Coulon de Villiers and his detachment of three hundred French and Indians who were to spend the winter in the region. A council of war was assembled, and all agreed that the enemy should be driven out of the town before they received reinforcements and erected a fort. Given that Ramezay had badly twisted his knee in an earlier march, he gave command of the expedition to Villiers. It would not be until the twenty-third that the preparations were complete, and the detachment moved forward on snowshoes dragging their supply behind them on wicker sleds.

By February 9, Villiers was at Piziguit (Windsor) on the St. Croix River, a dozen miles from Grand Pre. After speaking with several inhabitants, it became clear that about six hundred New Englanders had been quartered on the populace. The latter had abandoned their homes fearing a French attack, but the enemy troops, pointing to the miserable weather, scoffed at the idea. After consulting with the inhabitants, and determining that twenty-four homes had been occupied, Villiers formulated a plan. There were simply too many dwellings, and they were too widely scattered to attack all of them at once. Thus, he would break his forces into ten sections and simultaneously attack ten of the homesteads. He would personally lead the first and largest detachment of eighty-four men, while the remaining nine would each consist of an officer and twenty-eight men.

The war party returned to its march on the afternoon of the tenth and around 9:00 p.m. arrived before the Gaspereaux River, a little over a mile from Grand Pre. Guides were assigned to each of the sections, and twenty-five Acadian volunteers were distributed throughout the ranks. As the snowfall began to increase, the army ate and rested until the order to advance was given at 2 a.m. The war party reached Grand Pre an hour and a half later. The slanting snow from a nor'easter that would deposit four feet of snow over the next twenty-four hours made the march far more difficult than anticipated. Given the poor visibility, several sections, such as Villiers, found themselves before the wrong home with no time to locate the assigned one.[2]

It cannot be said that Noble's men were unprepared, as each home had a sentry posted, but the blizzard made it impossible to see for more than a few dozen yards. Suddenly war parties appeared out of the darkness and clouds of swirling snow. Most sentries were barely able to fire a warning shot before the howling charge swept them away. The sound of splintering wood and the shouts of the attackers rang through the homesteads as Villiers' men forced their way into the buildings. Although the timing of each individual attack was slightly off, it was over in a matter of thirty minutes, leaving Villiers in possession of ten homes, an eighty-ton schooner at the docks, and over sixty prisoners. Just as many lay dead, including Colonel Noble and several of his officers. With the element of surprise French casualties had been light, perhaps a dozen or so, but counted among these was Villiers, whose left arm had been shattered by a musket ball, requiring him to return to the encampment on the Gaspereaux River for medical attention.

As a few sporadic shots echoed through the howling wind, Captain Jean-Louis de La Corne, now in command, consolidated his holdings. The remaining 350 British had retreated into a stone building near the center of the village, which mounted several small cannons. A lull fell over the battlefield as the snow, wind, and darkness made any concerted action out of the question. At dawn La Corne was watching the enemy stronghold from the window of a nearby building when a series of flashes translated into a ripple of dull knocks as grapeshot struck his building. This was followed by a wild yell as two hundred New Englanders exited the stone structure and advanced on several nearby homes. The fighting raged door to door as the shrieking wind muffled the shouts and sound of muskets. The New Englanders captured a few dwellings but, taking fire and without snowshoes, finally gave up and retreated back into their stone haven around eleven o'clock.

Cramped in the small structure without firewood and with their ammunition running low, Captain Benjamin Goldthwait, now in command after Noble's death, requested a truce. La Corne, whose own men were exhausted, was happy to grant a ceasefire until nine o'clock the next morning. Talks then proceeded as to what terms the French would grant Goldthwait and his men. After holding a council of war La Corne and his officers agreed to offer the British full honors of war. While such a cache of prisoners would have been useful to exchange for French prisoners, the war party had no way to cope with so many captives. The New Englanders were to leave Grand Pre in forty-eight hours and pledge not to take up arms in this region for six months. Goldthwait could hardly argue with the terms and agreed to surrender. After extending the British departure by a day because of bad weather, on the morning of February 14 the captured garrison, numbering 348 in all, marched out of their stone building with their arms shouldered. After passing between two lines of French troops they were led to a home at the far edge of the town. Here they were fed, and then under the guidance of twenty Acadian volunteers, they were marched to the outskirts of Annapolis Royal, bringing the Battle of Grand Pre to an official end.

The French victory was clear on several levels. The numerically superior enemy force had been ejected from Grand Pre, demonstrating French strength not only to the British but also to the Acadians of the area. In addition, casualties had been light with seven killed and twice as many wounded. They now had sixty-nine prisoners in their hands, had captured and released another 348, and by British accounts, another seventy-five had been killed and almost as many wounded. For Mascarene it was a foolish disaster. Without a fortification to allow Noble's men to concentrate their strength, they were forced by necessity to be dispersed among the village, allowing detachments to be isolated and destroyed. Noble, who like many was killed in his night shirt, bears responsibility as well, but given the near perfect weather conditions for an attacker, it is doubtful that more sentries would have made any difference. For the moment there was little Mascarene could do but focus on the defenses of Annapolis Royal. It appeared the countryside would remain French.[3]

The other French theater of concern, the Champlain Valley, had also stabilized. For the moment Fort St. Frederic appeared secure, but it would not be until the depths of winter that Beauharnois was convinced of the fact. The governor was still lamenting the fate of the French fleet when Ensign Louis Repentigny returned from a scout of the area between Albany and Saratoga in mid-November 1746. He had encountered a column of British troops moving toward the latter location and had managed to ambush a few wagons, but from the size of the column and the encampments about Saratoga, it appeared that the British were preparing for a winter campaign.

The governor held the militia of Montreal in readiness, warned the commander of Fort St. Frederic, and dispatched additional scouts to the area. In early December a second scout returned with better news. They had found no signs of an upcoming campaign. The British fort at Saratoga had been enlarged and was well garrisoned, but the former troop encampments were abandoned. As January 1747 passed into February, Beauharnois still held his doubts. Toward the end of March, he finally received more proof. Lieutenant M. de Herbin and a war party of thirty French and Indians routed an British supply column near Saratoga. The attack had netted a number of prisoners who quickly subdued the governor's fears. The siege cannons and bateaux for an attack were in place, but sickness had decimated the British garrisons at Saratoga and Albany. The captives were also able to dispel the fear generated by Repentigny's report. The troops Repentigny had seen were three hundred men sent to garrison Fort Clinton, as the new fort at Saratoga was now called, in expectation of a French attack. This last bit of information surprised Beauharnois. After all their efforts it was now the British who were afraid of being attacked. How quickly the fortunes of war change.[4]

Herbin brought the governor conclusive proof of the British plight a month later. In late March he ambushed an British detachment on the road between Fort Clinton and Albany. The British retreated after a hotly contested affair, but he had managed to secure several prisoners from the engagement. For Beauharnois, the prisoners and their papers presented him with his first clear view of the British situation at Saratoga. The bulk of the garrison was sick, there was want of almost every necessity, no one had been paid, and the fort itself was in such a miserable condition that its commander wrote that he pitied the officer sent to relieve him. There were references to the campaign against Fort St. Frederic, but the tenor and tone of the letters made it clear that they were not the words of men about to undertake such an effort. Nor was the governor led to believe that the situation was any better at Albany. It seemed that for the moment, there was little to fear.[5]

The British may have been idle, but their allies were not. Primarily due to the efforts of William Johnson, the Mohawk had been enticed into raiding the French frontier. A new generation of Iroquois fell to the task, striking at the settlements about Montreal with the zeal and familiarity of their forefathers. In early April they scored their first real success. A party of twenty or so Mohawk led by Lt. Walter Butler left for a scout of Crown Point. For several days the group lay in the woods outside of the fort, seeing nothing beyond two canoes of men departing the fort. On the third day the party divided into two and approached the fort. The first group, consisting of thirteen, discovered a set of tracks and after following them for a time came across a French patrol resting on the remains of a fallen tree. Under the protection of an embankment the Mohawk crept closer, and when the time was judged right, they unleashed a volley upon their unsuspecting foes. Three of the French fell immediately; the rest, some thirty in number, bolted to their arms and launched a ragged response. A second Mohawk volley broke any resistance and sent the patrol reeling toward the fort. But the matter had yet to be settled. The French commander rallied his troops and returned to the scene. The contest was renewed upon a snow-patched entanglement of dormant trees. For a time, the two sides proved evenly matched, but when one of the French Indians fell, his comrades darted for the fort. The French troops had also seen enough, and ignoring the shouts of their leaders, sprinted for safety.

Soon all that remained of the French position was a pair of officers and a sergeant. The three men put up a gallant defense. One young officer dressed in a dark blue coat with broad gold lace fought with particular resolution. With his comrades fallen, he called for quarter in the Iroquois tongue after receiving his seventh wound. But these were not the fields of Flanders, and he and his two compatriots were given over to the scalping knife as the rest of the Mohawk raced after the retreating French. A strong detachment from the fort ended any pursuit and sent the victors scrambling back into the woods.[6]

As the "Petty War" moved forward, the leaders on both sides prepared for the coming campaign season. With every indication that the British would renew their plans against Fort St. Frederic, the task before Governor Beauharnois remained the same. In May he dispatched Ensign La Corne to the fort with two hundred men to continue scouting operations along the frontier. Major Rigaud would follow shortly with another nine hundred French and Indians and take command of the defenses. His orders were almost a duplicate of last year's: obstruct Wood Creek to delay the British advance, prepare the defenses of the fort as best as possible, and in lieu of any British attack strike at the New York-New England frontier.

For Governor Shirley and Governor Clinton, the matters at hand were quite different. Both fully expected that the previous year's campaign would go forward, but neither had received any orders from London along these lines. For Clinton there were other issues. The troops wintered along the New York frontier had yet to be paid. Desertion was widespread, and grumblings were turning into threats of a full-scale mutiny. In May, Lt. Colonel Johnathan Roberts, who commanded the four independent companies, informed the governor that a resolution had passed among the troops that if they did not receive their full pay soon, they would desert *en masse* and compensate their wages by plundering Albany. There were also provisioning issues both from New York, whose council had refused to pay for the movement of the supplies beyond Albany, and from the various governments involved, which had reached the end of their supply allotments. Temporary measures were undertaken in the form of pay and supplies, but they could only delay the inevitable. The Canadian expedition was on the verge of collapse. What was desperately needed at this point was word from London.[7]

By mid-June Rigaud and his forces were in place about Fort St. Frederic. Never content with defensive measures, Rigaud's attention drifted toward Fort Clinton. He mulled over the reports on the state of the British fort and spoke with Lt. Herbin and the other scouts who had recently returned from Saratoga. With its weakened and disgruntled garrison, the fort was a tempting target but by no means an easy one. Armed with cannons and garrisoned by several hundred men, it would require an actual siege to take the structure. Rigaud was not prepared to undertake such an operation, but he could exploit the fort's state of affairs. If he could pressure the defenders, catch them unaware, or draw them out into an open battle, there was a chance that the fort might be taken by storm or, better yet, simply surrender.

By late June he had decided to test the defenders of Fort Clinton. La Corne was given twenty French and two hundred Indians to carry out the task. The expedition arrived in the vicinity of the fort on June 28 and immediately set up a number of ambuscades. Seeing nothing, La Corne formulated a plan for the next day. He would arrange his forces in an ambush about one of the fort's gates, which opened toward the Batten Kill River. A handful of men would lay in wait behind the riverbank about eighty paces from the fort. If anyone left the fort, these forces were to rush forward and fire upon them. If the fort returned fire, they were to pretend to have suffered a number of casualties and show some difficulty in making good their escape. Many of the chieftains balked at the plan and complained that the expedition had already exposed itself too much. They must retreat now. There were rumors that four hundred of the fort's garrison had already surrounded them. La Corne dismissed the reports as nonsense. They had come to strike a blow against the enemy, and he meant to do just that. Many of his Native allies agreed with La Corne, and soon half a dozen volunteered to be the bait for his trap.

That night La Corne's forces took their positions. At dawn a pair of Englishmen exited the fort, and as planned, the six Natives darted forward and discharged their pieces. The French commander watched the unfolding masquerade. His scouts trampled back toward the riverbank, dragging a few of their number as scattered shots from the fort kicked up the dirt around them. There were then a few anxious minutes. La Corne stared at the fort's gate over short breaths, hoping to discern some sign that the garrison had taken the bait. If the British did not buy the act, or if one of his men showed himself prematurely, the whole plan would collapse.[8]

He was soon rewarded. The gate swung open, and close to a hundred of the garrison spilled through the opening, arraying themselves in line of battle before the fort. Their commander, a lieutenant named Chew, took his position before them and signaled an advance. La Corne cocked his double-barreled flintlock and signaled to those around him to wait. When the British line reached the spot where his troops had staged their ruse, La Corne rose from his concealment and fired into the line. Two hundred muskets followed, creating a tattered screen of smoke in front of Chew's men. The British line returned fire, but between the smoke and surprise, most missed their mark. They were not given a chance to reload. With a war whoop, La Corne signaled a charge, and with hatchet, tomahawk, and knife, his men fell upon the formation. A score of Chew's men toward the rear of the line bolted for the fort, whose cannons fired a few rounds to discourage any further pursuit. The rest, now enveloped and pressed between the enemy and the Batten Kill, fought back as best they could. Many threw themselves into the river only to be shot as they swam for safety. The remainder, with no recourse but annihilation or surrender, chose the latter.[9]

Chew called for quarter, and the request was granted. He and forty-five of his men now found themselves prisoners while another twenty-eight were killed in the engagement. La Corne wasted no time in collecting his captives and withdrawing to a safe distance. Upon the conclusion of the battle, another 150 men exited the gate and arrayed themselves beneath the walls of the fort but proceeded no further. La Corne's party spent the evening about the fort. A few Natives entertained themselves by launching flaming arrows at the structure in hopes of setting it ablaze but to little effect beyond provoking the occasional hail of grape shot from the fort's cannons. With nothing else to be accomplished, La Corne and his detachment returned to Fort St. Frederic the next day.[10]

As it turned out, Fort Clinton's days were numbered. Its destruction, however, would not be by French hands but by British. In mid-July Colonel Peter Schuyler's regiment relieved the beleaguered garrison. Of Captain Livingston's original complement of four hundred men, scarcely half remained to trek back to Albany. True to the captain's earlier words, Schuyler found the fort a wreck. Nothing could be kept dry, the palisades were falling down, and the barracks were too small to handle the entire regiment. Finding himself confined to such a structure, and at the end of a dwindling supply line, Schuyler opted to abandon the fort in late July. Upon its abandonment, Clinton directed Colonel Roberts of the independents to examine the fort and make a recommendation as to its future. Roberts did better. Finding the fort utterly useless, he had it burned to the ground in early November, much to the astonishment of the French, who upon the next visit to the site found nothing standing but twenty disembodied chimneys.[11]

Clinton struggled with Lt. Governor DeLancy and the New York council to hold the campaign and defenses of the frontier together. The Mohawk, who had taken up the cause against the French and had thus far scored the only successes against the enemy, were short on arms and supplies. The council sympathized but voted a mere £150 to support their effort. Nor could the council be persuaded to resolve the pay and supply issues haunting the campaign. Three months' supplies were voted upon, but the council would still only pay for the movement of supplies to Albany and no farther. As for the soldiers' pay, that was a matter to be resolved by the Crown, they informed the governor. Until then they would advance no money to settle this point. Clinton fired off letter after letter to Newcastle and the ministry over the council's conduct but to little avail.[12]

In late July 1747, Clinton received an express from Shirley concerning the prosecution of the Crown Point campaign. In lieu of any orders from London, the governor was calling together the Massachusetts Assembly in mid-August to advocate pressing forward with the expedition. He recommended to Clinton that he do the same so the two governments could coordinate their affairs. The prospect of more dealings with the New York Assembly must have depressed Clinton to no end. On August 15, the governor received another express from Shirley. When he opened the letter, he fully expected that it would be nothing more than an indication that the Massachusetts governor had summoned together his assembly and presented his case to them. Instead, he found shocking news. Due to commitments in Europe, London had ordered a halt to the Canadian campaign. The troops raised for the expedition were to be dismissed from service, and "as these American troops have done little or no service hitherto," it was expected that they would not be paid as if they had "actually been employed on service."[13]

Newcastle's message was clear: end the campaign, and get rid of the troops in the cheapest way possible. Shirley, Clinton, and the troops who had left their homes to suffer through the hardships of frontier duty, duty from which so many would not return, had all been betrayed with the stroke of a pen. Of course, the colonies were free to pursue the campaign at their own expense, but such matters, although proposed by Shirley, were nonsense. Most of the men needed for such a task were about to be deprived of their promised reward. After such an act it would be surprising if more than a regiment could be raised for the cause.

Almost fittingly, on Halloween the troops along the New York frontier were discharged from service. Most found no treats in their bags as they trudged off toward their homes, and it seemed the trick of the day was the withholding of their pay by the governments involved. A general mutiny was staved off by promises of compensation, and compensation was eventually forthcoming, although it was only partial at best and a fraction of what had been promised. For the colonies it was the culmination of a two-year journey that left most embittered and indebted. There would be more talk of a campaign against Fort St. Frederic, mostly in the taverns of New England and New York, and even a few words scrawled on official papers, but for all practical purposes, Canada and Fort St. Frederic were safe.[14]

For Beauharnois it had been a year of alarms and anxiety, but little had materialized in the way of real threats. The same could be said for his promised reinforcements. A fleet under the command of Admiral M. Grou de St. Georges consisting of seven warships and six transports departed La Rochelle in the company of Admiral Jonquiere, who with five warships and a number of armed transports was bound for Quebec to assume his earlier appointment as Beauharnois's replacement. The two admirals would not get far, as a pair of British squadrons under Admirals George Anson and Peter Warren converged on the convoy. On May 3, 1747, the two sides fought a running engagement that decimated the French flotilla. Six French warships were captured as well as over half a dozen transports. Some seven hundred French sailors and marines were killed in the battle, and another four thousand were taken prisoner including Jonquiere, who would once again have to wait to assume the position of governor.

A number of vessels that had escaped the carnage arrived at Quebec, as did the annual supply ships, although plying the Gulf of St. Lawrence was becoming more dangerous. Rumors of invasion, raids, and counter raids crisscrossed the French and British frontiers, with little of consequence coming from any of the actions. On September 19, 1747, Beauharnois welcomed his replacement, Roland-Michel de Galissoniere, the Marquis de Galissoniere. With Jonquiere still held by the British and Beauharnois's health deteriorating, the minister of the marine selected Galissoniere as the interim governor. Galissoniere was from a powerful and well-connected family, which, when combined with the marquis's natural talents, created an excellent naval captain with over thirty-five years of experience. Galissoniere did not seek the Canadian post and preferred to stay in command of the *Monarque*, which was preparing to depart with a squadron under the command of Marquis de L'Étenduère for the West Indies. Nonetheless he reluctantly accepted the post and departed for Quebec aboard the *Northumberland* in late July.[15]

The new governor knew very little about the colony and wisely spent his first few months under Beauharnois's tutelage. He spent his days visiting the fortifications at Quebec, Montreal, and Three Rivers, speaking with Beauharnois's officers, and studying piles of reports on the state of the colony and the war along its borders. While concluding that shortages and enemy threats abounded, precarious finances and impossible frontier defenses presented themselves, and British warships stationed at Louisbourg threatened maritime traffic in the Gulf of St. Lawrence, Galissoniere noted something else: New France still remained defiant.

Part Five

War, Privateers, and the Treaty of Aix-la-Chapelle

CHAPTER TWENTY-FIVE

The Privateers: The War of Jenkins' Ear

While French, Spanish, and British expeditions clashed on the mainland, another war was occurring offshore. This conflict was not primarily a naval endeavor, such as what was seen at the sieges of St. Augustine, Louisbourg, and the relief of Annapolis Royal, but a commercial venture with a naval component. Privateering was nothing new to the colonies of the New World. All sides had issued letters of marquis and raised vessels to raid the enemy's commerce during King William's War and Queen Anne's War. With a large seafaring base to draw upon, the American colonies had shown themselves to be particularly adept at converting their commercial maritime activities over to this task, and the decade of conflict that comprised the War of Jenkins' Ear and King George's War proved no exception.

The concept of privateering was centuries old by this time. It called for private citizens willing to sail under the banner of the king in return for a bounty on captured enemy vessels. The privateer assumed the costs of outfitting a vessel and raising the crew, although they could often get some level of support from the government. In return for accepting these financial and operational risks, a letter of marque was issued by the government authorizing the privateer's actions. Many viewed the idea of privatizing commerce warfare as sanctioned piracy. Even the renowned Admiral Horatio Nelson took a dim view of the subject, stating, "The conduct of all privateers is, as far as I have seen, so near piracy that I only wonder any civilised nation can allow them." Regardless of the ethics behind the approach few could deny the effects, both on the enemy, and just as importantly, on the economy of a port from which the privateers operated.[1]

By the time news of the War of Jenkins' Ear reached North America British privateering had entered a more professional stage. Gone were the exorbitant fees associated with condemning or legally securing the captured vessel at the local vice admiralty court. The reasons were simple. First, this taxation dissuaded privateering, which only helped the enemy's commerce, and second, these fees had pushed many privateers toward piracy. Other regulations had appeared as well. In order to discourage smaller privateers who might avoid the admiralty courts by working out of remote harbors, vessels under a hundred tons and with less than ten guns and forty men were excluded from the trade. This last effort also ensured that a sizable investment would be required to participate in this lucrative business, and individuals behind such efforts were not likely to bypass the vice admiralty court. In addition, the larger vessels were more capable of securing a prize and could cruise longer, which increased their chances of success.

Investors who wished to participate in this venture were almost all maritime merchants with access to money and vessels that could be converted to warships. Politically, these investors were well connected and would apply to the governor for a letter of marque and reprisal. This later document, and the regulations that went with it, were issued by the colonial governor and counter signed by the local judge of the vice admiralty court. While the fee for such an application was modest, it required a sizable bond be put forth, which would be forfeited if the vessel was found to have violated any of the attached regulations.

Once the letter of marque was issued, the colonial governors and vice admiralty judges, ordered by London to encourage such activities, would look to help in whatever way possible. This usually came in the form of small arms and munitions. The bulk of the effort, however, fell upon the investors, which usually consisted of several individuals so as to minimize the financial risk should the vessel be lost. While some privateers were built specifically for this task, the majority were converted merchantmen. To brace the vessel for cannons, an increased crew, and prolonged voyages required time and substantial funds. Even more crucial was the choice of a captain. At first, these were well-known merchant captains whose names would attract a crew, but if the captain proved successful, this task became much easier.

When it came to raising a crew, many found the position by word of mouth or were recommended by another crew member. After all, the harbors of North America were not that large at the time and most who participated in maritime occupations were aware of such efforts through their personal contacts. To supplement this, many newspapers of the time carried announcements that a privateer captain or a ship was looking for crew. A May 11, 1741, advertisement placed in the *Boston Post-Boy* for the Newport-based privateer *Revenge* typifies these efforts:

> The Sloop *Revenge*, burthen about One hundred and fifteen Tons, or there-abouts, mounting about Twenty-four Guns large and small, Capt. *Benjamin Norton*, Commands being bound on a cruising Voyage against the Spaniards: If any Gentlemen Sailors or others, have a mind to take a Cruize in said Sloop let them repair on board of said Sloop now lying at Mr. *Albert Taylors* Wharff, where they may see said Articles of Agreement and be kindly received. Said Sloop wants a Doctor at present.[2]

The fact that this ad for a Newport privateer was placed in a Boston paper speaks to one of the major problems faced by American privateers: experienced manpower. It was this element that restricted the bulk of privateering activities to the major coastal ports of Boston, New York, Newport, Philadelphia, and Charleston. Although well-known locations such as Portsmouth, New Hampshire, Perth-Amboy, New Jersey, Frederica, Georgia, Cape Fear, North Carolina, Norfolk, Virginia, and several others harbored privateers, the scarcity of manpower greatly limited their efforts. Even the five principal ports experienced shortages. Charleston, for instance, an ideal location for privateers looking to operate in the Caribbean, which was the vast majority of American privateers, did not have the experienced seamen or the vessels necessary to take advantage of its position. Part of this was because most of the vessels involved in South Carolina trade were not based in Charleston. In fact, at the opening of the War of Jenkins' Ear the colony only had thirty registered vessels, and of these, only half were greater than fifty tons. There were also competing interests for mariners, as the Royal Navy operated out of this port and was always in search of recruits via whatever means necessary.

Boston, which should have been a major player in the privateering business given its surplus of vessels and manpower, was actually less involved than South Carolina. Part of this was due to the northern theater during King George's War. Initially privateering efforts in the waters about Nova Scotia, Cape Breton, and the Gulf of St. Lawrence were quite successful, but most of the captures were smaller French fishing vessels. With the fishing fleet soon driven back into their ports, the only traffic in this area was in the Gulf of St. Lawrence. While intercepting French vessels was a crucial effort for the New England colonies who faced the brunt of French Canada's wrath, it was not a lucrative venture, especially after the fall of Louisbourg when Royal Navy vessels began to cruise the area on a more frequent basis.

Like Charleston, Boston also suffered manpower shortages. Here, however, the problem was slightly different. There was plenty of manpower, but with basic commerce, fishing, Royal Navy recruitment, and now the sudden lure of privateering, it was being stretched thin. This was particularly apparent during the Louisbourg Campaign of 1745. When Rhode Island could not provide more mariners and vessels for the campaign because of the colony's privateering efforts, Governor Shirley implied that the colony had placed the interests of the Crown subservient to those of profiteering. While this was not the case, and pointed more to the need of a centralized command in North America to better utilize the resources available, even after the fall of Louisbourg the lure of privateering made it difficult to man merchant vessels. This problem also extended to the colony's coast guard and the Royal Navy as well. Enticed by better pay and greater opportunities, desertion proved a constant problem for Royal Navy commanders, and on multiple occasions they appealed to the Massachusetts Assembly for help in the matter. While the latter attempted to comply, there was really little that could be done, as the directives from London called for encouraging privateers. As such, both the colonial navies and the Royal Navy resorted to impressment to fill out their ranks. When such actions led to riots and local unrest, Shirley suspended all impressment warrants, pointing out that they had only made matters worse. "Since the commencement of the War with France," he wrote the Duke of Newcastle on December 31, 1747,

> it has been found to drive away the other Seamen out of the Province into the neighbouring Colonies of New York and Rhode Island (but chiefly the latter) where they were shelter'd from Impresses, and ship'd themselves on board the Privateers and trading Vessels sailing out of those Harbours; by which means the Trade and Navigation of this Province, especially of the Town of Boston, was laid under great Difficulties, not only for want of Sailors to mann their Ships, but through the extravagant Wages that were exacted from the Merchants and Traders by means of the scarcity of Seamen.[3]

Philadelphia harbored a number of successful privateers, but the Quaker merchants, who dominated the maritime and financial markets there, were not interested in such speculative matters, limiting the number of investors. Even so, the city proved a fertile ground for sailors. By far, however, most American privateering centered on Newport, Rhode Island, and New York City. Newport had long been a center of privateering, first during King William's War (1689-1697) and then during Queen Anne's War (1702-1714). In this last conflict the Rhode Island privateers led the way. "The New Englanders must Confess," Rhode Island agent Richard Partridge wrote a friend at Whitehall, "that the Privateers from this Colony of Rhode Island did more Execution against the Privateers of the Enemy that infested their Coasts than all the Ships of War of the Massachusetts or indeed than of all the Colonys in those parts put together."[4]

While Rhode Island would demonstrate the same behavior during the War of Jenkins' Ear and King George's War, New York took a different approach toward the privateering business. Although the number of vessels operating out of the port rivaled Newport, the number of privateers that used this vice admiralty court to confirm their captures was near double that of Newport. The reason was Lewis Morris. Morris, who was judge of the vice admiralty court, was from a politically connected New York family, and at the time of the War of Jenkins' Ear was also speaker of the New York Assembly. His interests were not so much in profiting directly from the privateer trade but the financial impact it would have on the city and the colony as a whole, which certainly included his own investments.

Under privateering regulations any captures made had to be brought before the vice admiralty court, where evidence was submitted regarding the nationality of the prize and activities behind its capture. If all went well, the vessel was condemned, meaning that the capture had been validated as legal and a value assessed to the vessel and its cargo. If all did not go well, it could lead to long delays and even the forfeiture of the prize and restitution on the part of the privateer. What a privateer captain sought was a friendly admiralty judge and a receptive community. While the costs to process a claim hovered around 10 percent of the assessed value, any cargo captured would also face a colonial tax. As speaker of the assembly Lewis convinced his fellow New York representatives to suspend such a tax. While the savings were not significant, the message that New York was transmitting was clear: privateers welcome.

In Lewis, many a captain found a pro-privateer judge. Lewis was a lawyer by profession who had studied maritime law and had an extensive library partly inherited from his father. This combination allowed the judge to make rulings, which more times than not favored the privateer. One of the more common targets for this were captured Dutch vessels. While the Dutch were neutral, if they were visiting an enemy port, it could be construed as aiding the enemy, and thus, they would be a legitimate target. A number of Dutch captains threw their vessel's papers over the side when set upon by a British privateer in hopes of later claiming neutrality. Although there was often scant evidence that these vessels were aiding the Spanish or French, Lewis shrugged and pointed out that, since they could not prove who they were and had acted in a fashion to deceive, they were legitimate prizes and condemned them.

Lewis also dealt with competing claims to a vessel. By rule if another privateer appeared during the capture of a vessel it was entitled to part of the prize money. The idea behind this was that the appearance of another privateer would inspire the prize to surrender, thus avoiding a pitched battle. Here Lewis carefully looked at the accounts before making a judgment, which typically did not reward the privateer not engaged. To alleviate such instances, he promoted privateers sailing in concert where the distribution of the prize money was agreed upon ahead of time. A more difficult problem arose with the recapture of British vessels. Lewis gave the original owners twenty days to make a claim against the vessel, and if they did, he invoked a salvage approach to guarantee that the efforts of the privateers in this process were rewarded.[5]

For Lewis and the other colonial vice admiralty courts there were plenty of claims in 1740, the first full year of the War of Jenkins' Ear, as close to three dozen American privateers made forty-seven captures, all but two in Caribbean waters. With the business proving profitable, almost as many vessels went to sea next year but with only half as many captures to show for their efforts. The drop in captures, which could easily be explained by the enemy taking better defensive measures or limiting their activity, led to a decline in the number of vessels participating in the trade. Although fewer vessels would go to sea in 1742 (20) and 1743 (25) they proved far more successful, seizing thirty-nine vessels in 1742 and another thirty-three the following year. This decrease in privateers over 1742 and 1743 would lead to a more profitable market and the reestablishment of a capture-to-privateer ratio more along the lines of 1740.[6]

The mariners of Newport and Narragansett Bay, Rhode Island, were at the forefront of this early American privateering effort. When news of the War of Jenkins' Ear arrived, the colony quickly responded by equipping and dispatching the sloops *Revenge, Virgin Queen, Charming Betty, Victory,* and *St. Andrew* to raid Spanish shipping in the Caribbean. While there were sev-

A 1729 painting of the Boston Lighthouse and a 10-gun sloop. (*Boston Public Library*)

eral very successful privateers in this group and those that followed, the voyages of the *St. Andrew* are a good example of the extent of privateering and the perils that came with it. The *St. Andrew* was a ninety-five-ton sloop owned by Sueton Grant and John Godfrey of Newport. Armed with ten small cannons and a dozen swivel guns, the vessel carried eighty men under the command of Captain Charles Davidson and received its letter of marque from the governor on June 11, 1740. It was not until July that Davidson took the *St. Andrew* out to sea, but instead of steering south toward the rich hunting grounds in the Caribbean, the *St. Andrew* set a course east to the Canary Islands.

The hope was to catch the Spanish inhabitants of the islands off guard, which seemed to be the case when Davidson quickly captured a sloop anchored at Fuerteventura Island. With the plan seemingly intact, he sent a fifty-six-man landing party ashore to seize the nearby village. The prize sloop commanded by Davidson's quartermaster, Richard Ross, and the *St. Andrew* kept a close eye out for Spanish vessels as they awaited word from the detachment ashore. After three days it was clear to Davidson that something had gone wrong. He dispatched one of his prisoners to the island's governor and offered a prisoner exchange. The governor informed the Rhode Island mariner that he could not comply. While a few mortally wounded sailors were in his hands the rest, although surrounded, had yet to surrender. Davidson did not believe the response, but now facing the alerted militia of the island and with only two dozen men left to man a pair of vessels, there was little to do but sail away before a Spanish warship captured the rest of the *St. Andrew*'s crew.

Ross took the prize to Antigua where it was condemned, while Davidson sailed for Surinam (Dutch Guiana) with a skeleton crew. The *St. Andrew* arrived in late 1740, and after refitting, Davidson put back out to sea again in February 1741 worried about having not been able to add more men to his current crew complement of twenty-eight. On March 4 the undermanned Rhode Island privateer encountered a sloop near Crab Island on the southeastern side of Puerto Rico. As neither the unidentified sloop or the *St. Andrew* were flying a flag, Davidson maneuvered closer and hailed the vessel to come to. When it failed to do so, he fired a shot over the vessel as a warning. The sloop's response was a volley of small arms fire and a few shots from their cannons. A brisk engagement ensued but quickly came to an end when the better sailing *St. Andrew* positioned itself to unleash a broadside down the length of the enemy vessel.

The vessel proved to be the eighty-ton *Amiable Theresa*, armed with six cannons and commanded by a Frenchman, Simon Langoiran. Langoiran was dismayed to see that he had surrendered to an undermanned privateer but claimed he was at the helm of a French vessel chartered by the government of Martinique to act as a tender. There were several French gentlemen aboard with silver-hilted swords and pistols, which seemed to reinforce the French captain's claim. A quick search of the vessel, however, turned up letters speaking to the French West Indies fleet joining Spanish forces for a surprise attack upon Admiral Vernon's fleet. The correspondence was enough for Davidson to claim the *Amiable Theresa* as a prize. He put a portion of the French crew ashore on Crab Island and returned to Newport with the newly captured vessel.[7]

After a short cruise in search of a reported Spanish privateer near Block Island, Connecticut, in July the *St. Andrew* put back out to sea. After a series of problems that forced the vessel into Charleston for repairs, it was not until late December 1741 that the Rhode Island privateer was at anchor in a small harbor along the northern coast of Cuba. Davidson and his lieutenant were on watch the night of their arrival when a small craft loaded with eighteen men appeared out of the darkness and pulled alongside. As the Spanish sailors and marines scrambled to board the *St. Andrew*, their lieutenant stood and fired his pistol at Davidson. The shot missed and the Rhode Island captain replied with a musket shot that toppled the Spanish officer from his craft. Another shot followed and then another as the enemy troops emerged onto the privateer's deck with a shout. They were met with a rude reception as the crew began appearing from below decks with cutlasses, clubs, and pistols. The outnumbered Spanish fought hand to hand with the New Englanders until the end, with only one of their number being taken alive.

The next morning the Spanish privateer that had launched the attack could be seen in the distance. Davidson ordered the sails to be raised and steered for the enemy vessel. At first the Spaniard looked to run, but when it became clear that they could not outrun the Newport sloop it turned and offered battle. The two vessels exchanged cannon fire and musketry for almost an hour and a half before the Spanish vessel, with "'the Blood of the wounded and killed running over the Deck by Gallons," struck its colors. Davidson sent the prize to Newport and set sail for New Province, arriving there with the *St. Andrew* in early January 1742.

Here Davidson encountered Captain James Wimble, a privateer from London who had recently purchased a captured Spanish vessel, the *San Antonio*, and outfitted it for privateering under the very popular name, *Revenge*. The two captains agreed to sail together, and sometime in April the duo encountered a heavily armed Spanish privateer. A two-hour battle ensued as the three vessels exchanged fire. The smaller Rhode Island sloops finally closed and maneuvered along either side of the Spanish warship. With Wimble at their head a boarding party surged forward with a shout and perhaps might have seized the day were it not for Wimble falling mortally wounded in the initial charge. To the credit of the Spanish crew, they pushed the disheartened privateers back onto their craft, and having seen enough, the two Rhode Island sloops broke off the engagement allowing the Spanish vessel to make good its escape.

After returning to New Providence to careen the *St. Andrew*, by June Davidson had gone back out to sea, and on the fifteenth, he sailed into St. Nicholas Harbor, Hispaniola. Here he surprised and took the seventy-ton French sloop *St. Jean* lying at anchor. Technically a neutral vessel, the *St. Jean* was seized without a shot, its captain vehemently complaining that the action was illegal. He would prove correct. Davidson sent the *St. Jean* back to Newport with a prize crew only to have the vice admiralty court chastise the privateer's actions and release the vessel.

A few weeks later Davidson took the Dutch sloop *Nooyt Godagt*, which was without papers, and sent it to Newport. The vessel never arrived, likely being captured by a Spanish privateer on its voyage. Not long after, while at anchor in a river along the coast of Honduras, the *St. Andrew* was attacked by five Spanish perriaugers carrying 160 men. Under a barrage of musketry, the Spanish attackers boarded the stationary vessel. The matter quickly turned into a melee, and even Davidson thought that the privateer would be overwhelmed, but his crew was able to fight off the boarding parties with cutlass, pike, pistol, and the occasional flash of a blunderbuss. The Spanish retreated, but in doing so they exposed their craft to the *St. Andrew*'s cannons, which, loaded with grapeshot, tore through the small vessels causing yet more casualties. Davidson, who had survived yet another hand-to-hand clash, captured the small schooner *St. Francis* a few weeks later and by late October 1742 had returned to Newport. Davidson, perhaps in punishment for the capture of the *St. Jean*, or just as likely because he did not wish to press his luck any further after having survived several harrowing engagements, would not command another privateer, and the *St. Andrew* itself would be retired from the service.[8]

By early 1744 the American privateering market had gone through a series of oscillations. Early speculation into this market was partly driven by stories such as Captain John Lush of the 20-gun *Stephen and Elizabeth*. Lush departed New York on September 1, 1739, and by late November reports had reached the city that he had captured two valuable Spanish schooners off the northern coast of Cuba. The owners of the *Stephen and Elizabeth* took advantage of the situation to issue additional shares in the vessel, which reportedly were "bought and sold confidently." When Lush finally returned with his Spanish prizes on April 26, 1740, he was rowed to the crowded docks with both he and his men dressed in some of the expensive embroidered jackets they had captured. It was reported that each member of the crew had received 465 pieces of eight as their part of the captured monies found on the vessels, while the vessels themselves, along with their cargo, were "esteemed to be the richest taken by any privateer taken in this war."[9]

Of course, the war had just started, but urged on by these successful ventures early speculation into this market led to a profitable year in 1740, in part due to the poor defensive efforts on the part of the Spanish to protect their maritime commerce early in the war. This may explain 1741, the worst year for American privateers during either the War of Jenkins' Ear or King George's War, as more privateers were in operation than captures. The result was another correction, leading to fewer privateers in 1742 and an improved capture-to-privateer ratio of almost two, only surpassed in the final full year of King Georges War, 1747. This general success led to a few more privateers entering the business in 1743, but with a slightly reduced number of captures, profits were limited. It appeared that the market fluctuations were stabilizing and that a balance was being reached between the size of the American privateering fleet and the size of the Spanish merchant fleet.

In fact, American privateering was about to explode.

CHAPTER TWENTY-SIX

The Privateers: King George's War and the Blockade of Canada

NEWS OF WAR with France would transform the sagging privateer business. In Massachusetts, Governor Shirley's initial batch of five privateers under Captains Rous, Waterhouse, Ingerson, Gatman, and Loring quickly grew to nine and soon posted an impressive tally. By the fall of 1744 they had captured over forty French vessels. Most of these were fishing craft, but one was a store ship bound for Quebec and four others were supply ships destined for Louisbourg. Captain Rous in the recently up-gunned *Young Eagle* was one of the first Massachusetts privateers out of the harbor with their freshly signed letters of marque. Sailing along the coast of Nova Scotia and Newfoundland he entered St. Johns Harbor in late July with eight French fishing vessels in tow. While at the port Rous armed a captured schooner and obtained assistance from the Royal Navy vessels on station in manning and equipping a local privateer. On August 1, the trio of vessels departed for a cruise along the northern coast of the island. On the morning of August 24, Rous finally found what he was looking for, five French privateers at Fischot Island near the northernmost point of Newfoundland.

The French vessels had been warned of Rous's presence, and similarly armed, had anchored in a crescent formation that concentrated their fire on the harbor's entrance. Leaving the schooner behind Rous and the other British privateer advanced on the formation, paying the price as cannonballs splintered their hulls and chain shot tore through the rigging. The battle raged for five hours, during which both British vessels went aground several times. The French, finally having seen enough, abandoned their craft to Rous who, after seizing anything of value, put them to the torch. Rous would capture a 16-gun privateer not long after, before raiding the French fishing fleet and burning storehouses at several harbors along the coast of Cape Breton. The following spring Rous would find himself appointed to command the 24-gun Massachusetts frigate *Shirley* during the Louisbourg campaign. An appointment to Royal Navy lieutenant would follow, as would a career that would eventually see Rous in command of a ship during the last French and Indian War.

In contrast to Rous's success, Captain Loring's first cruise in the 14-gun, 120-man brigantine *Victory* would prove short. In August the small colonial craft encountered a pair of French warships off the coast of Cape Breton Island, and after a four-hour chase, which left the *Victory*'s rigging shredded and her topsail shot away, Loring struck his colors and along with his crew was carried prisoner into the French fortress of Louisbourg. While this would be one of the lowest moments for Loring, the captured privateer captain would later play a key role in the planning of the Louisbourg expedition.[1]

New York demonstrated a similar response to news of war with France. "The Merchants of this City have been extreamly active in fitting out privateers, at a very great expence, and have brought in several prizes," Governor Clinton informed London. On August 13 four New York privateers returned with six prizes, and after the captures were officially condemned a week later, "said Prizes saluted the Town with near 50 Guns." Other New York privateers such as the *Elizabeth*, *Ranger*, *Hester*, *Polly*, *Clinton*, *Greyhound*, and *Mary Ann* also took to the open sea to strike at French and Spanish commerce.

Philadelphia added the three-hundred-ton ships *Wilmington* and *Tartar*, the schooner *George*, and the sloop *Trembleur* to the growing list of privateers and pledged to outfit four more. Unfortunately, the race to put to sea combined with experienced manpower shortages would lead to perils far greater than the enemy. After departing Philadelphia on its maiden voyage, the privateer *Tartar* would capsize and sink in Delaware Bay on July 1 with the loss of almost a hundred of its crew. One account pointed to the vessel being poorly managed, "being (as tis said) over-masted, and not well ballasted, she was unfortunately overset, by a slight Flaw of Wind, near the Capes, and sunk immediately in about 8 Fathom Water." Others within these initial ranks were more successful.[2]

Privateering, of course, cut both ways, and with France and Britain now at war, New England's great fear of a nest of privateers operating out of Louisbourg had become a reality. This important point was successfully used to promote Governor Shirley's expedition against the French fortress in 1745, resulting in its capture, but when considering the year that proceeded the Louisbourg campaign (mid-1744 to mid-1745) the imagined maritime threat to New England's commerce never materialized. When the war began there were three types of commerce raiders using Louisbourg. The first, elements of the French Navy on station, would conduct patrols of the local waters, but this was primarily focused on anti-privateering efforts. Typically frigates or larger, these warships were more than a match for any privateer they encountered, and several American privateers were captured by these vessels. Even one of the local privateers, the 110-ton schooner *Succes*, commanded by Louisbourg's port captain Morpain, functioned in this role for a time. The commercial privateers came in two varieties: European or Caribbean ships using the port as a temporary layover or as replenishment point and a small group of local privateers that were based in Louisbourg. This last group, which was at the center of New England maritime concerns, consisted of only a handful of vessels, with the *Marie Joseph*, *Signe*, *Cantabre*, *St. Charles*, *Caesar*, *St. Joseph*, and *Succes* making up the preponderance of the force.

This small force started in an encouraging fashion when Captain Francois Bauchet de Saint-Martin in the *Signe* conducted the most successful cruise of any of the local Louisbourg privateers. Armed only with muskets, the crew of the *Signe* preyed on the enemy's fishing fleet along the coast of Nova Scotia and the Gulf of Maine, which in the early weeks of June were completely unaware of the declaration of war. On June 14, Saint-Martin, having done little more than fire a few warning shots, returned triumphantly to Louisbourg with a string of seven captured vessels in his wake. The *Marie Joseph* also took advantage of the enemy's ignorance as to the opening of hostilities and on one occasion was actually being invited aboard a fishing vessel before informing the crew that they were now French prisoners. Even the 2-gun *St. Charles* proved more than a match for a surprised fishing sloop. As a result of these initial efforts in local waters over a dozen enemy vessels had been brought into Louisbourg Harbor. It was saluted by the populace and viewed as a promising start, but such enthusiasm was tempered by the fact that the British vessels were now aware of the state of war and would not be so quick to yield. In addition to this, to be truly effective the Louisbourg privateers would need to move farther south into the main shipping routes for New England and New York, where they were likely to encounter far more resistance.[3]

Mid-June brought three of the more heavily armed French raiders into action, the *Succes*, *Caesar*, and *Cantabre*. The first, a 10-gun schooner under Morpain, who had been a successful privateer before his current posting, began patrolling the approaches and coastal waters around Louisbourg. The 8-gun sloop *Caeser*, commanded by Captain Philip Leneuf de Beaubassin, and the 8-gun sloop *Cantabre*, commanded by Joannis-Galand d'Olabaratz, who would later command a frigate in d'Enville's ill-fated expedition, agreed to sail in concert with the aim of preying on shipping near Boston.

Departing Louisbourg in mid-June 1744, the two vessels became separated in a heavy fog near Cape Cod. On the morning of July 4, d'Olabaratz found himself nearing Crab Ledge some fifty miles to the east of Cape Cod. Spying a snow at anchor, and having been out to sea for three weeks with little to show for the effort, d'Olabaratz ordered the crew to make ready and steered for the unknown craft. Unfortunately for the crew of the *Cantabre*, they discovered too late that the vessel was the 16-gun Massachusetts warship *Prince of Orange* under the command of Captain Tyng. Tyng, watching the motions of the *Cantabre*, rightly deduced it was a French privateer and had ordered the gunports shut and the crew to conceal themselves. With the wind dropping off d'Olabaratz fired at the *Prince of Orange* from a few hundred yards away. When the enemy's gunports opened to a cheer of its crew and the Union Jack was run up, the French captain ordered his vessel about, and with the wind now at a standstill the crew began to deploy the vessel's oars. Tyng had also sent his men to the oars, and a slow-speed chase ensued. The gunners at the bow chaser on the *Prince of Orange* scored nine hits on the *Cantabre* throughout the day, but it was not enough to slow the craft, and as the sun began to set, both Tyng and d'Olabaratz believed that the chase would soon come to an end.

Once darkness descended over the Gulf of Maine d'Olabaratz altered course, and after a few hours along this new heading he ordered his exhausted men to slow their pace around midnight. This proved a mistake, as yet another piece of misfortune would visit the French privateer. Four lanterns set aloft in the *Cantabre*'s rigging had not been extinguished. This guided Tyng's pursuit, and around 2 a.m. he came up upon the French sloop. Taken by surprise and separated by less than a pistol shot, d'Olabaratz steered the *Cantabre* toward the *Prince of Orange* in an attempt to board the British vessel. Tyng was not caught off guard and unleashed a broadside of 6-pounders firing chain and grape shot. With many of the *Cantabre* crew resting below deck, the volley had miraculously not caused any casualties, but the French sloop's mast had been fractured, and as the smoke from the *Prince of Orange*'s broadside cleared, half of the mast came crashing down onto the deck carrying the main sail with it. With control over the ship lost and the British certainly prepared to fire another broadside, d'Olabaratz signaled his surrender.

The *Caeser* would have better luck, capturing three vessels off the coast of Cape Cod before returning to Louisbourg in late July. On July 8, Morpain in the *Succes* added a pair of British privateers to the capture list, but even with this, the total in July was less than half of the previous month. It was quickly becoming apparent that New England and New York were raising privateers in numbers that Louisbourg could never hope to match, and working in conjunction with the provincial navies, they were seeking out the Louisbourg privateers.[4]

August and September produced little in the way of captures, with the French ship-of-the-line *Ardent* making the single capture in September as French warships stepped up their patrols in the face of growing numbers of enemy privateers. October brought four prizes into the harbor, but it also brought loss. On October 10 the *Signe* encountered the Massachusetts privateer *Ranger* near Cape Breton. Now mounting ten small cannons and a dozen swivel guns, the *Signe* dueled with the *Ranger* at half a pistol shot for an hour and a half in rough seas. The captain of the *Ranger* was wounded and the helmsman at his side shot dead during the engagement. In addition to this, several men on both sides were washed overboard by the boisterous waves. When the two sides broke off the action the *Ranger* had a dozen casualties onboard, and the *Signe*, which had also been struck hard, had a score of casualties, including Saint-Martin who had been killed late in the engagement. The captain of the *Ranger* thought that he had encountered Morpain, but when he found out it was Saint-Martin he wrote, "Let him be who he will, he fought very courageously. He ran fore and aft with his cutlass driving about his people and had a great number of marines." The loss of Saint-Martin, who had started the privateering efforts out of Louisbourg, coupled with the declining number of captures and the growing number of encounters close to the port made it clear that the reports of privateer activities and the advertisements for crews in colonial newspapers onboard the captured prizes were coming to fruition. A swarm of British privateers from the American eastern seaboard was descending on Louisbourg. The local privateers could not counter this, nor could they fulfill their intended function, as they were being hunted as well. Without French naval support, the approaches to the port would soon be in British hands.[5]

Farther south, in Newport, Rhode Island, the news of King George's War was greeted with enthusiasm. The *Revenge* and *Charming Betty* were at Newport being refitted for another voyage into the Caribbean. Alongside these were four more craft being readied for their new line of work—the *King George*, *Phoenix*, *Hector*, and *Queen of Hungary*—while the sloops *Prince Frederick* and *Prince William* had completed taking on supplies and were ready to set sail. They would not have to wait long. On June 7, 1744, three days after Governor William Greene had the declaration of war read publicly in Newport, the *King George*, *Prince William*, and *Prince Frederick* set sail, with the 12-gun, 115-ton *Revenge* following a week later. By fall the *Duke of Marlborough* and the *Prince Charles of Lorraine* had set out to sea as well. The effort, coupled with the colony's long tradition in such activities, attracted attention with one French informant who wrote of Newport that, "Perhaps we had better burn it, as a pernicious hole, from the number of privateers there fitted out, as dangerous in peace as in war."[6]

Among the Rhode Island privateers, many of whom had been operating against the Spanish in the Caribbean since the opening of the War of Jenkins' Ear in 1739, the exploits of Captain John Dennis stand in the forefront. When news arrived of war with France, Dennis was at Newport refitting the hundred-ton sloop *Prince Frederick*. He and his crew had just returned from a successful cruise in the Caribbean in which they had relieved one Spanish vessel of close to £10,000 and, working with another New England privateer, had captured the 6-gun Spanish schooner *Serena*.

The timing was such that the *Prince Frederick* was one of the first Newport vessels to put out to sea after word of war with France. Now carrying a crew of 120, the *Prince Frederick* steered south along the coast. On June 29 Dennis spotted three Spanish vessels about fifty miles south of St. Augustine. The trio scattered at the sight of the British sloop, and Dennis directed the helmsman to follow the largest of the three. The chase went on for a few hours with the Spanish schooner *Senora de San Jose y San Nicolas* occasionally firing a shot at the gaining *Prince Frederick* before realizing the futility of its flight and surrendering. The prize proved to be the former Philadelphia schooner, *Indian Queen Opess*. This vessel had been captured by the Spanish and converted into a privateer. Not long after it had then been badly damaged in an encounter with the Philadelphia privateer *Wilmington* near Jamaica and surrendered to a Jamaican government ship the next day. The vessel was repaired, returned to its original name, and sent to Bristol, England, with a cargo of trade goods. Unfortunately, the *Indian*

Queen Opess was once again captured by the Spanish, who noted the recent work done to the vessel. The craft was renamed the *Senora de San Jose y San Nicolas* and was fitted to carry fourteen guns when the *Prince Frederick* captured it a few weeks later. Dennis put a prize crew onboard the schooner and sent it back to Newport.

Continuing south Dennis overhauled a small forty-ton French sloop in the Lesser Antilles. The vessel was bound for Martinique with sugar, cocoa, and coffee. He sent this vessel back to Newport as well. After an aborted chase of another Spanish vessel, Dennis encountered fellow Newport privateer Captain James Allen of the *Revenge*, and after a brief discussion, the two captains agreed to sail together, or in concert as the agreement was referred to at the time. On July 23 near Cap-Francais, Haiti, the two Rhode Island captains encountered a pair of larger French privateers. Both French vessels steered for the *Prince Frederick*, one coming alongside while the other positioned itself on the opposite side a pistol shot away. The crew of the *Prince Frederick* fought back, but to make matters worse, the *Revenge* was now a few miles away due to a navigation error. Dennis and his men repelled a boarding attempt in a hand-to-hand melee and then a second before the French vessels moved off three hours later.

It is interesting to note that, while such gallant conduct against the enemy was saluted in colonial and British newspapers, and might be serving the general war effort, the privateer's investors and crews were more interested in profit than glory. The owners of the *Prince Frederick* likely would have expressed their feelings toward Dennis in this matter, were it not for the fact that after the engagement the two Rhode Island vessels steered for the Florida Keys where they captured the 150-ton Spanish snow *St. Fermin*, carrying flour, copper, and an ample amount of silver.[7]

Accounts of privateers such as Davidson, Rous, Dennis, and a host of others could easily fill several volumes. Most lived a more subdued existence, and success was not always the outcome. Captain Loring in the *Victory* was captured, as was the Newport privateer *Charming Betty*, the New York privateers *Humming Bird* and *Clinton*, along with many others. The joint cruise of the Rhode Island privateers *Fame* and *Industry* speaks to how quickly disaster could strike. The 250-ton topsail schooner *Fame*, commanded by Captain Thomas Thompson, was reported to be a double-decked vessel "built of Spanish Cedar, Mahogany and Madeira." With a crew of 170 and fitted with twenty-four carriage guns, eighteen of which were 9-pounders, as well as two-dozen swivel guns, the *Fame* was a powerful privateer compared to its sailing partner the schooner *Industry*. The latter, commanded by Captain John Ellis, carried a crew of sixty-five men and

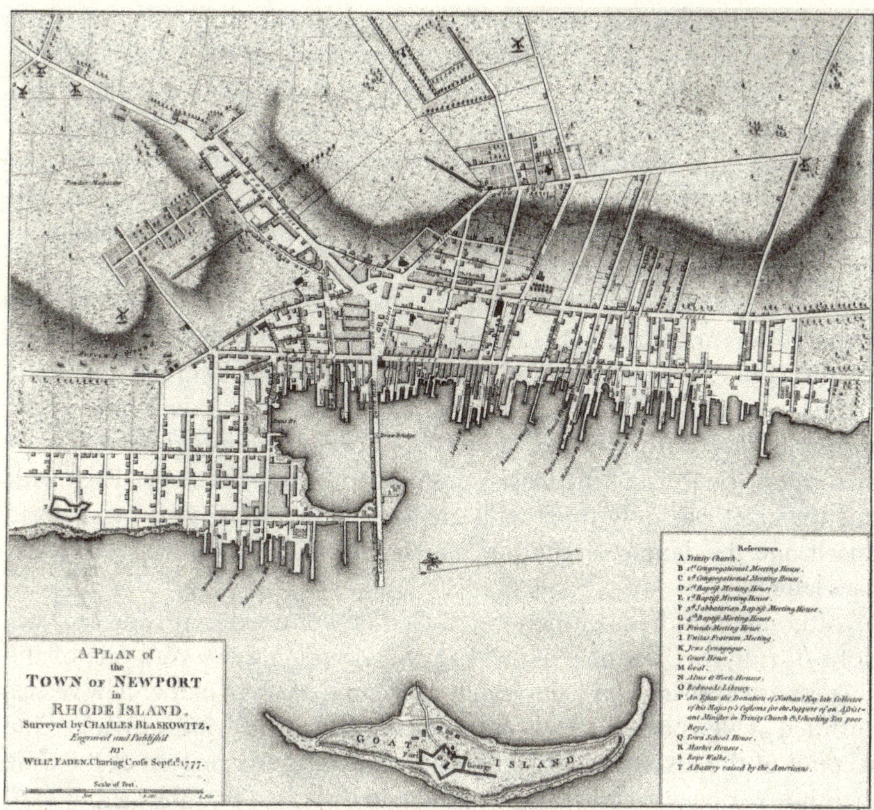

Newport, Rhode Island, by Charles Blaskowitz, 1777. This town, near the entrance of Narragansett Bay, was one of the primary American privateering ports during the War of Jenkins' Ear and King George's War. (*Library of Congress*)

mounted ten smaller 3- and 6-pound carriage guns as well as half a dozen swivels guns.

Operating within sight of the fortifications of Havana, the two privateers captured and burned a Spanish sloop carrying pitch and tar before sighting a Spanish privateer later that afternoon. Taking the lead Thompson steered the *Fame* directly for the enemy sloop and exchanged broadsides. The Spaniard, seeing itself outgunned and outnumbered, took flight. The *Fame* pursued and exchanged five more broadsides with the enemy privateer in a running fight. Thompson could see the effect of his cannons, and with his quarry slowing from the damage he steered the schooner toward the enemy in an attempt to board. No sooner had he done such when the *Industry* finally came up and fired on the damaged Spanish vessel. There were only a few cannons still operational on the enemy sloop, but one returned fire and found its mark, crashing through the side of the small schooner into the powder magazine. A thunderous explosion followed leveling part of the ship and sending men and debris whirling into the nearby waters. What was left of the schooner quickly slipped beneath the waves, leaving Captain Ellis and his crew floating in the nearby waters. Thompson aborted his attack and managed to rescue forty-four of the *Industry*'s crew, although almost half of these survivors were badly injured.

A few days later, on October 3, Thompson with the *Industry*'s survivors on board was anchored in the Florida Keys taking on wood and water. The weather looked threatening, and what was hoped to be a simple squall line turned into a sixteen-hour hurricane. The *Fame* was blown up on a reef and stuck fast. With no other choice, the hold was emptied, the cannons thrown overboard, and the masts cut down to lighten the vessel. Even with this the craft was only freed with great difficulty. Makeshift masts were raised, and the damaged schooner crawled into Charleston Harbor eleven days later.[8]

Although hundreds of men were killed or wounded in privateering actions during the War of Jenkins' Ear and King George's War, one of the greatest privateering losses during the two conflicts was a pair of new vessels outfitted at Newport, the *Duke of Cumberland* and the *Prince of Wales*. One account of the disaster claimed that, "according to the custom of the time their horoscope was cast and the figure had disclosed that they should sail on Friday, the 24th of December, 1745." While the weather did not appear good, most thought that it would break and trusted in their conjured prediction. This did not prove to be the case, and after they were out to sea, they realized it was just the beginning of a howling nor'easter that threw high seas and blinding snow at the craft. The storm would accelerate in fury and at some point sent both vessels to the bottom with all 260 hands aboard.

1745 would turn out to be the peak of American privateering, both in terms of captures and participants over the span of the War of Jenkins' Ear and King George's War. With over a hundred vessels involved in the trade in 1745, it became impossible to sustain this level of effort. The saturated market created manpower and material shortages with prices for common naval goods, if they could be obtained, increasing dramatically. Many not happy with their returns abandoned the business, and for the last three years of the war the number of vessels involved in the trade hovered just below sixty.

By the conclusion of King George's War, American privateers had accounted for 939 prize actions in American, Caribbean, and European waters. When combined with the captures made by Caribbean privateers, the colo-

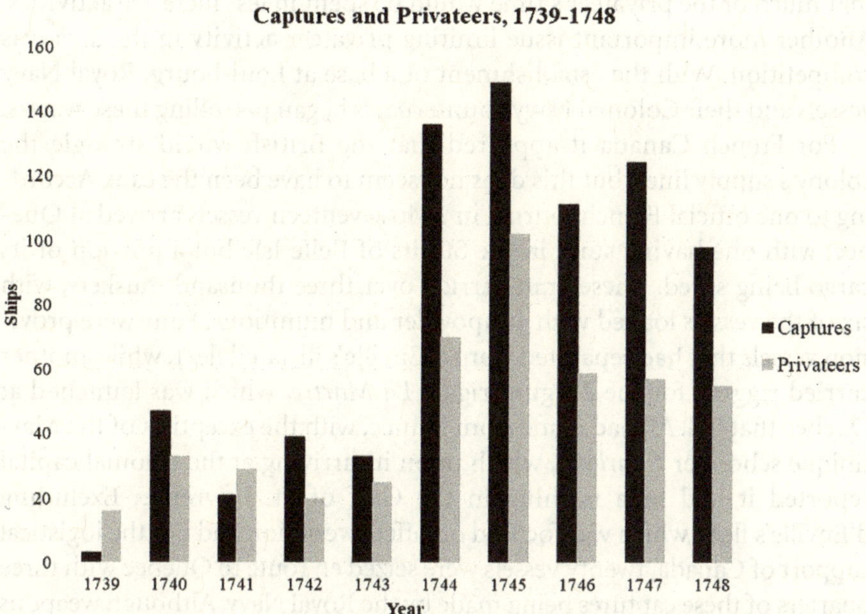

American privateers and their captures in the War of Jenkins' Ear and King George's War. Compiled from Swanson, *American Privateering and Imperial Warfare*, 371-374.

nial coast guards, and vessels operating out of the British Isles, the sum, far in excess of 2,500, demonstrates the value of these commerce raiders and the important role they played in crushing French and Spanish commerce.[9]

One particular element within this larger effort pertained to the blockade of Canada. With the fall of Louisbourg in the summer of 1745, French Canada was in peril of having its lifeline to France and the Caribbean cut. Now operating from this advanced post at the entrance to the Gulf of St. Lawrence, American privateers would flock to the Gulf of St. Lawrence to intercept French vessels from or bound for Quebec. While a reasonable assumption by the French governor and his council, two elements worked against an expansion of privateering in the area. The first was a lack of valuable targets. A few small coastal vessels might be seized, but the more desirable transports filled with supplies arriving from France were nowhere as numerous as traffic in the Caribbean, and unlike the Caribbean there was little to no activity in the winter. In addition to this, the French transports entering the Gulf of St. Lawrence tended to be clustered in the late spring/early summer and again in the fall. When taken together, it meant that much of the privateer's time would be spent in less lucrative activities. Another more important issue limiting privateer activity in the area was competition. With the establishment of a base at Louisbourg, Royal Navy vessels and their Colonial Navy counterparts began patrolling these waters.

For French Canada it appeared that the British would strangle the colony's supply lines, but this does not seem to have been the case. According to one official French journal in 1746 seventeen vessels arrived at Quebec, with one having sunk in the Straits of Belle Isle but a portion of its cargo being saved. These craft carried over three thousand muskets, with six of the vessels loaded with gunpowder and munitions. Four were provision vessels that had separated from d'Enville's ill-fated fleet, while another carried rigging for the 22-gun frigate *La Martre*, which was launched at Quebec that fall. All had come from France, with the exception of the Martinique schooner *Charlotte*, which upon its arriving at the colonial capital reported it had seen nothing in the Gulf of St. Lawrence. Excluding d'Enville's fleet, which was focused on offensive action and not the logistical support of Canada, twenty vessels were seized en route to Quebec with three quarters of these captures being made by the Royal Navy. Although weapons and munitions had arrived, a 55 percent loss rate was unsustainable. It was clear that if the British reinforced their blockade, the economy and defenses of French Canada would collapse.[10]

In early 1747 the French Court, looking to reinforce Canada, dispatched a fleet under the command of Admiral Jonquiere, who was to assume the role of governor once he reached Quebec. While many of the transports bound for Quebec would arrive, the admiral and six of his warships would be captured in a running fight near Cape Finnister. This naval loss made up a sizable portion of the inbound Canadian losses for the year. Nine other vessels were captured, including one carrying 150 small cannons, and one, *L'Alexander*, was wrecked on Anticoste Island. In contrast to this, twenty-six vessels dropped anchor at Quebec. Four of these were warships whose presence before the colonial capital was a major addition to the defenses of the city. What is perhaps more surprising is that two of the vessels were prizes and over half a dozen were from Martinique. With more ships arriving, the loss rate reduced by almost twenty points, and trade between Martinique and Canada revived, the government of Canada was not only surprised but delighted by the sudden turn of events. The mechanisms behind this, however, had little to do with French efforts. The unprofitable circumstances had chased away many privateers for the more lucrative hunting grounds of the Caribbean, while a reduction in the Royal Navy's presence at Louisbourg had also played a major role.

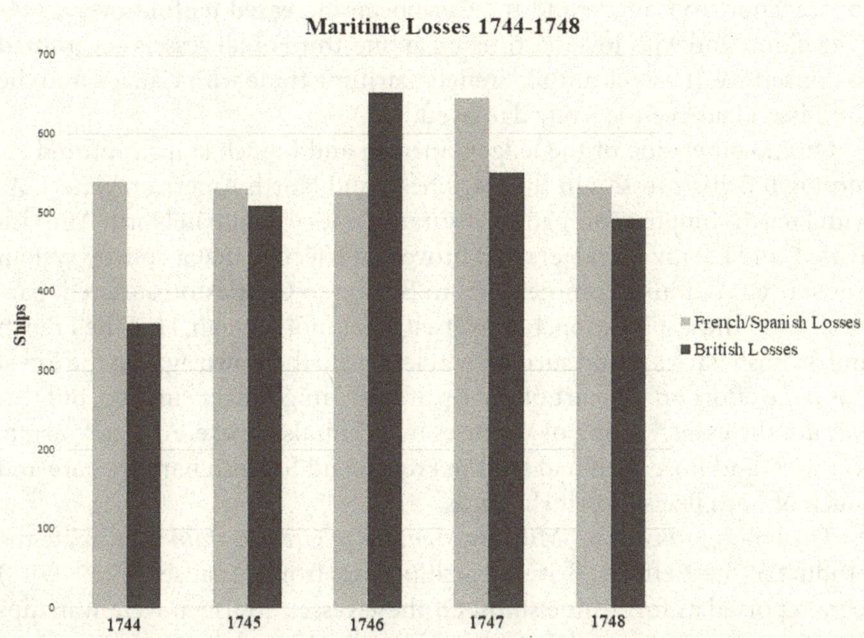

Overall maritime losses (privateers, merchants ships, and warships) during King George's War. While the final number separating the Franco-Spanish alliance and Britain is a little over 200 vessels in Britian's favor, the disparity in warship losses had a crippling effect on both France and Spain. (*Beatson,* Naval and Military Memoirs, I, 414, III, *82-85.*)

Excluding the loss of Jonquiere's warships, the success rate for vessels bound for Canada was close to 65 percent. While Canada's economy suffered, the effect on Canada's military position was not significant. Much of this was because the general approach toward the war was to remain on the defensive, and with the exception of d'Enville's descent on Nova Scotia, no large-scale operations were conducted against the British colonies. Governor Beauharnois wisely chose to husband his resources and pursue the policy of *petite guerre*, which by its very nature was cheap and required minimal resources to implement. The British might gnaw on his lifeline to France, but it would never prove to be enough to undermine the defense of the colony.

The real peril was the loss of the fur trade and the lack of trade goods for the allied nations on the frontier. This latter element threatened to destabilize the network of French trade and military alliances, as many of these allies began to look to the British to meet their needs. With insurance rates for transport to Canada and the Caribbean increased tenfold over 1744-1745 alone, and with losses estimated at one-third of all vessels committed to this service, it was clear that French maritime trade with Canada and the Caribbean had been severely damaged.[11]

On the other side of the ledger, Spanish and French ships captured almost 650 British vessels in the Caribbean and North American waters. As with French shipping companies, insurance rates went up in North America as well, and enemy privateers had proved so effective that a convoy system was started. Colonial commerce from Boston to Charleston suffered, particularly in the last location, but by itself it was not enough. Had the French and Spanish navies found success or at least held their own against the Royal Navy, the effort on the part of their privateers might have sufficed, but this was not the case. A string of victories by Admirals Hawke, Anson, Warren, Knowles, and Boscawen had left the French and Spanish harbors bare and much of both fleets in British hands.

The tables in *Beatson's Military Memoirs of Great Britain* illuminate the product of these efforts. British warship losses from all causes (1739-1748) were reported as forty-nine ships. Of these vessels fourteen were warships of fifty guns or more, which was considered a ship-of-the-line at the time. In contrast to this the Spanish Navy lost thirty-four warships during this period, sixteen of which were ships-of-the-line, and the French lost thirty-three warships, twenty-one of which were ships-of-the line, from 1744-1748. The clear disparity in losses, particularly in terms of capital ships, was even worse than portrayed by these numbers. Of the sixty-seven Spanish and French warships lost during the War of Jenkins' Ear and King George's War, over half were captured, including six Spanish and seventeen French ships-of-the-line. Many of these would soon be pressed into service against their former owners. In contrast, of the fourteen Royal Navy capital ships lost during this period only five were captured, and two of these were later retaken. The scope of the victory was clear. The Royal Navy was stronger than ever, the Spanish fleet lay in ruins, and according to one writer, "The Navy of France was so much reduced, as to be no longer formidable." When placed against the background of the terms of the Treaty of Aix-la-Chapelle, this same writer concluded that "this may truly be said to have been the only advantage that Britain gained by the war."[12]

CHAPTER TWENTY-SEVEN

The Treaty of Aix-la-Chapelle

As the calendar turned to January 1748, the war still had the better part of a year left, but as Galissoniere and Beauharnois had hoped, it would be a conflict dictated by the French. A war of dueling scouting parties, of raiders, and plunder. A war of pointless strikes against farmers whose goal in life was to stave off famine and hopefully pass something of worth on to their children. It left the homes of Western Massachusetts, the Chambly Basin, La Prairie, and Upper New York vacant shells or in ashes. William Johnson, one of its prime motivators, characterized it as a contest "resembling more the practices of banditti than the operations of civilized warfare, and tending to no other results than obscure individual suffering, and partial havoc and devastation." Neither side could win such a war. Both sides knew it, but to Canada the importance lay in survival. The French knew this type of war quite well. They had faced it for a hundred years, and still the colony remained. Given that, it was doubtful that a few more raids would change things one way or another.

In the west, along Lake Ontario, there was no fighting at all. Although plans were proposed to strike at either Oswego or Niagara and Fort Frontenac, in the end, both sides believed that doing so would draw the Seneca into the conflict against the attacker, and as such, these were put aside. The real discord that came out of the conflict was the disruption of trade on both sides. British traders refused to go to Oswego for fear that the Seneca might side with the French and descend upon the post, while for the French, a lack of supplies reaching the western posts due to the disruptions of King George's War had inflated trade good prices, aggravating their western allies. In the end, the Iroquois, and in particular the Seneca, path of neutrality worked to prevent an open conflict in this region. In a few years this would drastically change as Oswego, Fort Niagara, and Fort Frontenac would all be targets of major campaigns in the last French and Indian War.[1]

In French Louisiana, the new governor, Pierre Vaudreuil, the Marquis de Vaudreuil, did not face a direct military threat, in part because France had reinforced the vulnerable colony with several thousand troops. The primary threat faced by the new governor during the war was an old one, British attempts to disrupt the Franco-Native alliances in the region. From his experience as the son of the former governor of Canada, major of the Free Companies of the Marine in Canada, and governor of Three Rivers, Vaudreuil knew how to handle this form of attack. When a revolt inspired by Carolina traders broke out within the Choctaw, a nation that was the lynchpin of the Franco-Native alliance in the region, Vaudreuil pressured the other elements of the nation to squash the pro-English rebellion by cutting trade with them. While Governor James Glenn of South Carolina did not openly support the rebellious Choctaw Chieftain Red Shoe, he did attempt to exploit the instability by approaching the Cherokee and Chickasaw with the offer to build British forts in their territory to protect them from the French. Neither were interested in the forts or becoming involved in the conflict. As Vaudreuil had hoped, the Carolina traders could not deliver on their promises to supply trade goods, leading the chieftains of the Choctaw Nation to abide by the governor's request for Red Shoe's head. This would end the only real threat to French Louisiana during the conflict.[2]

In Quebec, Governor Galissoniere listened to reports from prisoners taken along the New York and New England frontiers as the snows melted and spring took hold of the land. He found no indications of an impending campaign against Canada, and in late June 1748, when reports of peace talks in Europe reached Quebec and Boston, it appeared to further reduce the probabilities of an attack on Canada. Even so, the governor had the small raiding parties continue their work, which netted a steady stream of prisoners to keep him apprised of events. In early August, official word of a truce reached Galissoniere. Although there appeared to be no immediate threat to the colony, the governor was relieved by the news and sent couriers to his commanders with orders to bring the hostilities to an end.

For Governor Shirley the early months of 1748 were spent pressing for another expedition against Montreal and Quebec, but there was even less interest than before. Nor was the colony interested in anything beyond defensive measures. The militia was exhausted and the colony's finances in ruins. Soon there was even more reason to adopt this approach as official word of a truce between the two nations began to circulate in Boston. A delegation of sagamores from the Penobscot and Norridgewock met with Shirley in Boston not long after, claiming they were tired of the war and that peace was being sought by all the Wabanaki nations, including the Abenaki at the St. Francois Mission. They wished for a truce until a conference could be convened to sign an official treaty. Shirley agreed to both the ceasefire and to meet with the leaders of all nations seeking a peace at Falmouth in the last days of September. After a brief but tense wait at Falmouth for the Native delegations to arrive, a treaty was finally signed on October 16, 1748, bringing yet another conflict between the Wabanaki and New England to an end.[3]

While both sides would still have to wait before the official announcement of a peace treaty arrived, for all practical purposes the conflict was at an end. In Europe the War of Austrian Succession had ended in a military stalemate. The French armies, under the leadership of Count Maurice de Saxe, had defeated every allied army thrown against them and stood on the throat of England's cross-channel allies, while in India, Joseph Dupleix and Admiral Bertrand-Francois Mahe de la Bourdonnias had captured Madras and threatened to expel the British from the subcontinent. On the other hand, British naval might had shattered French trade, disrupted its overseas markets by as much as 50 percent, and drained its treasury of the funds it desperately needed to keep Saxe's army in the field. Canada was slowly becoming isolated, the West Indies sugar islands were on the verge of collapse, and much of the French fleet rested quietly in British ports. With major belligerents Britain, the Dutch Republic, and France looking for an end to the conflict, a preliminary treaty between the three had been signed on April 30, 1748.

The Treaty of Aix-la-Chapelle would be officially signed between Britain, the Dutch Republic, and France on October 18, 1748. The other participants would sign two other treaties over the next three months, bringing an end to the conflict. For Britain and France, the Treaty of Aix-la-Chapelle was more a truce than a resolution of differences. Under the agreement all territories were returned to their prewar status, which meant Britain was compelled to return one of its few successes in the conflict, the fortress of Louisbourg, while the French gave back Madras and parts of the Austrian Netherlands in exchange.[4]

Although King George's War and the early parts of the War of Jenkins' Ear in the South did little to change the balance of power in North America, particularly given the provisions of the treaty that ended the conflict, it did point to a weakened New France. Louisbourg, the greatest French defeat in King George's War, demonstrated the sorry state of the French marine. Strangely, French warships were prized by the British for their speed and construction, but the organization itself was far removed from the days of King William's War when captains like Pierre Iberville could cast a net of fear over the American coast with just their names. With this reduced naval presence, coupled with the loss of Louisbourg early in the conflict, the vulnerable colonial lifeline through the Gulf of St. Lawrence proved no safer than in Queen Anne's War. Fortunately for Canada, the British blockade never truly materialized and the fortress of Louisbourg would be returned under the terms of the treaty.

Spurred forward by the opening of the War of Jenkins' Ear, the new colony of Georgia supported by South Carolina demonstrated that they were not strong enough to seize the Spanish stronghold of Castle San Marcos at St. Augustine, nor did the Spanish, with aid from Cuba, prove strong enough to capture the two British colonies. The failure of both efforts led to a stalemate. While this outcome did nothing to resolve the long-standing issues between the two sides, it meant that, regardless of Spanish claims, the colony of Georgia was there to stay.

Although King George's War was the shortest of the first three French and Indian Wars, it showed an escalation in scope and scale of operations that would foreshadow the last French and Indian War. The siege of Louisbourg and the revival of the Old Invasion Plan, calling for a simultaneous attack on Montreal and Quebec, as well as major commitment by the French Navy in terms of d'Enville's fleet, speak to this point.

The conflict also called into question British power in Nova Scotia, but here the colony was fortunate in that Governor Shirley had intervened, although one is left with the impression that it was more French mismanagement than New England reinforcements that saved Annapolis Royal. Even so, Shirley's response and talents were being recognized, and his successful gamble to strike at Louisbourg would make him something of a colonial expert. The governor would follow this the next year by calling for a campaign that targeted both Montreal and Quebec. The Old Invasion Plan was difficult to argue with and would ultimately be the plan that led to the collapse of New France in 1759, but the failure to execute, particularly on the part of Great Britain, undermined the operation.

When it became clear that the military elements from Britain would not arrive in time Shirley shifted focus to the capture of Fort St. Frederic. The French stronghold had already shown itself to be a threat to the New York and New England frontiers, and there was general agreement to proceed, but the presence of d'Enville's fleet off the coast of Nova Scotia ultimately led to the abandonment of this campaign. Shirley would press London to revive the plan in 1747, but events in Europe meant that there would be no support coming from Britain, and the colonies were too short of funds to attack Fort St. Frederic on their own. This failure to challenge the French for control over the Champlain Valley would have its consequences as testified to by the clusters of burned homes and demolished forts along the New York and New England frontiers.

While not successful in dealing with Fort St. Frederic, Shirley was proving to be the correct man for the time. His efforts in stabilizing the defenses of Annapolis Royal and in organizing the capture of Louisbourg point this out. As does his involvement in pushing for an attack on Quebec and, for that matter, continuing to press for an attack on Fort St. Frederic although one would not materialize. He was the leader New England had sought in Queen Anne's War, and had the governor been supported after his spectacular Louisbourg campaign, and St. Clair's fleet appeared as agreed upon, the history of the French and Indian Wars might well have ended in 1746. Given his knowledge and involvement Shirley would be selected for a peace commission in Paris that would demarcate the boundaries of the British and French colonies in North America. It proved a temporary foray. Shirley was not finished with Fort St. Frederic and New France.

For Canada the war ended with its survival, so in that sense it was a victory. The same could be said for Spanish Florida and Louisiana. However, the reality was Canada was in many ways fortunate. There had been crop failures in the colony in the three years leading up to the conflict, and while this had not occurred during the war, had it been longer, British naval dominance and a crop failure in the fall of 1748 would have further weakened the colony, leaving the door open to a thrust against Fort St. Frederic, Quebec, or both. The government was not prepared for either, and with the loss of Louisbourg early in the war an attack on the colonial capital seemed certain. Here New France can only be said to have benefited from matters in Europe, which diverted British resources away from pursuing this operation.

The French were also fortunate that, once the British controlled Louisbourg and possessed the ability to project naval dominance over the Gulf of St. Lawrence, they had not pressed this advantage. Although one in three vessels traveling to or from Quebec were lost in the voyage, had it not been for the shifting of naval resources away from Louisbourg, and the poor hunting grounds the gulf offered to privateers, these numbers would have been far worse. In fact, if the British had tightened the blockade, it would have proven beneficial if a campaign against Quebec and Montreal ever materialized, but just as importantly, the economic hardships from it would have made New France's Native allies vulnerable to British influence through the latter's ability to supply them with trade goods at far cheaper prices. The leaders of New France had avoided this situation, which might have upended French policy in the west, but it had been close, and whether or not the British increased their blockade, had the war gone on another year or two it seemed a likely scenario.

WHILE FRENCH CANADA would always be vulnerable in a long conflict, King George's War did not turn into a long conflict, and British mistakes or missed opportunities aside, the defenders of New France and their Native allies had fought the much larger American colonies to a standstill. True, Louisbourg had been captured, but this post fell outside of the domain of the governor of New France, and there was little that Quebec and Montreal could have done to prevent its loss. Nor was there much that Canada could due to mitigate Admiral d'Enville's disastrous naval campaign.

Elsewhere, New France had done well given its limited resources and manpower. The forts in Chignecto Neck, Nova Scotia, remained in French hands, and with the French victory at the Battle of Grand Pre, they had demonstrated that Nova Scotia was still a disputed territory, regardless of what any treaty said. French power in the Champlain Valley had been established with Fort St. Frederic, which now allowed war parties to strike deeper into New England and New York in pursuit of the philosophy of *petite guerre* and its perceived paralyzing effect on the American colonies. The number of successful raids on the New England and New York frontiers, the destruction of Fort Massachusetts, and the fact that the British colonies did not seriously challenge Fort St. Frederic were viewed as confirmation that *petite guerre* was working.

Yet, the French were not understanding the new response to this type of warfare along the frontier. Whereas in the past, the resources and will to respond to this approach had seldom resulted in an operation that threatened the existence of the French colony, the campaigns of 1690, 1709, and 1711 being the few exceptions over the course of a quarter century of fighting during King William's and Queen Anne's Wars, this time the immediate response, and that throughout the conflict, was to besiege Montreal and Quebec. Louisbourg was the first step toward the latter, and when this opportune event came to fruition, the campaign of 1746 saw a colonial commitment to the reduction of Montreal and Quebec on a level never seen before. Over seven thousand colonials responded to the call with colonies as far away as Virginia sending men. While these troops waited in vain for St. Clair's forces, the scare created by the French fleet ballooned their numbers to over fifteen thousand with an ample reserve standing by—numbers that astonished the defenders of Canada.

Even though the campaign of 1746, and a continuation of the idea the following year, failed to materialize, it was clear that the frontier raids no longer had a paralyzing effect but one of unity of purpose, albeit coupled with failure of execution. It was the solidification of the idea that New France and the British colonies could not coexist in North America. Governor Shirley was at the forefront of this growing movement. "The Reduction of that Country to the Obedience of his Majesty seems to be the most effectual means of securing to the Crown of Great Britain not only Nova Scotia," he wrote the Duke of Newcastle in the fall of 1745, "but the whole Northern Continent as far back as the French Settlements on the River of Missisippi."[5]

Although three French and Indian Wars, the War of the Quadruple Alliance, the Anglo-Spanish War of 1727, the War of Jenkins' Ear, and numerous proxy conflicts had failed to resolve the basic issues between Spain, France, Britain, and their North American colonies, a fourth conflict, the Old French War or as it is more commonly known, the French and Indian War (1754-1763), and a brief Anglo-Spanish War in 1762 would decide matters in North America. Nor would the wait be long. Just six years after signing the Treaty of Aix-la-Chapelle the peace was ruptured, not in Europe but in the Ohio Valley, when a twenty-two-year-old Virginia colonel by the name of George Washington started the last chapter in the contest for North America.

Glossary

Bastion. A small blockhouse structure, typically diamond in shape, located at the junctions of the fort's walls. While platforms on the bastions were used for the fort's cannons, the primary purpose of the structure was to provide flanking fire against any troops attempting to storm the adjacent curtain walls.
Bateau. Small wooden shallow draft boats, similar to whaleboats, which could either be rowed or powered under a simple square sail arrangement. In some cases, these vessels would also be armed with small cannon on their bow and/or stern.
Bomb. An exploding mortar round.
Bombproof. A shelter with overhead cover built to withstand the impact of an exploding mortar round.
Breastwork. A field fortification made of earth and timber.
Brig. A two-masted square rigger vessel.
Brigantine. A two-masted vessel where the main (forward) mast is square sail rigged and the rear mast is inline rigged.
Cannon. Eighteenth-century cannons were muzzle-loading guns, classified simply by the weight of the shot they used, with perhaps the caveat of long or short, which pertains to the barrel length. They were manufactured in two materials: brass and iron. Brass guns were lighter and better withstood the metal fatigue that came with repeated firing, but because of the construction costs they were typically limited to 6-pound cannons or smaller. These qualities made brass guns popular on small naval vessels, where weight was an issue, and among field artillery units. Iron cannons were heavier but cheaper to produce and came in all sizes from swivel guns up to large naval and fortress guns, such as the French 42-pound naval cannons employed at Louisbourg. Weight was always a consideration with larger cannons. For instance, a 24-pound cannon, which would be considered a

siege gun at this time, weighed two and a half tons. So too did two hundred rounds of ammunition for the gun, not to mention the gunpowder, which could easily exceed another ton. Landing and moving such artillery, particularly over an open beach, would prove a trying task.

Cannon Type	Point Blank Range (yards)	Effective Range (yards)	Maximum Range (yards)
3-pounder	400	400-600	2,000
6-pounder	650	500-600	3,300
9-pounder	700	900	3,500
12-pounder	730	800-1,000	3,650
18-pounder	600	800-1,000	3,100
24-pounder	650	700-900	3,250
32-pounder	630	1,000-1,300	3,100
42-pounder	580	1,000-1,300	2,900
5 ½ Howitzer	300	500-700	1,350
8-inch mortar	250	800-1,000	2,550
13-inch mortar	300	900-1,400	2,800

Table 1. Range of eighteenth-century cannon.

Mid-eighteenth-century artillery types and ranges. Point-blank range is the distance a cannonball would travel with a standard powder load and the barrel at zero elevation. For cannons up through 24-pounders, the effective range, which is the range at which the cannon could strike targets at a repeatable rate, was a band of a few hundred yards beyond the point-blank range. The exception to this are the 32- and 42-pounders, which have effective ranges around twice their point-blank range. In the case of mortars, the point-blank range denotes a minimum range, and they have effective ranges on the order of two to four times their point-blank ranges. Fire beyond the effective range up to maximum range was typically reserved for the bombardment of a city or a fortress, where accuracy could be sacrificed for range.

Cannons of this time fired solid shot, chain shot, bar shot, and grapeshot. The solid shot or simply "ball" was by far the most common type employed. In siege operations the shot was sometimes heated in an attempt to start fires within the enemy stronghold. Chain shot and bar shot were designed to damage the rigging of enemy vessels, and as such, they were typically reserved for naval use. Grapeshot was used in both land and sea operations with deadly effect. It consisted of hundreds of musket balls discharged in a short-range blast that struck fear into any attacker.

Reload rates for cannons depended on the size of the gun and the experience of the gun crew. A 3-pound gun with a trained crew could fire three to four aimed shots in a minute, while a 12-pound gun with a crew of ten could manage three shots every two minutes, and the larger siege and naval guns, 24- through 42-pounders, could typically fire one shot a minute. Although under ideal conditions one could fire at this rate, or even faster if aiming was not involved, in reality such circumstances were seldom encountered, nor could such a rate of fire be sustained without damaging the gun at some point, thus much slower firing rates are actually encountered in practice.

The direct fire applications of cannons were supplemented by mortars. These squat wide-mouthed guns were designed to lob an explosive projectile, aptly referred to as a "bomb," over a wall or other obstruction. Manufactured in sizes ranging from a few inches in bore to siege guns thirteen inches in diameter, the projectiles from this weapon could create havoc within the interior of a fort and were one of the besieger's principal options.

There were two other types of artillery that were popular at the time: swivel guns and wall guns. Swivel guns were 1- or 2-pound cannons that could be serviced by one or two men. Their names derived from the cannon's mount which allowed it to be placed along the side of a ship or along the wall of a fortification and easily directed by a single man. Wall guns were swivel-mounted heavy muskets that were often positioned along sections of the fort's wall to provide accurate long-range fire, especially against sappers and pioneers digging siege trenches. Easily transportable, these guns could be quickly moved around the fort's perimeter to either concentrate their fire or take advantage of an opportune firing angle.

Casemate. A bombproof shelter designed to either protect the garrison or the fort's magazine from mortar fire.

Cheval de frise. This defensive structure is a row of sharpened stakes driven into the ground and angled toward the attacker. Often trees were used in place of stakes with their branches sharpened to points. This field fortification was originally used to repel cavalry charges, but it was also used in conjunction with brush and other debris to slow an infantry attack.
Covered Way. This is a platform cut into the ditch side of the glacis to allow for troop movement and protected small arms fire.
Curtain Wall. An interconnecting wall between two bastions.
Demilune. A smaller crescent-shaped fortification typically placed in front of a curtain wall to protect it from bombardment. Such structures are small forts unto themselves and are frequently connected to the nearby wall via a drawbridge.
Embrasures. Openings cut into the parapet to allow for either musket or cannon fire. (See merlons.)
En Barbette **or Barbette.** A cannon mounted such that it can fire over the parapet. While such an arrangement does not offer as much protection for the gun or its crew it does allow the gun to be trained over a much greater field of fire.
Fascine. A bundle of small branches of wood. These were used to support earthworks and in particular to brace the walls of a siege trench or to fill in a ditch to allow for crossing.
Gabion. A barrel filled with earth. Gabions were typically used as temporary field fortifications or as temporary repairs to damaged or incomplete fortifications.
Glacis. Sloping ground placed in front of the fort's walls to reduce the amount of wall that can be seen and targeted by enemy cannon fire. Shots that are too short deflect off the glacis and over the fort's wall.
Grapeshot. Bags of musket balls fired out of cannons. This type of shot was used to repel an infantry attack.
Grenade. The idea of a thrown explosive, or a hand grenade as it would become known, had become popular in seventeenth-century armies. In fact, the term grenadier traces its name to this idea. While a commonplace idea today, the use of early grenades on the battlefield, which had to be lit just moments before its use, proved impractical. For the defenders of fortifications, however, the grenade was an ideal weapon. It could be safely tossed over the ramparts to clear the base of a fort's walls of attackers or used against an enemy that had advanced into the ditch before the fort. Most forts stocked an ample supply of these devices, which certainly created yet another obstacle for anyone looking to take the stronghold by storm.
Machicolation. These are extended portions of a wall or tower designed to

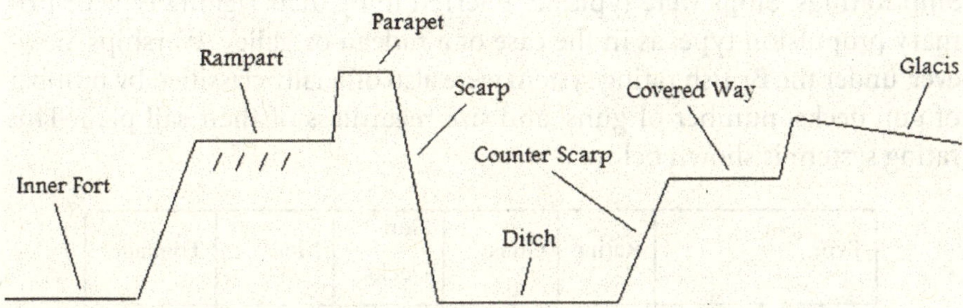

Cross section of a fort's outer works.

allow the defender to shoot down or drop objects on attackers at the base of the supporting wall.

Merlons. The solid portion of the parapet. These may be pieced with slit embrasures to allow for covered musket fire, or they may be located on either side of a larger embrasure, which allowed for cannon fire.

Mortar. An artillery piece designed to fire exploding rounds (bombs) in an arching trajectory so they will clear the fort's walls.

Palisade. A wooden wall typically made of trees placed vertically in a filled ditch and then bound together.

Parallel. A perpendicular, or near perpendicular, extension of the main sap designed to employ a battery of guns from which the besieged fort can be bombarded.

Place of Arms (or **Parade Ground**). This is the open interior portion of the fort where the garrison can be assembled.

Ravelin. A redan.

Redan. A "V"-shaped fortification where the point is aligned with the direction of an enemy attack. Redans were typically employed as outworks or field fortifications as well as in fort walls to provide flanking fire down the length of the wall.

Redoubt. A self-contained fortification with a ditch about its perimeter and earth and timber walls.

Sap. A trench.

Sap Roller. A large cylinder, typically made of bound branches, which is placed in front of the sap being dug to provide shelter for the work crews. The device is then rolled forward as the trench advances.

Scarp and **Counterscarp.** The scarp is the slope of the ditch adjacent to the fort while the counterscarp is the slope on the ditch opposite the fort.

Ship Ratings. Ships were typically referred to by their rigging type or primary propulsion type, as in the case of a radeau or galley. Warships, however, under the British rating system were also officially classified by number of gun decks, number of guns, and size regardless of their sail plan. This rating system is shown below.

Type	Rating	Guns	Gun Decks	Men	Tonnage
Ship-of-the-Line	1st	100 to 120	3	850-875	2,500
	2nd	90-98	3	700-750	2,200
	3rd	64-80	2	500-650	1,750
	4th	50 to 60	2	320-420	1,000
Frigate	5th	32 to 44	1	200-300	700-1,450
	6th	20 to 28	1	140-200	340-450
Sloop-of-War	none	16 to 18	1	90-125	380
Brig, Sloop, Cutter, or Schooner	none	4 to 14	1	20-90	220 or less

Table 2. Eighteenth-century British naval vessel rating system.

Schooner. A two-masted vessel with an inline sail plan. Some would employ a small square sail at the top of the main mast and hence were referred to as topsail schooners.
Ship. A three-masted vessel square sail rigged.
Sloop. A single-masted vessel employing an inline sail plan. These vessels were favored for their ability to get underway in light or variable winds, such as those often encountered on lakes and rivers.
Snow. A two-masted square-rigged vessel with a smaller third mast just aft of the second, which deploys an inline sail.

Notes

ABBREVIATIONS

Cal. A&WI (*Calendar American & West Indies Papers*)
CMNF (*Collection de manuscrits contenant letters, mémoires, et autres documents historiques relatifs à la Nouvelle-France...*)
DCB (*Dictionary of Canadian Biography*)
Doc. Hist. Maine (*Documentary History of the State of Maine*)
FHQ (*Florida Historical Quarterly*)
MHSC (*Massachusetts Historical Society Collections*)
NAC (*National Archives of Canada, Ottawa*)
NY Col. Doc. (O'Callaghan, *Documents Relative to the Colonial History of the State of New York*)
RAPQ (*Rapport de l'Archiviste de la Province de Quebec*)
RFL (*Researching the Fortress of Louisbourg (http://www.krausehouse.ca/krause/FortressOfLouisbourgResearchWeb*)

CHAPTER 1: FROM CAPE BRETON TO ÎSLE ROYALE

1. Chalmers, *A Collection of Treaties between Great Britain and Other Powers*, I (Treaty of Utrecht), 340-390, vol. II (Peace of Utrecht), 40-107.
2. Lunn, "Agriculture and War in Canada," 123-136; McLennan, *Louisbourg*, 22-31; Charlevoix, *History*, V, 285-292; Pitcher, *Louisbourg's Labourer-Soldiers*, 33-34; Lanctot, *History of Canada*, II, 159-160.
3. McLennan, *Louisbourg*, 11-13; Chard, "The Impact of Ile Royale on New England," 5-7.
4. *Cal. A&WI*, XXVIII, 39-40, 125-128, 194; McLennan, *Louisbourg*, 14-18.
5. Murdoch, *History of Nova Scotia*, I, 336-337; *CMNF*, III, 3, 5-6. "I dare say that with regard not only to these Indians," Vaudreuil informed the French court, "but to all the nations which are in our interests, that war with England was more favorable than peace." (*CMNF*, III, 5.)
6. Pitcher, *Louisbourg's Labourer-Soldiers*, 38-39; McLennan, *Louisbourg*, 19-20.
7. *Cal. A&WI*, XXVIII, 42-43; McLennan, *Louisbourg*, 21; Akins, *Pub. Doc. Nova Scotia*, 6.

8. McLennan, *Louisbourg*, 21-22. The French minister of the marine was not only responsible for the French Navy but the French colonies as well.
9. *Charlevoix*, V, 282-285, 294-296; McLennan, *Louisbourg*, 33-34; Johnston, "From port de peche," 4-6.
10. McLennan, *Louisbourg*, 35, 53.
11. Fry, "The Fortifications of Louisbourg," 20-21; Thorpe, "Verville, Jean-Francois de," *DCB*, II; McLennan, *Louisbourg*, 50-52.

CHAPTER 2: NOVA SCOTIA

1. *Cal. A&WI*, XXVIII, 124-128, 181-182.
2. McLennan, *Louisbourg*, 14-18; Akins, *Pub. Doc. Nova Scotia*, 3-4.
3. Akins, *Pub. Doc. Nova Scotia*, 5-7; *Cal. A&WI*, XXVIII, 42-43.
4. Richard, *Acadia*, I, 99-103; Akins, *Pub. Doc. Nova Scotia*, 3-4, 7-8; *Cal. A&WI*, XXVIII, 63-64, 67-68.
5. *Cal. A&WI*, XXVIII, 128-129.
6. Akins, *Pub. Doc. Nova Scotia*, 7-8.
7. *Cal A&WI* XXVIII, 114, 128-129.
8. *Cal A&WI* XXVIII, 179-180,195-196, 214-215, 281-282, XXIX, 28. Caulfield would inform the Board of Trade in May 1716 that the clothing issue had reached a point that "there is butt five soldiers that mount the Gard that have either shooes, stockings, or shirts." (*Cal A&WI*, XXIX, 76.)
9. Akins, *Pub. Doc. Nova Scotia*, 8-10; *Cal. A&WI*, XXVIII, 114.
10. Akins, *Pub. Doc. Nova Scotia*, 11-12; *Cal. A&WI*, XXIX, 25.
11. Lanctot, *History of Canada*, III, 42-45; *Cal A&WI*, XXX, 97-99; Akins, *Pub. Doc. Nova Scotia*, 12-16.
12. Pothier, "Monbeton de Brouillan, St. Ovide, Joseph de," *DCB*, III; *Cal A&WI*, XXX, 269-270.
13. *Cal A&WI*, XXX, 269-270, 325-326, 405-406. Douchett wrote newly appointed Governor Richard Philipps, "I hope sir that you will put a stop to their proceedings, or else they will claim everything to within cannon shot of this Fort." (Ibid., 405-406.)
14. Hutchinson, *Hist. Mass.*, II, 217-218; *CMNF*, III, 28-32, 36-38; Murdoch, *History of Nova Scotia*, I, 357-358; *Cal A&WI*, XXX, 285-286, 403, XXXI, 1.
15. *Cal A&WI*, XXXI, 67-69, 99-100, 102-106.
16. McLennan, *Louisbourg*, 62-64; *Cal A&WI*, XXXI, 102, 105-106, 115-116, 120.
17. Akins, *Pub. Doc. Nova Scotia*, 18-35; *Cal A&WI*, XXXII, 78-82, 84-90; Murdoch, *History of Nova Scotia*, I, 357-361; Charlevoix, *History*, V, 297-299.
18. *Cal A&WI*, XXXII, 227.
19. McLennan, *Louisbourg*, 68-69; Murdoch, *History of Nova Scotia*, I, 374-375; *Cal A&WI*, XXXII, 148-153; Akins, *Pub. Doc. Nova Scotia*, 49-57; Hutchinson, *Hist. Mass.*, II, 240-241.
20. *Cal A&WI*, XXXII, 148, 153-155.
21. *Cal A&WI*, XXXII, 155-159, 198-199; Murdoch, *History of Nova Scotia*, I, 384-385.

CHAPTER 3: THE ROAD TO WAR

1. Penhallow, *Indian Wars*, 74-80; *Cal A&WI*, XXVII, 229-231.
2. Williamson, *History of Maine*, II, 80-89; *Doc. Hist. Maine*, IX, 351-352, 351-355, 361-

362, XXIV, 234-240; Penhallow, *Indian Wars*, 81-83; Wheeler, *History of Brunswick*, 625-627.
3. *Doc. Hist. Maine*, XXIII, 80-82.
4. Hutchinson, *Hist. Mass.*, II, 217-218; *Cal A&WI*, XXIX, 262.
5. Schuyler, "The Apostle of the Abenaki," 164-170; Charland, "Rale, Sabastian," DCB, II; *Doc. Hist. Maine*, IX, 363; Baxter, *Pioneers of New France*, 34-40.
6. Bouton, *N.H. Prov. Papers*, III, 693-698.
7. Hutchinson, *Hist. Mass.*, II, 218-221; Bouton, *N.H. Prov. Papers*, III, 698-701; Baxter, *Pioneers of New France*, 68-84. This agreement is referred to as the Arrowsic Treaty of 1717, although it is just an affirmation of the Treaty of Portsmouth.
8. *NY Col. Doc.*, IX, 878-879; *Cal A&WI*, XXX, 101-102, 357-358; *Doc. Hist. Maine*, IX, 374-382.
9. *NY Col. Doc.*, IX, 880-881.
10. *NY Col. Doc.*, IX, 880-881.
11. *Doc. Hist. Maine*, XXIII, 97-99; Williamson, *History of Maine*, II, 97-102.
12. *Doc. Hist. Maine*, XXIII, 99-100.
13. Ibid., 100-103.
14. *Mass. Acts & Resolves*, 1720-1726, 14; *Doc. Hist. Maine*, XXIII, 103-108; Williamson, *History of Maine*, II, 100-103.
15. Sprague, *Sabastian Rale*, 125.
16. *CMNF*, III, 40.
17. Hutchinson, *Hist. Mass.*, II, 236-237; Williamson, *History of Maine*, II, 104-107; Baxter, *Pioneers of New France*, 294-297.
18. *Doc. Hist. Maine*, XXIII, 108-110; Penhallow, *Indian Wars*, 84-85.
19. Williamson, *History of Maine*, II, 107-109; *Cal A&WI*, XXXII, 406-407, 500, XXXIII, 27-30; Hutchinson, *Hist. Mass.*, II, 243-247; Sylvester, *Indian Wars of New England*, III, 187-191; Charlevoix, *History*, V, 273-277.

CHAPTER 4: THE THREE YEARS' WAR

1. *Cal A&WI*, XXXIII, 27-30.
2. Charlevoix, *History*, V, 273-277; Penhallow, *Indian Wars*, 85-86; Williams, *History of Maine*, II, 114-115; *Mass Arch.*, vol. 72, 55.
3. Penhallow, *Indian Wars*, 86; Sylvester, *Indian Wars of New England*, III, 192-193.
4. Williams, *History of Maine*, 116; *Cal A&WI*, XXXIII, 407-408, Charlevoix, *History*, V, 277-278; "Vaudreuil Report," *CMNF*, III, 85-88; *Doc. Hist. Maine*, X, 150-152; Wheeler, *History of Brunswick*, 54-55.
5. *Cal A&WI*, XXXIII, 89-90, 117, 420-421; *Mass. Acts and Resolves*, X, 200-201, 204; *Doc. Hist. Maine*, X, 152-153, XXIII, 116-122; Hutchinson, *Hist. Mass.*, II, 276-278.
6. *Doc. Hist. Maine*, X, 106-108. The Pennacook, Androscoggin, and Pequawket were the southernmost Abnaki tribes, while the Kennebec were Catholic converts who resided at Father Rale's Norridgewock mission. Shute does not mention the Passamaquoddy and likely wraps their numbers into the fighting strength of the Penobscot.
7. *NY Col. Doc.*, IX, 880; *Cal A&WI*, XXXIII, 97-98.
8. *New England Courant*, June 18-25, 1722; *Cal. A&WI Papers*, XXXIII, 96-98, 102-104, 122; Calnek, *Annapolis*, 71.
9. Penhallow, *Indian Wars*, 91-92; *Cal. A & WI Papers*, XXXIII, 122-123, 126, 142; Mur-

doch, *History of Nova Scotia*, I, 400-402; Hutchinson, *Hist. Mass.*, II, 295-296.
10. Williams, *History of Maine*, II, 117-118.
11. *Doc. Hist. Maine*, X, 153-156; Penhallow, *Indian Wars*, 95; Williams, *History of Maine*, II, 118-119.
12. *Cal. A&WI Papers*, XXXIII, 324-330, 337-341; *Mass. Archives.*, vol. 72, 56-68; Hutchinson, *Hist. Mass.*, II, 278-288.
13. Penhallow, *Indian Wars*, 96-97; *Doc. Hist. Maine*, X, 146-147; Williams, *History of Maine*, II, 120-121; Trask, *Westbrook Letters*, 10-15; *Mass Arch.*, vol. 72, 152, gives a list of posts on the Maine frontier from Ft. St. George's to York and their garrisons, which as of January 1724 only amount to 123 men.
14. *NY Col. Doc.*, IX, 933-934; "Vaudreuil to Dummer, 28 Oct. 1723," *Mass. Archives.*, vol. 51, 381.
15. *NY Col. Doc.*, IX, 934-935.

CHAPTER 5: LOVEWELL'S POND AND THE TREATY OF CASCO

1. Trask, *Westbrook Letters*, 62-63; Penhallow, *Indian Wars*, 96-97.
2. Williams, *History of Maine*, II, 125-128; Sylvester, *Indian Wars of New England*, III, 227; *Mass. Archives*, vol. 72, 270; *Cal. A & WI Papers*, XXXIV, 429-432, 439. Penhallow noted that in one instance a large Wabanaki war party "surprized eight [vessels] with little or no opposition." (Penhallow, *Indian Wars*, 101.)
3. *Doc. Hist. Maine*, XXIII, 163-167; *Cal. A & WI Papers*, XXXIV, 429-432. Father Etienne Lauverjat, who accompanied this war party, claimed that the enemy blockhouse did catch on fire but that the garrison came out of the fort to extinguish the fire. The Wabanaki, not expecting such an action, were not in a position to fire on this damage control party. (*Cal. A & WI Papers*, XXXIV, 431.)
4. *Mass. Archives*, vol. 63, 406-408; Williams, *History of Maine*, II, 128. Writing a friend on July 19, 1724, Samuel Hicks of Portsmouth noted that "the fishermen don't go East of this Place or scarce to sea." (Salter, *John Salter, Mariner*, 10.)
5. *Mass. Acts and Resolves*, X, 556; *Mass. Archives*, vol. 52, 20-21; Sylvester, *Indian Wars of New England*, III, 228; Penhallow, *Indian Wars*, 102; *New England Courant*, July 13-20, 1724. Dummer would commission several more vessels shortly thereafter.
6. Potter, *Military History of the State of New Hampshire*, 44-45; Williams, *History of Maine*, II, 128; *Boston News-Letter*, July 23-30, 1724; Bouton, *N.H. Prov. Papers*, IV, 7-8; Both Salter and Mannery were brought before New Hampshire Lt. Governor John Wentworth and his council to explain their conduct. The testimony pointed to Salter's actions, but little seems to have come of the matter. (Bouton, *N.H. Prov. Papers*, IV, 7-8.)
7. *Boston News-Letter*, July 30–Aug 6, 1724; *New England Courant*, August 3-10; *Mass. Acts and Resolves*, X, 495, 524, 542; *Mass. Archives*, vol. 72, 188-189. It is unclear if the captured schooner was the same one engaged by Lakeman and Jackson a week before. The petitions of Cox's wounded crewmen can be found in *Mass. Acts and Resolves*.
8. Hutchinson, *Hist. Mass.*, II, 308-311; Baxter, *Pioneers of New France*, 251-252.
9. Hutchinson, *Hist. Mass.*, II, 311-314; Williams, *History of Maine*, II,129-132; Allen, *History of Norridgewock*, 40-41; Charlevoix, *History*, V, 278-279; Baxter, *Pioneers of New France*, 258-265. Charlevoix is in error as to the number of New England troops involved, and both his and Allen's accounts of Rale's death are fictitious. Moulton, who

had ordered the Jesuit taken alive, questioned Jaques's actions, but nothing more would come of the matter.

10. *Cal. A&WI Papers*, XXXIV, 351-352; Williams, *History of Maine*, II,132-134; Trask, *Westbrook Letters*, 80-83; Baxter, *Pioneers of New France*, 266.

11. Belknap, *Hist. N.H.*, 208-209; Sylvester, *Indian Wars of New England*, III, 243-247, 259-260; Potter, *Military History of the State of New Hampshire*, 46-48; Bourne, *History of Wells*, 323-324.

12. Sylvester, *Indian Wars of New England*, III, 261-265; *Doc. Hist. Maine*, X, 268; Penhallow, *Indian Wars*,112-113.

13. *Doc. Hist. Maine*, X, 269-273, 278-279, 289; Belknap, *Hist. N.H.*, 210-212; Sylvester, *Indian Wars of New England*, III, 265-274; Penhallow, *Indian Wars*,113-116; Williams, *History of Maine*, II, 137-141; *Mass. Arch.*, vol. 72, 239.

14. *NY Col. Doc.*, IX, 939-940.

15. *NY Col. Doc.*, IX, 939-940.

16. *Cal A&WI*, XXXIV, 437-441; *N.Y. Col. Doc.*, IX, 941-945; Penhallow, *Indian Wars*, 108-110.

17. Penhallow, *Indian Wars*, 108-110, 117-128; *Mass. Arch.*, vol. 29, 191-193, 230-249, vol. 34, 2; Hutchinson, *Hist. Mass.*, II, 316-318; Williams, *History of Maine*, II, 143-150.

18. *NY Col. Doc.*, IX, 949-950.

CHAPTER 6: A STONE SENTINEL

1. Murdoch, *History of Nova Scotia*, I, 408-410.

2. *Cal. A&WI*, XXXIV, 413-415.

3. Murdoch, *History of Nova Scotia*, I, 428-430, 435-437; *Cal. A&WI*, XXXV, 162-164.

4. *Cal. A&WI*, XXXIV, 34-37, XXXV, 197-199, 288, 300.

5. Akins, *Pub. Doc. Nova Scotia*, 70-72; *Cal. A&WI*, XXXV, 27, 269-270, XXXVI, 376.

6. Murdoch, *History of Nova Scotia*, I, 454-457; *Cal. A&WI*, XXXVI, 485-486, XXXVII, 251-252.

7. *Cal. A&WI*, XXXVIII, 286-289.

8. *Cal. A&WI*, XL, xxxvii-xxxix, XLI, 161-162, XLII, 15.

9. McLennan, *Louisbourg*, 71-72, 76-77; Johnston, "From port de peche," 33-38.

10. *NY Col. Doc.*, V, 960-962; McLennan, *Louisbourg*, 79-82. When the French vessels arrived at New York, Governor William Cosby agreed to help but quickly noted that "a Garrison at so great a distance from France from whence they are supplyed with Beef and Pork, and the uncertain crops of grain in Canada from whence they are to expect their bread (for on Cape Breton they raise nothing from the earth) must make that place in time of War very precarious especially, if our Men of war which must necessarily be on that coast to Guard our settlements at Annapolis and Canso and our fishery, are active and constant in their Cruises between Cape Breton and Newfoundland, for they can hardly fail of intercepting all vessells that are sent from France with supplys for them or with Merchandize to Canada." (*NY Col. Doc.*, V, 962.)

11. Krause, "Construction Chronology of the Royal Battery," *RFL*; "Devis de La Grande Batterie, Aug 8, 1723" NAC, C11B, vol. 6, 298-308, *RFL*.

12. Krause, "Chronology of the Island Battery," *RFL*.

13. Downey, *Louisbourg: Key to a Continent*, 25-31; Bourinot, *Cape Breton*, 26-28; Krause, "Construction Chronology for the Royal Battery," *RFL*; Krause, "Domestic

Building Construction at the Fortress of Louisbourg," *RFL*; Fry, "The Fortifications of Louisbourg," 22-24. Fortunately for the reader interested in a more detailed account of the construction and life at Louisbourg, the fortress has been restored as a Canadian national park. A comprehensive number of papers and original documents concerning the location have been archived and placed online at "Researching the Fortress of Louisbourg" (see bibliographical entry RFL under abbreviations).
14. Johnston, "From port de peche," 35-39; Wrong, *Lettre Habitant Louisbourg*, 30-32; Greer, "The Soldiers of Isle Royal, 1720-1745," *RFL*. One British ship that had anchored at the French port in 1735 reported that, "The grand battery mounts 44 guns of 48 pounders and the two towers 4 of the same nature. The island at the entrance of the harbour mounts 26 guns of 36 pounders. The Dauphin's battery at the town gate mounts 24 guns of 24 pounders. The Queen's Battery 16 guns of 18 pounders, and on the key are 6 guns of 18, there are likewise 12 guns to be mounted on the Fort." (*Cal. A&WI*, XLII,108-109.)
15. McLennan, *Louisbourg*, 80-84.
16. Dunn, "The Louisbourg Lighthouse," *RFL*.

CHAPTER 7: THE HUDSON AND CHAMPLAIN VALLEYS

1. *NY Col. Doc.*, IV, 967-971, 1057, 1128-1129; V, 631, 923-924, 927; *Cal. A&WI*, XLI, 136-142, 449-454.
2. Brandow, *Old Saratoga*, 28-29; *NY Col. Doc.*, VI, 374-375; Pearson, *A History of the Schenectady Patent*, 310-317; *Journal of the Legislative Council of New York, I, 1691-1743*, 391-392, 471,631, 641. At the same time Fort Cosby was constructed the old stone church in the center of the town was modified to act as a defensive strongpoint.
3. *NY Col. Doc.*, IV, 967-971, V, 279-280, VI, 648. By the fall of 1736 Fort Hunter was in such a state that Governor George Clarke recommended abandoning the post, but fear that the Mohawk might abandon the British cause prevented this. (*Journal of the Legislative Council of New York*, I, 661, 731.)
4. *NY Col. Doc.*, IV, 836-837, 929, VI, 184-186, VII, 341; *Cal. A&WI*, XLIV, 129, 209.
5. Memoire anonyme, Nov. 6, 1702, MG1-C11A, vol. 20, 253-254; Beaudet, *Archaeology at Fort Chambly*, 11-12, 41-42, 51-69; *NY Col. Doc.*, IX, 841, 846, 851; Vaudreuil to Minstre, Nov. 12, 1712, MG1-C11A, vol. 33, fols. 15-37; Memoire de M. de Lery – fort de Chambly, Oct. 26, 1720, MG8-A1 serie 3, vol. 7, 741-744 ; "The value of the fort," de Lery wrote in an assessment, "resides above all in the strength of its garrison, but this had always been one of its major deficiencies." (Beaudet, *Archaeology at Fort Chambly*, 12.)
6. *NY Col. Doc.*, IX, 400, 1021-1023; Roy, *Hommes et Choses du Fort Saint-Frederic*, 9-13. At this time Pointe-a-la-Chevelure or Scalp Point referred to the peninsulas on both sides of the lake, today known separately as Crown Point and Chimney Point. The British and Dutch also did not distinguish between the two sides of the lake at this time, referring to the whole region as Crown Point, with the term "crown" referring to the top of one's head.
7. *NY Col. Doc.*, IX, 1021-1023.
8. Ibid., 1024-1025.
9. Roy, *Hommes et Choses du Fort Saint-Frederic*, 20-21; Plan du Terrain de la Pointe a la Chevelure, Oct. 25, 1731, MG1-C11A, vol. 54, fols. 346-346v; Conseil de Marine à M. Rocbert de Morandière, April 22, 1732, MG1-B, vol. 57, fol. 644; *NY Col. Doc.*, IX, 1034,

1037; For the initial colonial reaction to the French fort see *Cal. A&WI*, XXXVIII, 312-314, 331-332.

10. Beauharnois et Hocquart au Ministre, Nov 14, 1731, Oct 1 & Oct 14, 1733, MG1-C11A, vol. 54, 338-342, 385-386v, 423-424; Memoire de Chaussegros de Lery , Oct 25, 1731, ibid., 344-345. Also, Roy, *Hommes et Choses du Fort Saint-Frederic*, 22-32, which contains portions of the above correspondence and excerpts of several additional letters.

11. Lery au Ministre, Oct 30, 1735, MG1-C11A, vol. 64, fols. 259-261.

12. Work continued on the structure for several more years. The covered way was improved, as was the garrison's accommodations and the outer ditch. In 1742 a dockyard was added to accommodate a barque and additional works placed to defend it. (Beauharnois et Hocquart au Ministre, Oct 5, 1740, & Oct 31, 1742, (two letters) MG1-C11A, vol. 73, 19-20v, vol. 77, 72-73v, 141-142; Etat estimatif des ouvrages necessaries a faire au fort Saint-Frederic, Oct 10, 1740, ibid., vol. 73, 24-25v; Lery to Ministre, Oct 30, 1742, ibid., vol. 64, fols. 259-261)

13. Kalm, *Travels*, III, 36-37.

14. Beauharnois et Hocquart au Ministre, Oct 5, 1740, MG1-C11A, vol. 73, 19-20v; Projet de dépense pour la construction et armement d'une gabare ou bateau plat... à faire naviguer dans le lac Champlain, ibid., vol. 73, fol. 21-22; Lery to Minister, Oct 26 & Nov 7, 1744, ibid., vol. 82, fol. 296-303v, fol. 306-307v .

15. *Cal. A&WI*, XLIV, 126-136.

CHAPTER 8: NIAGARA AND OSWEGO

1. Severance, *Old Frontier of France*, I, 42-45; Charlevoix, *History*, III, 201-202; Hulbert, *The Niagara River*, 172-176.
2. Lanctot, II, 104-107; Laramie, *King William's War*, 77-87.
3. Hulbert, *The Niagara River*, 189-195; Preston and Lamontagne, *Royal Fort Frontenac*, 175.
4. Severance, *Joncaire*, 3-7, 22-24; *NY Col. Doc.*, IX, 747, 828-830; Laramie, *Queen Anne's War*, 273-274, 311.
5. Severance, *Joncaire*, 13, 29-32; *NY Col. Doc.*, IX, 885-886, 897-898.
6. *Cal. A&WI*, XXXII, 29, 202-204; Severance, *Joncaire*, 32-34.
7. *NY Col Doc.* IX, 899-903.
8. *Cal. A&WI*, XXXII, 202-207, 215-216, 441-442.
9. *NY Col. Doc.*, V, 630-640; *Cal. A&WI*, XXXII, 179-180.
10. *NY Col. Doc.*, V, 949-950; Severance, *Joncaire*, 62-65.
11. Severance, *Old Frontier of France*, I, 226-228.
12. Severance, *Joncaire*, 65-66.
13. "Chaussegros de Lery, Gaspard-Joseph," DCB, III; *NY Col. Doc.*, IX, 977-978; Severance, *Old Frontier of France*, I, 231-241.
14. *NY Col. Doc*, V, 783-801.
15. *Cal. A&WI Papers*, XXXV, 277; *NY Col. Doc*, IX, 973-975.
16. *NY Col. Doc.*, V, 818-822, IX, 1048-1049; Preston and Lamontagne, *Royal Fort Frontenac*, 67-68, 222-225; *Cal A&WI*, XXXV, 340-341, 384-385; *Doc. Hist. N.Y*, I, 447-448. While King Louis did not disagree with the economic argument regarding the sale of liquor, he also pointed out that poor administration would explain it as well. (*Royal Fort Frontenac*, 225.)

17. *Journal Legislative Council New York, 1691-1743*, 589-626; *Cal A&WI*, XXXVII, 398-400; Severance, *Old Frontier of France*, I, 347-349.

CHAPTER 9: THE YAMASSEE WAR

1. Gallay, *Indian Slave Trade*, 288-292; Crane, *The Southern Frontier*, 94-97; La Salley, *Journals S.C. Assembly, Oct. 1707-Feb. 1708, 50.*

2. Sherman, *Robert Johnson*, 16-18; McCrady, *South Carolina*, 531-532; Gallay, *Indian Slave Trade*, 329-334; *Journal Comm. S.C. Indian Trade*, 12-18, 43, 45, 47, 51. Internal conflicts within the Board of Indian Commissioners would damage the board's credibility and resolve in such matters.

3. Carroll, *Hist. Coll. S.C.*, I, 193-195; *Cal. A&WI*, XXVIII, 166-167; Crane, *The Southern Frontier*, 167-168; *Journal Comm. S.C. Indian Trade, 1710-1715*, 85-86.

4. *Cal. A&WI*, XXVIII, 166-167, 227-228; Rivers, *Early South Carolina*, 260-263.

5. *Cal. A&WI*, XXVIII, 167-168, 227-228; Carroll, *Hist. Coll. S.C.*, I, 195-197.

6. McCrady, *South Carolina*, 534-536; Carroll, *Hist. Coll. S.C.*, II, 571-572; *Journal Dr. Francis Le Jau*, 151-154; *Cal. A&WI*, XXVIII, 228.

7. "Rodd Letter," *Year Book Charleston 1894*, 319-320; Rivers, *Early South Carolina*, 264-265; *Cal. A&WI*, XXVIII, 297-299; Carroll, *Hist. Coll. S.C.*, I, 194-197.

8. *Cal. A&WI*, XXVIII, 229, 232-238; Sherman, *Robert Johnson*, 19; McCrady, *South Carolina*, 536-537. The Board of Trade requested that 300 barrels of powder, 1,500 muskets, 40 Coehorn mortars, 6 field guns, and 500 men be immediately dispatched to aid the colonists with the lord proprietors of the colony paying for a portion of the transport costs. (Syfert, "Proprietary Misrule in South Carolina," 20.)

9. *Cal. A&WI*, XXVIII, 199-201, 296-302; "Rodd Letter," 320-322; "A Working Definition of Periauger," *Underwater Archaeology*, 22-28.

10. *NY Col. Doc.*, V, 437-447; Crane, *The Southern Frontier*, 178-180.

11. *Cal. A&WI*, XXIX, 50-51, 135-138, 157-158; Crane, *The Southern Frontier*, 180-183; "Chicken Journal," *Year Book Charleston 1894*, 341-348.

CHAPTER 10: PROPRIETORS AND PIRATES

1. *Cal. A&WI*, XXIX, 218-222, 280; Williams, *Letters from the Clergy*, 304; Crane, *The Southern Frontier*, 183-184.

2. McCrady, *South Carolina*, 578-579; *Cal. A&WI*, XXIX, 206-207, 239, 266-267.

3. Carroll, *Hist. Coll. S.C.*, II, 144-146; *Cal. A&WI*, XXIX, 130-139, 144, 157-158; Sherman, *Robert Johnson*, 22-23.

4. *Cal. A&WI*, XXIX, 250, 258-259, 303, 321-323, XXX, 232-233, 246-247; Rivers, *Early South Carolina*, 31-33.

5. *Cal. A&WI*, XXX, 224,264-266, 285; Rivers, *Early South Carolina*, 133-135.

6. McCrady, *South Carolina*, 589-592; *Cal. A&WI*, XXX, 266-267, 336-338; *Pirates Own Book*, 312-314; Ravenel, *Charleston*, 70-71.

7. Johnson, *Pyrates*, 91-93; McCrady, *South Carolina*, 592-596; *Cal. A&WI*, XXX, 366; Howell, *State Trials*, 1241-1242, 1249-1258.

8. McCrady, *South Carolina*, 598-599; Johnson, *Pyrates*, 93-98; Stockton, *Pirates*, 228-232.

9. *Cal. A&WI*, XXX, 366-367; Johnson, *Pyrates*, 98-100; Stockton, *Pirates*, 233-242; McCrady, *South Carolina*, 599-604.

10. Johnson, *Pyrates*,100-101; *Cal. A&WI*, XXXI, 10; McCrady, *South Carolina*, 606-609. "This undertaking, besides that it has been a considerable expence to us, will (wee apprehend) very much irritate the pirates who infest this coast in great numbers," Johnson wrote the Board of Trade a few weeks after Bonnet's capture. He then asked once again for a Royal Navy warship to deal with the pirates and safeguard the colony's commerce. (*Cal. A&WI*, XXX, 367.)
11. McCrady, *South Carolina*, 610-617; Howell, *State Trials*, 1299-1302; Sherman, *Robert Johnson*, 32-36; Stockton, *Pirates*, 246-252.
12. *Cal. A&WI*, XXXI, 80-81, 259-260.

CHAPTER 11: LOUISIANA AND FLORIDA

1. Swanton, *Early History of the Creek*, 101-102; Tepaske, "Economic Problems of Florida's Governors," *FHQ*, vol. 37, no. 1, 42-46; Grady, *Anglo-Spanish Rivalry*, 256-257. In 1716 a new governor, Pedro de Olivera y Fullana, arrived at St. Augustine, but he would die of illness three months later, leaving Ayala interim governor.
2. Hann, "St. Augustine's Fallout from the Yamassee War," *FHQ*, vol. 68, no. 2, 180-184; Grady, *Anglo-Spanish Rivalry*, 258-262; Wright, *Anglo-Spanish Rivalry in North America*, 69-71; Tepaske, "Economic Problems of Florida's Governors," *FHQ*, vol. 37, no. 1, 46-47.
3. *Charlevoix*, VI, 17-18; Remonville, "Journal," *Hist. Coll. Louisiana and Florida*, 112-114; Allain, 1-3.
4. *Hist. Coll. Louisiana*, III, 38-45; Crane, *Southern Frontier*, 97-104; *Charlevoix*, VI, 18-25.
5. Remonville, "Journal," *Hist. Coll. Louisiana and Florida*, 130-135; *Hist. Coll. Louisiana*, III, 45-47, 84.
6. *Miss. Prov. Archives*, III, 240-242; Remonville, "Journal," *Hist. Coll. Louisiana and Florida*, 137-148; *Hist. Coll. Louisiana*, III, 54-66; Chalmers, *Collection of Treaties*, I, "The Quadruple Alliance, 1718," 257-310.
7. Faye, "Spanish Fortifications of Pensacola," *FHQ*, vol. 20, no. 2, 151-158; Griffen, "Spanish Pensacola," *FHQ*, vol. 37, no. 3 & 4, 244-248, 251-254; Faye, "The Contest for Pensacola Bay," *FHQ*, vol. 24, no. 3, 184-190.
8. *Hist. Coll. Louisiana*, III, 63-64, V, 4-7; Faye, "The Contest for Pensacola Bay," *FHQ*, vol. 24, no. 3, 190-195, #4, 302-304; Remonville, "Journal," 147-148; Campbell, *Colonial Florida*, 41-44.
9. Faye, "The Contest for Pensacola Bay," *FHQ*, vol. 24, #4, 303-308; *Miss. Prov. Archives*, III, 251-253, 269-270; Griffen, "Spanish Pensacola," *FHQ*, vol. 37, no. 3 & 4, 254-255.
10. *Miss. Prov. Archives*, III, 242-251, 254, 262, 270-273; Remonville, "Journal," 148-149; Faye, "The Contest for Pensacola Bay," *FHQ*, vol. 24, no. 4, 308-313.
11. *Histoire Maritme France*, IV, 197-198; Remonville, "Journal," 149-150; *Hist. Coll. Louisiana*, III, 65-66, V, 6-14.
12. Faye, "The Contest for Pensacola Bay," *FHQ*, vol. 24, no. 4, 313-317; *Miss. Prov. Archives*, III, 273-275, 281-283; Chalmers, *Collection of Treaties*, II, 3.

CHAPTER 12: THE NATCHEZ AND CHICKASAW WARS

1. Carroll, *Hist. Coll. S.C.*, I, 224-226, II, 161-166; Hewatt, *South Carolina & Georgia*, I, 255-258; *Cal. A&WI*, XXXI, xi-xiii, 287-291, 315-316, 332-343.

2. Hewatt, *South Carolina & Georgia*, I, 259-270; *Cal. A&WI*, XXXI, xi-xiii, 287-291, XXXII, 97-98; Carroll, *Hist. Coll. S.C.*, I, 236-239, II, 180-181.
3. Carroll, *Hist. Coll. S.C.*, II, 190-191; *Cal. A&WI*, XXXII, 302.
4. McCrady, *South Carolina*, 663-664; *Cal. A&WI*, XXXII, 271, 301-302; Sherman, *Robert Johnson*, 50-54; Hewatt, *South Carolina & Georgia*, I, 287-288.
5. *Cal. A&WI*, XXXII, v-vi, 74-75, 179-180, 216, 229-231; Clowes, *Royal Navy*, III, 42-45; Chalmers, *Collection of Treaties*, II, 219-228.
6. *Hist. Coll. Louisiana*, V, 47-56; *Miss. Prov. Archives*, III, 375-377, 385-387.
7. Milne, *Natchez Country*, 156-163, 173-177; Gayarre, *Hist. French Louisiana*, 396-405, 412-418; *Hist. Coll. Louisiana*, III, 151-157, V, 58-75, 79-83; *Miss. Prov. Archives*, I, 54-60, 76-77, 122-128; Bunner, *Hist. Louisiana*, 85-89.
8. *Miss. Prov. Archives*, I, 64-72; *Hist. Coll. Louisiana*, III, 157-158, V, 89-90; Gayarre, *Hist. French Louisiana*, 420-429.
9. *Hist. Coll. Louisiana*, V, 90-94; King, *Bienville*, 279-282; Harris, *Old Fort Mobile*, 48-51; Gayarre, *Hist. French Louisiana*, 429-434; *Miss. Prov. Archives*, I, 77-81.
10. *Hist. Coll. Louisiana*, V, 94-98.
11. Gayarre, *Hist. French Louisiana*, 442-448; King, *Bienville*, 282-284; *Hist. Coll. Louisiana*, V, 101-102; Ferland, *Canada*, 464-466; *Miss. Prov. Archives*, I, 117-122, 134-136.
12. Gayarre, *Hist. French Louisiana*, 448-452; *Miss. Prov. Archives*, I, 164-170.
13. *Miss. Prov. Archives*, I, 193-200.
14. *Hist. Coll. Louisiana*, V, 102-105; *Miss. Prov. Archives*, I, 206-207, 211-213, 229-237; Gayarre, *Hist. French Louisiana*, 459-460.
15. Gayarre, *Hist. French Louisiana*, 470-472; *Miss. Prov. Archives*, I, 268-269, 273-276, 311-314, III, 665-667. Bienville admitted in his letter to the minister of the marine concerning D'Artaguette's detachment that, "I have difficulty in reconciling all the accounts I have received on the subject." (*Miss. Prov. Archives*, I, 311.)
16. Harris, *Old Fort Mobile*, 65-74; Ferland, *Canada*, 466-468; King, *Bienville*, 303-305; *Hist. Coll. Louisiana*, V, 113-114.
17. King, *Bienville*, 293-301; *Hist. Coll. Louisiana*, V, 106-110; *Miss. Prov. Archives*, I, 294-308. Bienville wrote of the attack that, "We were expecting to deal with Indians who we knew were brave to be sure, but incapable of fortifying themselves to the extent that it almost impossible to take them without artillery." (*Miss. Prov. Archives*, I, 314.)
18. King, *Bienville*, 301-303; *Miss. Prov. Archives*, I, 308-310, 314-320; *Cal. A&WI*, XLII, 242-244, 271-272.
19. *RAPQ, 1922-1923*, 156-178, 180-183; Ferland, *Canada*, 469-472; *Hist. Coll. Louisiana*, V, 114-118; *Miss. Prov. Archives*, I, 379-388, 419-421, 428-461; Claiborne, *Mississippi*, 64-85; Gayarre, *Hist. French Louisiana*, 505-513.

CHAPTER 13: GEORGIA AND JENKINS' EAR

1. *Coll. Georgia Hist. Soc.*, I, 204-232; *Cal. A&WI*, XXXVII, 357-358, 394-397, XXXIX, 138-146, 183, 205, 217, 220; Phillips, "New Light upon the Founding of Georgia," *Georgia Hist. Quarterly*, VII, no. 4, 277-284.
2. Jones, *Georgia*, 113-121; *Cal. A&WI*, XL, xxiv, 10, 15-20, 29, XLII, 234-242; *Coll. Georgia Hist. Soc.*, I, 94-95, 100-103; Anon., "Oglethorpe's Treaty with the Lower Creek," *GHQ*, IV, no. 1, 3-16.

3. Clowes, *Royal Navy*, III, 50-51; *Cal. A&WI*, XLI, 398-401, 442-443, XLIV, x-xi, 28; Wright, *Anglo-Spanish Rivalry in North America*, 69-71.
4. Tailfer, *Narrative of Col. Georgia*, 27-29; Ivers, *British Drums of the Southern Frontier*, 72-74; *Cal. A&WI*, XLIII, vii-viii, 104-105. Oglethorpe's regiment was to consist of six companies, each composed of 113 officers, NCOs, and soldiers, which, when added to the regimental staff, gave 684 officers and men at full strength. (Ivers, *British Drums of the Southern Frontier*, 78-79.)
5. Lannen, "James Oglethorpe," *GHQ*, vol. 95/2, 213-218; Wright, *Oglethorpe Memoir*, 190-205; *Cal. A&WI*, XLIV, 245-246. Two hundred fifty men of the 42nd were drawn from the garrison of Gibraltar and formed with an independent company already in Georgia to create three of the six companies. The other companies were recruited in England. (Ivers, *British Drums of the Southern Frontier*, 78-79.)
6. *Cal. A&WI*, XLV, 33-34, 122.
7. Lecky, *History of England*, I, 414-419; Hoffman, *Florida's Frontiers*, 190-193.
8. Berson, "Stono Rebels," *S.C. Hist. Magazine*, vol. 110, no. 1 & 2, 53-68; *Gentleman's Magazine*, X (Mar 1740), 127-129; *Col. Rec. State of Georgia*, vol. 22/2, 25-31; 232-236; *St. Augustine Expedition*, 17-19; *Cal. A&WI*, XLV, 268.
9. *St. Augustine Expedition*, 137-139; *Col. Rec. State of Georgia*, vol. 22/2, 217-218.
10. *Col. Rec. State of Georgia*, vol. 22/2, 266-269.
11. Torres-Reyes, *The British Siege of St. Augustine*, 9-17; Goggin, "Ft. Pupo," *FHQ*, XXX, no 2, 150-152; Ivers, *British Drums of the Southern Frontier*, 91-92; *Col. Rec. State of Georgia*, vol. 22/2, 284-290, 312-316; *Coll. Georgia Hist. Soc.*, VII/1, 32-34.
12. Goggin, "Ft. Pupo," *FHQ*, XXX, no. 2, 150-152; Mereness, *Travels in the American Colonies*, 224-227; *Coll. Georgia Hist. Soc.*, VII/1, 35-37; *St. Augustine Expedition*, 23-24, 133, 139-140; *Cal. A&WI*, XLV, 267-271; Wright, *Oglethorpe Memoir*, 226-238.

CHAPTER 14: OGLETHORPE'S CAMPAIGN

1. *St. Augustine Expedition*, 22-29, 138-150; Ivers, *British Drums of the Southern Frontier*, 99-102; Wright, *Oglethorpe Memoir*, 239-243. Many of these units did not materialize. The independent company from Georgia settlers was too small, and their ranks were absorbed into the South Carolina regiment. The highland company was formed but with only 70 of the projected 115 men. The ranger companies followed the same line. Neither had more than 25 men in their ranks when Oglethorpe departed for the siege and only a few dozen horses could be obtained, in part because the officer sent to purchase them was robbed en route. (Ivers, *British Drums of the Southern Frontier*, 99-102.)
2. *Coll. Georgia Hist. Soc.*, VII/1, 37-43.
3. Torres-Reyes, *The British Siege of St. Augustine*, 19-22; *Coll. Georgia Hist. Soc.*, VII/1, 43-51. Before the galley's arrival Montiano listed his garrison as 462 soldiers and 151 militia and Native scouts. During the siege these numbers would be augmented by another 50 or so prisoners, friars, and volunteers. (*Coll. Georgia Hist. Soc.*, VII/1, 48-49.)
4. *St. Augustine Expedition*, 28-32, 147-148; Hewatt, *South Carolina & Georgia*, II, 76-77; Clowes, *Royal Navy*, III, 268-269. Pearce's fleet consisted of the frigates *Squirrel* (20), *Flamborough* (20), *Hector* (44), *Tartar* (22), *Phoenix* (20), and the smaller brigantines *Wolf* (8) and *Spence* (6). Added to this were over half a dozen armed colonial sloops and schooners that could easily clear the main bar at St. Augustine. (*Royal Navy*, III, 269.)

5. Torres-Reyes, *The British Siege of St. Augustine*, 28-31; *St. Augustine Expedition*, 32-34, 150-152; Jones, *A Report on Fort Diego*.
6. Torres-Reyes, *The British Siege of St. Augustine*, 31-33; *St. Augustine Expedition*, 34-37, 150-157.
7. *Coll. Georgia Hist. Soc.*, VII/1, 54-55.
8. *St. Augustine Expedition*, 38-43, 166-167, 171-177.
9. McCall, *Georgia*, 100-102; *St. Augustine Expedition*, 43-45, 162-165. One South Carolina ranger who acted as an interpreter to the Creek scoffed at Oglethorpe's fear of attacking the town, later testifying "that it was very easy to have been done." (*St. Augustine Expedition*, 167.)

CHAPTER 15: THE SIEGE OF ST. AUGUSTINE

1. *St. Augustine Expedition*, 44-46; *An Impartial Account of the Late Expedition*, 22-23.
2. *St. Augustine Expedition*, 46-48, 52-53, 166-167, 176-177; Herson, "A Joint Operation Gone Awry," 16-18.
3. Wright, *Oglethorpe Memoir*, 247-251; *St. Augustine Expedition*, 54-58; Mereness, *Travels in the American Colonies*, 227-229.
4. *Coll. Georgia Hist. Soc.*, VII/1, 54-55.
5. *St. Augustine Expedition*, 172-173; Ivers, *British Drums of the Southern Frontier*, 114-116.
6. Torres-Reyes, *The British Siege of St. Augustine*, 43-56; *Coll. Georgia Hist. Soc.*, VII/1, 56-57; *St. Augustine Expedition*, 60-66, 172-176; *Col. Rec. Georgia*, IV, 621-622; Fairbanks, *Spaniards in Florida*, 82-87. Captain MacKintosh, who was captured in the engagement, later claimed that, "They did not surprise us, for we were all under arms, ready to receive them." (Fairbanks, *Spaniards in Florida*, 85.)
7. Torres-Reyes, *The British Siege of St. Augustine*, 55-56.
8. *St. Augustine Expedition*, 65-68, 159-160; Torres-Reyes, *The British Siege of St. Augustine*, 57-59.
9. *St. Augustine Expedition*, 68-70.
10. *St. Augustine Expedition*, 70-71.
11. Torres-Reyes, *The British Siege of St. Augustine*, 59-63; Herson, "A Joint Operation Gone Awry," 21-23; *St. Augustine Expedition*, 71-77; Arana, *History Castillo de San Marcos*, 41-45; Subhash, Janotti, "Impact response of Coquina," *Dynamic Behavior of Materials*, I, 1-27. "The extreme durability and endurance of the fort has been attributed to a unique indigenous rock, called 'coquina' from which the fort walls were constructed. Unlike other structural materials of the day (e.g., stone), when the cannon balls impacted the fort walls, the coquina absorbed the impact without causing large cracks or catastrophic failure of the wall. Instead, the cannon balls became embedded several inches deep into the wall, with no large cracks emanating from the impact site or fragments being ejected from the wall." (Subhash, "Impact response of Coquina," 2.)
12. *Coll. Georgia Hist. Soc.*, VII/1, 57-60; *St. Augustine Expedition*, 84-85.
13. Torres-Reyes, *The British Siege of St. Augustine*, 63-75; *St. Augustine Expedition*, 85-91; Herson, "A Joint Operation Gone Awry," 24-27.
14.*St. Augustine Expedition*, 92-93.
15. Torres-Reyes, *The British Siege of St. Augustine*, 76-82; Wright, *Oglethorpe Memoir*, 253-255; *St. Augustine Expedition*, 106-111. "And thus ended this most disgraceful and

unfortunate Expedition," the author of *An Impartial Account of the Late Expedition under General Oglethorpe* would conclude. (*An Impartial Account of the Late Expedition*, 26)

CHAPTER 16: THE INVASION OF GEORGIA

1. *Coll. Georgia Hist. Soc.*, VII/1, 59-62.
2. Ibid.
3. *St. Augustine Expedition*, 92-93, 111-126; *An Impartial Account of the Late Expedition*, 36-37. A committee formed by the government of South Carolina to examine the cause of the expedition's failure concluded after consulting scores of witnesses and placing 139 documents in evidence that, "Neither the General nor the Commodore have taken any proper or Vigorous Step towards the Reduction of St. Augustine, or done what they engaged to do, and therefore they are of opinion that this Government hath been greatly misled by both." (*St. Augustine Expedition*, 126.)
4. *Coll. Georgia Hist. Soc.*, VII/1, 62-70.
5. Clowes, *Royal Navy*, III, 52-69; Hart, "Attacks upon the Spanish Main," 1-3; Beatson, *Naval and Military Memoirs*, I, 43-53, 61-70, 84-89, III, 24-27.
6. *Papers Relating to the Expedition against Cartagena*, 12-15; Clowes, *Royal Navy*, III, 69-74; Beatson, *Naval and Military Memoirs*, I, 89-103;
7. *Account of the Expedition to Cartagena*, 29-46; Beatson, *Naval and Military Memoirs*, I, 103-115; *Papers Relating to the Expedition against Cartagena*, 50-51, 57-79; Clowes, *Royal Navy*, III, 74-78.
8. *Coll. Georgia Hist. Soc.*, VII/3, 20-26.
9. *Coll. Georgia Hist. Soc.*, VII/3, 25-27.
10. McCall, *Georgia*, 120-122; Wright, *Oglethorpe Memoir*, 291-298; *Coll. Georgia Hist. Soc.*, II, 84-85, III, 130-132.
11. Wright, *Oglethorpe Memoir*, 297-298.
12. Jones, *Georgia*, 344-346; Wright, *Oglethorpe Memoir*, 299-301; McCall, *Georgia*, 122-123; Mereness, *Travels in the American Colonies*, 232-233.
13. *Col. Rec. Georgia*, XXIII, 332-335, 377-378; *Gentleman's Magazine*, Dec. 1742, 661; *Coll. Georgia Hist. Soc.*, VII/3, 39-47, 65-68, 88-89.
14. Wright, *Oglethorpe Memoir*, 301-303; *Gentleman's Magazine*, Sept, 1742, 494-495, Dec., 661; McCall, *Georgia*, 122-124; *Coll. Georgia Hist. Soc.*, VII/3, 68-69, 89-90; *London Magazine*, Sept. 1742, 461.
15. Jones, *Georgia*, 346-347; Mereness, *Travels in the American Colonies*, 233-234; *Coll. Georgia Hist. Soc.*, III, 133-135; *Gentleman's Magazine*, Sept. 1742, 494-495.

CHAPTER 17: THE GENERAL'S FINEST HOUR

1. *Coll. Georgia Hist. Soc.*, VII/3, 69-70, 90-91.
2. Ibid., III, 134-135, VII/3, 70-72; Jones, *Georgia*, 347-348.
3. *Coll. Georgia Hist. Soc.*, VII/3, 72-73, 90-91.
4. Mereness, *Travels in the American Colonies*, 234-235; Wright, *Oglethorpe Memoir*, 303-307; McCall, *Georgia*, 124-126; *Coll. Georgia Hist. Soc.*, VII/3, 91, 110-111; *Gentleman's Magazine*, Oct. 1742, 550; Jones, *Georgia*, 348-349.
5. *Coll. Georgia Hist. Soc.*, VII/3, 76-83, 92-96; *Gentleman's Magazine*, sup. 1742, 693-696; *Col. Rec. Georgia*, XXIII, 384-385.

6. *Gentleman's Magazine*, sup. 1742, 696.
7. Wright, *Oglethorpe Memoir*, 317-319.
8. *Gentleman's Magazine*, sup. 1742, 696-697; Mereness, *Travels in the American Colonies*, 235-236.
9. Wright, *Oglethorpe Memoir*, 320-321, 327-337; *London Magazine*, July 1743, 356-357; *Coll. Georgia Hist. Soc.*, III, 149-153.

CHAPTER 18: KING GEORGE'S WAR

1. Browning, *The War of Austrian Succession*, 137-161; McLennan, *Louisbourg*, 109; *CMNF*, III, 196-201.
2. Rawlyk, *Yankees at Louisbourg*, 1-5; McLennan, *Louisbourg*, 110-112; *CMNF*, III, 201-202; "Lettre d'un Habitant Louisbourg," in Wrong, *Louisbourg in 1745*, 17-18.
3. *CWS*, I, 112-126; Wood, *William Shirley*, 181-197.
4. *Pub. Doc. Nova Scotia*, 128-131; *CWS*, I, 131-132.
5. Godfrey, "Bastide, John-Henry," *DCB*, III; Porter, *Hist. Royal Engineers*, I, 156-157; *CWS*, I, 131; *Pub. Doc. Nova Scotia*, 129.
6. *NH Prov. Papers*, V, 223; *Journal of Mass. House*, vol. 20 (March 1743), 371.
7. *CWS*, I, 131, 134-137; *Pub. Doc. Nova Scotia*, 131-133, 140-141.
8. Johnston, *Summer of 1744*, 50-56, 64-67; McLennan, *Louisbourg*, 113-114; Murdoch, *History of Nova Scotia*, II, 29-32; *Pub. Doc. Nova Scotia*, 134-135.
9. "Lettre d'un Habitant Louisbourg," 19-21; *NY Col. Doc.*, IX, 1107; Murdoch, *History of Nova Scotia*, II, 32-43; McLennan, *Louisbourg*, 114-116; Johnston, *Summer of 1744*, 79-82; *Pub. Doc. Nova Scotia*. 131, 141-146; Calnek, *History of Annapolis*, 101-105; *New American Magazine, 1744*, 613-614. De Gannes would later justify his conduct by pointing to the request by the inhabitants of Minas to leave. Duvivier disputed this, but nothing came of the matter. (McLennan, ibid.).
10. Wood, *William Shirley*, 216-219; *CWS*, I, 145-151.
11. *CWS*, I, 138-141.
12. Wood, *William Shirley*, 209-212, 231-232; *CWS*, I, 134-141, 144-147; Johnston, *Summer of 1744*, 39-42, 55-56.

CHAPTER 19: A MAD SCHEME

1. *NY Col. Doc.*, VI, 226-229; Wood, *William Shirley*, 225-229. Such proposals were nothing new and date back to the early days of Louisbourg's construction.
2. *Memoirs of the Last War*, 31-33; *CWS*, I, 151-152, 161; Wood, *William Shirley*, 235-239, 244-245, 254.
3. *CWS*, I, 159-160; Wood, *William Shirley*, 244-246.
4. McLennan, *Louisbourg*, 130-132; *Memoirs of the Last War*, 34-37; *CWS*, I, 161-165; *The Importance of Cape Breton*, 127-129.
5. *CWS*, I, 167-168.
6. *Mass. Acts and Resolves*, XIII, 425; Rawlyk, *Yankees at Louisbourg*, 35-37, 41-44; Wood, *William Shirley*, 272-276; *Memoirs of the Laste War*, 37-39, 42; *CWS*, I, 193-194. Pepperrell was also aware of his lack of military experience and politely declined the initial offer to command the expedition, claiming his wife's health and his own business affairs prevented this. He was eventually convinced to accept the offer when Shirley and the Massachusetts council informed him that without his involvement it would be unlikely

that they could raise the men needed, and as such, the expedition would probably be cancelled. (Rawlyk, 43-44.)

7. Wood, *William Shirley*, 257-261.

8. "Bidwell Journal," *NEHGR*, XXVII, no. 2, 159-160; *Memoirs of the Last War*, 37-40; Chapin, *New England Vessels Against Louisbourg*, 3-6.

9. *Memoirs of the Last War*, 40-42; Clowes, *Royal Navy*, III, 109-110.

10. *Pepperrell Papers*, 4-8, 124-126; Chapin, *New England Vessels Against Louisbourg*, 6-11; *Pepperrell's Journal*, 7-9.

11. "Green's Journal," 146-147; *Pepperrell's Journal*, 9-10; McLennan, *Louisbourg*, 139-140; Clowes, *Royal Navy*, III, 114-115.

CHAPTER 20: THE DUNKIRK OF THE WEST

1. "Green's Journal," 147; Kimball, *Corr. Gov. Rhode Is.*, I, 329-330; Chapin, *Rhode Is. Privateers*, 191-193.

2. At the time the British used the Julian calendar while the French and Spanish had converted to the more accurate Gregorian calendar. This means that British dates are eleven days behind the French/Spanish dates. As it is easier to trace the documents using the date employed by the various sources, I have kept these original dates and in any instances of confusion I have used the format (British date, French/Spanish date).

3. Rawlyk, *Yankees at Louisbourg*, 67-71; McLennan, *Louisbourg*, 122-123; Bower, *Louisbourg: A Focus of Conflict*, *RFL*.

4. "Du Chambon Journal," Downey, *Louisbourg*, 204-206; *Pepperrell's Journal*, 10; Rawlyk, *Yankees at Louisbourg*, 67-71, 77-83; *D. Bradstreet's Diary*, 10-11. The author of "Lettre d'un Habitant Louisbourg" was amazed with the New Englanders' good fortune when it came to the normally stormy weather, saying they, "appeared to have enlisted Heaven in their interests." (Wrong, "Lettre d'un Habitant Louisbourg," 35-36.)

5. *Pepperrell's Journal*, 10-12; "Lettre d'un Habitant Louisbourg," 38; "Du Chambon Journal," 205-206; McLennan, *Louisbourg*, 148-150; *D. Bradstreet's Diary*, 10-11; "Green's Journal," 148-149.

6. "Du Chambon Journal," 206-207; Rawlyk, *Yankees at Louisbourg*, 89-91; "Lettre d'un Habitant Louisbourg," 38-40.

7. *Pepperrell Papers*, 138-140; *The Importance of Cape Breton*, 129-131; "Cleaves' Journal," 118; "Du Chambon Journal," 207; "Giddings Journal", 298; *D. Bradstreet's Diary*, 11.

8. *Pepperrell Papers*, 139-144; *D. Bradstreet's Diary*, 12; "Green's Journal," 150-151.

9. "Giddings Journal," 298; "Bidwell Journal," 154; *Pepperrell Papers*, 141-149; "Du Chambon Journal," 207; *D. Bradstreet's Diary*, 12; "Craft's Journal," 184.

10. *Pepperrell Papers*, 13-14, 151-158; "Cleaves' Journal," 118; *D. Bradstreet's Diary*, 12.

11. "Green's Journal," 151-152; *Pepperrell Papers*, 14-15; "Du Chambon Journal," 207-208.

12. *Pepperrell Papers*, 15-17; Rawlyk, *Yankees at Louisbourg*, 109-111.

CHAPTER 21: THE FALL OF LOUISBOURG

1. *Pepperrell Papers*, 157-158, 166-168;

2. *Pepperrell Papers*, 17-20, 162; *D. Bradstreet's Diary*, 13-14; "Craft Journal," 184-185; "Cleaves' Journal," 118.

3. *Gibson's Journal*, 17; "Green's Journal," 152-153; *Pepperrell Papers*, 163, 166-167.
4. Chapin, *New England Vessels Against Louisbourg*, 16-17; Wood, *William Shirley*, 287; *Pepperrell Papers*, 187-188; *Gibson's Journal*, 17-18.
5. Rawlyk, *Yankees at Louisbourg*, 121-122.
6. *D. Bradstreet's Diary*, 14-15; "Green's Journal," 154-156; *Pepperrell Papers*, 181-187; "Cleaves' Journal," 119.
7. "Lettre d'un Habitant Louisbourg," 46-49; Chapin, *New England Vessels Against Louisbourg*, 17-19; McLennan, *Louisbourg*, 155-157; Hutchinson, *Hist. Mass.*, II, 417-418; Clowes, *Royal Navy*, III, 114-115.
8. *Pepperrell Papers*, 20, 189, 192-200, 213-214; "Du Chambon Journal," 210-211; *Gibson's Journal*, 18-19.
9. *Pepperrell Papers*, 20-23, 213, 220-223; *D. Bradstreet's Diary*, 16.
10. "Du Chambon Journal," 213; *Pepperrell Papers*, 226, 231-233; "Curwen Journal," 14; *D. Bradstreet's Diary*, 16; Rawlyk, *Yankees at Louisbourg*, 129-130; "Green's Journal," 158-159; *Gibson Journal*, 21.
11. *CWS*, I, 222-225; *Pepperrell Papers*, 241-245; "Green's Journal," 158-159.
12. "Du Chambon Journal," 209.
13. *Pepperrell Papers*, 244-245; "Du Chambon Journal, 210-212; "Lettre d'un Habitant Louisbourg," 51-55.
14. "Du Chambon Journal," 210-215; *Pepperrell Papers*, 230-231, 238-245; *CWS*, I, 221-225. In a March 2, 1745, letter to Governor Wentworth of NH, Shirley had Bastide overseeing the landing operations. (*CWS*, I, 190. Note: date should read 1744/45.)
15. *Pote's Journal*, 1-5, 28-32, 40-47; Chapin, *Privateering during King George's War*, Murdoch, 49-52; *History of Nova Scotia*, II, 72-75; *Pepperrell Papers*, 230-231. Captain Donahue was killed a few weeks later when his landing party was ambushed by a large French and Indian war party. (Chapin, 52.)
16. *Gibson's Journal*, 22-26; Wolcott's Journal, 132-136; *Memoirs of the Last War*, 48-49; *Pepperrell's Journal*, 21-24; "Green's Journal," 161-165; *Pepperrell Papers*, 27, 270, 280-285, 290-291; "Du Chambon Journal," 214-219. A later survey of French armaments after the surrender of the fortress reported 384 barrels of gunpowder remaining. (McLennan, *Louisbourg*, 408.)
17. *Memoirs of the Last War*, 49-52; "Du Chambon Journal," 216; McLennan, *Louisbourg*, 408; *Pepperrell Papers*, 299-302.

CHAPTER 22: THE RAIDERS OF SCALP POINT

1. Brandow, *Old Saratoga*, 31; *NY Col. Doc.*, X, 38.
2. Brandow, *Old Saratoga*, 32-38; *NY Col Doc.*, X, 38-39, 76. A number of the prisoners were given to the allied Indians while the rest were carried back to Montreal where Marin arrived on December 9. Many of the former were later ransomed back to the French.
3. *NY Col. Doc.*, X, 32, 39.
4. *NY Col. Doc.*, X, 32-34.
5. Deerfield, Massachusetts.
6. Present-day Boscowen, NH.
7. Bougainville, *Journal*, 41.
8. Shirley to Newcastle, 29 Oct, 1745, C.O. 5/900; *C.W.S.*, I, 293-300; *NY Col. Doc.*, VI,

284-288. Shirley's plan called for the Crown to pay for the raising and equipping of a combined force from North Carolina (600), Virginia (2,100), Maryland (1,000), Pennsylvania (2,500), New Jersey (1,000), New York (4,500), Connecticut (2,100), New Hampshire (700), Rhode Island (1,000) and Massachusetts (4,500). ("Shirley to Newcastle Oct 29, 1745," C.O. 5/900.)

9. *CWS*. I, 307-325; *Conn Hist Soc Coll*, XIII, *Law Papers*, II, 180-181, 201-204. Of the eight British regiments assigned to the venture three were slotted to relieve the colonial garrison at Louisbourg. (*Law Papers*, II, 201-204.)

10. *Law Papers*, II, 201-204; *CWS*, I, 323-24; *N.H. Prov. Papers*, V, 430-432; *NY Col. Doc.*, VI, 314; *Penn Archives*, V, 52-54; Parkman, *A Half Century of Conflict*, II, 152.

11. *CWS*, I, 330, 342-354; *Journal of the Legislative Council of New York*, II, 927 (June 6, 1746); The force destined to join Gooch's force was to consist of 2,900 men, New Jersey (500), New York (1,600), Virginia (100), Maryland (300), Pennsylvania (400), far short of Shirley's initial numbers. (*NY Col. Doc*, VI, 314, 657; *Boston Post Boy*, 22 Sept., 20 Oct., 3 Nov. 1746.)

12. *NY Col. Doc.*, X, 41, 43-44, 48, 51-55.

13. *NY Col. Doc.*, X, 34, 51-52, 56.

14. Journal de la campagne de M. Rigaud de Vaudreuil en 1746, F3, 11 (Moreau St. Mery) fol. 220; Parkman, *A Half Century of Conflict*, II, (1909), 235-241; *NY Col. Doc.*, X, 35, 77.

15. Perry, *Origins in Williamstown*, 107-109; Norton, *The Redeemed Captive being a Narrative of the Rev. John Norton*, 3.

16. Rigaud, Journal, F3, 11 (Moreau St. Mery) fol. 220 ; Norton , *The Redeemed Captive*, 4-6.

17. Norton, *The Redeemed Captive*, 6-7.

18. Parkman, *A Half Century of Conflict*, II, 246-247; Rigaud, Journal, F3, 11 (Moreau St. Mery) fol. 220; Norton, *The Redeemed Captive*, 8.

19. Parkman, *A Half Century of Conflict*, II, 247-248; Rigaud, Journal, F3, 11 (Moreau St. Mery) fol. 220; Norton, *The Redeemed Captive*, 8-9; There is a discrepancy between the British and French accounts on the parley. Rigaud says that it was the British who instigated the parley while Hawks and Rev. Norton claimed that it was the French who acted first. This discrepancy also carries over to exactly who met whom outside the fort.

20. Parkman, *A Half Century of Conflict*, II, 248-249; Rigaud, Journal, F3, 11 (Moreau St. Mery) fol. 220; Norton, *The Redeemed Captive*, 8-10.

21. Norton, *The Redeemed Captive*, 10-12; Dolittle, *A Short Narrative of Mischief done by the French and Indian Enemy on the Western Frontiers…*, 8-9; Parkman, *A Half Century of Conflict*, II, 255. One of Hawk's garrison was killed during the siege and another died shortly thereafter, while Rigaud listed his final casualties as one killed and sixteen wounded (Norton, *The Redeemed Captive*, 7; Rigaud, Journal, F3, 11 (Moreau St. Mery) fol. 220. Another French report gives Rigaud's casualties as three Indians killed, four French and eleven Indians wounded. (*NY Col. Doc.*, X, 35.)

22. Parkman, *A Half Century of Conflict*, II, 253; Rigaud, Journal, F3, 11 (Moreau St. Mery) fol. 220; *NY Col. Doc.*, X, 35, 77.

23. Dolittle, *Short Narrative of Mischief done by the French*, 10.

CHAPTER 23: FLEETS, FORTS, AND FRUSTRATION

1. *The Colden Papers*, vol. III, 229.

2. Johnson, William, c.1715-1774, *DCB*, Vol. IV; *NY Col. Doc.*, VI, 314, 358; *JP*, I, 59-60.

3. *NY Col. Doc.*, VI, 313-314, 317-326; Stone, *Life and Times of Sir William Johnson*, vol. I, 204-207.

4. *NY Col. Doc.*, VI, 314, 340-341, 653.

5. *CWS*, I, 342-345.

6. *Boston Post Boy*, 22 Sept., 20 Oct., 3 Nov., 1746; *Journal of the Legislative Council of New York*, II, 946 (Oct 17, 1746); *NY Col. Doc.*, VI, 314; *JP*, I, 60-61, 64.

7. *CWS*, I, 346-353; *Law Papers*, II, 301-302, 307-312, 313-315; Shirley to Newcastle , 29 Sept. 1746, C.O. 5/ 901.

8. Minister to Beauharnois et Hocquart, 24 Jan., 1746, F3, 11 (Moreau St. Mery) fol. 210; Pritchard, *Naval Disaster*, 74-75, 81-89, 100; Taillemite, "Jean-Baptiste-Louis-Frederic De, Marquis de Roucy, Duc d'Anville," DCB, III; *NY Col. Doc.*, X, 42-43.

9. Pritchard, *Naval Disaster*, 80-81, 103, 106-111; *NY Col. Doc.*, X, 44-47, 50-57; Murdoch, *History of Nova Scotia*, II, 88-90.

10. *NY Col. Doc.*, X, 61-62; *Collection de Documents Inedits*, II, 16-31; Parkman, *A Half Century of Conflict*, II, 157-168.

11. Pritchard, *Naval Disaster*, 176-185; Lanctot, III, 66-69; Murdoch, *History of Nova Scotia*, II, 91-96; *NY Col. Doc.*, X, 68-74; *Maritime Hist. France*, IV, 268-271; *Boston Post Boy*, 27 Oct., 1746; *CWS*, I, 366-367.

12. Secretary Cadwallader Colden of New York summarized the ministry's decision not to send St. Clair's forces by saying in a letter to a friend that "Any Expedition against Canada was thought to be laid aside at this time for this reason that the making conquests abroad can be of little use while the French remain superior in Europe because in such case they will make what terms of peace they shall think proper…" (*Colden Papers*, III, 312). For an in-depth analysis of the politics behind, and ultimate failure, of St. Clair's mission the reader is directed to Arthur H. Buffinton's "The Canadian Expedition of 1746," *American Historical Review*, Vol. 45, No. 3 (April 1940).

13. *Colden Papers*, III, 268-269, 272; *Journal of the Legislative Council of New York*, II, 946. When Shirley first broached the plan to shift colonial efforts toward Crown Point Clinton was advised by his council in Albany, "That whether the attempt on Crown Point be made or not at all the forces now levied must be kept on foot paid and clothed and supported with provisions and placed on the frontiers towards Canada so that the reduction of Crown Point can occasion a very small additional expense…" The council also recommended using these troops to build whatever forts were deemed necessary for securing the army's supply and communications lines and "to prevent the incursions of the enemy." (*Colden Papers*, Vol. III, 264.)

14. *CWS* I, 368-369, 373; *Law Papers*, II, 334-338,340-343, 345-348, III, 3-4, 7, 10. In a letter to Governor Green of Rhode Island Shirley expressed his concern that not pressing forward with the expedition against Crown Point after Iroquois assistance had been secured would jeopardize losing the Six Nations to the French "which will e of the most fatal consequences to all the northern English colonies." (CWS, I, 378.)

15. Major John Rutherford, stationed at Albany throughout the winter, wrote to his friend Cadwallader Colden, "I think the governor has been ill advised in not allowing

us to assist the New England troops against Crown Point, the winter proved extremely favorable for such an attempt and the troops very healthy and in good spirits and wanting for nothing." (*Colden Papers*, III, 365.)
16. Doolittle, *Short Narrative of Mischief done by the French*, 10. *NY Col. Doc.*, X, 75.

CHAPTER 24: STALEMATE

1. *Memoirs of the Last War*, 68-71; *Journal of Mass. House*, vol. 23 (1746-1747), 206-208; *Collection de Documents Inedits*, II, 32-57; *London Magazine*, July 1747, 309; Murdoch, *History of Nova Scotia*, II, 104-105; Wood, Shirley, 353, 359-361.
2. *Collection de Documents Inedits*, II, 10-13, 58-62; Murdoch, *History of Nova Scotia*, II, 105-107; *NY Col. Doc.*, X, 89-91.
3. Williamson, *History of Maine*, II, 249-250; *Memoirs of the Last War*, 71-73; Murdoch, *History of Nova Scotia*, II, 107-110, 114-115; *Collection de Documents Inedits*, II, 13-16, 62-71; *NY Col. Doc.*, X, 89-94; *London Magazine*, June 1747, 292, July 1747, 310.
4. *NY Col. Doc*, X, 75, 89, 93; *Boston Post Boy*, 20 April 1747.
5. *NY Col. Doc*, X, 95-96; *Boston Post Boy*, 20 April, 1747; Brandow, *Old Saratoga* , 42; *Colden Papers*, III, 370-371. British losses were stated at nine killed, nine wounded, and six missing, of which at least three were taken prisoner. French losses were not stated, but at least one Frenchman was taken prisoner. He reported that there were only a hundred men at Fort St. Frederic, causing one Englishman on the scene to lament "I wish we had orders to march tomorrow." (*Boston Post Boy*, 20 Oct. 1747.)
6. *Boston Post Boy*, 11 May 1747; *NY Col. Doc.*, VI, 343-344, X, 96. The officer in blue referred to by the Iroquois braves in this incident seems to have been named LaPlante. (*NY Col. Doc.*, X, 96.)
7. Ibid., X, 98-99, 101-102, VI, 340-343, 349-350, 357-358; *Journal of the Legislative Council of New York*, II, 963-964. Beyond how the current troops stationed along the New York frontier were to be employed Shirley was anxiously awaiting a reply to a plan he proposed that called for eight thousand British regulars and twenty thousand colonials to descend upon Canada during the summer of 1747. (Shirley to Newcastle , 12 Oct. 1746, C.O. 5/901.)
8. *NY Col. Doc.*, X, 79-80.
9. *NY Col. Doc.*, X, 79-80.
10. *NY Col. Doc.*, X, 79-80; *Boston Post Boy*, 6 July, 1747; St. Luc claimed the British force amounted to 120 or so, of which 45 were captured and 28 killed. British reports make the numbers 102, of which 47 were captured and 15 killed. St. Luc reported his losses as one killed and five wounded. (*Boston Post Boy*, 6 July 1747; *NY Col. Doc.*, X, 80.) Rigaud wanted to follow up this success with an assault by several hundred men. His Indian allies, however, refused to join the campaign, which brought an end to the idea. (*NY Col. Doc.*, X, 133.)
11. *Boston Post Boy*, 13 July 1747; *NY Weekly*, 6 July 1747; *NY Col. Doc.*, VI, 629-630, X, 132-133, 147-148; Brandow, *Old Saratoga*, 57-59.
12. *NY Col. Doc.*, VI, 352-357, 360-362, 364, 378-380; JP, I, 83, 93-94; Stone, *Life and Times of Sir William Johnson*, 237-238. Also see the New York Assembly's reply to the governor on these matters. (*NY Col. Doc.*, VI, 365-374.)
13. *CWS*, I, 386-389, 392-394.
14. *Law Papers*, III, 99-101; *NY Col. Doc.*, VI, 408-410; *Journal of the Legislative Council*

of New York, II, 988; *New York Weekly Journal*, 7 Dec. 1747. Commissioners from several of the leading northern colonies met and formulated a plan for future operations against Canada, but little came of the idea. (*Journal of the Legislative Council of New York*, II, 984-987.)

15. Clowes, III, 124-126; *Collection de Documents Inedits*, I, 33-36; *Maritime Hist. France*, IV, 291-296.

CHAPTER 25: THE PRIVATEERS: THE WAR OF JENKINS' EAR

1. Statham, *Privateers and Privateering*, 11-12; Lester, *Privateering in the Colonial Chesapeake*, 24-27; Moats, *Navigating Neutrality*, 12-13; Starkey, *Pirates and Privateers*, 126-128.
2. Swanson, "American Privateering," *William & Mary Quarterly*, vol. 42/3, 363-366; Chapin, *Rhode Island Privateers*, 33; Lester, *Privateering in the Colonial Chesapeake*, 33-35; Watson, "Judge Lewis Morris," *NY History*, vol. 78, no. 2, 127-128; Bartlett, *Records of Colony of Rhode Island*, IV, 560-561.
3. *CWS*, I, 420-423; Swanson, "The Competition for American Seamen," *Man and Nature*, I, 119-129.
4. Kimball, *The Correspondence of the Gov. of Rhode Island*, I, 372-373.
5. Watson, "Judge Lewis Morris," *NY History*, vol. 78, no. 2, 117-146.
6. Swanson, "American Privateering," 371-374.
7. Chapin, *Rhode Island Privateers*, 6-8, 73-76; Sheffield, *Privateersmen of Newport*, 12, 44, 48.
8. Chapin, *Rhode Island Privateers*, 76-81.
9. Chapin, *Privateering during King George's War*, 131-133.

CHAPTER 26: THE PRIVATEERS: KING GEORGE'S WAR AND THE BLOCKADE OF CANADA

1. *The American Magazine, 1744*, 528, 571-572; *CWS*, I, 148; Chapin, *Privateering during King George's War*, 42-43.
2. *The American Magazine, 1744*, 481. By "over-masted" the writer means that the masts were either too long or too heavy for the craft.
3. Johnston, *Summer of 1744*, 31-34.
4. McLennan, *Louisbourg*, 118-124; Johnston, *Summer of 1744*, 47-50; Chapin, *Privateering during King George's War*, 74-76. Governor Shirley discovered that the lure of easy profits often undermined his approach to employ these vessels in anti-privateering operations, and on several occasions he reprimanded captains who passed on an opportunity to attack an enemy privateer. (McLennan, *Louisbourg*, 121.)
5. Chapin, *Privateering during King George's War*, 44-46.
6. Sheffield, *Privateersmen of Newport*, 11-12; Chapin, *Rhode Island Privateers*, 10-11.
7. Chapin, *Rhode Island Privateers*, 108-114; *The American Magazine, 1744*, 482-483, 570-571. After an explosion in a Newport warehouse, which killed the owners of the *Prince Frederick*, the vessel was not refit for another voyage.
8. *Boston Post Boy*, Oct. 27, 1746; Chapin, *Rhode Island Privateers*, 171-172.
9. Sheffield, *Privateersmen of Newport* 18, 45-47, 52; Chapin, *Rhode Island Privateers*, 172-173; Swanson, "American Privateering," 370-382.
10. *NY Col. Doc.*, X, 38-75; *Gentleman's Magazine*, vol. 16 (1746).

11. *NY Col. Doc.*, X, 89-131; *Gentleman's Magazine*, vol. 17 (1747); Swanson, "American Privateering," 372-374; 379-380.
12. Swanson, "American Privateering," 380-382; Beatson, *Naval and Military Memoirs*, I, 414, III, 82-85. According to the tables in Beatson, the French fleet lost nearly half its strength from 1744 to 1748. (Beatson, *Naval and Military Memoirs*, I, III, 82-85.)

CHAPTER 27: THE TREATY OF AIX-LA-CHAPELLE

1. Stone, *Life and Times of Sir William Johnson*, II, 255.
2. Caldwell, "The Southern Frontier During King George's War," 37-54.
3. Williams, *Hist. of Maine*, II, 256-259.
4. Chalmers, *A Collection of Treaties between Great Britain and Other Powers*, I, (Treaty of Aix-la-Chapelle), 424-467.
5. *CWS*, I, 284.

Bibliography

Manuscript Sources

Canada. National Archives. (Ottawa)
Manuscript Division
MG1: Fonds des Colonies
Sèrie C11A, Canada et Dépendances (Lettres des Gouverneurs, Intendants, officers et autres)
Sèrie C11B, Correspondence generale
Sèrie F3 Collection Moreau de Saint-Méry
Massachusetts Archives (Boston)
Volumes – v29, v34, v51, v72
Great Britain, Public Record Office (London)
Colonial Office
C.O.5, America and West Indies, Correspondence, originals on microfilm.

Published Sources

Akins, Thomas (ed.). *Selections from the Public Documents of Nova Scotia.* Halifax: Charles Annand, 1869.

Allain, Mathe. "Plus ca Change, Plus c'est la meme Chose: Premier Acte: Cadillac and Duclos," *Proceedings of the Meeting of the French Colonial Historical Society*, vol. 12 (1988), 1-9.

The American Magazine.

Ames, Ellis (ed.). *The Acts and Resolves of the Province of Massachusetts* Bay. Vol. IX, X, XI, XII, XIII. Boston: Wright & Potter, 1902-1907.

Anon. "Oglethorpe's Treaty with the Lower Creek," *Georgia Historical Quarterly*, IV, no. 1, 3-16.

Anon. *The Importance of Cape Breton*. London: John and Paul Knapton, 1746.

Anon. *Authentic Papers Relating to the Expedition against Cartagena*. London: L. Raymond, 1744.

Anon. *Report of the Committee appointed by the General Assembly of South Carolina in 1740 on the St. Augustine Expedition under General Oglethorpe*. Reprinted in *Collections of the Historical Society of South Carolina*, IV. Charleston: Walker, Evans, & Cogswell, 1887.

Arana, Luis. *History Castillo de San Marcos*. St. Augustine: Historic Print and Map Co., 2005.

Baker, Raymond. *A Campaign of Amateurs: The Sige of Louisbourg, 1745*. Ottawa: Canadian Parks Service, 1995.

Bartlett, John Russell (ed.). *Records of the Colony of Rhode Island and Providence Plantations in New England*. 10 vols. Providence: A. C. Greene, 1856-65.

Baxter, James. *The Pioneers of New France in New England, with contemporary letters and documents*. Albany: J. Munsell and Sons, 1894.

Beatson, Robert. *Naval and Military Memoirs of Great Britain from 1727 to 1783*. 6 vols. Aberdeen: J. Chalmers & Co., 1804.

Beaudot, Pierre and Cloutier, Céline. *Archaeology at Fort Chambly*. Ottawa: Canadian Parks Service, 1989.

Belknap, Jeremy. *The History of New Hampshire*. Dover: Stevens, Ela, and Wadleigh, 1831.

Berson, Joel. "How the Stono Rebels Learned of Britain's War with Spain," *South Carolina Historical Magazine*, vol. 110, no. 1 & 2, 53-68.

Bidwell, Adonijah. "Expedition to Cape Breton: Journal of the Rev. Adonijah Bidwell," *NEHGR*, XXVII, no. 2 (April 1873), 153-160.

Boston News-Letter.

Boston Post Boy.

Bougainville, Louis Antoine. *Adventure in the Wilderness: The American Journals of Louis Antoine de Bougainville, 1756-1760*. (Trans. and ed.) Edward P. Hamilton. Norman: University of Oklahoma Press, 1964.

Bourinot, J.G. *Historical and Descriptive Account of the Island of Cape Breton*. Montreal: W. Foster Brown and Co., 1892.

Bourne, Edward. *The History of Wells and Kennebunk*. Portland: B. Thurston & Co., 1875.

Bouton, Nathaniel. *Documents and Records Relating to the Province of New Hampshire*, 7 vols. Manchester: John B. Clarke State Printer, 1867-1873.

Bower, Peter (March 1970). *Louisbourg: A Focus of Conflict*, ch. III, unpublished report, *RFL*.

Bradstreet, Dudley. *Diary kept by Lt. Dudley Bradstreet of Groton, Mass. at the Siege of Louisbourg.* Cambridge: John Wilson and Son, 1897.

Brandow, John Henry. *The Story of Old Saratoga and History of Schuylerville.* Saratoga Springs, New York: Robson & Adee, 1906.

Brodhead, John. *History of the State of New York.* 2 vols. New York: Harper & Brothers, 1853, 1871.

Browning, Reed. *The War of Austrian Succession.* New York: St. Martin's Press, 1993.

Buffington, Arthur H. "The Canadian Expedition of 1746," *American Historical Review*, vol. 45, no. 3 (April 1940).

Caldwell, Norman. "The Southern Frontier During King George's War," *The Journal of Southern History*, VII, no. 1 (Feb. 1941), 37-54.

Calnek, W.A. *History of the Country of Annapolis.* Toronto: William Briggs, 1897.

Campbell, Richard. *Historical Sketches of Colonial Florida.* Cleveland: Williams Publishing, 1892.

Candler, Allen (ed.). *Colonial Records of the State of Georgia.* 26 vols. Atlanta: C. Byrd, State Printer, 1904-1916.

Carroll, B.R. *Historical Collections of South Carolina.* 2 vols. New York: Harper & Brothers, 1836.

Chalmers, George (ed.). *A Collection of treaties between Great Britain and other powers.* 2 vols. London: J. Stockdale, 1790.

Chapin, Howard. *Rhode Island Privateers in King George's War, 1739-1748.* Providence: Rhode Island Historical Society, 1926.

Chapin, Howard. *New England Vessels Against Louisbourg.* Boston: New England Historical Society, 1923.

Chapin, Howard. *Privateering during King George's War.* Providence: R.A. Johnson. 1928.

Chard, Donald. *The Impact of Ile Royale on New England.* Ph.D. thesis, University of Ottawa. 1976.

Charlevoix, Pierre-François-Xavier de. *History and General Description of New France.* 6 vols.; Paris: 1744. (Trans. and ed.) John Gilmary Shea. New York: Francis P. Harper, 1900.

Chicken, George. "Journal," *City of Charleston Year Book, 1894.* Charleston: Walker, Evans, and Cogswell (1894), 315-317, 324-352.

Claiborne, J.F.H. *Mississippi as a Province, Territory, and State*, I. Jackson, Miss: Power and Barksdale, 1880.

Clowes, William. *The Royal Navy: A History from the Earliest Times to the Present.* 6 vols. London: Sampson, Low, Marston, and Co., 1897-1902.

Collection de Documents Inédits sur le Canada and L'Amérique, II. Quebec: Demers and Frére,1889.

Collection de manuscrits contenant letters, mémoires, et autres documents historiques relatifs à la Nouvelle-France, recueillis aux Archives de la Province de Québec, ou copies à l'étranger. 4 vols.; Québec, 1883-1885.

Collections of the Connecticut Historical Society, XIII: The Law Papers, Vol. II. Hartford: Connecticut Historical Society, 1911.

Collections of the Georgia Historical Society, I, II, III, VII. Savannah: The Society, 1890-1911.

Collections of the New-York Historical Society for the Year 1919: Cadwaller Colden Papers, III, 1743-1747. New York: The New York Historical Society, 1919.

Collections of the Nova Scotia Historical Society for the year 1878. Halifax: Morning Herald, 1879.

Collections of the Nova Scotia Historical Society for the year 1884. Halifax: Morning Herald, 1885.

Cook, Stephen R. "The Chickasaw Villages," www.thechickasawvillages.com.

Crane, Verner. *The Southern Frontier, 1670-1732.* New York: W.W. Norton & Co. (1928), 1981.

Crowley, T.A. "The Forgotten Soldiers of New France: The Louisbourg Example," *Proceedings of the Meeting of the French Colonial Historical Society*, vol. 3 (1978), 52-69.

Crowley, T.A. *Louisbourg: Atlantic Fortress and Seaport.* Ottawa: Canadian Historical Association, 1990.

Documentary History of the State of Maine. 24 vols. Portland: Bailey and Noyes, 1869-1916.

Doolittle, Benjamin. *A Short Narrative of Mischief done by the French and Indian Enemy on the Western Frontier.* Boston: S. Kneeland, 1750.

Downey, Fairfax. *Louisbourg: Key to a Continent.* Englewood, N.J.: Prentice-Hall, 1965.

Dunn, John. (July 1971) "The Louisbourg Lighthouse," *RFL.*

Ellms, Charles. The *Pirates Own Book.* Portland, ME: Francis Blake, 1856.

Fairbanks, George. *The Spaniards in Florida.* Jacksonville: Columbus Drew, 1868.

Faye, Stanley. "The Contest for Pensacola Bay, Part I," *FHQ*, vol. 24, no. 3, 167-195.

Faye, Stanley. "Spanish Fortifications of Pensacola, 1698-1763," *FHQ*, vol. 20, no. 2, 151-168.

Ferland, J.B.A. *Cours D'Histoire du Canada.* Quebec: Augustine Cote, 1865.

Forbes, Allyn (ed.). *Journals of the House of Representatives of Massachusetts*, vol. 20 (1742-1744). Boston: Massachusetts Historical Society, 1945.

French, B.F. *Historical Collections of Louisiana and Florida*. 2 vols., New York: Sabin & Sons, 1869 and Albert Mason, 1875.

French, B.F. (ed.) *Historical Collections of Louisiana*, 5 vols., New York: Appleton & Co., 1846-1853.

Fry, "An Appearance of Strength: The Fortifications of Louisbourg," *Aspects of Louisbourg*. Sydney, Nova Scotia: University of Cape Breton Press (1995), 19-69.

Gallay, Alan. *The Indian Slave Trade*. New Haven: Yale University Press, 2002.

Gayarre, Charles. *History of Louisiana*, I. New York: Redfield, 1854.

Gentleman's Magazine.

Ghere, David. "European Diplomacy with the Eastern Abenaki, 1725-1750," *Proceedings of the Meeting of the French Colonial Historical Society*, 1994, vol. 19 (1994), 87-100

Gibson, James. *A Journal of the Siege of Louisbourg and Cape Breton in* 1745. Washington, D.C: James Bowen Johnson, 1894.

Godfrey, W.G. "John Bradstreet at Louisbourg: Emergence or Re-emergence?" *Acadiensis*, vol. 4, no. 1 (Autumn 1974), 100-120.

Goggin, John. "Ft. Pupo: A Spanish Frontier Outpost," *FHQ*, vol. 30, no. 2, 139-192.

Grady, Timothy. *Anglo-Spanish Rivalry and the development of the colonial Southeast, 1670-1720*. PhD. Thesis, College of William and Mary, 2006.

"Green's Journal," *Proceedings of the American Antiquarian Soc.*, XX, no. 1, (1909), 133-176.

Greer, Allan. (1976) "The Soldiers of Isle Royal, 1720-1745," *RFL*.

Griffen, William. "Spanish Pensacola, 1700-1763," *FHQ*, vol, 37, no. 3 & 4, 242-262.

Guerin, Leon. *Histoire Maritime de France*. 6 vols. Paris: Boulanger et Legrand, 1851-1856.

Hann, John. "St. Augustine's Fallout from the Yamassee War," *FHQ*, vol. 68, #2, 180-200.

Hart, Francis. *Attacks upon the Spanish Main by Admiral Vernon*. New Haven, CT; Associated Publishers, 1908.

Herson, James P. "A Joint Operation Gone Awry: The 1740 Siege of St. Augustine." Thesis, U.S. Army Command College, Fort Leavenworth, Kansas, 1997.

Hewatt. *South Carolina & Georgia*, I, 255-258.

Hoffman, Paul. *Florida's Frontiers*. Bloomington: Indiana University Press, 2002.

Howell, T.B. *A Complete Collection of State Trials*, vol. XV. London: T.C. Hansard, 1816.

Hulbert, Archer. *The Niagara River*. New York: G.P. Putnam's Sons, 1908.

Hutchinson, Thomas. *The History of the Province of Massachusetts Bay*. 3 vols. London: M. Richardson, 1765-1828.

Ivers, Larry E. *British Drums on the Southern Frontier: The Military Colonization of Georgia*, 1733-1749. Chapel Hill: University of North Carolina Press, 1974.

Jau, Dr. Francis Le. *The Carolina Chronicles of Dr. Francis Le Jau, 1706-1717*. Los Angeles: University of California Press, 1956.

Johnson, Charles. *A General History of the Pyrates*. London: 1724.

Johnston, A.J. B. "From port de peche to ville fortifiee: The Evolution of Urban Louisbourg, 1713-1758," *Proceedings of the Meeting of the French Colonial Historical Society*, 1993, vol. 17 (1993), 24-43.

Johnston, A.J.B. *The Summer of 1744: A Portrait of Life in 18th-Century Louisbourg*. Ottawa: Canadian Parks, 2002.

Jones, Charles. The History of *Georgia*. 2 vols. Boston: Houghton, Mifflin, and Company, 1883.

Jones, William. *A Report on Fort Diego*. Jacksonville: Private Printing, 1993.

Journal of the Legislative Council of the Colony of New York, I, Begun the 3rd day of April 1691 and ended the 27th of September, 1743. Albany: Weed, Parsons & Co., 1861.

Journal of the Legislative Council of the Colony of New York, II, Begun the 8th day of December 1743 and ended the 3rd of April 1775. Albany: Weed, Parsons & Co., 1861.

Kalm, Peter. *Travels into North America*. Trans. John Reinold Forster. 3 vols. London: T. Lowndes, 1771.

Kimball, Gertrude. *The Correspondence of the Colonial Governors of Rhode Island*. 2 vols. Boston: Houghton, Mifflin, and Co., 1902.

King, Grace. *Jean Baptiste Le Moyne, Sieur de Bienville*. New York: Dodd, Mead, and Co., 1893.

Kingsford, William. *The History of Canada*. 10 vols. London: Trubner & Co., 1888-1898.

Knowles, Charles. *An Account of the Expedition to Cartagena*. London: M. Cooper, 1743.

Krause, Eric. (1982, Sept.) "Construction Chronology for the Royal Battery, Actual and Proposed," *RFL*.

Krause, Eric. (1996) "Domestic Building Construction at the Fortress of Louisbourg, 1713-1758," *RFL*.

Krause, Eric. (December 2005) "The Chronology of Historical Events at the Island Battery, 1713-1768," *RFL*.

Lanctot, Gustave. *A History of Canada, 1600-1763.* 3 vols. Trans. Josephine Hambleton and Margaret Cameron. Cambridge: Harvard University Press, 1963-65.

Lannen, Andrew. "James Oglethorpe and the Civil Military Contest for Authority in Colonial Georgia, 1732-1749." *GHQ*, vol. 95, no. 2 (summer 2011), 203-231.

Lanning, John. "The American Colonies in the Preliminaries of the War of Jenkins' Ear." *GHQ*, vol. 11, no. 2 (June 1927), 129-155.

Lanning, John. "American Participation in the War of Jenkins' Ear." *GHQ*, vol. 11, no. 3 (Sept. 1927), 191-215.

Laramie, Michael G. *Queen Anne's War*. Yardley, PA: Westholme, 2021.

Lecky, William Edward Hartpole. *A History of England in the Eighteenth Century.* 8 vols. New York: D. Appleton and Co., 1878-1917.

Lester, David Alan. *Privateering in the Colonial Chesapeake.* Thesis. William and Mary, 1989.

Lincoln, Charles H. (ed.). *The Correspondence of William Shirley, Governor of Massachusetts and Military Commander in America, 1731-1760.* 2 vols. New York: The Macmillan Co., 1912.

London Magazine.

Lunn, Jean Elizabeth. "Agriculture and War in Canada, 1740-1760," *Canadian Historical Review,* 16 (1935), 123-136.

McCall, Hugh. *The History of Georgia.* 2 vols. Savannah: Seymour and Williams, 1811.

McConnell, David. *British Smooth-Bore Artillery: A Technological Study to Support Identification…* Ottawa: National Parks Service, 1988.

McCrady, Edward. *The History of South Carolina under the Proprietary Government, 1670-1719.* New York: Macmillan Co., 1897.

McDowell, W.L. (ed.). *Colonial Records of South Carolina: Journals of the Commissioners of the Indian Trade, 1710-1718.* Columbia: South Carolina Archives, 1955.

McLennan, J.S. *Louisbourg, from its Foundation to its Fall, 1713-1758.* Toronto: Macmillan and Co., 1918.

Mereness, Newton. *Travels in the American Colonies.* New York: Macmillan Co., 1916.

Milne, George. *Natchez Country: Indians, Colonists, and the Landscapes of Race in French Louisiana.* Athens: University of Georgia Press, 2015.

Moats, Sandra. *Navigating Neutrality: Early American Governance in the Turbulent Atlantic.* Charlottesville: University of Virginia Press, 2021.

Murdoch, Beamish. *History of Nova Scotia*. 3 vol. Halifax: J. Barnes, 1865-1867.

New American Magazine.

New England Courant.

New York Weekly.

Norton, Rev. John. *The Redeemed Captive. Being a Narrative of the taking and carrying into Captivity of the Rev. John Norton*. Boston: 1748.

O'Callaghan, E.B. (ed.). *Documents Relative to the Colonial History of the State of New York*. 15 vols. Albany: Weed, Parsons & Co., 1856-1877.

O'Callaghan, E.B. (ed.). *Documentary History of New York*. 4 vols. Albany: Weed, Parsons & Co., 1849-1851.

Parkman, Francis. *A Half Century of Conflict*, 2 vols. Boston: Little, Brown, and Company, 1914.

Pearson, Jonathan. *A History of the Schenectady Patent*. Albany: Munsell and Sons, 1883.

Pecorelli, Harry, Alford, Michael, & Babits, Lawrence, "A Working Definition of Periauger," *Underwater Archaeology* (1996), 22-28.

Penhallow, Samuel. *The History of the Wars of New England with the Eastern Indians*. Boston: T. Fleet (1726) 1924.

Pepperrell Papers: Collections of the Massachusetts Historical Society. 6th ser., vol. X (1849).

Pepperrell, William. *An accurate journal and account of the proceedings of the New-England land-forces, during the late expedition against the French settlements on Cape Breton*...London: A. and S. Brice, 1746.

Perry, Arthur Latham. *Origins in Williamstown*. New York: Charles Scribner's Sons, 1894.

Pitcher, Daniel. *Louisbourg's Labourer-Soldiers.* Master's Thesis Dalhousie University, Halifax, Nova Scotia, 2014.

Porter, Whitworth. *The History of the Corps of Royal Engineers*. Vol. I. London: Longmans, Green, & Co., 1889.

Pote, William. *The Journal of Captain William Pote, Jr.* New York: Dodd, Mead, and Company, 1896.

Potter, Chandler E. *The Military History of the State of New Hampshire*. 2 vols. Concord: McFarland & Jenks, 1866.

Preston, Richard, and Lamontagne, Leopold. *Royal Fort Frontenac*. Toronto: The Champlain Society, 1958.

Pritchard, James. *Anatomy of a Naval Disaster: The 1746 French Expedition to North America.* Montreal: McGill-Queen's University Press, 1995.

Ramsey, William. "Something Cloudy in Their Looks: The Origins of the Yamassee War Reconsidered," *Journal of American History*, vol. 90, no. 1 (June 2003), 44-75.

Rapport de L'Archiviste de la Quebec pour 1922-1923. Quebec: Redempti Paradis, 1923.

Rawlyk, George. *Yankees at Louisbourg*. Orono: University of Maine Press, 1967.

Ravenel, Harriet. *Charleston*. New York: Macmillan Co., 1912.

Richard, Edouard. *Acadia*, I. New York: Home Book Company, 1895.

Rivers, William. *A Sketch of the History of South Carolina*. Charleston: McCarter & Co., 1856.

Rodd, George. "Letter," *City of Charleston Year Book, 1894*. Charleston: Walker, Evans, and Cogswell (1894), 319-323.

Rogers, Greg. *Rhode Island's Wars: Imperial Conflicts and Provincial Self-Interests in the Ocean Colony, 1739-1748*. Thesis, California Polytechnical University, San Louis Obispo, 2010.

Rowland, Dunbar, and Sanders, A.G. *Mississippi Provincial Archives, 1729-1740, French Dominion*. vols. I, II, III. Jackson: Mississippi Department of Archives, 1927-1932.

Roy, Pierre-George. *Hommes et choses du Fort Saint-Fréderic*. Montreal: Les Editions Dix, 1946.

Sainsbury, W. Noel et al. (eds.). *Calendar of State Papers, Colonial Series, American and West Indies, Preserved in Her Majesty's Public Records Office*. 45 vols. London: His Majesty's Stationery Office, 1860-1964.

Salley, A.S. *Journals of the Common House of Assembly of South Carolina for Oct. 1707-Feb. 1708*. Columbus: The State Company, 1941.

Salter, William T. *John Salter, Mariner*. Philadelphia: John Highlands, 1900.

Schuyler, Henry. "The Apostle of the Abenaki." *The Catholic Historical Review*, first series, I (1910), 164-174.

Severance, Frank. *The Story of Joncaire*. Buffalo: Buffalo Historical Society, 1906.

Severance, Frank H. An *Old Frontier of France: The Niagara Region and Adjacent Lakes under French Control.* 2 vols. New York: Dodd, Mead, and Company, 1917.

Sheffield, W.P. *Privateersmen of Newport*. Newport: John P. Sanborn, 1883.

Sherman, Richard P. *Robert Johnson: Proprietary and Royal Governor of South Carolina*. Columbia, South Carolina: State Printing Co., 1966.

Shirley, William. *Memoirs of the Principal Transactions of the Last War*. London: Green and Russell, 1748.

Starkey, David. *Pirates and Privateers*. Exeter, UK: University of Exeter Press, 1997.

Statham, E.P. *Privateers and Privateering*, New York: James Pott & Co., 1910.

Stockton, Frank. *Buccaneers and Pirates of our Coasts.* New York: Macmillan Co., 1898.

Stone, William L. *The Life and Times of Sir William Johnson, Bart.* 2 vols. Albany: J. Munsell, 1865.

Subhash, Janotti, "Impact response of Coquina," *Dynamic Behavior of Materials: Proceedings of the Society for Experimental Mechanics 2015*, I, 1-27.

Sullivan, James, and Hamilton, Milton W. (eds.). *The Papers of Sir William Johnson.* 14 vols. Albany: University of the State of New York, 1921-65.

Swanson, Carl. "The Competition for American Seamen during the War of 1739-1748," *Man and Nature*, I (1982), 119-129.

Swanson, Carl. "American Privateering and Imperial Warfare, 1739-1748," *William & Mary Quarterly*, vol. 42, no. 3, 357-382.

Swanton, John. *Early History of the Creek Indians and their Neighbors.* Washington, DC: Government Printing Office, 1922.

Swanton, John. *Indian Tribes of the of the Lower Mississippi Valley.* Washington, DC: Government Printing Office, 1911.

Syfert, Samuel R. "Proprietary Misrule in South Carolina, 1700 to 1720," Masters Thesis, Eastern Illinois University, 1961.

Sylvester, Herbert. *Indian Wars of New England*, vol. III. Boston: W.B. Clarke Co., 1910.

Tailfer, Patrick. *A True and Historical Narrative of Colony of Georgia.* Charleston: P. Timothy, 1741.

Tepaska, John. "Economic Problems of Florida's Governors," *FHQ*, vol. 37, no. 1, 42-52.

Topping, Aileen (ed.). *An Impartial Account of the Late Expedition under General Oglethorpe.* Gainesville: University of Florida Press, 1978.

Torres-Reyes, Ricardo. *The British Siege of St. Augustine in 1740.* Denver: National Park Service, 1972.

Trask, William (ed.). *Letters of Colonel Thomas Westbrook*, 1722-1726. Boston: George Littlefield, 1901.

Watkins, Walter. "Massachusetts in the Intended Expedition to Canada in 1746," *Yearbook of the Massachusetts Society of Colonial Wars for 1900*, 49-106.

Watson, Michael. "Judge Lewis Morris, the New York Vice-Admiralty Court, and Colonial Privateering, 1739-1748," *New York History*, vol. 78, no. 2 (1997), 117-146.

Weeden, William. *Economic and Social History of New England*, 2 vols. Boston: Houghton, Mifflin, and Co., 1891.

Wheeler, George and Henry. *History of Brunswick.* Boston: Alfred Mudge and Sons, 1878.

Williams, George (ed.). *Letters from the Clergy of the Anglican Church in South Carolina*. College of Charleston, spec. coll.

Williamson, William D. *The History of the State of Maine*, 2 vols. Dallowell, Maine: Glazier, Masters and Co., 1832.

Wiseman, Frederick. *The Voice of the Dawn: An Autohistory of the Abenaki Nation*. Hanover, NH: University Press of New England, 2001.

Wood, Arthur. *William Shirley, Governor of Massachusetts,1741-1756*. New York: Columbia University, 1920.

Wright, J. Leitch Jr. *Anglo-Spanish Rivalry in North America*. Athens: University of Georgia Press, 1971.

Wright, Robert. *A Memoir or General James Oglethorpe*. London: Chapman and Hall, 1867.

Wrong, George M. *Louisbourg in 1745: The Anonymous Lettre D'un Habitant De Louisbourg*. Toronto: Warwick Bro's & Rutter, 1897.

Zoltvany, Yves. "The Frontier Policy of Philippe de Rigaud de Vaudreuil, 1713-1725," *Canadian Historical Review*, XLVIII, no. 3 (Sept. 1967), 227-250.

Acknowledgments

Thank you, Lord. And to be clear, thank you again. When I first started, I would have never imagined that I would actually reach this point. Your hand is in this. My thanks to my wife Pam and my children Ryan, Andrew, Brittany, and Nathanael for their unwavering support throughout this effort. My original hopes were to write on the first three French and Indian Wars. Why? In part, because long ago, I once read in one of Francis Parkman's works that he hoped someone would do so. Thank you for the idea, Mr. Parkman, and thank you for your works. To the personnel of the University of Arizona Library, the University of Vermont Library, and the Baker-Berry Library at Dartmouth, my many thanks for your help and professionalism. And of course, a shout out to Folgers. Nothing happens without you guys. Lastly, if you have reached this section and still have not cast this book aside, I thank you as well and hope that I have sparked or continued an interest in a seldom-recounted part of American history.

Index